WatchKit by Tutorials

By the raywenderlich.com Tutorial Team

By Ryan Nystrom,
Scott Atkinson, Soheil Azarpour, Matthew Morey,
Ben Morrow, Audrey Tam, and Jack Wu

WatchKit by Tutorials: Updated for Swift 1.2

Scott Atkinson, Soheil Azarpour, Matthew Morey, Ben Morrow, Audrey Tam, and Jack Wu

Notice of Rights

Notice of Liability

Trademarks

ISBN: 978-1-942878-06-3

Table of Contents:

Dedications

"To my amazing wife and family, who encourage me to never stop."
– Ryan Nystrom

"To my parents and teachers, who set me on the path that led me to the here and now."
– Audrey Tam

"To my lovely, always supportive wife Elnaz, and our son Kian."
– Soheil M. Azarpour

"To Patrick Maruthmmotil, who listened relentlessly and inspired joy each and every day."
– Ben Morrow

"To my amazing wife Tricia, and my parents – thank you for always supporting me."
– Matthew Morey

"To my loving parents and supportive wife, Scarlett."
– Jack Wu

"To Kerri, my beautiful and supportive wife, who gave me a Mac and encouraged me to do something different."
– Scott Atkinson

Introduction

Imagine you're back at September 9, 2014. Tim Cook has been talking to a packed audience about the finer details of the new iPhone 6 and 6+, as well as the just-announced Apple Pay service. Just when things appear to be wrapping up, the familiar "One more thing…" keynote slide appears.

The lights dim and a video begins to play. A short time into the video, the penny drops for each and every person in the room—it's the eagerly anticipated Apple Watch.

The video ends and the room bursts into rapturous applause, followed by a standing ovation with many whoops and cheers. The watch looks every inch the polished article we expected it to be, and there is a genuine feeling of excitement in the air.

As Tim continues to talk about the intricacies of the design, the multitude of sensors and other hardware flourishes, every developer watching the live stream likely has the same question spinning in their head—"What about the apps?"

A little later in the event and Kevin Lynch is on stage introducing WatchKit, announcing it will be made available to developers at some point in November. He's a little coy with the details, but it appears as though in the initial release of WatchKit, we'll be able to build both glances—quick and lightweight views providing timely information—and custom notifications. The tools to create fully native apps will come in late 2015. We are ecstatic!

OK, enough reminiscing – let's move back to the present. :]

Apple made good on its promise and released the first beta of WatchKit on November 18, 2014. But to our surprise, we got a whole lot more than we'd been led to expect. Along with the promised glances and notifications came unique hybrid apps, where the assets and interface run from the watch, but the code is executed as an app extension on the iPhone, with communication between the two taking place wirelessly. As mystifying as these apps are, they appear to be the WatchKit equivalent of web apps on the first generation iPhone.

And that sets the scene for this initial release of WatchKit. Any developers who were building apps for the first generation iPhone will notice a lot of familiarities between the system access and the hardware they got back then, and what they're getting now with the Watch. But certainly don't let that put you off—WatchKit is full of many wonderful new things, backed by a brand new platform rich with opportunity.

You can build hybrid apps, glances, custom short and long look notifications, and you can implement Handoff, sync data between devices and even have the containing iPhone app execute tasks in the background on behalf of the Watch app. All pretty magical stuff.

Prepare yourself for your own private tour through the amazing new features of WatchKit. By the time you're done, your WatchKit knowledge will be completely up to date and you'll be able to benefit from the amazing new opportunities presented by the Apple Watch.

Sit back, relax and prepare for some high-quality tutorials!

What you need

To follow along with the tutorials in this book, you'll need the following:

- **A Mac running OS X Mavericks or later**. You'll need this to be able to install the latest version of Xcode.
- **Xcode 6.3 or later**. Xcode is the main development tool for creating iOS and WatchKit apps. You'll need Xcode 6.3 or later for all tasks in this book, as Xcode 6.3 is the first version of Xcode to support WatchKit and Swift 1.2. You can download it for free from the Mac app store here: https://itunes.apple.com/app/xcode/id497799835?mt=12.
- **To run the samples on physical hardware, you'll need an iPhone running iOS 8.3 or later, an Apple Watch and a paid membership to the iOS development program.** Almost all of the chapters in the book let you run your code on the iOS and Apple Watch simulators that come bundled with Xcode.

Once you have these items in place, you'll be able to follow along with every chapter in this book.

Who this book is for

This book is for intermediate or advanced iOS developers who already know the basics of iOS and Swift development and want to broaden their horizons by exploring Apple's new smart watch platform.

- **If you are a complete beginner to iOS development**, we recommend you read through *The iOS Apprentice, 3rd Edition* first. Otherwise, this book may be a bit too advanced for you.
- **If you are a beginner to Swift**, we recommend you first read through either *The iOS Apprentice, 3rd Edition* (if you are a complete beginner to programming), or *Swift by Tutorials* (if you already have some programming experience).

If you need one of these prerequisite books, you can find them in our store, here:

- http://www.raywenderlich.com/store

Please note that the tutorials in this book are written exclusively in Swift.

How to use this book

We recommend you read this book from cover to cover. Each chapter in this book builds on the concepts and materials covered in the previous one, and once finished, you'll have built a rich, engaging, full-featured WatchKit app that manages recipes, grocery lists and cooking instructions—aptly called SousChef.

However, if you don't have time to go through sequentially, you can alternatively pick and choose the chapters that interest you the most, or the chapters you need immediately for your upcoming WatchKit projects This is the more familiar approach we usually recommend for our other "by Tutorials" books. Just remember that these chapters aren't self-contained, and were written with the intention that the book would be read through in a sequential order.

If you chose the latter approach and are looking for some recommendations of which chapters to begin with, here's our suggested Core Reading List:

- Chapter 2, Architecture
- Chapter 3, UI Controls
- Chapter 4, Layout

- Chapter 5, Navigation
- Chapter 6, Tables
- Chapter 8, Sharing Data
- Chapter 12, Image Caching and Animation

That covers the "Big 7" topics of WatchKit; from there, you can dig into other topics of particular interest to you.

Important: As mentioned above, each chapter in this book builds on the chapters that precede it. If you jump straight to a chapter that comes after chapter 8 and use the accompanying starter project, you'll need to set up the necessary provisioning profiles and enable App Groups before you're able to run each of the targets in that project.

For more information, please consult Chapter 8, "Sharing Data".

Book overview

The Apple Watch is a brand new platform, and WatchKit a brand new SDK, built on a unique architecture, with lots of new concepts and paradigms. Here's what you'll be learning about in this book:

Section I: Beginning WatchKit

In this section, you'll quickly get up to speed with the underlying architecture of WatchKit apps and the new layout paradigm, as well review each and every interface element at your disposal. You'll learn how to build navigation stacks, tables and context menus, and come to understand how they differ from their iOS counterparts.

By the end of this section, you'll have a firm grasp of WatchKit's core concepts and will have built the foundation of the SousChef sample app.

Here's a quick overview of the chapters in this section:

1. **Chapter 1, Hello, Apple Watch**: Dive straight in and build your first WatchKit app—a very modern twist on the age-old "Hello, World" app.
2. **Chapter 2, Architecture**: You'll learn about the unique architecture of WatchKit apps, and how it's unlike anything we've seen before.
3. **Chapter 3, UI Controls:** There's not a `UIView` to be found! You'll dig into the suite of brand new interface elements that ship with WatchKit.
4. **Chapter 4, Layout**: Auto Layout? Nope. Springs and Struts? Nope. Get an overview of the new layout system behind the interfaces of WatchKit apps.
5. **Chapter 5, Navigation**: You'll learn about the three different modes of navigation available in WatchKit, as well as how to combine them.
6. **Chapter 6, Tables**: Deep dive into tables in WatchKit and learn how to set them up, how to populate them, and how they differ considerably from `UITableView`.
7. **Chapter 7, Menus:** Context menus are the WatchKit equivalent of action sheets in iOS. You'll get your hands dirty and learn everything you need to know about creating them and responding to user interaction.

Section II: Intermediate WatchKit

It's paramount that your Watch app and containing iPhone app share data; what use is the convenience of the Watch if it doesn't display the same up-to-date data as your iPhone? In this section, you'll start by learning exactly that—how to share data between the phone and the watch—and update the SousChef app to share its recipes between both devices.

After that, you'll create a glance, which is the WatchKit equivalent of a Today extension, before getting your glance and Watch app talking via Handoff. You'll finish off the section by taking a look at how to handle incoming notifications, both local and remote.

Here's a quick overview of the chapters in this section:

8. **Chapter 8, Sharing Data**: You'll learn how to take advantage of app groups and shared containers to sync data between your WatchKit app and the containing iOS app.
9. **Chapter 9, Glances**: Think of a glance as a read-only, quick and lightweight view of your app, providing your users with timely information. You'll learn about the interface of a glance, as well as how to provide the underlying data.
10. **Chapter 10, Handoff**: With the glance in place, you'll want to advertise what it's displaying to the main Watch app so the app can respond accordingly when the user taps the glance. You'll learn just how to do that in this chapter by using Handoff.
11. **Chapter 11, Notifications**: WatchKit offers support for several different types of notifications and allows you to customize them to the individual needs of your WatchKit app. In this chapter, you'll get a complete overview.

Section III: Advanced WatchKit

In this section, you'll approach the more advanced topics of WatchKit, beginning with how WatchKit handles animation—spoiler: there's no Core Animation!—as well as how to cache images on the Watch itself. Then, you'll move on to adding iCloud sync by updating both the iPhone and Watch SousChef apps to use `UIDocument`. Finally, you'll take a deep dive into some of the pitfalls you may stumble upon when creating apps for the Watch, and how to work around them.

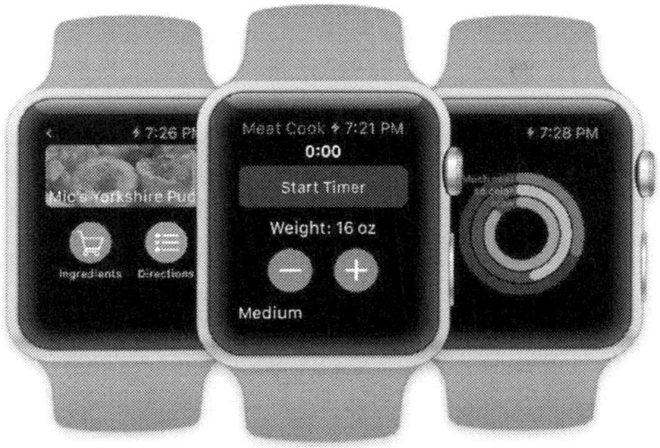

Here's a quick overview of the chapters in this section:

12. **Chapter 12, Image Caching and Animation**: You'll learn how to make use of the on-device image cache, and then move on to look at how WatchKit handles animations and how you can go about generating them.
13. **Chapter 13, iCloud**: Take your device-to-device syncing to a new level by introducing iCloud into the mix. You'll learn the intricacies of `UIDocument`, as well as what to do when iCloud isn't available.
14. **Chapter 14, Performance, and Tips & Tricks**: It's a brand new platform; it's a first-generation device—there are bound to be pitfalls you'll find yourself tripping over. This chapter has your back! Plus it's packed full of other cool stuff.
15. **Chapter 15, Localization**: Learn how to expand your reach and grow a truly international audience by localizing your Watch app using the tools and APIs provided by Apple.

Book source code and forums

You can get the source code for the book here:

http://www.raywenderlich.com/store/watchkit-by-tutorials/source-code

Almost all of the chapters have starter projects or other required resources, so you'll definitely want these close at hand as you work through the book.

We've also set up an official forum for the book at raywenderlich.com/forums. This is a great place to ask questions about the book, discuss WatchKit in general, share challenge solutions or submit any issues or errors you come across.

PDF Version

We also have a PDF version of this book available, which can be handy if you ever want to copy and paste code, or search for a specific term within the book as you're developing.

And speaking of the PDF version, we have some good news!

Since you purchased the print version of this book, you're eligible to buy the PDF version at a significant discount. For more details, open the following page in your favorite web browser:

http://www.raywenderlich.com/store/watchkit-by-tutorials/upgrade

License

By purchasing *WatchKit by Tutorials*, you have the following license:

- You are allowed to use and/or modify the source code in *WatchKit by Tutorials* in as many apps as you want, with no attribution required.
- You are allowed to use and/or modify all art, images or designs that are included in *WatchKit by Tutorials* in as many apps as you want, but must include this attribution line somewhere inside your app: "Artwork/images/designs: from the WatchKit by Tutorials book, available at http://www.raywenderlich.com".
- The source code included in *WatchKit by Tutorials* is for your personal use only. You are NOT allowed to distribute or sell the source code in *WatchKit by Tutorials* without prior authorization.
- This book is for your personal use only. You are NOT allowed to sell this book without prior authorization, or distribute it to friends, co-workers or students; they must purchase their own copy instead.

Acknowledgements

We would like to thank many people for their assistance in making this book possible:

- **Our families**: For bearing with us in this crazy time as we worked all hours of the day and night to get this book ready for publication!
- **Everyone at Apple**: For developing an amazing new smart watch platform, for constantly inspiring us to improve our apps and skills, and for making it possible for many developers to have their dream jobs!
- **InfinitApps**: For creating Bezel, which has allowed us to create some wonderful screenshots instead of having to rely on the Apple Watch simulator.
- And most importantly, **the readers of raywenderlich.com—especially you**! Thank you so much for reading our site and purchasing this book. Your continued readership and support is what makes all of this possible!

About the authors

Ryan Nystrom is the lead author of this book, and a software engineer at Facebook. He is a passionate open source contributor where he builds UI controls and frameworks for others to use and learn from. In his spare time, he enjoys flying planes as a private pilot.

Audrey Tam retired at the end of 2012 from a 25-year career as a computer science academic. Her teaching included several programming languages as well as user interface design and evaluation. Before moving to Australia, she worked on Fortran and PL/1 simulation software at IBM. Audrey now teaches short courses in iOS app development to non-programmers.

Soheil Azarpour is an independent iOS developer. He's worked on iOS applications for clients as well as his own personal apps. He enjoys making apps, hanging out with his family and watching movies.

Ben Morrow is a developer, author and hackathon organizer. Within the Apple Watch community, he's been teaching the tools and techniques for the past few months to help others be ready to launch their apps when the new device is finally released.

Matthew Morey is an engineer, developer, hacker, creator and tinkerer. As an active member of the iOS community and a lead developer at ChaiOne, he has led numerous successful mobile projects worldwide. He's the creator of Buoy Explorer, a marine conditions app for water sports enthusiasts, and Wrist Presenter, an app that lets you control presentations with your smart watch.

Jack Wu is the lead mobile developer at Extreme Innovations. He has built dozens of iOS apps and enjoys it very much. Outside of work, Jack enjoys coding on the beach, coding by the pool, and sometimes just having a quick code in the park.

Scott Atkinson is a software developer in Alexandria, Virginia. USA. For a day job, Scott is the iOS developer for Homesnap, a really great real estate discovery app. He also has two personal apps in the App Store: Metrownome, a coaching tool for rowing, and Preplist-K, a tool to help chefs create work lists for their employees. When he's not developing, Scott rows on the Potomac River, explores new restaurants and cooks great food.

About the editors

Mike Oliver is a tech editor of this book. He has been a mobile junkie ever since his first "Hello, World" on a spinach-screened Blackberry. Lately, he works primarily with iOS, but is always looking for new ways to push the envelope from your pocket. Mike is currently the director of engineering at RunKeeper, where he tries to make the world a healthier place, one app at a time.

Eric Cerney is a tech editor of this book. He is the head of iOS at Monsoon, where he works to bring client ideas to reality. He enjoys pushing the bounds of user interaction and finding ways to create awesome reusable components within a mobile environment. He likes tinkering with hardware, exploring San Francisco, and regretting endless Netflix marathons.

Greg Heo is QA for the source code of this book. He is an iOS developer and trainer, and has been on the raywenderlich.com editorial team since 2012. He has been nerding out with computers since the Commodore 64 era in the 80s and continues to this day on the web and on iOS. He likes caffeine, codes with two-space tabs, and writes with semicolons and the Oxford comma.

Bradley C. Phillips is the editor of this book. He splits his time between the full volume of New York City and the enchanting, dark and quiet Catskill Mountains. He was the first editor to come aboard raywenderlich.com, and he makes sure you've got the clearest, most engaging programming material available, whether you're reading the site's books or tutorials.

Mic Pringle is the final pass editor of this book. He is a developer, editor, podcaster and video tutorial maker. He's also Razeware's third full-time employee. When not knee-deep in Swift or standing in front of his green screen, he enjoys spending time with his wife Lucy and their daughter Evie, as well as attending the football matches of his beloved Fulham FC.

About the artists

Vicki Wenderlich created many of the illustrations in this book. Vicki discovered a love of digital art three years ago, and has been making app art and digital illustrations ever since. She is passionate about helping people pursue their dreams, and makes affordable app art for developers available on her website, http://www.gameartguppy.com.

Section I: Beginning WatchKit

In this section, you'll quickly get up to speed with the underlying architecture of WatchKit apps and the new layout paradigm, as well as review each and every interface element at your disposal. You'll learn how to build navigation stacks, tables and context menus, and come to understand how they differ from their iOS counterparts.

By the end of this section, you'll have a firm grasp of WatchKit's core concepts, and will have built the foundation of the SousChef sample app.

Chapter 1: Hello, Apple Watch!

By Audrey Tam

I'm sure I'm not alone in seeing the Apple Watch as absolutely the coolest device ever to come out of Cupertino. Many of us are excited about developing Watch apps—as you likely are if you're reading this book! I don't even wear a watch, but I'm going to get one as soon as possible and seize the excuse to upgrade my faithful old 4S to a 6. :]

In this chapter, you'll get comfortable with the basics of creating a Watch app and running it in the simulator. You'll start by changing the background color, just to get quick confirmation that your Watch app is running.

Then, you'll add a label to display the traditional "Hello, World!" text. Just for fun, you'll change the label to show:

And finally, you'll update your app so it displays random emoji fortunes, just like this one:

That fortune suggests you're in for a chapter that is fun, successful, rewarding, exciting and cool, so let's get started!

Getting started

Create a **New Project** in Xcode and select the **iOS\Application\Single View Application** template.

Set the **Product Name** to **HelloAppleWatch**, make sure the **Language** is set to **Swift**, **Devices** is set to **iPhone**, **Core Data** is unchecked, and click **Next**. Choose a folder in which to save your project and click **Create**.

> **Note:** You won't actually add anything to the empty template iPhone app in this chapter, but currently you can only create a Watch app as an extension of an iPhone app. You'll learn more about the relationship between iPhone apps and Watch apps in "Chapter 2: Architecture".

Run your app in the iPhone 6 simulator and you should see the default launch screen, then a blank white window.

In the iOS Simulator menu, select **Hardware\External Displays** and then select one of the Apple Watch screen sizes. A small black window appears:

When you run your Watch app target, you'll interact with the Watch display in this secondary window.

In the same way that an iPhone app needs a storyboard and a view controller to display and control its UI, an Apple Watch app needs a storyboard and an interface controller. To create these, you'll add a Watch app target to your project.

Adding a Watch app target

Select **File\New\Target...** from the Xcode menu:

In the target template window, select **iOS\Apple Watch\WatchKit App**:

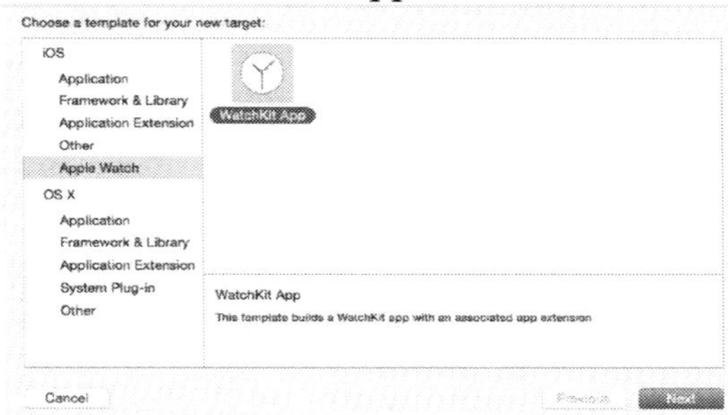

Click **Next**. In the target options window, <u>un</u>check **Include Notification Scene** and leave everything else as it is:

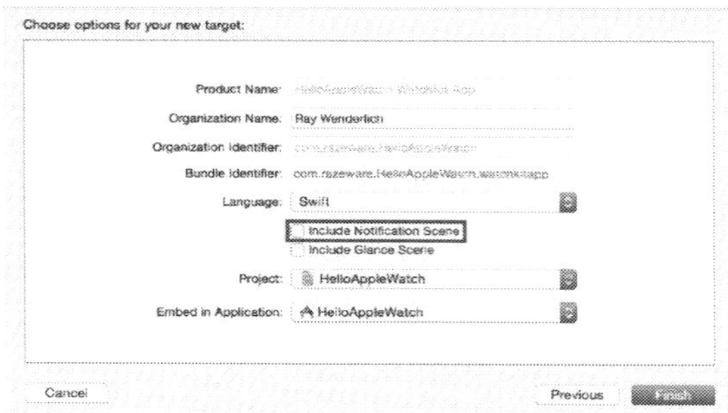

Click **Finish**. A pop-up window appears:

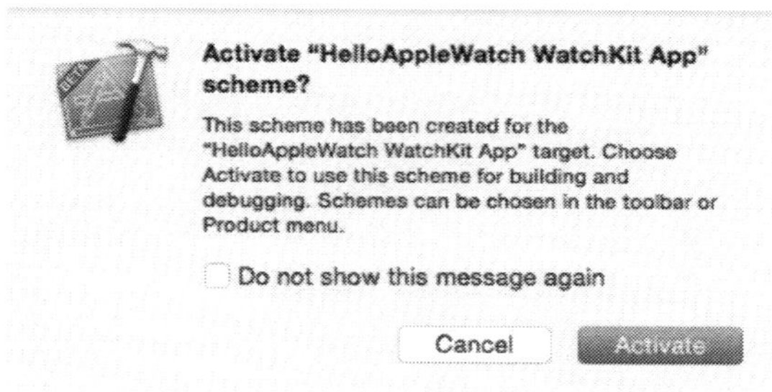

You are *absolutely* going to click **Activate**! This is the key step to making your Watch app appear in iOS Simulator. If you want this step to happen automatically whenever you add a WatchKit target, tick the checkbox for *Do not show this message again*, then click **Activate**.

> **Note:** This pop-up removes a major pain point for WatchKit newbies. In the early WatchKit betas, you had to remember to set the scheme manually, and as a result there were numerous anguished forum posts by devs wondering why their Watch apps weren't running in the simulator.

Two new groups now appear in the **project navigator**: a **WatchKit Extension** group and a **WatchKit App** group. Open these to see that **InterfaceController.swift** is in WatchKit Extension and **Interface.storyboard** is in WatchKit App:

The workflow for creating a Watch app is similar to that of an iPhone app: You set up the UI in the storyboard, and then connect the UI objects to outlets and actions in the controller.

Add-target shortcuts

Xcode provides two other ways to add a target to your project. These take advantage of the fact that a new Xcode project always opens with the project displayed in the editor—making these methods quicker than using the Xcode menu.

When the project is displayed in the editor, the Projects and Targets list is either open or closed.

If the **Projects and Targets** list is open, click the **+** icon in its lower-left corner:

If the **Projects and Targets** list is closed, click the project/target menu:

And select **Add Target...**

Showing the Watch app in the simulator

Before going much further with your Watch app, check that you can see the results of your labors in the simulator.

Open **Interface.storyboard** and then select the interface, either in the storyboard canvas or in the document outline.

Then, in the **Attributes Inspector**, change the **Color** to something other than **Default**:

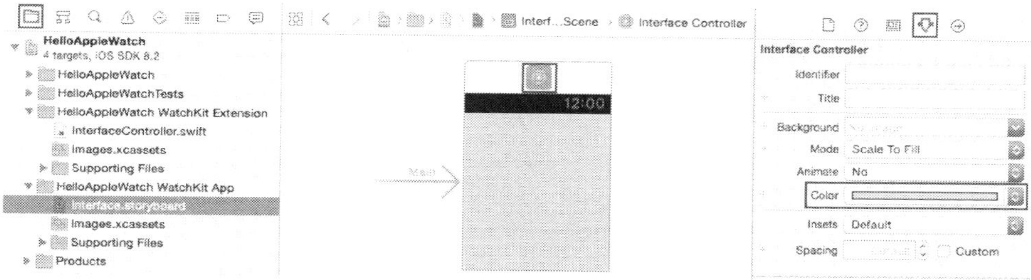

This will change the background color of the top-level interface.

Next, check that the active scheme is set to **HelloAppleWatch Watch App**:

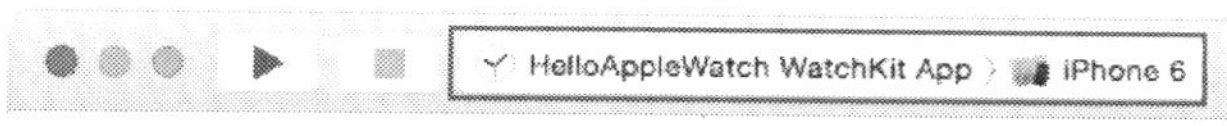

Run the app and… wait. What? The first time you run your Watch app, it might take a while to appear as Apple has gone to great lengths to make the simulator reflect the performance of the real device as closely as possible.

> **Note:** If you don't see a Watch display at all, then from the iOS Simulator menu, select **Hardware\External Displays** and then select one of the Apple Watch screen sizes. Then stop the app and run it again.

Hello, World!

This is the traditional "Hello, World!" first app. :]

It will simply be a label, the text of which you set in the Attributes Inspector, but it will give you a taste of the capabilities and limitations of the Apple Watch interface. You'll learn more about creating Apple Watch UIs in Chapter 3, "UI Controls".

Open **Interface.storyboard** and select the interface. Change the background color back to **Default** to start.

Drag a **label** from the Object Library onto the single interface controller:

By default, the label sits at the top-left of the interface. Unlike when designing for iOS, you can't move the label by simply dragging it around in the interface—if you try, it just reverts back to the top-left position. What you can do is drag the resizing handle to widen the label to fill the width of the interface. Do this now:

With the label still selected, in the **Attributes Inspector** change the **Text** to **Hello, World!** And the **Alignment** to **Centered** (the middle button of the five). The label resizes to fit the new Text value:

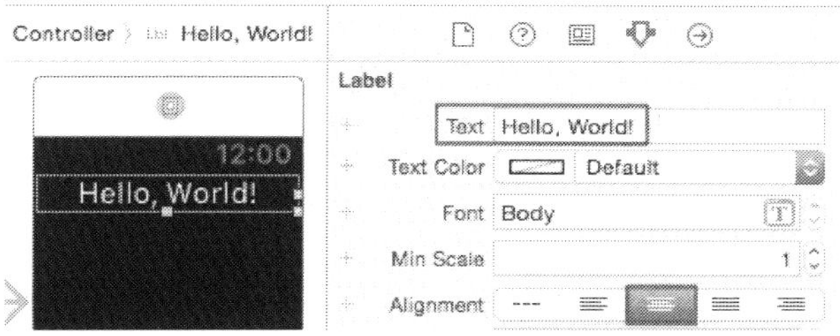

> **Note:** When you edit the Text field in the Attributes Inspector, the change doesn't take effect until you press the Return key. Another way to change the text is to double-click on the label itself to select the text and then change it there.

Build and run the Watch app. If you display the 38mm Watch, it looks fine, but if you display the 42mm Watch, the text is not centered:

There's a more convenient way to compare how your UI looks on both Watch sizes: You can preview them side by side using the **Assistant Editor's preview**. Close the project navigator and the utilities pane to give yourself some screen space, then open the **Assistant Editor** and in the drop-down menu, change **Automatic** to **Preview**:

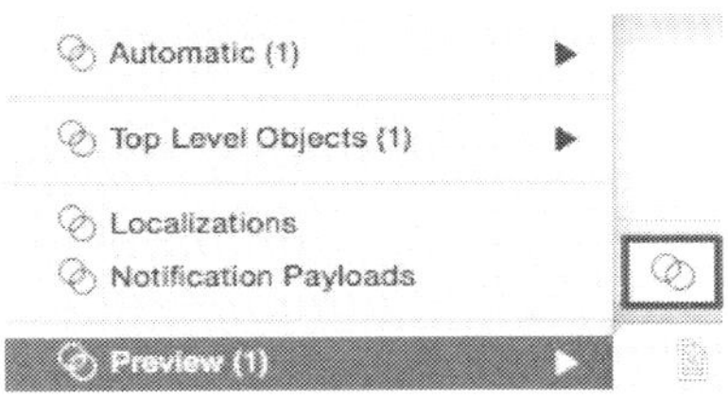

> **Note:** In this screenshot, the pop-up menu is hiding the button—it looks like the **Automatic** item in this menu.

Preview shows you the 38mm Watch face. Click the + button in the lower-left corner to add the 42mm Watch face:

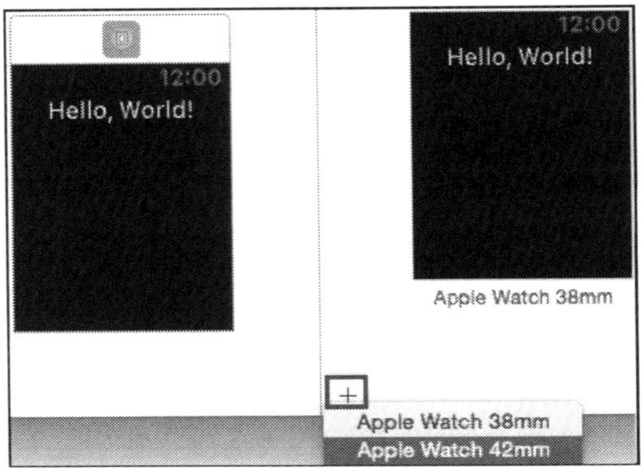

Now you can see both sizes, side by side, with the off-center text in the larger Watch face:

Now you need to open the utilities pane again to properly center the label, but it's awkward with the assistant editor taking up so much space between the editor and the Attributes Inspector. Fortunately, you can change where Xcode places the assistant editor. From the Xcode menu, select **View\Assistant Editor\Assistant Editors on Bottom**:

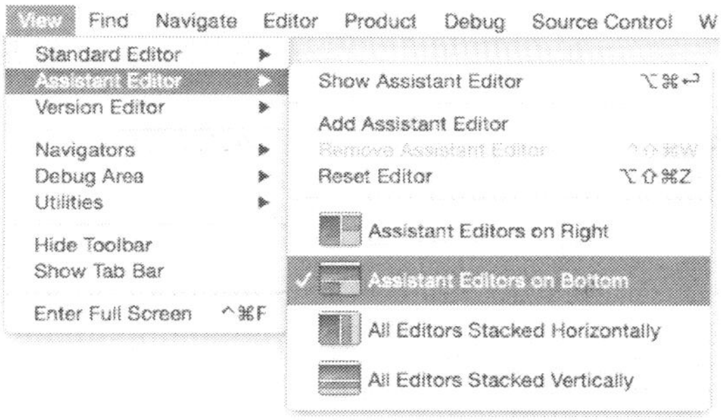

Ah, that's much better! Now, in the storyboard, select the **label** and scroll to the bottom of the **Attributes Inspector** until you can see the **Position** and **Size** sections of the label's attributes. Change the **Horizontal** position to **Center**—hey, presto! You've centered the text in the 42mm Watch face. And the 38mm Watch face still looks fine.

Since the label is the only thing in your interface, change the **Vertical** position to **Center**. Also, change **Width** to **Size To Fit Content**.

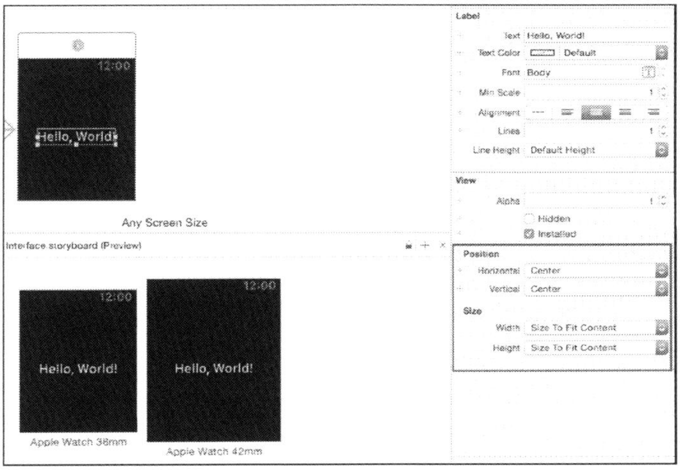

Note: There was actually no need to widen the label back near the start of this tutorial, as the width setting **Size To Fit Content** informs WatchKit to adjust the label's width so it accommodates its content, and that's the default value for new labels. I just needed an excuse to show you how to preview both Apple Watch sizes, and that required a fixed, full-width label with centered alignment to show the off-center text in the 42mm Watch face. All for a good cause. :]

Set label text in code

You'd probably like your Watch app to be a little more dynamic—at the very least, you'd want to set the label's text in the controller code. To do that, you need to set up the label as an *outlet* in **InterfaceController.swift**.

Move the **assistant editor** back to its original position on the right and set it to either **Automatic** or **Counterpart**, so that it displays **InterfaceController.swift**:

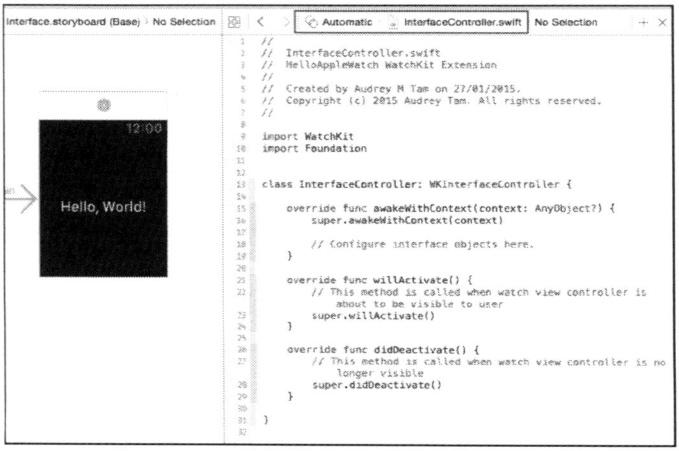

Select the **label** and, holding down the **Control** key, drag from the **label** into **InterfaceController.swift**, to that open line just below the class title. Xcode will prompt you to **Insert Outlet**. When you release the cursor, a pop-up window will appear, as shown in the following screenshot. Check that **Type** is set to `WKInterfaceLabel`, then type **label** in the **Name** field and click **Connect**:

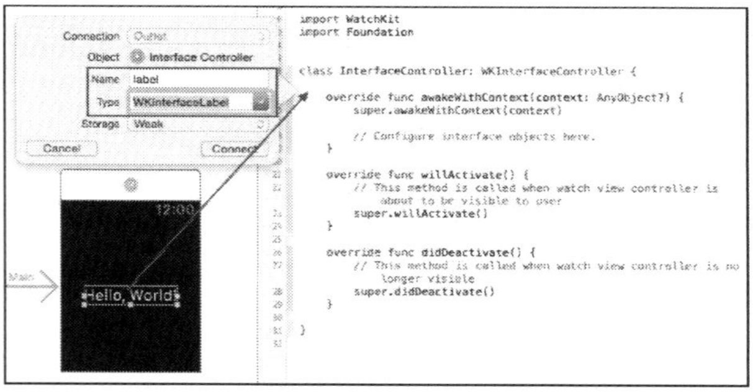

The following `@IBOutlet` declaration appears in **InterfaceController.swift**:

```
@IBOutlet weak var label: WKInterfaceLabel!
```

Your code now has a reference to the label in your Watch app interface, so you can use this to set its text.

Add the following line to `willActivate()`, below `super.willActivate()`:

```
label.setText("Hello, Apple Watch!")
```

Build and run your app:

Fantastic! You've added a label to the Watch interface, and set its text from code. This is pretty impressive stuff; remember that the storyboard and interface controller actually reside on different devices, but the outlet connection appears seamless and works as if everything were local.

The Apple Color Emoji font

This text is a tight squeeze on the smaller Watch face. If you want to make the font bigger or the text longer, you could change the label's **Lines** attribute from **1** to **0**, which informs WatchKit to give the text as many lines as it needs.

However, you don't need to do that for *this* app, because you're going to use emoji instead, which use much less space and are way more fun!

First, with the label selected in the storyboard, delete the text "Hello, World!" Next, click on the **T** icon in the Font attribute in the Attributes Inspector to invoke the font pop-up. Change **Font** to **System** and increase **Size** to **24**, then click **Done**:

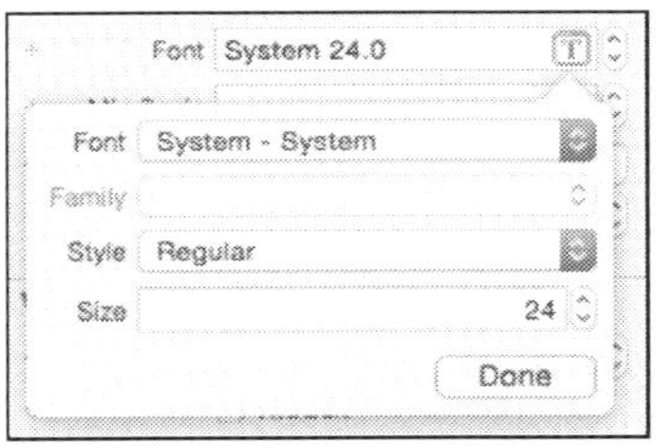

Next, edit the `Hello, Apple Watch!` string in **InterfaceController.swift**:

1. Select `Hello` and press **Control-Command-Space** to pop up the emoji character viewer beneath the selected text.
2. Scroll up in the emoji viewer to show the **Search** field, click in it and type *"waving"*—the **waving hand** emoji will appear. Click it and it will replace `Hello`.

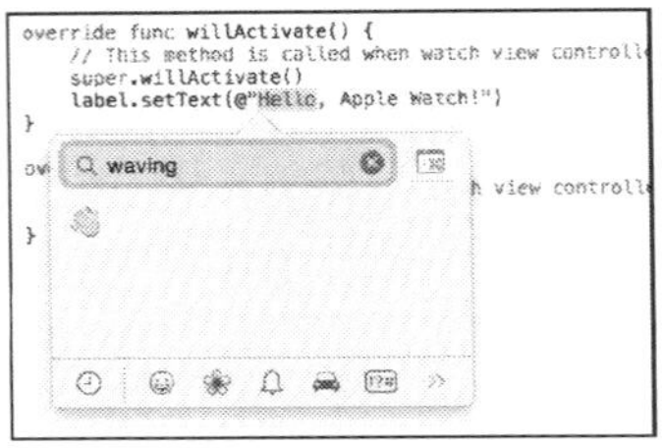

Repeat these steps to replace `Apple`, `Watch`, and the exclamation mark with suitable emojis.

Delete the comma and spaces, so your string looks like this:

"👋🍎⌚!"

Build and run your app:

An ultra-cool greeting to an über-cool gadget!

Now you're going to take this font and run with it.

Emoji fortunes

On April 9 2014, @nrrrdcore tweeted *"Free idea: Emoji Fortune Cookies"*, and on May 14, Luke Karrys launched emojifortun.es:

Wouldn't that look cool on an Apple Watch? Just the emojis, not the words, and more is better:

In **InterfaceController.swift**, do the following:

1. Below the `@IBOutlet` statement, just above `awakeWithContext(_:)`, create five arrays of emojis: `people`, `nature`, `objects`, `places` and `symbols`. You can use the emojis I've picked or have fun selecting your own, and feel free to add as many emojis as you want to each array:

```
let people = ["😆", "😘", "😌", "😔", "😑", "👯", "👩"]
let nature = ["🐣", "🍀", "🌺", "🌴", "⛄", "🐳", "🐴"]
let objects = ["👕", "⌛", "🍅", "🎵", "💰", "⏰"]
let places = ["✈", "♨", "🎡", "🚲", "📈"]
let symbols = ["🆗", "🆖", "▶", "◀", "🆒"]
```

> **Note:** I added some of these after seeing this article: http://www.theage.com.au/lifestyle/life/top-10-emojis-official-meaning-vs-best-use-20141211-1253v7.html

2. In `willActivate()`, replace the `label.setText()` call with these lines:

```
// 1
let peopleIndex = Int(arc4random_uniform(UInt32(people.count)))
let natureIndex = Int(arc4random_uniform(UInt32(nature.count)))
let objectsIndex = Int(arc4random_uniform(UInt32(
  objects.count)))
let placesIndex = Int(arc4random_uniform(UInt32(places.count)))
let symbolsIndex = Int(arc4random_uniform(UInt32(
  symbols.count)))
// 2
label.setText("\(people[peopleIndex])\(nature[natureIndex])
  \(objects[objectsIndex])\(places[placesIndex])
     \(symbols[symbolsIndex])")
```

The `arc4random_uniform()` function is a pseudo-random number generator. This code:

1. Generates a random number between 0 and the array's `count` property, for each array;
2. Uses the five random numbers to pick emojis from the arrays to create the label text.

Build and run your Watch app and have fun trying to figure out whether your fortune is good, bad, indifferent or just unfathomable:

Where to go from here?

At this point, you have hands-on experience making a simple WatchKit-based app.

If you're new to iOS, you've also learned how to set up and use storyboard outlets—these work exactly the same way in plain old iOS apps—and you've learned a few tricks while making your way around Xcode.

I hope this chapter has whetted your appetite to try out all the cool stuff in the rest of this book, as well as boosted your confidence that *you can do this!*

In the next three chapters, you'll learn about architecture, basic UI controls and layout to get you started with using WatchKit to build more complex interfaces and apps.

Chapter 2: Architecture

By Ryan Nystrom

The Apple Watch provides a unique challenge for engineers due to its form factor and the fact that it's the first version of a major product. Developers who used the first version of the iPhone OS SDK can recall how limited, buggy, and *different* it was. Instead of AppKit, developers had to learn how to use this shiny new framework called UIKit. They also found themselves confined to a strange, foreign space known as the app sandbox.

Of course, most of what was puzzling then is now commonplace for iOS developers, and the OS itself is considerably improved. The tools and frameworks are more robust, the app sandbox is widely accepted and devices are faster and more efficient.

The WatchKit framework is in a situation similar to the early days of iOS. There are new tools, frameworks and methods for building Apple Watch apps. To build quality Watch apps now and in the years and updates to come, you'll need a solid foundation in the architecture of both the Watch and the WatchKit framework, and that's what this chapter aims to provide you.

Exploring the Watch

Before jumping into WatchKit, take a few minutes to get familiar with what the Apple Watch is, and—more importantly—what it isn't.

Operating system

So what is the power behind the face of the Apple Watch? Is it iOS? Is it another flavor of OS X, like iOS is? Or did Apple come up with a brand new operating system that is different from anything that's come before?

Well, it turns out that Apple Watch *is* running iOS! This is somewhat of a surprise because of how different the Watch works and looks, when compared to an iPhone or iPad. But some folks have opened up the SDK and gotten a look at some of the internals of the Apple Watch. While outside the scope of this book, a quick search on Google for "PepperUICore" will return several articles detailing what's running under-the-hood, and the differences between the more elaborate, bundled Apple Watch apps and those you're able to build using WatchKit.

Interaction

Among the coolest features of the Apple Watch are the ways in which users can interact with it. Taken from the Apple Watch Human Interface Guidelines, there are four ways users can interact with your apps:[1]

- **Action-based events**: These are what you're likely already familiar with: things like table row selection and tap-based UI controls.
- **Gestures**: The gesture system for the Apple Watch is a lot more limited than the bountiful gesture options developers have in iOS, supporting only vertical and horizontal swipes and taps. Currently, the Watch *does not* support multi-touch gestures like pinching.
- **Force touch**: This is an interesting new gesture. The Apple Watch has special tiny electrodes around the display to determine if a tap is light or has more pressure and force behind it. This is likely a nice trade-off for losing multi-finger gestures.
- **The digital crown**: The excellently designed crown on the Apple Watch is a fine-tuned scrolling replacement. Since the Watch screen is so small, your fingers will likely hide where you're scrolling. The crown let's you see where you're scrolling and what you're scrolling to.

---

[1]https://developer.apple.com/library/prerelease/ios/documentation/UserExperience/Con

The Watch display

Out of the gate, you'll need to support multiple screen sizes for the Apple Watch.

- The **38mm** Watch screen is 272 pixels wide by 340 pixels tall.
- The **42mm** Watch screen is 312 pixels wide by 390 pixels tall.

Luckily for developers, both Watches share an aspect ratio of 4:5, so, at least for the time being, you won't have to do a ton of extra work to support both screen sizes.

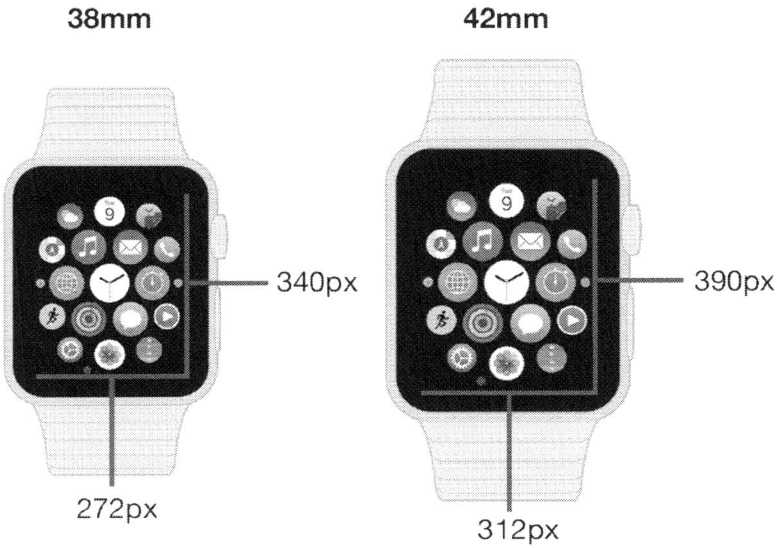

38mm and 42mm screen sizes

> **Note:** That doesn't mean you should hardcode your interfaces for this aspect ratio. Apple is notorious for adding further screen sizes to their products. Always design and build your interfaces to be screen-size agnostic!

Introducing WatchKit

A couple of months after announcing the Apple Watch, Apple provided eager developers the tools to start building Watch apps. The primary framework, called WatchKit, was bundled with Xcode 6.2.

Even though Apple released Swift only a few months before it released WatchKit, right away the framework had both Swift and Objective-C support.

What it is

Viewed from a high level, WatchKit is nothing more than a group of classes and Interface Builder additions that you can wire together to get an Apple Watch app working. Some of the important classes are:

- **WKInterfaceController**: This is the WatchKit version of `UIViewController`. Later in this chapter, you'll learn more about this class and how to use it.
- **WKInterfaceObject**: Instead of shipping with a Watch version of UIKit, WatchKit provides what would best be described as proxy objects for dealing with the user interface. This class is the base from which all of the Watch interface elements, like buttons and labels, inherit.
- **WKInterfaceDevice**: This class provides all of the information about the Watch, like screen size and the locale.

And whether you love them or hate them, you'll build all of your user interfaces in storyboards. That is currently the only way to create interface controllers.

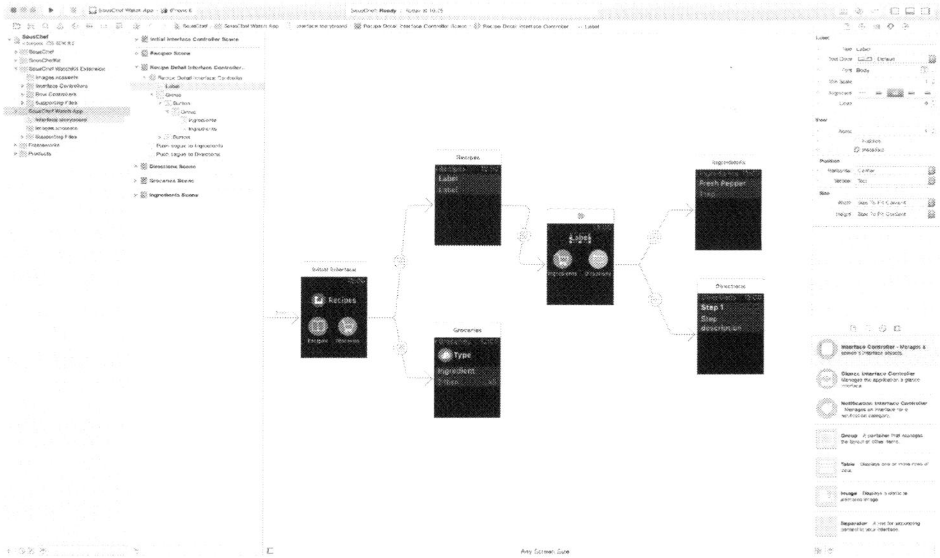

Building a Watch app in Interface Builder

What it isn't

When Apple announced the Apple Watch to developers, the company made it clear that it would deploy WatchKit in two phases: the first with simple notification-based apps, and the second with more robust apps.

WatchKit actually launched with both notification support and an interesting extension-based API. This means you and I can create Watch apps from the beginning! But it's very important to know that what we can currently build and run as *extensions* are 100% dependent on an iPhone running the containing app.

> **Note:** If you're interested in reading about building regular app extensions, check out this tutorial on building an iOS 8 Today extension:
> http://www.raywenderlich.com/83809/ios-8-today-extension-tutorial

The code that you write for the Watch is also executed *on the phone* that's paired with the Watch.

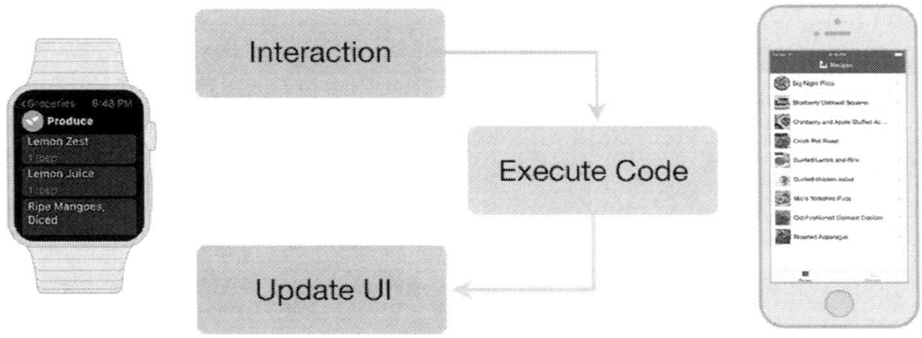

A simplified diagram of what the Apple Watch and iPhone do

The idea of Watch apps running as iOS extensions has probably got you more than a little intrigued; carry on reading, as in the next section I'll try to answer some of the questions that are already springing to mind.

WatchKit apps

The initial launch of WatchKit apps running as app extensions reveals many interesting architectural decisions. For instance, if a WatchKit app is an extension of an app that has to live on another device… *what runs the code?*

In fact, it is the iPhone that the Apple Watch connects to for Internet access and GPS data that executes the code! This means that your iPhone will execute all of the code that you end up writing for your Watch apps.

Even though the Apple Watch runs its own version of iOS, it doesn't execute any of the code you write. The Watch has its own graphics and interaction software, but that is hidden beneath the WatchKit extension SDK.

You should plan on putting a lot of effort into designing your app to be quick, efficient, and simple to use. Watch apps are not meant to be long-lived processes. You can imagine that if your code takes a while for the extension to execute, the Watch will just be sitting there not doing anything, especially if it's blocking the main thread.

> **Note:** If there's one thing to take away from this chapter, it's that **the phone executes your code** and the Apple Watch displays the interface and handles interactions. However, expect the Watch to begin executing its own code sometime around iOS 9. If you're wondering about the implications of this for such things as performance and battery life, read on.

Storyboards and resources

Though it is another device that executes code for the Apple Watch, the Watch performs all resource management and UI assembly. This architectural decision helps keep data transfer low so that the executing device (for now, an iPhone) isn't sending the Watch bits of information that are known before compile time.

> **Note:** The Watch only stores local resources, like images and files. Images downloaded from the web will have to be downloaded to the phone and then sent across to the Watch.

Apple Watches are shipping with Retina screens from day one. Their screens are 2x resolution at the moment, so Apple recommends only using @2x image resources.

However, that doesn't save you from having to supply a bunch of different icon sizes. App and menu icons require several sizes because the 38mm and 42mm Watches have different widths and heights.

From the Apple Watch Human Interface Guidelines:

Image	Apple Watch 38mm	Apple Watch 42mm
Notification center icon	29 pixels	36 pixels
Long Look notification icon	80 pixels	88 pixels
Home screen icon and Short Look icon	172 pixels	196 pixels
Menu icon canvas size	70 pixels	46 pixels
Menu icon content size	80 pixels	54 pixels

If you ever need to dynamically create a resource, like a custom image drawn with Core Graphics, or to download something from the web, you'll have to fetch it and then send it to the Watch. As you can imagine, this could become incredibly expensive to do and is likely to ruin your user's experience.

Make sure to bundle as much as you can ahead of time! It's also worth noting that you don't perform the sending of resources to the Watch manually; WatchKit handles this behind the scenes, meaning you have no control over transfer rate, priority or timing.

Code execution

You've seen that the Watch manages the interface while depending on another device, like an iPhone, to do the code execution. But why is that? And how can you best design your Watch apps so that they're still fast and useable?

First, take a moment to understand how the runtime of the WatchKit extension works. WatchKit performs what's called a **remote procedure call** (RPC), which Wikipedia describes as:

> *...an inter-process communication that allows a computer program to cause a subroutine or procedure to execute in another address space (commonly on another computer on a shared network) without the programmer explicitly coding the details for this remote interaction.*[2]

If all code had to be completed before the Watch could display any data, blocking the main thread, developers would throw a fit. It would make the Watch slow and clunky, with users having to wait for images to download before seeing any bit of an interface.

Luckily, the engineers at Apple are smart cookies. You can still make use of thread management APIs such as Grand Central Dispatch and NSOperation. Remember that all of the local resource loading is done on the Watch. The phone only has to do things like configure the controllers and parse data. As long as you write efficient code, you should be OK.

Take a look at all of the events that take place when the user taps on your app's icon.

---

[2] http://en.wikipedia.org/wiki/Remote_procedure_call

App launch lifecycle

Because data is transferred between the Watch and phone over the air, you should expect there to be some natural delays. Nothing should ever take more than a few hundred milliseconds to compute and transfer, though.

Implications

It might seem ludicrous to have an iPhone execute code and send data over the air to the Apple Watch. There is a higher chance of data loss and inconsistency, sure, but there are also a lot of advantages to this strategy:

- **CPU:** The CPU on an iPhone is likely much faster than that of the Apple Watch. Heavy-lifting code will be faster.
- **Battery:** It's critical that the first version of the Apple Watch has good battery life. Having the iPhone handle code execution removes a lot of power consumption from the smaller battery on the Watch.
- **Storage:** Files that aren't bundled in the WatchKit extension will be housed on the iPhone, so you won't need a terabyte SSD stuffed into a tiny watch.

Sharing data

Because it is the iPhone—running iOS 8—that executes the code for the Apple Watch, WatchKit uses exactly the same mechanism introduced in iOS 8 to share data between extensions and the parent application. So instead of giving the Watch its own Core Data stack, syncing it with iCloud or enabling it to manage its own file system, you simply need to use a **shared app group**.

Apple recommends architecting your apps so that the main app manages syncing and updating all of the data in the shared app group. If new data comes in from the web, the main app should update the shared group in the background so that the new data is ready to use when the Watch needs it.

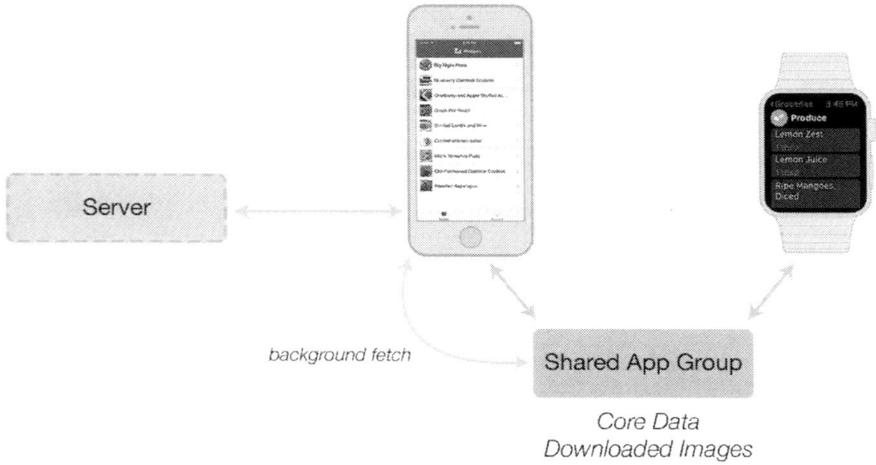

An example shared data solution

In Chapter 8, "Sharing Data", you'll learn how to set up a shared app group as well as sync data between both the main app and the WatchKit extension.

WatchKit classes

WatchKit consists of a group of entirely new classes. There is `WKInterfaceController` to act as the controller in the familiar model-view-controller pattern, and there are `WKInterfaceObjects` that are used to update the UI. All of the new WatchKit classes follow typical Apple class-naming conventions and are prefixed with "WK". Try to figure out what that stands for. :]

> **Note:** The move to prefix the WatchKit classes with "WK" has upset some developers who have already been using that prefix—for example, because they have the same initials. Now that Swift has namespacing, developers were expecting more succinct naming conventions. Maybe next year!

WKInterfaceController

`WKInterfaceController` is essentially WatchKit's `UIViewController`. Only this time, Apple engineers have taken notice of all the `UIViewController` pain points developers have struggled with, like passing data between controllers, handling notifications, and context menus.

Lifecycle

`WKInterfaceController` has a lifecycle, just like `UIViewController`. It is much simpler, though—there are only three methods you need to know.

`awakeWithContext(_:)` is called on `WKInterfaceController` immediately after the controller is loaded from a storyboard. This method has a parameter for an optional context object that can be whatever you want it to be, like a model object, an ID or a string. Also, when this method is called, WatchKit has already connected any `IBOutlets` you might have set up. That means no juggling property getters, empty initializers or waiting for `viewDidLoad()`!

Another important method to know in the `WKInterfaceController` lifecycle is `willActivate()`. When this method is called, WatchKit is letting you know the controller is about to be displayed onscreen. You only need to use this method to run any last minute tasks, or anything that needs to run each time the controller is displayed, as just like with `viewWillAppear(_:)` on iOS, you can call this method repeatedly while a user is interacting with your Watch app.

Finally, there's `didDeactivate()`, which will be called when the controller's interface goes off-screen, such as when the user navigates away from the interface controller or when the Watch terminates the app. You should perform any cleanup or save any state here.

Segues

Since you're using storyboards to build your interfaces and connect your controllers, you probably won't be surprised to hear that segues play a big part in managing the transition between two instances of `WKInterfaceController`.

Segues work in WatchKit very similar to the way they work in iOS: They are still *stringly* typed, meaning that they each need their own identifier string, and you create them by Control-dragging between controllers in Interface Builder.

Instead of `performSegueWithIdentifier(_:sender:)`, WatchKit provides several amazingly convenient new methods you can override to pass context data in-between controllers:

- `contextForSegueWithIdentifier(_:)` returns a context object of type `AnyObject`. Use this to pass custom objects or values between controllers.
- `awakeWithContext(_:)` is called when your `WKInterfaceController`'s UI is set up. Controllers can receive context object from methods like `contextForSegueWithIdentifier(_:)`.

With these methods, you can simply check the identifier of the segue that is being performed and then return a relevant context, which could be a model object, a string or just about anything else you might want!

Here's an example of using a segue to pass a context object to the next controller:

```
override func contextForSegueWithIdentifier(
  segueIdentifier: String) -> AnyObject? {
  if segueIdentifier == "RecipeIngredients" {
    return recipe?.ingredients
  }
  return nil
}
```

Interface objects

For dealing with user interfaces on iOS, UIKit provides an assortment of controls and objects that all seem to inherit from classes like `UIView`, `UIControl` and eventually `UIResponder`. This provides each view with basic functionality like touch handling, while allowing classes to add their own advanced features and overrides.

WatchKit is somewhat of a different story. There are only 11 interface-related classes available, and they all inherit from `WKInterfaceObject`, which then inherits from… `NSObject`?

Where's my responder chain?!

This is because you're not dealing with real objects, in the usual sense, but rather with proxy objects.

Proxy objects

Remember that all of your code is executed on the iPhone and *then* transmitted to the Watch. That means the code you write isn't immediately committed to the UI for display. The WatchKit extension on the phone has to run the code, package up all of the UI state and then transmit it over the air.

Because of this, instead of having some sort of `WKView`, you'll be working with `WKInterfaceObject`s that act as *proxy objects* for the view state on the Watch. Each class that inherits from `WKInterfaceObject` gets a handful of helpful methods:

- `setHidden(_:)` hides and shows the object. Note that this method works by collapsing the space the object was taking up in the Watch layout system. More on this later.
- `setAlpha(_:)` changes the alpha of the object.
- `setWidth(_:)` and `setHeight(_:)` manually set the width and height of the object, respectively.
- `setAccessibilityLabel(_:)`, `setAccessibilityHint(_:)` and `setAccessibilityValue(_:)` configure the accessibility options for each object.

> **Note:** You might notice that all of the previous methods are *setters*: that is, they are used to set values like `hidden` and `alpha`. Because `WKInterfaceObjects` are proxies, you don't have direct access to get and set the properties themselves.

WatchKit views and controls

You will never add a `WKInterfaceObject` directly to any of your interfaces. Instead, you'll use these 11 subclasses:

- `WKInterfaceButton`: Your standard button. These come stocked with a background and a label, but through the use of groups and layouts, you can make really complex button styles.

The stock WKInterfaceButton

- `WKInterfaceDate`: This class, unique to WatchKit, is a label built to display dates and times. That means no more fussing with `NSDateFormatter`!

Showing the current date and time

- `WKInterfaceGroup`: This is another special WatchKit class that handles all of the interface layout and grouping. You can add other objects to a group to lay them out horizontally or vertically, and adjust their spacing and padding.

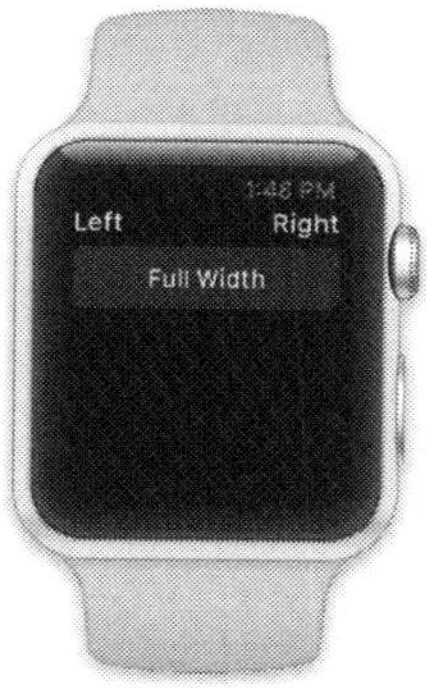

Nested groups with labels and buttons

- `WKInterfaceImage`: This subclass is almost exactly the same as `UIImageView`. The one special quality of `WKInterfaceImage` is that you can set multiple images and *animate* them. *The GIF is dead, long live the GIF!*

A simple image

- `WKInterfaceLabel`: This is your run-of-the-mill label, just like `UILabel`. You'll use this class anywhere you need to display text.

A plain old label

- `WKInterfaceMap`: This is a peculiar object. Maps on WatchKit are *not* interactive. In your controllers, you'll set a `MKCoordinateRegion` (which is basically just a latitude, longitude and zoom level) and the map will configure a static view of that location. You can still add things like pins and custom annotations, but they're not interactive.

Showing a location with WKInterfaceMap

- `WKInterfaceSeparator`: If you've been making iOS apps for a while, you've probably run into the scenario where you add a `UIView` or `CALayer` just to change the appearance of a table's separators. Now you have a fully-configurable `WKInterfaceSeparator` that you can use in tables and views, and that even works for vertical separation!

A simple separator

- `WKInterfaceSlider`: This is a slimmed-down version of `UISlider` in that it offers more limited functionality and shouldn't be subclassed. You can still customize the slider with min and max values, min and max icons and the number of steps. There is a new **Continuous** property that you set in Interface Builder to make the bar solid. With this property turned off, the bar is etched in the number of steps.

A stock WKInterfaceSlider with six steps

- `WKInterfaceSwitch`: This object is also similar to its iOS counterpart, `UISwitch`, except now you get a handy built-in label.

The stock WKInterfaceSwitch

- `WKInterfaceTable`: Tables in WatchKit are quite useful, and it's likely you'll use them all over the place. `WKInterfaceTable`s are automatically paired with `WKInterfaceController`s for interaction events and segues. Tables are *row-based* and have no notion of sections. You'll make a relatively complex table later in this book and get a feel for how to use multiple row styles.

A complex table with different row types

- `WKInterfaceTimer`: This is another special WatchKit interface object. Since watches traditionally handle time, Apple created a class that is basically a label that counts down to a specific date. You can configure what units to display: seconds, minutes, hours, days, weeks, months and even years.

A WKInterfaceTimer showing hours, minutes and seconds

Layout

Auto Layout has been a controversial tool among developers because of its coupling with Interface Builder, verbose syntax and foreign-looking visual format language. But with the introduction of varying device sizes and size classes, Apple has been pushing Auto Layout heavily.

Most developers were expecting Apple to force us to use Auto Layout in WatchKit. Just by taking a look at `WKInterfaceObject`'s methods, you can see that there isn't any way to change the position of the object, so that must mean you're going to have to brush up on Auto Layout, right?

Visual.Format.Language! What the...?

Auto Layout be gone! WatchKit provides its very own layout system that abstracts away most of the pain of layout and sizing and lets you focus on building your app. The WatchKit layout system defaults to sizing objects based on their content size and putting everything into either horizontal or vertical layout groups.

This works in much the same way as HTML and CSS layout, if you have any experience with those languages. Content is king, and interface elements are spaced and laid out relative to the content that comes before them.

Things like the number of lines a label has, font sizes and image sizes are all automatically calculated to lay out surrounding objects and even size table row heights!

No more calculating text height for table views!

Take a look at this more complex interface for a `WKInterfaceTable` with multiple row types. You're going to build this exact interface later in the book. All of the work is done in the storyboard, and the `WKInterfaceController` code only has to worry about wiring the data to the interface objects.

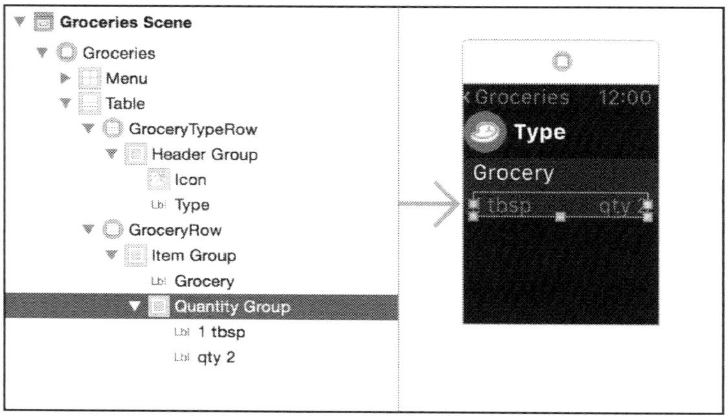

Animations

Almost as intriguing as the decision to make the WatchKit extension work with remote procedure calls is the way that WatchKit performs animations.

When Apple announced the Apple Watch, they demoed videos with tons of beautiful animations. Most developers couldn't wait to get their hands on the Watch and start playing with `UIView` animations or libraries like Facebook's Pop.

Each of these interfaces has delightful and fluid animations

But the WatchKit extension handles animations in a very *non-dynamic* way. To display animations in WatchKit, you'll need both a `WKInterfaceImage` and a series of images that, when combined, create a smooth animation, just like a GIF!

That means you can't easily create custom animations. Remember that this is only the first iteration of WatchKit, and fully-fledged Watch apps are likely to come later, hopefully bringing with them many of the features currently missing from WatchKit, such as a Core Animation equivalent.

Example of individual progress fill animation frames

> **Note:** Some developers are already trying to solve the problem of generating dynamic animations in WatchKit. Check out the project Flipbook for one approach: https://github.com/frosty/Flipbook

Notifications and glances

Alongside your typical Watch apps built with controllers and segues, WatchKit includes two other ways that users can interact with the Watch and your apps.

Notifications

Notifications should be a familiar topic, as they've been around since iOS 3, which was introduced in 2009. On Apple Watch, notifications work almost exactly the same as they do on iOS. If the Watch receives a local or remote notification, it displays an alert, along with a vibration and an optional noise, and it lights up the screen.

WatchKit introduces two new types of notifications: the **short look** and the **long look**. While both notification types are triggered by a remote or local notification, the source of the notification can determine which, or both, of the notification types should be used.

The short look

A short look is a very simple notification. It's comparable to the notifications that were available to iOS prior to iOS 8: The user sees only your app's icon, some text and the title of your app. If the user taps on the short look notification, then the Watch, like the iPhone, launches the full app.

The only real differences between the short look and pre-iOS 8 notifications are in layout and appearance.

A short look notification for a new recipe

The long look

A long look notification has a more complex interface that you can completely customize. The top part of the notification is called the "sash" and contains the name of your app and the icon, on top of a translucent, blurred bar.

Beneath the sash, you can add any content you want. Text content is driven by the notification and is either dynamic or static. With static notifications, you must bundle any image resources as part of the WatchKit extension. With dynamic notifications, you can customize the interface a bit more, but if you take too long, the system will fall back to the static notification.

You can also add any action items to the notification, so the user can jump into your app immediately and have it carry out the corresponding action. The user can dismiss your notification or tap anywhere in the content area to simply open your app.

Building a long look notification in Interface Builder

One interesting feature of short and long look notifications is that users can toggle in between the different types using a wrist-based gesture, if you've made both types available for your app. Apple claims that after receiving a notification, the Watch will first display the short look, and if the user brings their wrist up to look at the notification, the Watch will change it to a long look.

This feature can provide more context and flexibility to your users, so they don't have to fumble around navigating the tiny screen.

> **Note:** You'll have the opportunity to build your own custom notifications in Chapter 11, "Notifications".

Glances

Another interaction point in WatchKit are glances, which provide a "quick look" into your app, similar to Today extensions in iOS 8. The user gets a consumable, single-screen interface that tells them something about the state of the app, like the temperature outside or how much time is left before the roast in the oven is cooked to perfection.

In the WatchKit Programming Guide, Apple gives a couple of great examples of appropriate uses for glances:

> *The glance for a calendar app might show information about the user's next meeting, while the glance for an airline app might display gate information for an upcoming flight.*

Glances use `WKInterfaceController` just like a normal WatchKit interface controller. Apple recommends you keep glances simple, though: scrolling, and any interactive interface objects like buttons and switches, aren't permitted.

An example groceries glance

You can also use `updateUserActivity(_:userInfo:)` to advertise contextual information so your Watch app knows what to do when the user taps your glance. Using this method in your glance, and `handleUserActivity(_:)` in your app, you'll be able to open the app and configure its interface accordingly. These two methods are collectively known as Handoff.

Note: If you're eager to jump into making your own glance, skip to Chapter 9, "Glances", to learn what's involved!

WatchKit limitations

The first versions of the Apple Watch and WatchKit are exciting, but there are a few things that these newcomers cannot and should not do. These limitations are important to keep in mind as you're thinking about building your first app.

Intended for lightweight apps

From the Apple Watch Human Interface Guidelines:

> *Apps designed for Apple Watch should respect the context in which the wearer experiences them: briefly, frequently, and on a small display.*

You should look at building an Apple Watch app as literally extending an iPhone app to the user's wrist. The Watch is meant for quick and ephemeral interactions.

Small in size

The Apple Watch is small—really small. Developers are used to having at least 320 points in width, amazingly sharp Retina displays and a screen big enough for four-finger gestures.

Remember that the Apple Watch takes extremely limited input and is stuck to the user's wrist. Your interfaces should be big and simple. Make your fonts and buttons large and use very few of them.

Limited capabilities

Since the first version of WatchKit is an extension, you'll have limited capabilities if you don't rely on the features of an iPhone. Things like background fetching, Core Location and cameras are all out of the question.

If you need any advanced features, think about building them into the containing iPhone app and saving the data to a shared group that WatchKit can access.

Where to go from here?

This has been an overview of the design and features of WatchKit—what it can and cannot do. There are many exciting, new and unique tools for building Apple Watch apps, and the best way to get familiar with them is to pick them up and try them. What's more, I think we all know this is just the beginning for WatchKit!

In the following chapters, you'll get your hands on many of the different interface controls and objects in WatchKit, as well begin construction of a larger Apple Watch app that will take you through building custom layouts, navigation, tables and much more!

Chapter 3: UI Controls

By Ryan Nystrom

Apple delivered 11 interface controls with WatchKit, all of which inherit from `WKInterfaceObject`, which itself inherits from `NSObject`. Many of the interface controls have UIKit counterparts, but some are unique to WatchKit.

In this chapter, you'll get your hands on several of WatchKit's new interface controls providing you experience of how to start piecing together a functional Apple Watch app. Indeed, you'll build such an app: a cooking companion that will do all the timing and calculating so you can prepare the perfect steak!

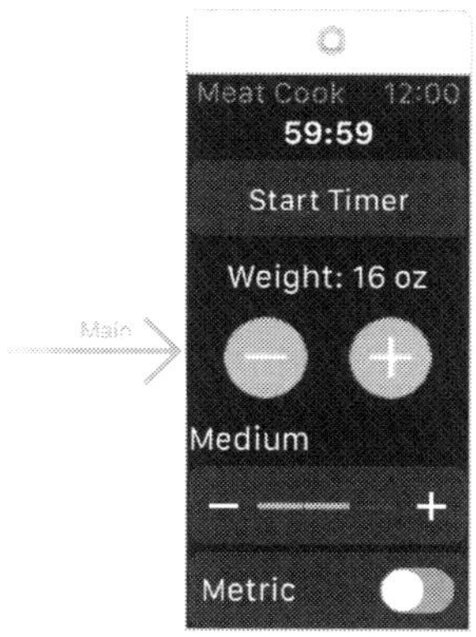

Storyboard of your cooking app

> **Note:** If you want a detailed review of each of the new controls, please refer to Chapter 2, "Architecture".

Getting started

To jump right into building and using the new interface objects, grab the **MeatCooker** starter project; this is mostly bare, but we've provided it so you don't have to waste any time on setup and configuration.

Open **MeatCooker.xcodeproj** and have a poke around. When you're done select the **MeatCooker** target, as well as the iPhone 6 simulator. **Build and run** to launch the app and you'll see an empty, white screen.

Blank MeatCooker iPhone app

Take a look at the targets and the project files. You'll see that we've already created the WatchKit App **scheme** for you, as well as **groups** for the MeatCooker WatchKit Extension and the MeatCooker WatchKit App.

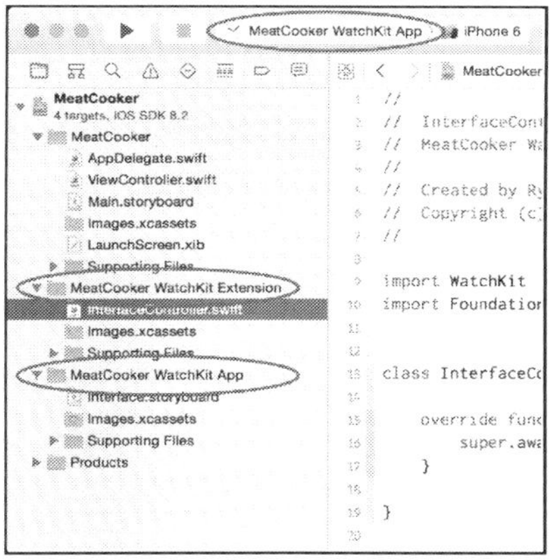

WatchKit target and groups

Groups are a great way to ring-fence code and resources that belong to a particular target, keeping your project neatly organized.

Select the **MeatCooker WatchKit App** scheme and **build and run** to launch the Watch app in the Apple Watch simulator. You'll see a lot of empty space for you to work with.

First run of MeatCooker on the Watch simulator

> **Note:** If you want to know how create a WatchKit app from scratch, please see Chapter 1, "Hello, Apple Watch!"

Next, take a look at the **MeatCooker WatchKit Extension** and **MeatCooker WatchKit App** groups in the project navigator. You'll see the following files and groups in each:

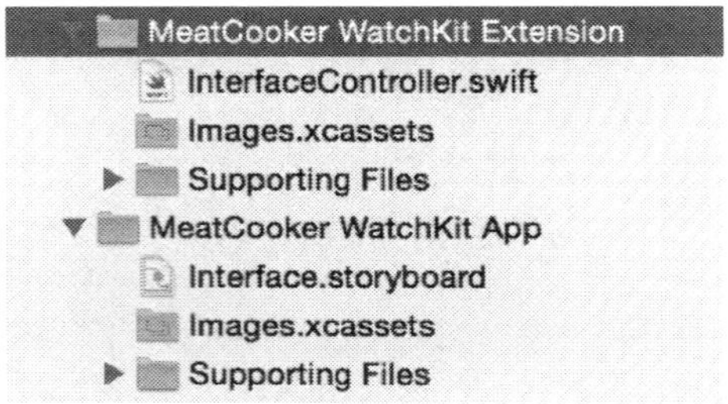

Starter project Extension and app

Each group of files corresponds to an individual app target with the same respective name. This helps organize your files while also keeping them accessible. It's a much cleaner setup than having a bunch of different Xcode projects crammed into a single workspace.

Make sure you understand the purpose of each group or target:

- **MeatCooker WatchKit Extension:** This target houses all of the code that runs as an extension on your iPhone. Refer back to Chapter 2, "Architecture" for more.
- **MeatCooker WatchKit App:** This target is for all of the resources that are physically stored on the Watch, including images, files and the interface storyboard.

Open **Interface.storyboard** from the **MeatCooker WatchKit App** group and take a look at the default, blank interface controller:

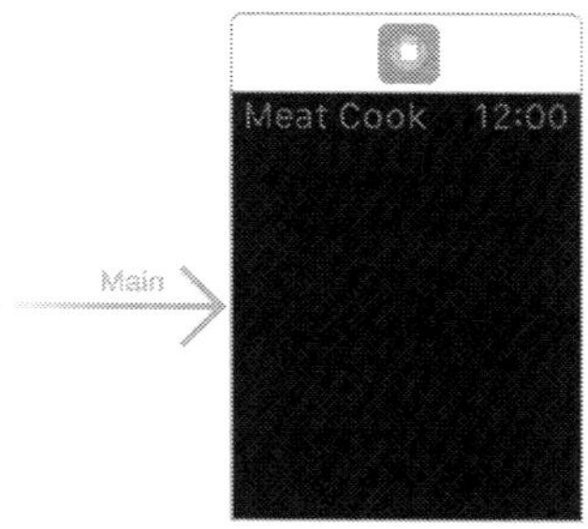

MeatCooker blank interface controller

If you've worked with iOS storyboards, this should look pretty familiar. There is a main entry point arrow designating that this is the controller that the OS will load when the app launches.

There is also the title of the controller, similar to a navigation bar title, and a time placeholder.

Select the interface controller, open the **Attributes Inspector**, and check out some of the available attributes for `WKInterfaceController`. This is where you can change things like the title, insets and spacing.

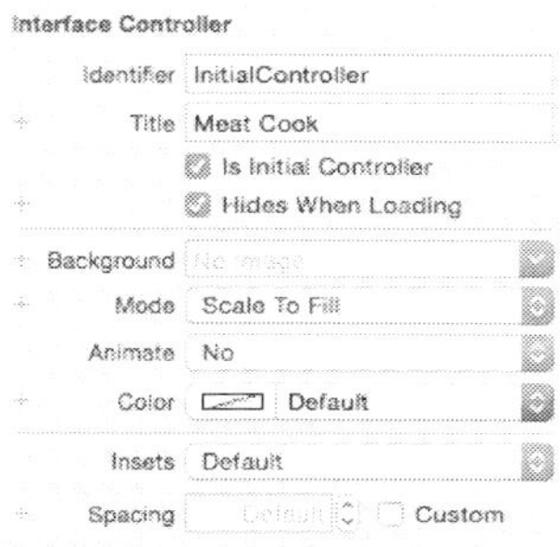

Attributes Inspector for the initial controller

For now, you don't need to change any these settings. Enough poking around—it's time to put some stuff on the screen!

Let there be controls

Throughout the rest of this chapter, you're going to create all of the interface elements for the app, one by one. While you won't use all 11 UI controls provided by WatchKit, pay attention while you're working and you'll see just how powerful WatchKit storyboards can be.

The timer object

To cook the perfect steak, you need to know a couple of things about your meat and the preferences of whoever is going to eat it, so you can determine just the right amount of time to leave the meat in the oven—and for the sake of simplicity, we are assuming you are cooking with an oven!

All in all, you're going to need to be able to:

- Start and stop a timer;
- Increase and decrease the weight of the meat;
- Select the diner's cooking preference, from rare to well done;

- Toggle between metric and imperial units.

With **Interface.storyboard** open, find **Group** in the Object library and drag one onto the interface controller.

You'll see a dashed border with the word "Group" in the middle. This is just a placeholder. If you were to run the app now, you wouldn't actually see anything new on the screen.

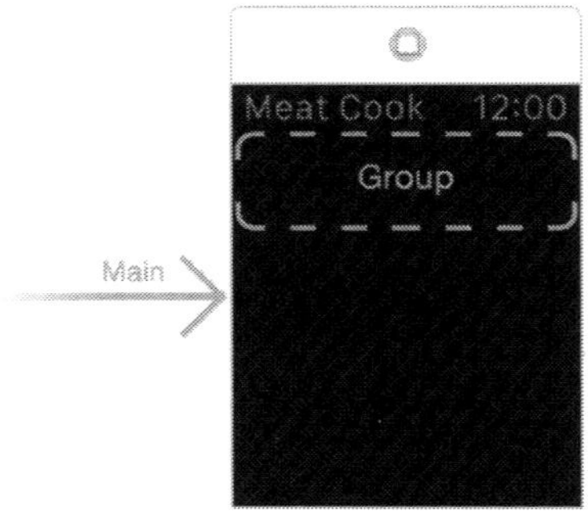

An empty Group interface object

> **Note:** Groups are unique interface objects in that they occupy the space of their contents. You can specify a width and height for a group, but the real magic is in how they automatically lay themselves out. You can read more in Chapter 4, "Layout".

Next, drag a **Timer** into the group. Timers also have placeholder text to give an idea of how their contents will be formatted.

With your new timer selected, open the **Attributes Inspector** and change the following attributes:

- In **Units**, select only **Second** and **Minute**;
- Change **Font** to **Text Styles – Headline**;
- Set **Alignment** to **Center** (the middle of the five buttons);
- Change the **Horizontal** position to **Center**.

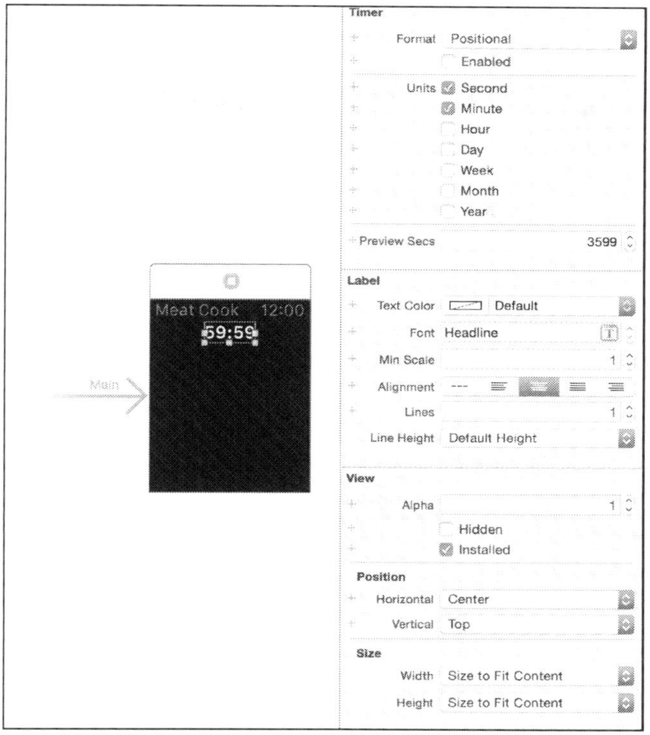

Setting up the Timer interface object

Wow, that's a lot of setup for such a tiny interface element! What exactly did you do?

The **Units** attribute configures what time units the timer will display. If you were to select Day, Month, Year and set a date of two months, three days and one year into the future, then the timer would read "1y 2m 3d". The timer is *really smart* in how it displays the time, and no more fussing around with `NSDateFormatter`.

Timers also have text properties, just like labels. You can configure the font, number of lines, alignment, color, height, etc.

Position is a new type of attribute that's unique to WatchKit and is extremely powerful. It lets you lay out objects to the left, center or right of their container.

It might seem like a lot of setup, but take a look at all the steps you would have to do in an iOS app to get a similar interface object:

- Use `NSDateFormatter` to get a string representation of an `NSDate`;
- Subclass `UILabel`;

- Set up the necessary Auto Layout constraints on the label;
- Use an `NSTimer` to update the label every second.

Using `WKInterfaceTimer` saved you from writing a whole lot of code and from running any number of tests!

With the MeatCooker WatchKit App scheme selected, **build and run** the app to see your new timer.

Hmm. That looks kind of… *lame*. Why isn't it doing anything?

Well, in your storyboard you've given the timer a placeholder number of seconds, but this doesn't carry over when you run the app; it's purely for design time purposes. For the timer to work, you need to wire it up and trigger it in code.

First, you need something to trigger the timer. Find a **button** in the Object library and drag it next to the timer, or just below it if you're dragging it into the document outline. Make sure you add the button to the *same group* that contains your timer. You can confirm this by checking the document outline.

But wait! Where did your timer go?

The problem is, all Groups have a horizontal layout by default. You need to change your group to make it vertical.

Select the **Group** in the document outline.

Then in the **Attributes Inspector**, change the **Layout** to **Vertical**.

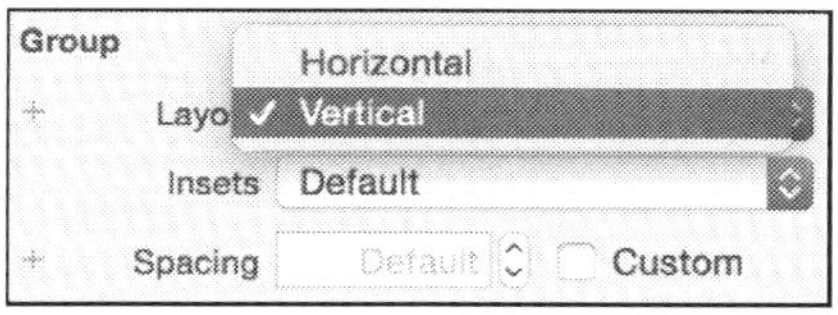

Now you should see your timer on top, with your new button underneath.

Double-click on the text in the button and change it to **Start Timer**. You can also do this by selecting the button and changing the text in the **Title** field of the Attributes Inspector.

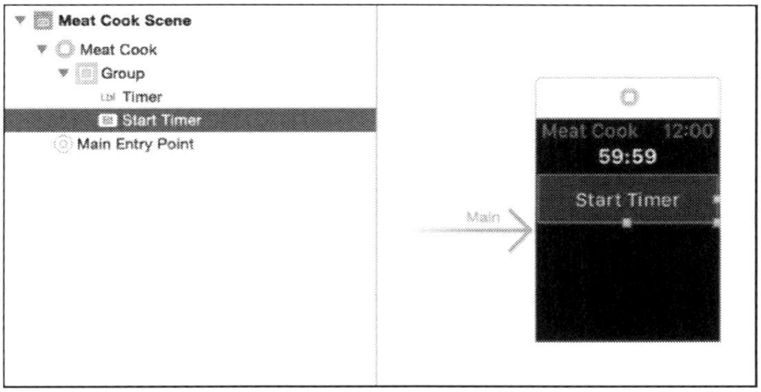

Your button and timer in a perfect layout!

Build and run your Watch app to see the new button. You'll be able to tap on the button and see the app both highlight it and depress it in 3D space. Now let's make that button do something!

Wiring the timer

Option-click on **MeatCooker WatchKit Extension\InterfaceController.swift** to open the controller in the assistant editor. You should see the storyboard and controller's Swift code side-by-side.

> **Note:** When you have `Interface.storyboard` and `InterfaceController.swift` open together, remember that you have files of *different targets* open together. WatchKit gives still lets you connect outlets between targets, but it's easy to make a mistake and add files to the wrong target, or outlets to the wrong file.

Control-drag from the timer in **Interface.storyboard** into **InterfaceController.swift** to create a new IBOutlet. In the pop-up, name the outlet `timer`, make it of type `WKInterfaceTimer` and give it a **weak** connection.

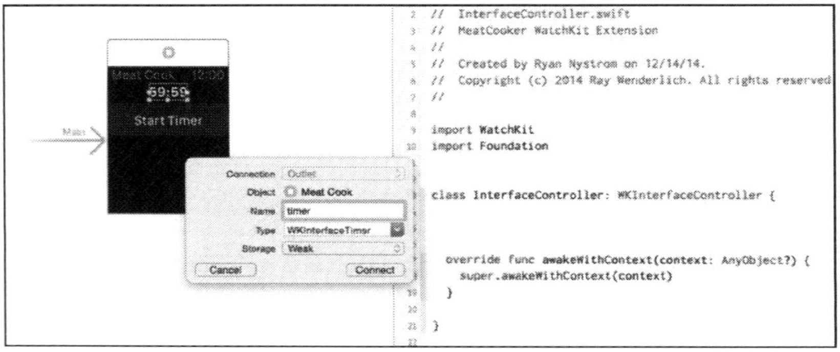

Connecting the timer to the controller

Now **Control-click** the **button**. Click on the **selector** option under **Sent Actions** and drag over to **InterfaceController.swift**. In the pop-up, name the new action `onTimerButton`.

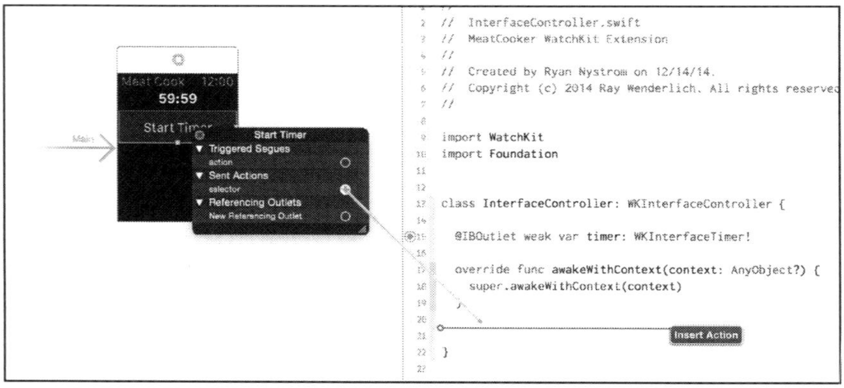

Inside `onTimerButton()`, add a print statement to test that this method is wired up and working. Your method should look like this:

```
@IBAction func onTimerButton() {
  println("onTimerButton")
}
```

Build and run your app. Tap on the **Start Timer** button a couple of times and make sure you see some output in your console log.

Now that you're confident the button is wired up properly, how about using it to make the timer work?

Replace the contents of `onTimerButton()` with the following code:

```
// 1
let countdown: NSTimeInterval = 20
let date = NSDate(timeIntervalSinceNow: countdown)
// 2
timer.setDate(date)
timer.start()
```

Here's what you're doing with the above code:

1. You set a 20-second countdown variable and use it to instantiate an `NSDate` object. `WKInterfaceTimer` always uses date objects, not primitives, to count time.
2. You set the date for the timer and then start the timer. A timer won't do anything until you call `start()` on it. Any time that passes between setting the date and calling `start()` will be subtracted from the timer.

Build and run the app, then tap on the button. Now, instead of some boring console output, you'll see the timer start, and count down all the way to zero!

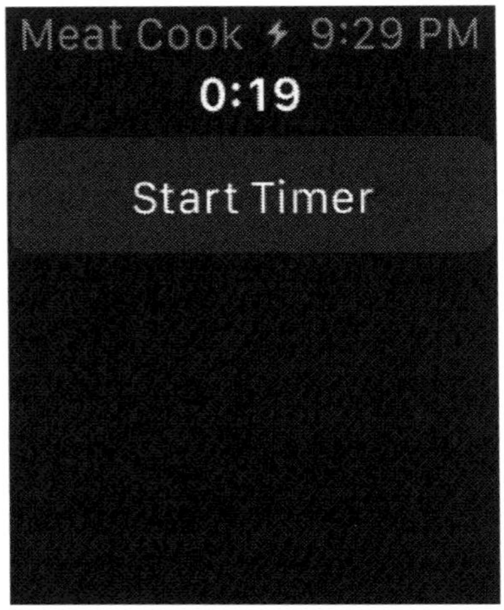

Timer counting down

Using a label and buttons to control weight

You've seen how to add interface objects to your storyboard as well as how to wire them into your controller. It looks like it's time to build out this app!

Open **Interface.storyboard** and drag a **Label** from the Object Library to just below the first group that contains the timer and button. That's *below* the group, not inside it! Change the **Text** to **Weight: 16 oz** and the **Horizontal** position to **Center**.

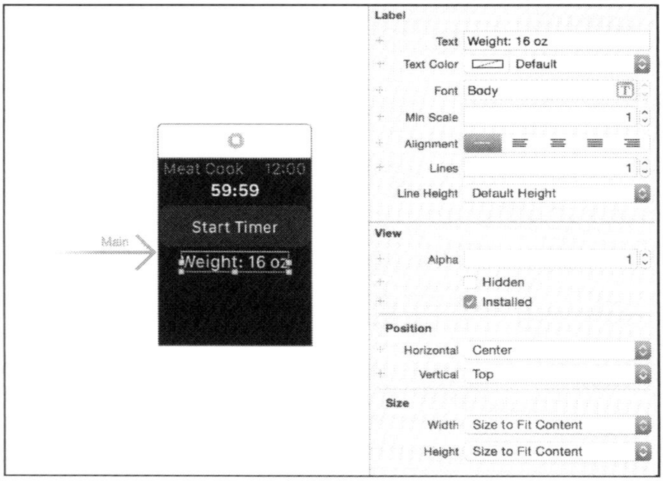

Weight label configuration

Next, drag another **Group** beneath the label you just added. You can leave the Layout setting of this group as Horizontal.

Now drag a **button** into the group. With this new button selected, change the following attributes in the Attributes Inspector:

- Clear the **Title** field;
- Set the **Background** image to **minus**;
- Change the **Horizontal** position to **Center**;
- Set the **Width** size to **Size to Fit Content**.

You'll end up with a button that looks just like the following:

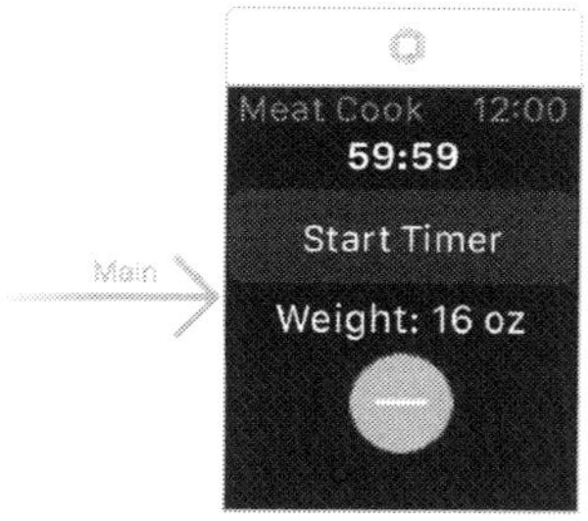

Next, click on your new button, **copy** and then immediately **paste**. This will paste a new button with the same configuration directly after the selected button, and within the same group.

Select this new button and change the **Background** image to **plus**.

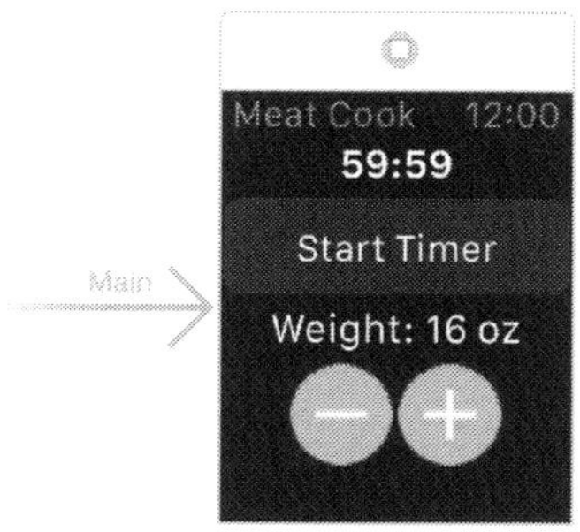

If you're a fan of Apple design and documentation, you've probably run across the Human Interface Guidelines at least a couple of times. Apple puts a lot of emphasis on interactive element sizes and spacing. You can probably tell that those two blue buttons are *way* too close for comfort.

Groups have powerful attributes that make layout extremely easy. In the case of items being too crowded, there's an attribute called *spacing* that fixes just this.

Select the **group** that contains your two blue buttons. You might have to use the document outline to select it. Change the **Spacing** attribute from Default to **20**. Tap the Return key to commit the change and see Interface Builder update automatically.

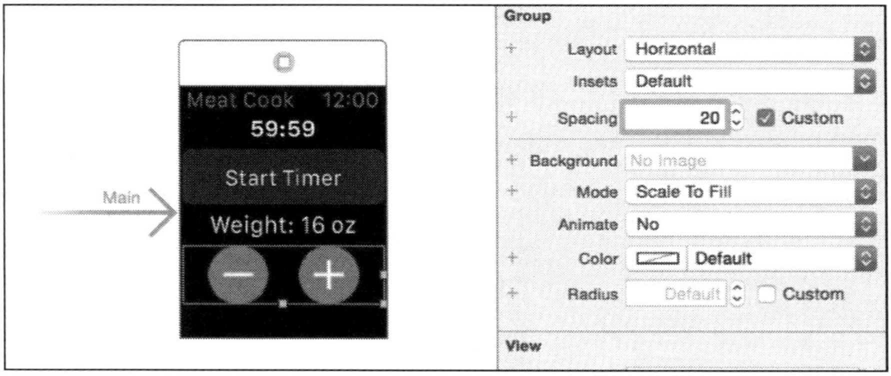

Ah, much more comfortable

While you're at it, all of the items are getting a little tight vertically. Well, it turns out that the contents of `WKInterfaceController` are already in one big layout group! We know this because WKInterfaceControllers contain other interface objects, are vertical, and even have spacing and inset options.

Select the interface controller by clicking on the white header above all of your interface objects. In the **Attributes Inspector**, change **Spacing** to **10** and hit Return. This will add a little vertical padding so your UI doesn't feel too crammed.

Open **InterfaceController.swift** in the assistant editor so you can see both it and **Interface.storyboard** at the same time. You're going to add a couple of outlets and actions.

Control-click on the **weight label** and drag to create an IBOutlet. Name it `weightLabel`, give it a type of `WKInterfaceLabel` and make it a **weak** connection.

Next, just as you did for the Start Timer button, add an **IBAction** for both the **plus** and **minus** buttons. Name them `onMinusButton` and `onPlusButton`, respectively.

If you did this correctly, you should have added the following code to your `InterfaceController` class:

```
@IBOutlet weak var weightLabel: WKInterfaceLabel!
@IBAction func onMinusButton() {
```

```
}
@IBAction func onPlusButton() {
}
```

Now it's time to make the buttons functional. Close the assistant editor and open **InterfaceController.swift** in the main editor. Add a new variable to the top of the class:

```
var ounces = 16
```

This will keep track of the selected weight for your meat. A default of 16 ounces, or one pound, is a good starting point.

Add a new function just below `awakeWithContext(_:)`:

```
func updateConfiguration() {
  weightLabel.setText("Weight: \(ounces) oz")
}
```

This simple function updates your label with the current weight. You will be adding a lot to this function in due course to update the interface to reflect to the app's current state.

In `onMinusButton()`, add the following code:

```
ounces--
updateConfiguration()
```

And in `onPlusButton()`, add the following code to increase the current weight:

```
ounces++
updateConfiguration()
```

Thanks to Swift, this code is short, clean and very readable!

Lastly, to make sure the app updates the interface with the proper state from the beginning, add a call to `updateConfiguration()` to the end of `awakeWithContext(_:)`:

```
override func awakeWithContext(context: AnyObject?) {
  super.awakeWithContext(context)

  updateConfiguration()
}
```

Build and run the app, and click on the plus and minus buttons to see your label update accordingly.

Now you can cook lean or heavy!

Using a slider object to control doneness

People have their own preferences when it comes to cooking meat, from rare to well done, to cremated. To please your diners, you need to be able to regulate the cooking temperature.

Open **Interface.storyboard** and drag another **Group** from the Object Library to just below the group containing the two blue buttons. Make sure it's in the same hierarchy level as the buttons, weight label and timer groups.

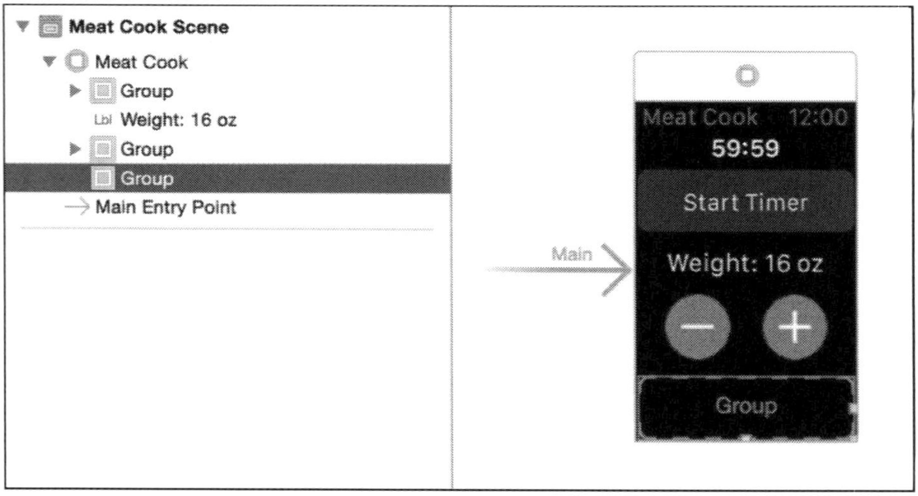

Drag a **Label** and a **Slider** into your new group. Since the group is horizontal by default, select the group, open the **Attributes Inspector** and change **Layout** to **Vertical**.

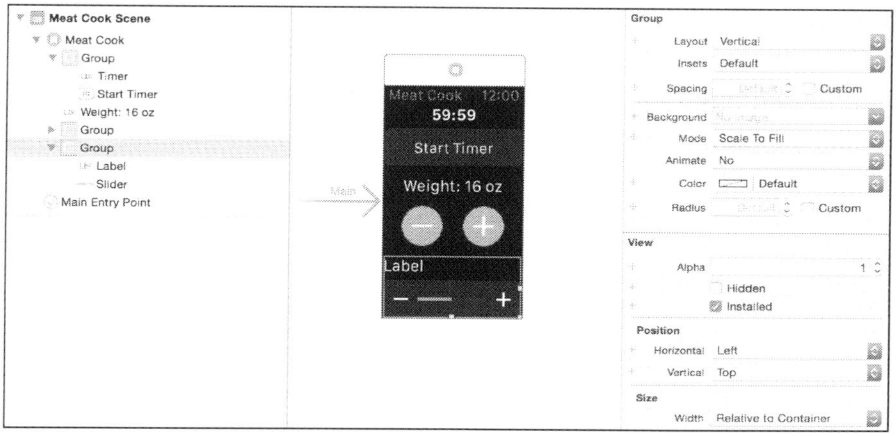

The laid out label and slider group

You will have four cooking temperatures: Rare, Medium Rare, Medium and Well Done. For the user to select one of these options, you'll have to configure the slider appropriately.

Select your new slider and, in the Attributes Inspector, make the following changes:

- Change the **Slider Value** to **2** to select medium by default;
- Change the **Slider Minimum** to **0** for rare;
- Change the **Slider Maximum** to **3** for well done;
- Set the number of **Slider Steps** to **3**. There is also an empty state, which actually makes four steps, but you need to set the number of values *in addition* to the value zero.

Make sure that **Continuous** is **unchecked**. This will give you step dividers on the slider to make the available options and means of selection more obvious to the user.

Open **InterfaceController.swift** using the **assistant editor**. **Control-drag** from the new label to create an IBOutlet. Name the outlet `cookLabel`, make the type `WKInterfaceLabel` and make it a **weak** connection.

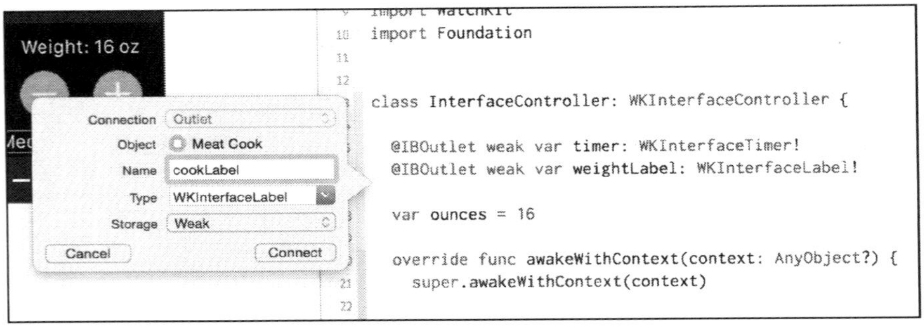

Wiring up the cookLabel

Control-click on the **slider** and drag the **selector** option into InterfaceController.swift to create an IBAction. Name the new action `onTempChange`.

To represent the cooking temperature, you could simply remember that rare is the integer 0, medium rare is 1 and so on, but Swift makes creating an `enum` to represent data structures like this way too easy to pass up!

Select the **MeatCooker WatchKit Extension** group. Click **File\New\File...** (⌘N), select **iOS\Source\Swift File** and click **Next**. Name your new file **MeatTemperature.swift** and make sure that it's being added to the **MeatCooker WatchKit Extension Target**, then click **Create**.

Lots of new targets in WatchKit apps

Note: WatchKit projects have a lot of targets. You can have even more targets if you're also building a shared library or framework. Make sure when adding new files that you add code to the WatchKit Extension, and images and other static resources to the WatchKit App.

Open **MeatTemperature.swift** and add the following `enum` at the top of the file:

```
enum MeatTemperature: Int {
  case Rare = 0, MediumRare, Medium, WellDone
}
```

This creates an `enum` that captures all four types of cooking temperature. `MeatTemperature` is of the type `Int`, so you can set the first case, `.Rare`, to `0`. Swift then infers the values of the rest of your cases by incrementing by 1, so `.MediumRare` is 1, `.Medium` is 2 and `.WellDone` is 3. All of these values correspond well with how you configured your slider when you set up the interface.

But integers aren't very user-friendly. How about getting a readable string value for the enum, as well? Add the following computed property to the `MeatTemperature` enum:

```
var stringValue: String {
  let temperatures = ["Rare", "Medium Rare", "Medium",
    "Well Done"]
  return temperatures[self.rawValue]
}
```

You create an array of strings, each associated with a `MeatTemperature` value. Then, you pluck the correct value by using the `rawValue` of the enum. Even though the enum is an `Int`, Swift's strong typing makes your code more declarative.

Ultimately, you're going to want the cooking temperature to affect the time spent cooking your meat. Add another computed property, just like `stringValue`, to get a cooking time modifier:

```
var timeModifier: Double {
  let modifiers = [0.5, 0.75, 1.0, 1.5]
  return modifiers[self.rawValue]
}
```

The entire `MeatTemperature` enum should now look like this:

```
enum MeatTemperature: Int {
  case Rare = 0, MediumRare, Medium, WellDone

  var stringValue: String {
    let temperatures = ["Rare", "Medium Rare", "Medium", "Well
       Done"]
    return temperatures[self.rawValue]
  }

  var timeModifier: Double {
    let modifiers = [0.5, 0.75, 1.0, 1.5]
    return modifiers[self.rawValue]
  }
}
```

Great! You not only have a way to represent cooking temperatures, but now you're supplying a readable string and a time modifier. Let's plug this into the app.

Go back to **InterfaceController.swift** and add another variable, just under the `ounces` variable you added earlier:

```
var cookTemp = MeatTemperature.Medium
```

This sets your default cooking temperature to `.Medium`, which is in my experience is a popular choice.

Find the `onTempChange()` method that you connected to the slider earlier and add the following code:

```
if let temp = MeatTemperature(rawValue: Int(value)) {
  cookTemp = temp
  updateConfiguration()
}
```

This code does two things:

- It creates a `MeatTemperature` variable. `WKInterfaceSlider` changed values are always of the type `Float`, so you have to cast it to an `Int` before initializing.
- Set the current cooking temperature and update the interface if a `MeatTemperature` variable was created.

To update the interface, add the following line to `updateConfiguration()`:

```
cookLabel.setText(cookTemp.stringValue)
```

Build and run, swipe down to the slider and tap around to change its value. Check out how the label updates every time you tap the plus or minus buttons on the slider!

Some like it charred

Integrating the timer

What good are these interface objects if you they don't tell you the correct amount of time to cook your meat? Looks like it's *time* to make the timer functional.

Since your app has variables for the weight and cooking temperature, add the following method to **InterfaceController.swift**:

```
// 1
func cookTimeForOunces(ounces: Int, cookTemp: MeatTemperature)
  -> NSTimeInterval {
  // 2
  let baseTime: NSTimeInterval = 47 * 60
  let baseWeight = 16
  // 3
  let weightModifier: Double =
  Double(ounces) / Double(baseWeight)
  let tempModifier = cookTemp.timeModifier
  return baseTime * weightModifier * tempModifier
}
```

1. Pass in parameters for the weight, in ounces, and the desired `MeatTemperature`. You could just use the `ounces` and `cookTemp` variables directly, but by using a simple function, you make your code much more *testable*. You are testing, right?
2. Create some standards that represent the time it takes to cook a 16-ounce steak in an oven at 400F.

3. Create modifiers that return a cooking time based on the provided weight and cooking temperature.

> **Note:** There are *lots* of ways to cook meat, and different meats have different cook times. This app is purely for introducing you to WatchKit controls, and doesn't aim to be culinary accurate or exhaustive!

One interesting feature of `WKInterfaceObject` is that it doesn't have very many ways to get the current state. This is because, as you read in Chapter 2, the code is executed on the phone. The state of the UI might have changed in the time that the phone has spent executing, so you need to keep track of any state yourself, like whether your timer is running.

Near the top of **InterfaceController.swift**, where your other properties are declared, add another to track the status of the timer:

```
var timerRunning = false
```

Your timer is not running when the controller is initialized, so it is safe to set its default value to `false`.

The timer counting down isn't enough to reflect the state of your app. It's a good idea to update the Start Timer button when the user taps it.

Open **Interface.storyboard** in the main editor and **InterfaceController.swift** in the assistant editor. **Control-click** and drag from the **Start Timer** button to create an outlet named `timerButton`.

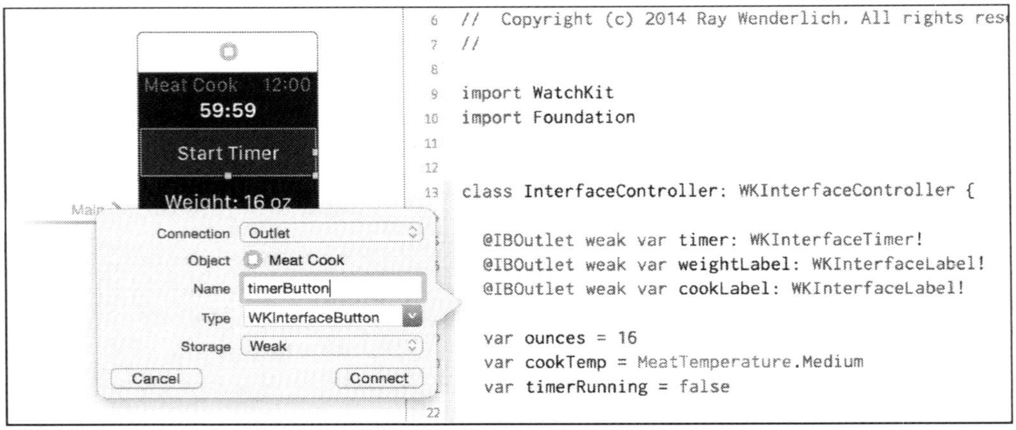

Replace everything inside `onTimerButton()` so that it looks like this:

```
@IBAction func onTimerButton() {
  // 1
  if timerRunning {
    timer.stop()
    timerButton.setTitle("Start Timer")
  } else {
    // 2
    let time = cookTimeForOunces(ounces, cookTemp: cookTemp)
    timer.setDate(NSDate(timeIntervalSinceNow: time))
    timer.start()
    timerButton.setTitle("Stop Timer")
  }
  // 3
  timerRunning = !timerRunning
}
```

1. Upon a user tap, if the timer is already running, you stop it and update the button title. This causes the timer to stop updating its UI.
2. If the timer isn't running, you create a cooking time interval using the new `cookTimeForOunces(_:cookTemp:)` method and use it to create an `NSDate`. Then, you start the timer and update the button title.
3. As the timer state has changed with the user tapping the button, you reflect that in your variable.

Build and run your app and change your cooking configuration. Tap the Start Timer button and watch the title change and the timer begin to count down. You can stop and restart the timer as many times as you like.

Now you're cooking!

Using the switch to change units

Since only three countries in the world use imperial units, it would be best to be able to toggle between imperial and metric. This is a perfect use-case for a `WKInterfaceSwitch`!

> **Note:** Liberia, Myanmar and the United States, if you were curious, although in the US, they are called United States customary units.

Open **Interface.storyboard** and drag in one last **Group** beneath the slider you added earlier. Make sure that you add the group to the same hierarchy as your other groups.

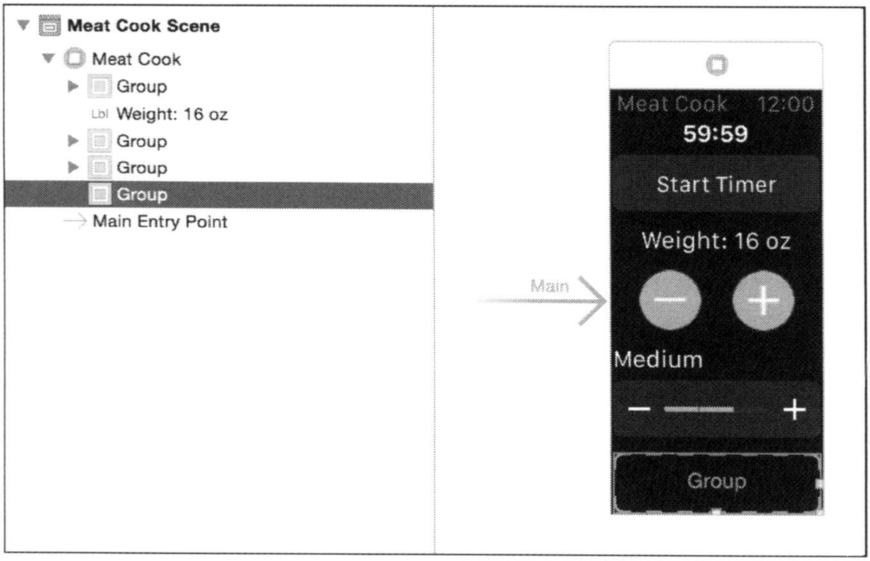

Drag a **Switch** object into the new group. Open the **Attributes Inspector** and change the **Title** attribute to **Metric**. Also change the **State** to **Off**. Remember you're using imperial units by default.

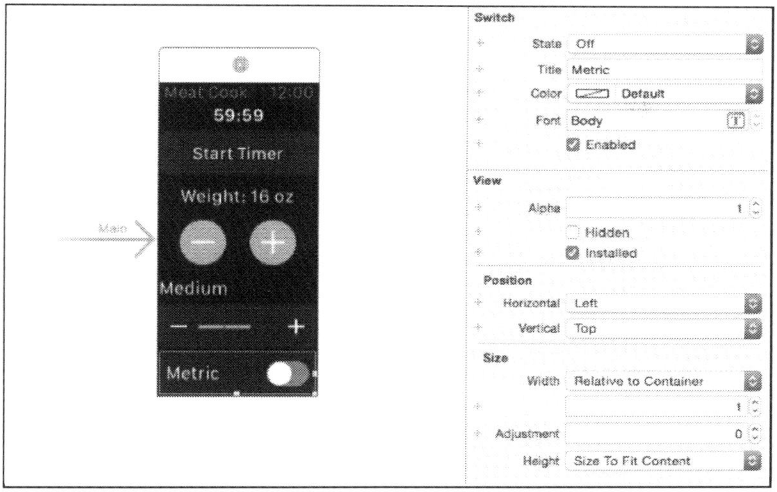

Adding and configuring an instance of WKInterfaceSwitch

Open **InterfaceController.swift** in the **assistant editor**, and just as you've been doing, **Control-click** the new switch and **drag** from the **selector** option to create a new IBAction. Name this action `onMetricChanged`.

Near the top of **InterfaceController.swift**, where your other variables are in the `InterfaceController` class, add another variable:

```
var usingMetric = false
```

This variable will keep track of which unit system, imperial or metric, your user prefers.

Go back to the method `onMetricChanged(_:)` that you just added and make it look like the following:

```
@IBAction func onMetricChanged(value: Bool) {
  usingMetric = value
  updateConfiguration()
}
```

You simply change your new variable whenever the user taps the switch and then tell the app to update the interface accordingly.

Find `updateConfiguration()` and change it to look like the following:

```
func updateConfiguration() {
  // 1
  cookLabel.setText(cookTemp.stringValue)
```

```
    var weight = ounces
    var unit = "oz"

    if usingMetric {
      // 2
      let grams = Double(ounces) * 28.3495
      weight = Int(grams)
      unit = "gm"
    }
    // 3
    weightLabel.setText("Weight: \(weight) \(unit)")
  }
```

1. The measurement system doesn't affect the cooking temperature, so you don't alter this line.
2. There are 28.3495 (roughly) grams per ounce, so if you're in metric mode, you need to convert your units. Notice that the `ounces` variable is *always* in ounces; you only use the metric state when it comes to configuring the interface objects.
3. Set the text of the `WKInterfaceLabel` with the converted weight and the proper unit abbreviation.

Build and run the app, and play around with the different settings. You should see your cooking weight change whenever you tap the switch!

The finished app with metric units (left), imperial (center), and the new switch (right)

Where to go from here?

You've learned a ton about new and familiar interface controls in this chapter: groups, labels, buttons, images, switches, sliders and timers. There are still several other controls you can explore.

Try adding a `WKInterfaceMap` to show your current location, a `WKInterfaceDate` object to show the current day and time or a `WKInterfaceSeparator` for a little design flare.

You could also extend the app by adding interface objects to change the oven temperature, which will affect the cooking time, or even to select between different meats and vegetables. Make the app work just how you like to cook!

In the next couple of chapters, you're going to begin building a much larger and more complex Apple Watch app that will demonstrate how to create more advanced layouts, navigate between interfaces and use tables.

Chapter 4: Layout

By Ryan Nystrom

When the iOS SDK was first released in 2008, it originally had a primitive layout system, implemented with *springs and struts*, that constrained views to their parent's edges. Soon after with the release of the iOS 6 SDK in 2012, Apple delivered a powerful new system called Auto Layout that it continues to improve, most recently in iOS 8. Auto Layout is still largely driven by the sizes of a view's parents and the positions of neighboring views.

WatchKit introduces an entirely new layout system. Instead of deriving layout from parent and neighbor views, WatchKit relies heavily on content size and spacing to lay out interface elements.

In this chapter, you'll learn the reasoning behind this new layout system, as well as begin building an interface that's far more complex than the one in the previous chapter.

A preview of what you will build in this chapter

Sticking with the food theme from the previous chapter, this app manages a collection of recipes approved by the raywenderlich.com team, and helps the user cook, track ingredients and even grocery shop! Are you salivating yet?

Understanding layout in WatchKit

Before you start dragging, dropping and clicking in Interface Builder, let's take a quick tour of the features of the layout system in WatchKit.

There are only three new concepts you need to understand to get started building awesome interfaces: **groups**, **content sizing** and **relative spacing**.

Layout groups

If you went through the previous chapter, you probably remember using several interface elements called **groups**. Groups are instances of `WKInterfaceGroup`, which inherits from `WKInterfaceObject`, just like `WKInterfaceLabel` or `WKInterfaceTimer`.

An empty WKInterfaceGroup

If, on iOS, you've ever used an empty view as nothing more than container to group other views in order to achieve a particular layout, then groups will feel instantly familiar. And just like `UIView`, `WKInterfaceGroup` is much more than a simple container for other interface elements. You can configure the appearance and behavior of a group in many different ways!

Open the header file **WKInterfaceGroup.h** and get a feel for all the things you can with a group.

> **Note:** To open **WKInterfaceGroup.h**, in Xcode open the **Open Quickly** dialog (**⌘-⇧-O**) and type **"WKInterfaceGroup"**. When the autocomplete shows **WKInterfaceGroup.h**, press Return to view the file. Notice that the class is in Objective-C!

Remember that groups already inherit from `WKInterfaceObject`, so there are even more things you can do than what's listed below:

- `setBackgroundColor(_:)` changes the background color.
- `setCornerRadius(_:)` changes the corner radius. No more fumbling with the `CALayer` property of a `UIView`!
- `setBackgroundImage(_:)` sets the background image using an image from the extensions asset catalog. It's nice to not have to add a `UIImageView`.
- `setBackgroundImageData(_:)` sets the background image data, usually when adding a series of images to animate.
- `setBackgroundImageNamed(_:)` sets the background image using an image from the Watch app's asset catalog.
- `startAnimating()` begins animating through the background images, if there is more than one.
- `startAnimatingWithImagesInRange(_:duration:repeatCount:)` is like `startAnimating()` but gives you a lot more control.
- `stopAnimating()` stops any image animations.

Looking at the group-specific attributes in the Attributes Inspector in Interface Builder, you'll see even more options you can use to create really interesting layouts.

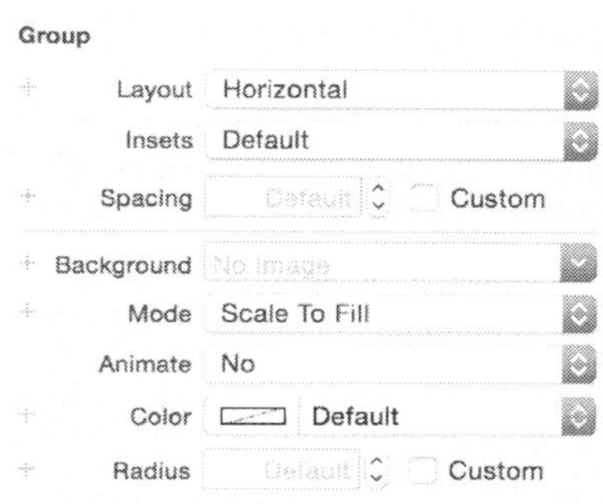

The group attributes in Interface Builder

Layout is likely one of the most important attributes for groups. It lets you change how interface elements inside the group are positioned. You can use either **Horizontal** or **Vertical**.

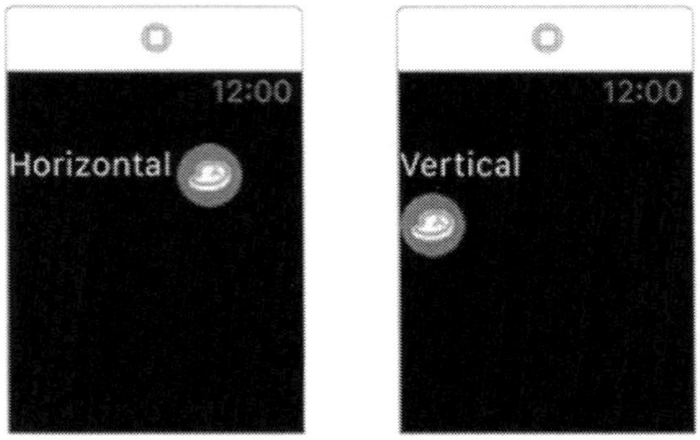

Horizontal and vertical groups with the same content

> **Note:** If you use a horizontal layout, make sure to pay attention to the sizes any dynamic interface elements like labels. If they grow too big they'll push any sibling elements off screen.

Insets let you create a margin between the group and its contents. If you've ever worked with `UIEdgeInsets` before, such as with `UIScrollView`, this should feel familiar. You can change the top, bottom, left and right insets independently for groups.

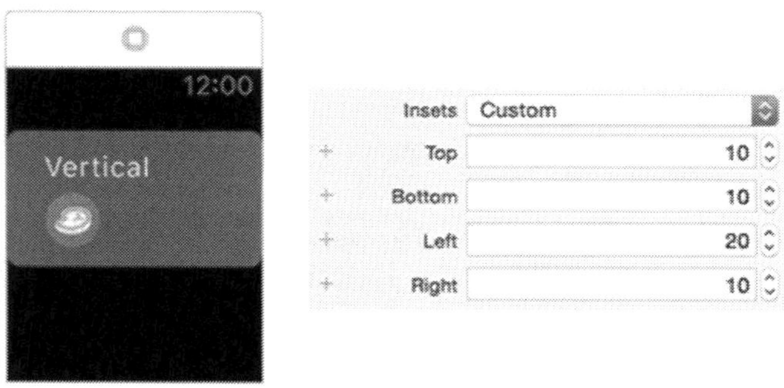

A group with custom insets

The Apple Watch Human Interface Guidelines recommend that interface elements in your interface controllers hug the side of the screen, because there's a black edging around the screen that affords a natural margin. However, when you're dealing with content toward the middle of the screen, it can be useful to add a little extra space so your interfaces aren't too crammed.

Spacing is similar to Insets, except that instead of adjusting the space from the edges of the group to its content, spacing adjusts the distance *between* the elements within a group.

If your group is vertical, spacing adds space to the y-axis, and if your group is horizontal, spacing adds space to the x-axis.

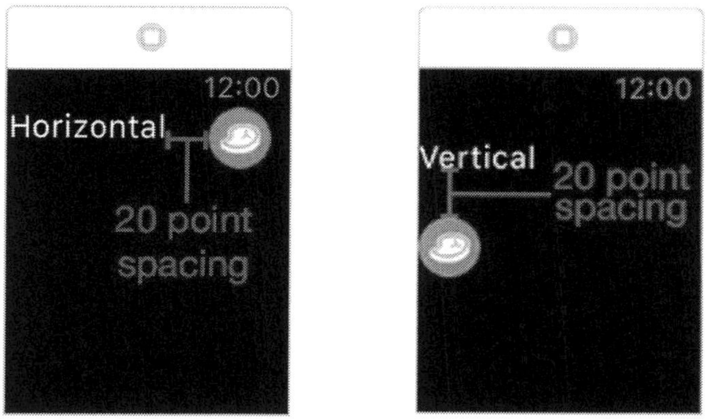

A vertical and horizontal group with 20 points of spacing

The next section of group attributes should be fairly obvious. You can change the **Background** image, the drawing **Mode** for the image, decide whether to **Animate** the background image, or simply select a background **Color**.

The last attribute in the section is the **Radius**, which changes the corner radius of the group. Never before have you been able to change the corner radius of something in Interface Builder without hacks or creating an entire framework that makes use of `@IBDesignable`.

The default radius value is 6 points, but this is only applied when you set either a background color or a background image, otherwise the group doesn't use rounded corners at all.

A group with a radius of 15

> **Note:** When changing the radius attribute, pay attention to the layout and size of your content. Groups will automatically clip anything that falls outside the bounds of clipped corners. This is a great example of when adjusting the insets would be useful.

Content size

Another interesting feature of the layout system in WatchKit is that it's driven by content size; the combined size of all the content within each group in the interface.

In WatchKit, the size that text takes up is determined by an `NSAttributedString`, which contains attributes like the font, line spacing and color. WatchKit renders the text offscreen, determines the height and width based on the strings bounding box and then applies that to the layout.

What's different about WatchKit as opposed to iOS is that in WatchKit, all of the layout is handled for you automatically.

Take a look at the example below. The labels contained in each group have had their fonts, styles, and line heights adjusted. Instead of fussing with text bounding sizes and line numbers, the groups are simply set to Size To Fit Contents and WatchKit takes care of the rest!

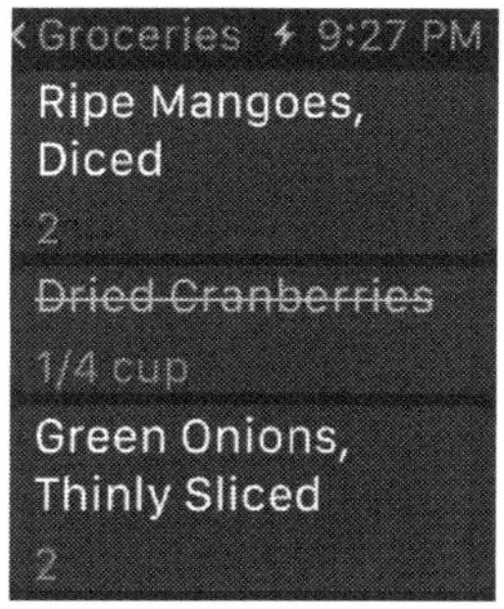

NSAttributedStrings and automatic content sizes

The **Lines** attribute is an important attribute when configuring any interface element that contains text, such as a label. This attribute informs the element to truncate any text where the number of lines exceeds the value you set here. Setting this property to 0 will allow as many lines as needed to lay the text out without truncating.

You can also set instances of `WKInterfaceObject` to respond to their background image size. WatchKit will automatically determine the appropriate dimension of the image based on the device resolution and pixels per inch, and then lay out the interface. As a general rule of thumb, if you create your images following the Apple Watch Human Interface Guidelines, your images will be set up appropriately in Interface Builder.

For instance, the images in the example below are simply set to size based on their contents. Both the *Recipes* and *Groceries* icons are the same dimension, so the text beneath them is aligned. This creates pixel-perfect objects based on their content instead of resizing the actual images.

Images laid out based on their size

Relative layout

The last important feature of WatchKit's layout system is the way it allows you to size and position an interface element based on its parent's size and position. In WatchKit, the parent will always be a group.

Even when you're in Interface Builder, the root interface element of `WKInterfaceController` is a group.

Below you can see the available attributes when editing any type of `WKInterfaceObject` in Interface Builder:

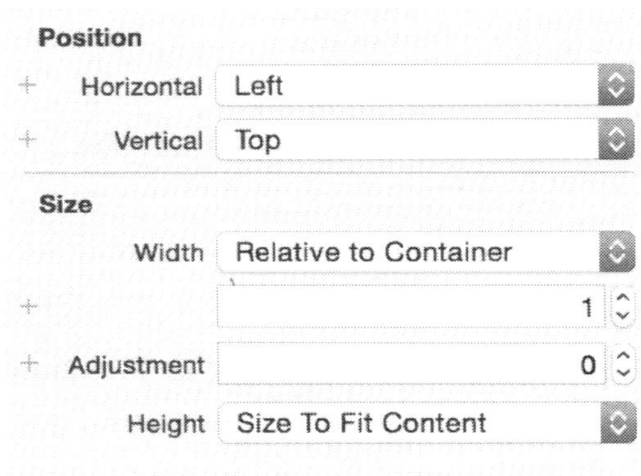

Size and position attributes in Interface Builder

You can change both the Horizontal and Vertical position attributes. You can align the Horizontal position to the left, right or center and the Vertical position to the top, center or bottom.

A label with center horizontal and vertical positions

The layout system updates the position of any interface elements when the interface is first loaded, any time the content, like text or background image, changes, and when sibling elements are hidden or unhidden.

You can change the **Height** and **Width** attributes of an interface element to fit their content, be relative to their container, or be fixed to a certain value.

If you change either to **Size To Fit Content**, the layout system decides how tall and wide the interface element needs to be to fit its content. With a label, if you set the width to fit its content, the label won't grow beyond the size of its containing group.

For images, you should almost exclusively use Size To Fit Content along with appropriately sized images. This results in pixel-perfect layout of your interfaces.

A label with Size To Fit Content width and height

The setting **Relative to Container** lets you change a multiplier value between 0 and 1. This value gets multiplied against the parent group's height or width, depending on which is being set, to determine the size of that axis of the interface element. You can also change the adjustment value, which offsets the final position.

```
Parent(width|height) * multiplier + adjustment = value
```

For example, if you had a parent group with a width of 250 and set your multiplier to 0.8 (or 80%) and the adjustment to 10, your interface element would have a width of 210 pixels.

The last size setting, **Fixed**, allows you to manually set a value for the width or height that the interface element will adhere to, no matter what its content size is.

The below image demonstrates a label nested in a group with a fixed width and height. Notice how the label is truncated because the group is too small to fit the text in a single line.

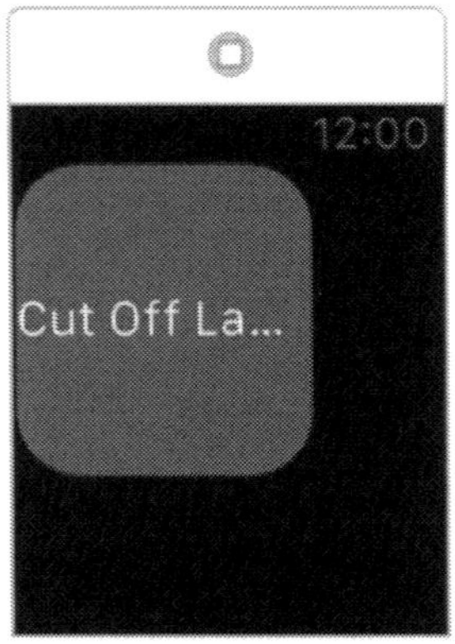

Fixed size is a good option to have in your tool belt, but use it with caution. Remember the Watch will come in two different sizes with two different pixel dimensions. Using a fixed size on one screen may not look as good on another.

Getting started with SousChef

It's time to grab the starter project, crack your knuckles and get down to business.

Before jumping into building your first complex layout, let's take a look at the starter project you're going to work with in this and the next few chapters.

The starter project

Open **SousChef.xcodeproj**, which you can find in the starter project folder in this chapter's resources. Select the **SousChef** scheme and then **build and run** the project with the iPhone 6 Simulator.

When the app launches, you'll be greeted with a list of hand-curated recipes from the raywenderlich.com team. You can tap on any of the items to open up the recipe.

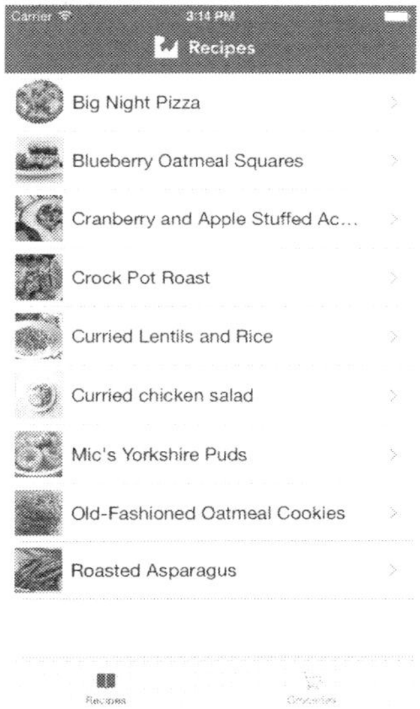

The first screen of the SousChef app

You can switch between the ingredients list and the directions by selecting one of the options in the header. Tap the action button to add the ingredients to a grocery list, or tap any instruction with a time in it to start a kitchen timer!

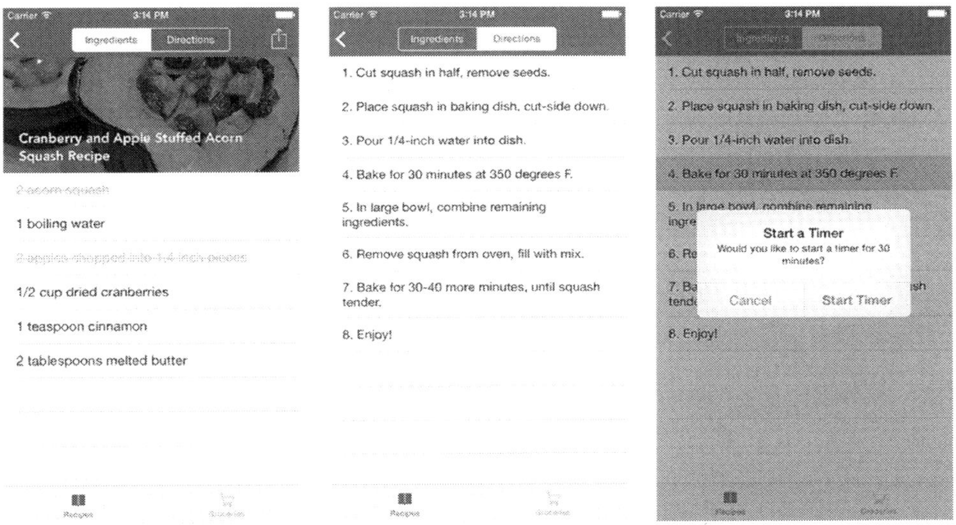

Viewing a recipe's ingredients and directions

Select the **Groceries** tab, and you'll see a list of all of the ingredients you have saved. Check off items as you purchase them, or tap the action button to clear any ingredients that you've purchased, or the entire list.

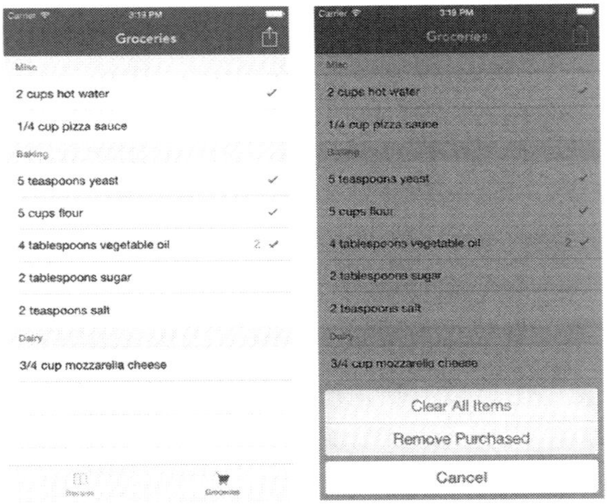

Buying ingredients and clearing your list

Show the **project navigator** (⌘-1) and look at the project hierarchy. You'll see four groups that all begin with "SousChef":

- **SousChef** holds the files of the containing iPhone app.
- **SousChefKit** has all the code that's shared between the extension and the iPhone app. You'll take a closer look at these files in a bit.
- **SousChef WatchKit Extension** is all the code that powers the WatchKit app you're going to build. Right now, there's only a empty `WKInterfaceController` in there.
- **SousChef Watch App** contains all the files and resources that will be physically stored on the Watch when the app is installed. This includes images and the Interface.storyboard file.

SousChefKit

Expand the **SousChefKit** group, and then expand the **Models** and **Storage** groups. These groups contain all the code that the iPhone app uses to get the list of recipes, as well as keep track of what items are on the grocery list.

Open **IngredientType.swift** to see the enum that categorizes ingredients. You can have ingredients that are meat, dairy, produce, baking-related, drinks, condiments, pasta or miscellaneous. Using an enum for the different ingredient types keeps your code safe and lets you quickly grab a string to display in your interfaces.

> **Note:** You'll notice the `public` keyword in front of `enum IngredientType`. The SousChefKit framework is shared with both the WatchKit app and the iPhone app. By default, Swift uses `internal` for all `classes`, `structs` and `enums`, which would not allow either app to see any of the objects in SousChefKit.

Open **Ingredient.swift** and take a look at the properties that represent an `Ingredient`: a quantity `String` for quantities like "1 tablespoon", a name `String` and a type that is an `IngredientType enum`.

At the bottom of the `Ingredient` class is a lot of code that conforms to `NSCoding`, so that you can easily serialize an `Ingredient` and store it in a file, in a format understood by `NSData`. This persists the grocery list between app sessions.

The very bottom of the `Ingredient` class has an operator overload of == to make it easy to equate `Ingredient` objects.

Open **Recipe.swift** to see the model that represents an entire recipe. This is a simple class that houses a bunch of different values. Some of the properties are worth noting:

- `ingredients` is an array of all of the ingredients in a recipe.
- `steps` is a list of cooking instructions.
- `timers` is an array of integers that correspond to each `step`. The general rule is that a cooking instruction can have a time in it, such as "boil for 10 minutes". If a step doesn't have a time, you just use 0.

There are two files in the **Storage** group. `GroceryList` is a class that manages syncing your list of ingredients and saving them in between app sessions. `RecipeStore` helps fetch a list of recipes from a data source.

Laying out a complex interface

By now, you have a good understanding of what you can do in WatchKit to design complex but user-friendly layouts for your Watch apps.

You're going to spend the rest of this chapter building the interface for the initial interface controller that's displayed when you run the SousChef Watch app. This controller will be responsible for showing the title and logo of the app as well as a couple of buttons.

The layout you will build in this chapter

Open **SousChef Watch App\Interface.storyboard** and you'll find a lone interface controller.

The only controller in Interface.storyboard

You want the top part of the interface to show an image and a title for SousChef. The default layout for an interface controller is vertical, so to get an image and a label to be laid out side by side, you need to add a new group with a horizontal layout.

Drag a **group** from the Object Library onto the interface controller. As we covered earlier, the default layout of a group is horizontal, so you don't need to make any changes.

Take a quick look at the **Width** and **Height** attributes in the Attributes Inspector. The default width will match the parent group (the interface controller) and the default height will size to fit the contents.

Drag an **Image** into the group that you just created. The image has a placeholder size at design time, but it won't actually have a size at runtime unless you add an image or set a fixed width and height.

Select the image and open the **Attributes Inspector**. Change the **Image** attribute to **rw-circle**.

The app logo image

Change the scheme to **SousChef Watch App** and select a simulator device. **Build and run** to make sure the app launches and correctly displays the logo.

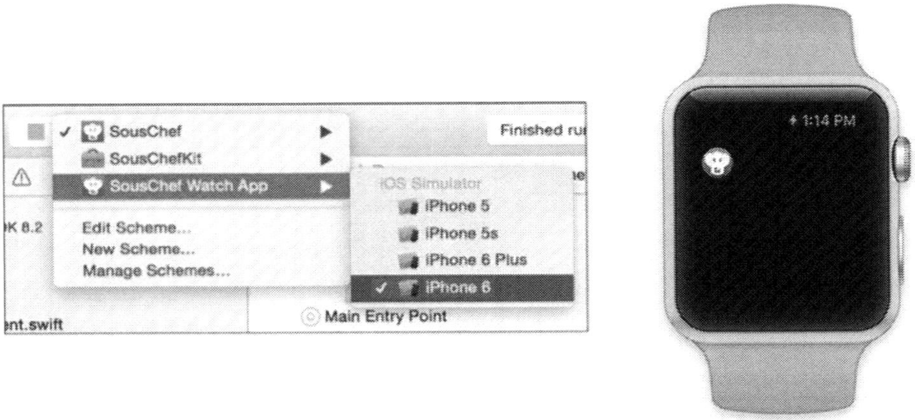

Selecting a target and running the app for the first time

Back in **Interface.storyboard**, drag a **label** into the same group as the image. Note that the interface guide will show up to the right of the image. This is a friendly helper that reaffirms the group has a horizontal layout.

Double-click the label and change the text to **SousChef**.

Label and image with a horizontal layout

The layout of the image and label is a little awkward, isn't it? It would be far more visually appealing if everything were centered, both horizontally and vertically.

Thankfully, WatchKit makes this super easy!

Select both the **image** and **label** by pressing **Command** and clicking on each object. This will make editing the interface objects really simple because you're going to apply the same settings to both objects at once.

Change both the **Horizontal** and **Vertical** positions to **Center**.

You should see both the image and label become centered in their container, like in the image below:

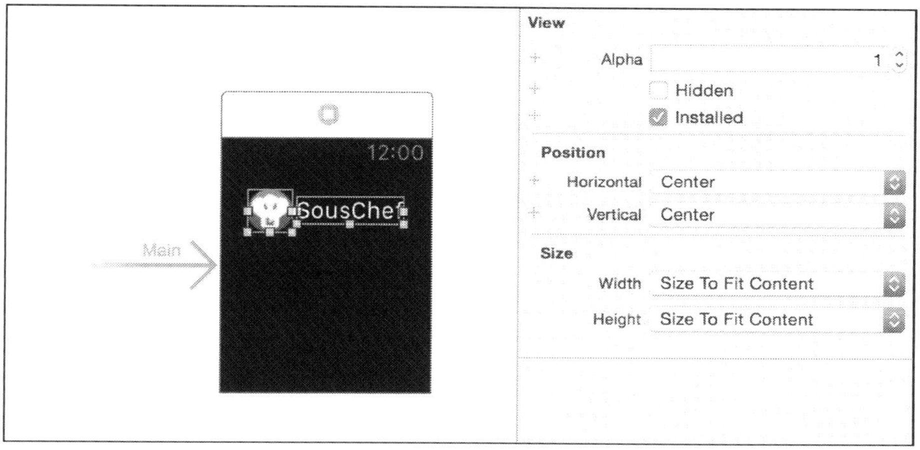

Build and run again to make sure that what you see in Interface Builder is what shows up on the simulator.

> **Note:** Interface Builder with WatchKit is really good about auto-updating the interface every time you change any settings or content. You will quickly get comfortable seeing the same thing on the Watch as you see in Interface Builder.

The image and logo look as though they're being squashed together. It would be great to add a little padding between them. Again, WatchKit to the rescue!

Select the **group** that contains both the image and the label. Open the **Attributes Inspector** and find the **Spacing** attribute. Change the value to **5**. This will automatically check the custom box.

You should now see space between the image and label. The WatchKit layout system takes care of all the layout math for you so that the image and label are still centered.

Next, you're going to add two buttons side by side. Tapping one button will show the grocery list and tapping the other will show the recipes. The buttons will look good but won't do anything yet; you'll add navigation in Chapter 5, "Navigation".

Still in **Interface.storyboard**, drag in another **group**. Make sure you add it *below* the group that has the image and label. A guide should show up immediately below the other group before you drop the object into the controller.

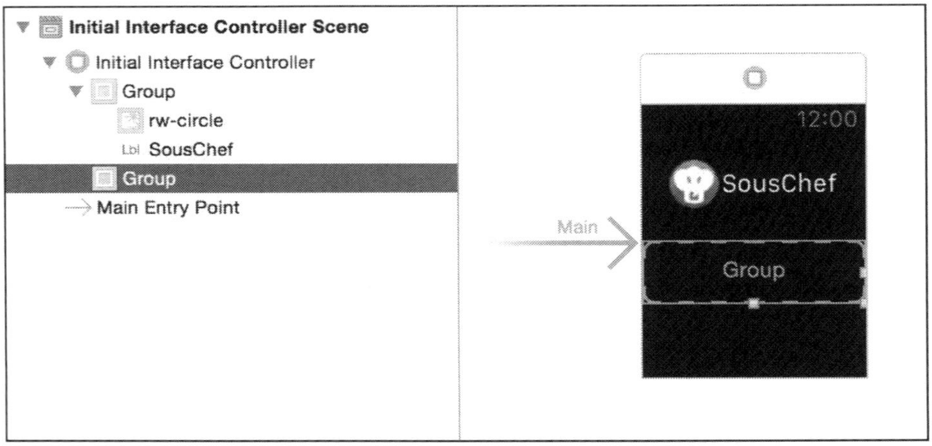

Next, drag a **button** into this new group. You'll see the default button label and style.

Your new, default button

The default buttons look OK, but definitely not as aesthetically pleasing as the stuff Apple showed off in the keynote when they announced the Apple Watch! Time to spruce things up a bit.

Select the **button** you just added and open the **Attributes Inspector**. Find the **Content** drop-down and change it to **group**. The preview of the button in Interface Builder should look like a normal group like in the image below:

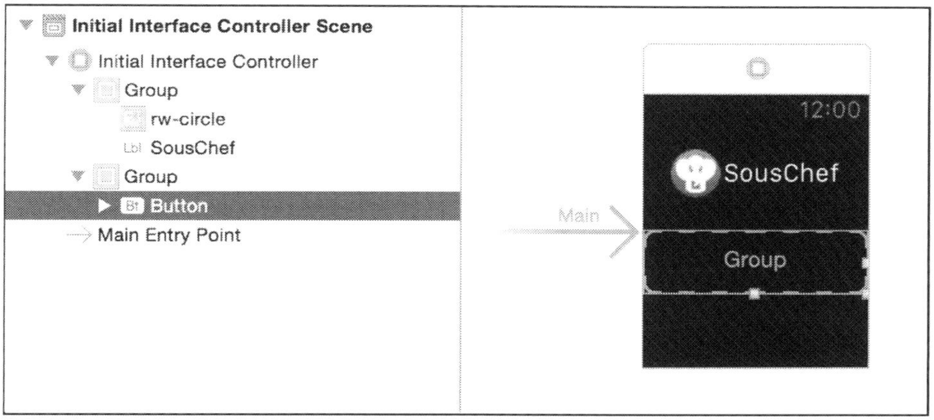

This special feature of buttons allows you to toggle between a standard button with a label and background image, and a button with a custom layout group. The custom layout group setting lets you create more complex buttons while still retaining all of the functionality.

Drag an **image** and then a **label** into the new button. Select the image and change its **Image** attribute to **bookmark-button**.

Select the **label** and change its **Text** attribute to **Recipes**. And while you're in the **Attributes Inspector**, click on the "T" next to **Font**, then change the **Font** to **System** and the **Size** to **11**.

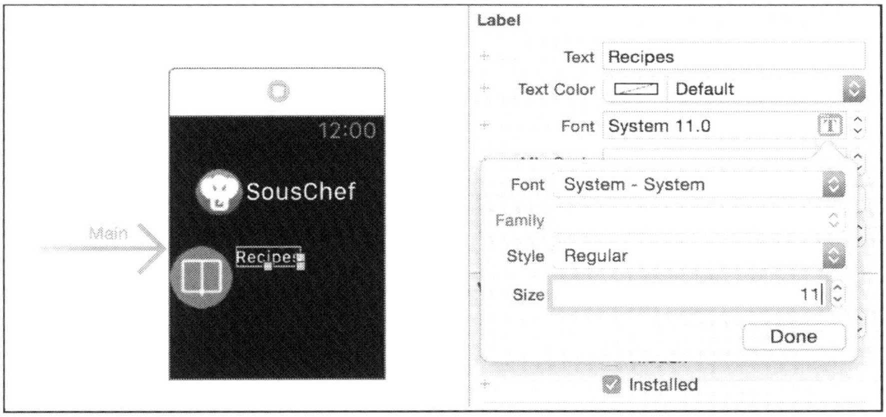

Setting up the recipes label

It would be great if the label could be underneath the icon; this type of layout is a good pattern to follow—users start to learn how to navigate the app based on visual recognition: color, shape (like the icon) or text.

Groups make this really simple! Select the group that's within the button. You can click on the blank space around the image or label, or use the document outline to find it.

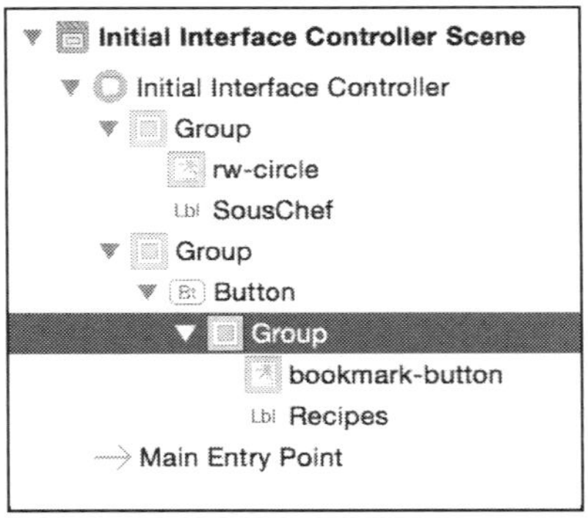

Finding the button group in the document outline

Open the **Attributes Inspector** and change the **Layout** of the group to **Vertical**.

Voila! The label falls nicely underneath the image.

To make sure everything is centered, you need to center both the image and the label. Select both and change the **Horizontal** position attribute to **Center**.

Build and run to double-check that the app looks just the same running as it does in Interface Builder.

If everything checks out, go back to **Interface.storyboard**. You want to place another button right next to the Recipes button.

To make this easy, select the button in the **document outline**, **copy** it and then immediately **paste**. This will paste a copy of the button directly next to it, in the parent layout group.

Take a look at your controller. Where is your new button? There's an outline if you select it, but a button isn't actually displayed?

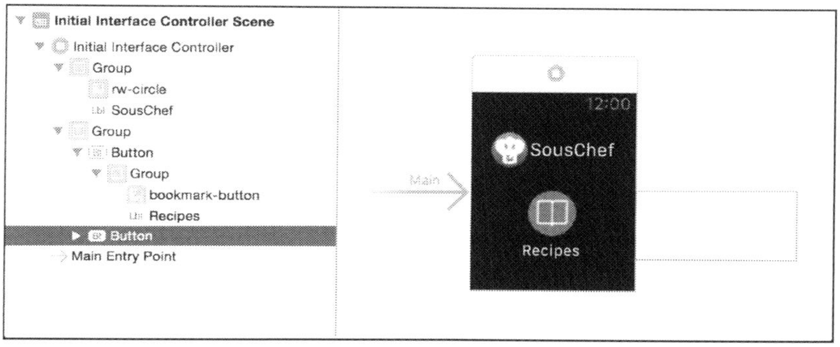

Search for the missing button

The parent group has a horizontal layout, so that can't be the issue. But wait—remember how groups have a default width relative to their container? That means your Recipes button is pushing the other one off the screen!

To fix this, select both button groups by cmd+clicking them in the **document outline**.

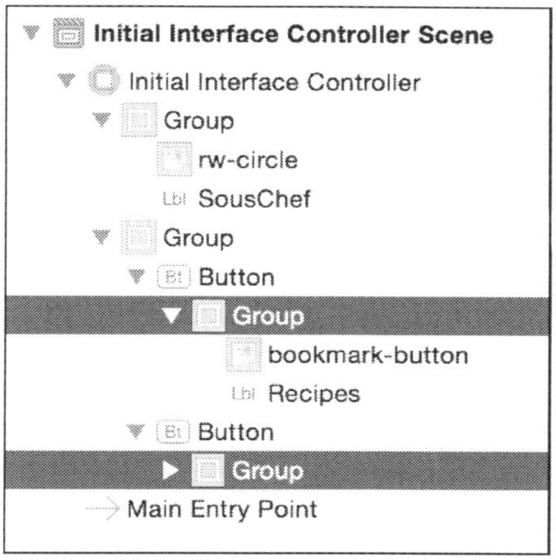

Selecting both button groups

In the **Attributes Inspector**, change the **Width** attribute to **Size To Fit Content**. This will make the groups width adjust to the width of its content.

It would also be nice to position the buttons so that they're a little more visually appealing. But since the groups you've selected are embedded in the button, they don't have their own position attribute. Instead, you need to select both of the buttons; again cmd+click them both.

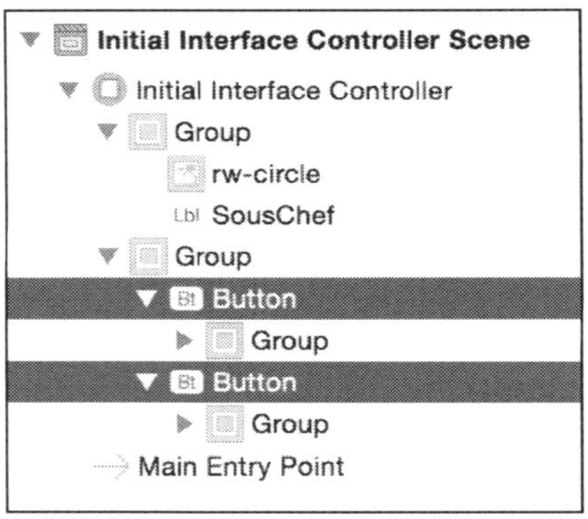

Now you can open the **Attributes Inspector** and change the **Horizontal** position to **Center**.

Next, select the image in the second buttons layout group and change its **Image** attribute to **ingredients**.

Double-click the **label** in the same group and change its text to **Groceries**.

Ah, that's better! But just like the header image and label, the buttons look a bit too close together. To give them a little space, select the group containing both of the buttons and change the **Spacing** to **15**.

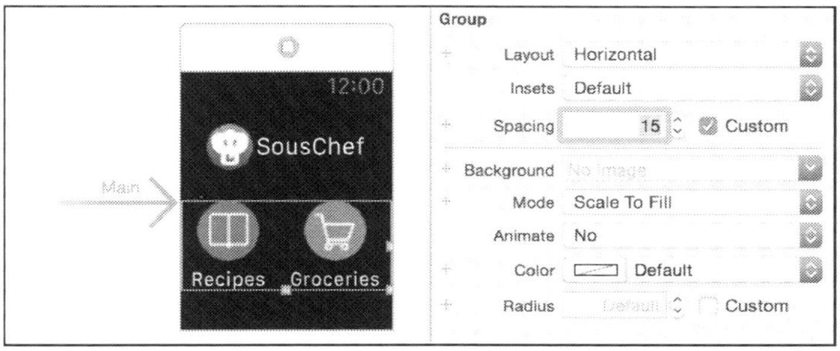

Build and run to see your beautiful new interface! Try tapping both the Recipes and Groceries buttons to see how WatchKit automatically animates and highlights buttons when they're interacted with.

The finished interface

Where to go from here?

Try playing around with groups to come up with even more unique and complex interfaces. Almost anything that a wild-eyed designer can create in Photoshop is easy to make thanks to WatchKit's advanced layout system!

In the following chapter, you'll further build out the SousChef app. You will connect interface controllers and learn how the navigation system works in WatchKit, build table views to browse lists of groceries and ingredients, and create actionable context menus to edit your grocery list and start timers.

Chapter 5: Navigation

By Ryan Nystrom

To build anything more than a single-screen app for the Apple Watch, you're going to need some means of navigating around the Watch app itself.

You're likely used to the many ways of navigating in iOS— navigation controllers, modal presentations, tab controllers, page controllers and so forth. On top of the built-in means of navigation, you can also take matters into your own hands and build your own custom `UIView` and `UIViewController` containers.

Navigation in WatchKit uses familiar concepts and takes the following forms:

- **Hierarchical**: similar to `UINavigationController`.
- **Page-based**: similar to `UIPageViewController`.
- **Modal**: any type of presentation or dismissal transition.

In WatchKit, unlike in iOS, you are strictly limited to these three methods. There is no custom navigation. In fact, you can't even mix and match hierarchical navigation and page-based navigation.

You can, however, use modals with either type. All you need to do is pick a base navigation type for your app and then decide whether mixing navigation is appropriate.

In this chapter you will explore the different navigation methods: modal, page based, and hierarchical. After that, you will dive into implementing navigation in the SousChef app from the previous chapter.

Getting around in WatchKit

Since WatchKit's navigation systems are so limited, it's definitely worth taking a moment and familiarizing yourself with each type of navigation before you dive in and build anything.

Hierarchical navigation

Hierarchical navigation will be one of the most familiar concepts to developers coming from iOS development. In iOS, you have `UINavigationController` that manages pushing and popping child controllers, and their animations.

WatchKit has a very similar system:

- You can push instances of `WKInterfaceController` onto the navigation stack.
- Swipe gestures and back buttons are built-in.
- You can use storyboards to set up the navigation, or you can do it in code.

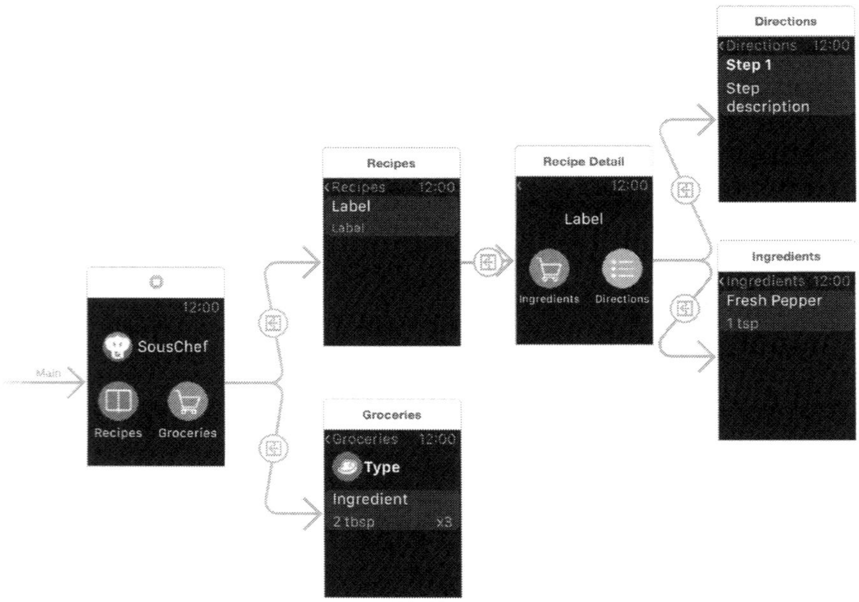

A hierarchical navigation tree in a storyboard

Instead of having a master navigation controller, WatchKit handles all of the navigation for you. You can simply Control-drag from a button to a controller or just call `pushControllerWithName(_:context:)` in your code.

There is an important concept that Chapter 2, "Architecture" touched on briefly: When using a hierarchical navigation system, WatchKit gives you an optional `context` parameter that you can pass between controllers as you navigate.

You'll most commonly use the context parameter when you're pushing from a master controller to a detail controller in the navigation stack. Instead of intercepting stringly-typed segues or adding lots of custom methods and properties, you can simply pass context objects between controllers.

UIKit has a great architecture for creating views, laying out their subviews, and separating the concerns between controllers and views. However, communication between controllers has always been difficult. Using context-passing in WatchKit will keep your app's architecture clean and expressive.

> **Note:** You'll get your hands on context objects later in this chapter, and throughout the rest of the book!

Page-based navigation

The second main form of navigation in WatchKit is page-based. This is essentially a group of `WKInterfaceController` instances strung together laterally that you can swipe between. Pages should each be unique chunks of information, and perform unique functionality. In iOS, this is most similar to a `UIPageViewController`, which manages several instances of `UIViewController`, as seen in the Weather application.

When building a page-based WatchKit app, you aren't able to pass a context object between the different controllers in the group, nor are you able to use a hierarchical navigation within its pages, *ever*. It's one or the other.

> **Note:** You *can* get a mix of page-based navigation and hierarchical navigation by presenting either one modally from the other. Skip ahead to the "Modal Navigation" section to learn more.

Apple presented an example WatchKit page-based app at the Apple Watch announcement—a timepiece app that has pages containing different representations of time, like digital, analog and solar.

Some of the Apple Watch clock app faces

To wire up a page-based interface, you simply have to connect each `WKInterfaceController` in Interface Builder, defining it as the next page. There isn't an option to define a previous page, because the list of controllers should be one-way. You'll have an initial controller (the one that is shown when the page-based controller is first shown) and a list of other controllers to which you can swipe.

A list of controllers connected in a page-based navigation

You do have limited control of a page-based navigation app's hierarchy in code. There are two methods you can call:

- `becomeCurrentPage()`: Call this from within an instance of `WKInterfaceController` to animate that controller into view.
- `reloadRootControllersWithNames(_:contexts:)`: You can use this method to dynamically load different controllers into your interface. This can be useful for enabling or disabling certain controllers based on data availability or user settings.

Modal navigation

The last possible means of getting around in WatchKit is by modal navigation. This is a familiar concept to anyone who's built iOS and Mac apps: think full-screen pop-ups.

When you present a `WKInterfaceController` modally, it animates from the bottom of the screen up into view, taking up the entire interface. Controllers presented modally build in a means to get back to the underlying controller by providing a Cancel button. You can change the title of this button to something such as "Done" or "Finished", depending on the context of your modal.

A modal transition in Interface Builder

You can display a `WKInterfaceController` modally by either wiring it up in Interface Builder, or calling one of the following methods in code:

- `presentControllerWithName(_:context:)`: This method displays a single `WKInterfaceController` modally. Note that you can pass a `context` object just like with hierarchical navigation.
- `presentControllerWithNames(_:contexts:)`: This method lets you display several instances of `WKInterfaceController` modally using page-based navigation, as previously discussed. In the event that your modal has multiple pages, use this method to provide easy access. This is an example of how you can combine multiple types of navigation.
- `dismissController()`—Use this method to dismiss the modal interface controller.

You should reserve modal navigation for context-specific interfaces, option selection or quick actions. These allow you to interrupt the current workflow for a specific purpose.

Page-based and modal navigation in practice

Now that you have some familiarity with the different types of navigation in WatchKit, you'll try your hand at building something with them. In this chapter, you'll explore both page and modal based navigation to get a feel for how they work. In the next section, you will then build the hierarchical navigation that is used in the SousChef application.

Before you get started, make sure you open **SousChef.xcodeproj** —this can be either the one you've been working on through the book so far, or the starter project for this chapter.

Flipping pages

Select the **SousChef Watch App** scheme and **build and run** to see the app in the simulator. It will look something like this:

You're going to add a couple of pages to this interface, which will give you a feel for how they work.

Open **SousChef Watch App\Interface.storyboard** to see the Interface Builder equivalent of the screen you were just looking at on the simulator.

From the **Object Library** drag in two **interface controllers**.

Two new controllers for paging

Drag a **label** into the first new controller and a **button** into the second. Feel free to give the label and button any placeholder text of your choosing.

To wire together these new controllers, select the **Initial Interface** and **Control-drag** to the controller with the label in it.

To avoid accidentally selecting any of the interface objects in the controller, you can select the Initial Interface and Control-drag from the yellow controller icon. In the dialog that appears once you've let go, click **next page**.

That's all it takes to connect your controllers for page-based navigation!

Realizing how easy page-based navigations are!

Repeat the process above to connect the two new controllers, using a **next page** segue. When you're done, your storyboard will look something like this:

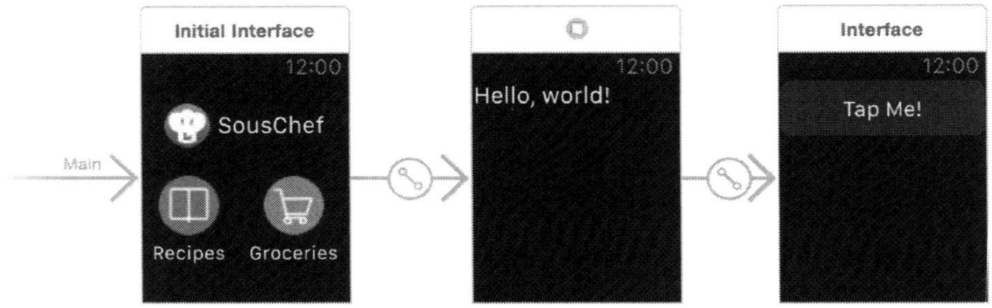

Notice the segues connecting the controllers

Build and run your WatchKit app. As soon as the app has launched, swipe left to see the interface controller containing the label. Now swipe once more and you'll see the interface controller containing the button!

Notice also how WatchKit provides a nice little page indicator at the bottom of the screen. This is an essential visual indication of how many pages there are, and where the user is in the group.

> **Note:** Apple is making page-based navigation this easy because it wants you to build simple apps with it. Be mindful of how easy it should be to using your WatchKit app. Avoid clunky and busy interfaces at all costs.

Even watches have pop-ups

Pages are great, but what if you're swiping through pages and come to an item on which you need to, say, change a setting. Instead of making another page that won't always be in the group, this is the perfect opportunity to use a modal interface controller instead!

Modals in WatchKit are extremely similar to their iOS counterparts. If you're familiar with iOS, just think back to how you would call `presentViewController(_:animated:completion:)` whenever you wanted to present a new controller modally.

Still in **Interface.storyboard**, find the **initial interface** that contains the logo and two buttons. Drag in another **interface controller** from the **Object Library** just above it, so that your storyboard looks something like this:

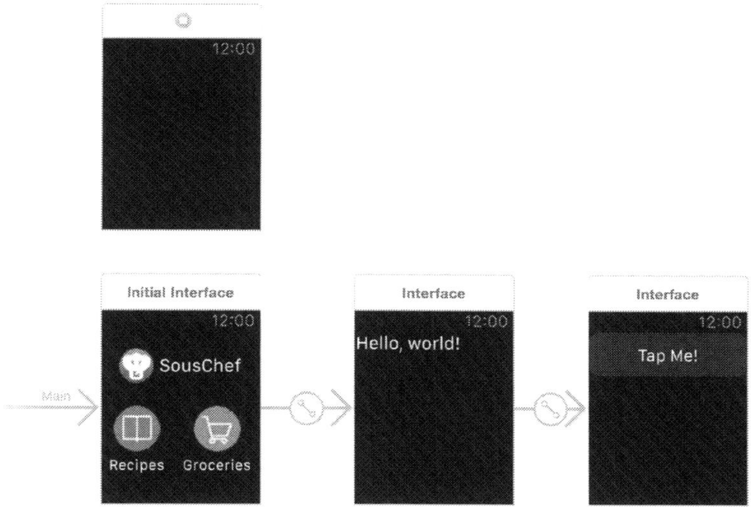

Select the **Recipes** button and **Control-drag** from it to your new controller. When you let go, select the **modal** action segue.

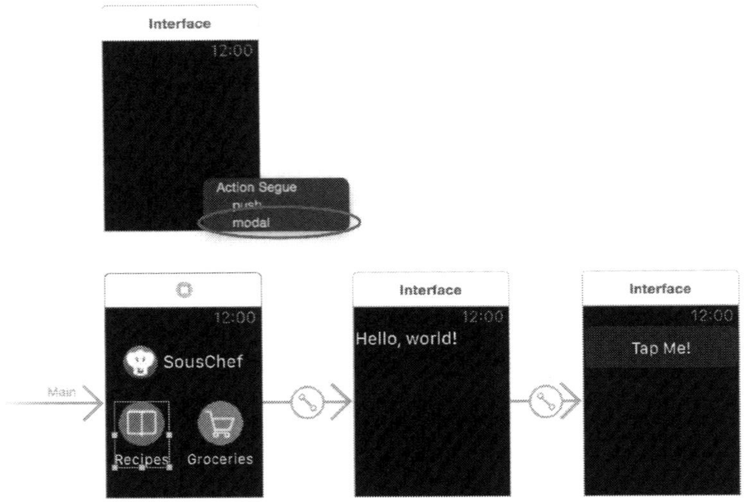

> **Note:** If you have any trouble getting the Control-drag to work with the complex button group, try opening the **document outline** and dragging directly from the **button** object.

Select your **new segue** and open the **Attributes Inspector**. Give the segue the identifier **DemoModalSegue**.

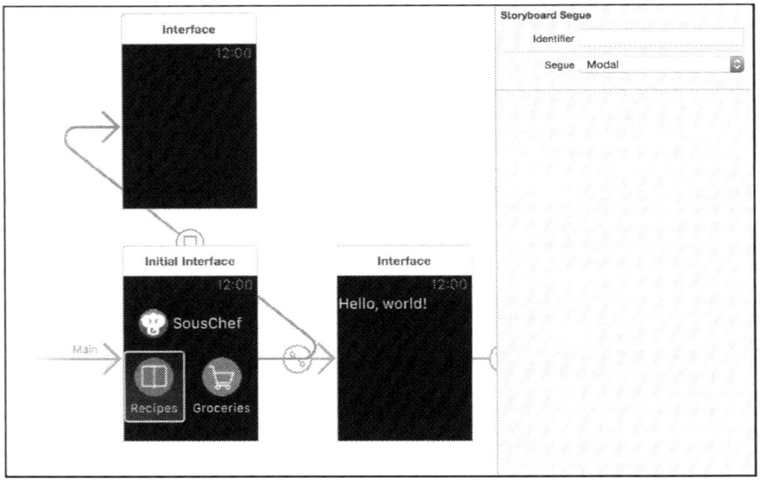

Build and run your Watch app. Tap on the Recipes button to display your new modal.

You'll see a black controller appear with the word "Cancel" in the upper-left. This is the default dismiss button title.

Go back to **Interface.storyboard**, select the interface controller you just added and open the **Attributes Inspector**. Change the **Title** attribute to **Done**, which changes the string of the dismiss button used by modal controllers.

Build and run again. This time you'll see the new dismissal text.

Riveting modal, isn't it?

Modal navigation includes the ability to pass a `context` object between segues. The calling controller, in this case the Initial Interface controller, can override `contextForSegueWithIdentifier(_:)` and return any object. It could be a string, a number, a custom object or even `nil`!

The modal controller then needs to override `awakeWithContext(_:)` to receive the context object, and can then decide what to do with it. In the current example, you might pass a string to tell the modal that it's being presented for Recipes.

Hierarchical navigation in practice

Hierarchical navigation is likely the form you're most familiar with, even if you haven't made a single iOS app. Hierarchical navigation means traveling in between nodes in a navigation hierarchy, or linear tree.

Most parts of SousChef that you'll build throughout this book use a hierarchical navigation, so it's time to dive into exactly how to implement it.

Setting up the hierarchy

Open **Interface.storyboard** and delete all of the page and modal interface controllers you added in the previous section. Make sure to leave the **Initial Interface** controller. Your storyboard will then contain just a single controller, as shown in the image below:

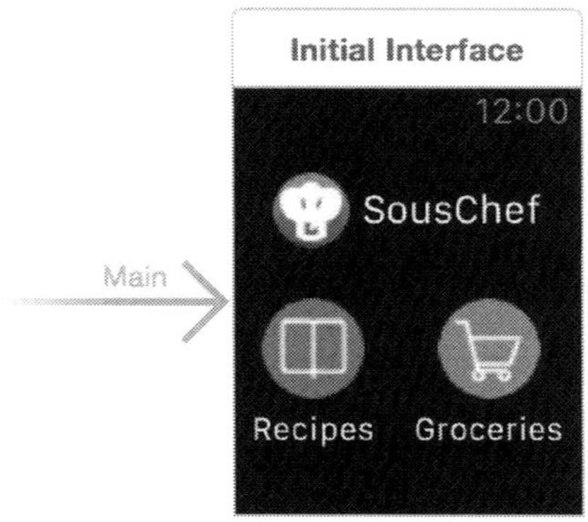

This controller is a little lonely

From the **Object Library** drag in two **interface controllers**. You're going to use these controllers to represent a list of recipes and a list of groceries, respectively.

Select the first controller you added. Open the **Attributes Inspector** and change the **Title** attribute to **Recipes**.

Select the second controller you added and change its **Title** attribute to **Groceries**. You will then have something resembling the following:

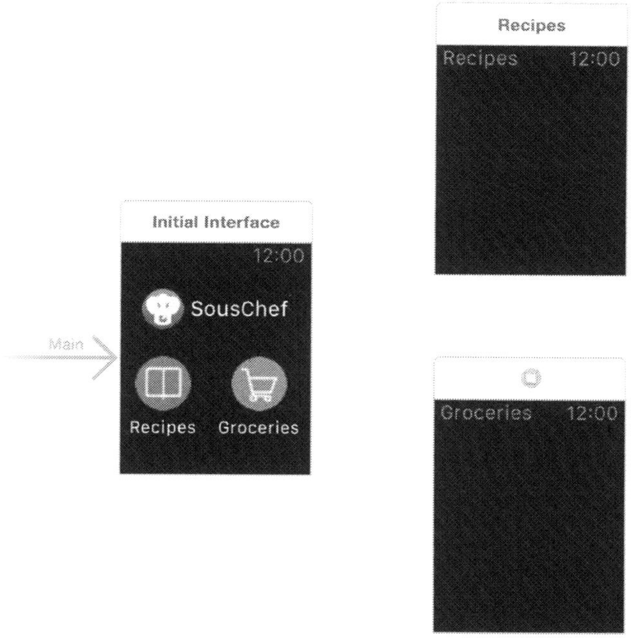

New controllers with titles set

Select the **Recipes** button, then **Control-click** and drag to the interface controller titled **Recipes**. Like before, you might have to use the **document outline** to properly select the Recipes button rather than the image inside the button.

When the action segue modal appears, select **push**. A new segue should appear connecting the initial controller to the recipes controller.

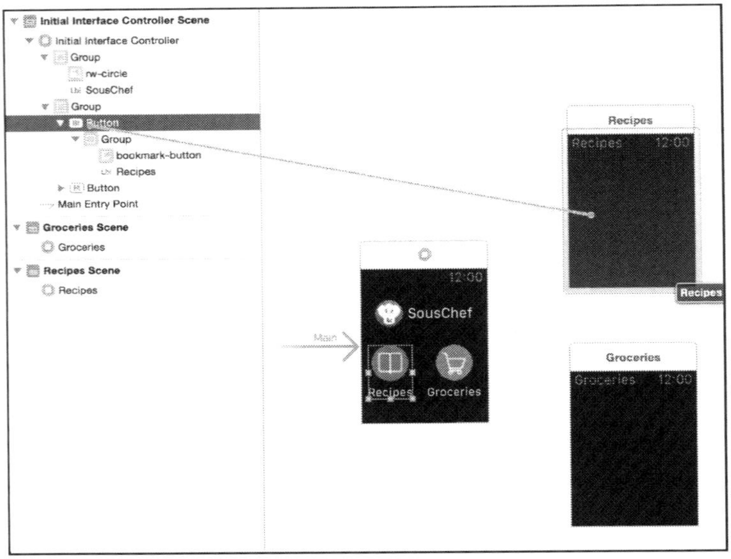

Creating the segue with the document outline

Repeat the process connecting the **Groceries** button to the **Groceries** controller using a **push** segue.

Build and run. Tap on the Recipes and Groceries buttons. You should see the blank controllers pushed onto the stack.

Notice how WatchKit automatically adds a small back arrow next to the title of the controller if it's part of a navigation hierarchy.

Since the Recipes and Groceries buttons are static, their segues are static, so you don't need to add a segue identifier or pass any context objects in between the controllers.

Still in **Interface.storyboard**, drag in three more **interface controllers** onto the canvas:

- One controller should sit next to the **Recipes** controller.
- The next two should sit to the right of the first, and you'll push these onto the first new controller.

Your storyboard will now look something like this:

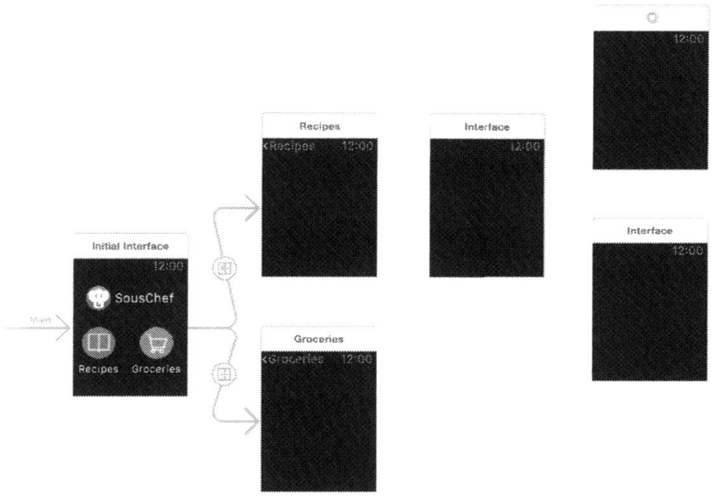

> **Note:** Try to organize your storyboard so that it makes sense simply by looking at the arrangement of your controllers. It will be easier to figure out what's happening, and if someone else needs to work on your app, such as when you're part of a team, they'll be able to understand the navigation hierarchy faster.

Tables and navigation

When you're done with this chef's companion app, you'll be able to select a recipe from the Recipes controller, which will then push a detail controller onto the stack. For that to happen, you need to implement **context passing**, one of the coolest features of WatchKit navigation.

With **Interface.storyboard** open, select the **Recipes** controller and drag a **Table** from the **Object Library** onto it. This will leave you with an empty table row group.

Control-click and then drag from the **Table Row** to the new interface controller that you placed closest to the Recipes controller. Select the **push** segue from the pop-up.

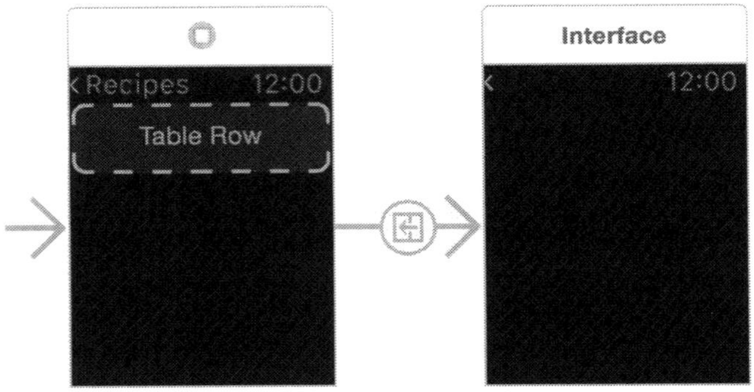

If you were to run the app right now and navigate to the Recipes controller, nothing would have changed. This is because the controller doesn't use a custom subclass and there is no data being supplied to populate the table.

Right-click the **SousChef WatchKit Extension\Row Controllers** group and click **New File...**. Select **iOS\Source\Swift File**, click **Next** and name your new subclass **RecipeRowController.swift**.

Make sure to select the **SousChef WatchKit Extension** directory, select the same-named target and click **Create**.

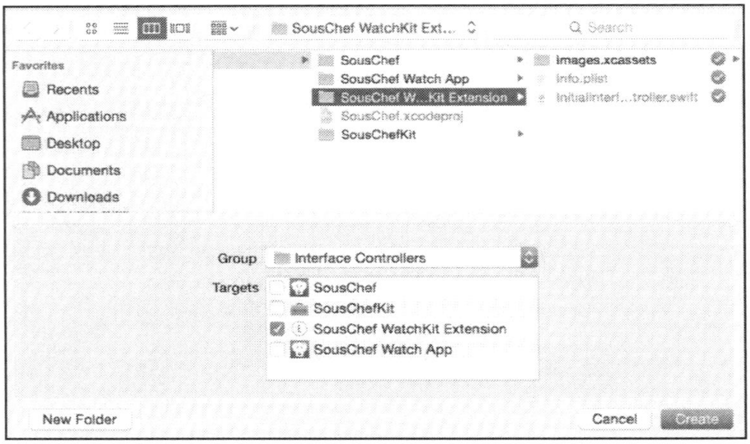

> **Note:** You're about to touch lightly on WatchKit table concepts. This chapter focuses on the navigation aspects of WatchKit and skims over the fundamentals of tables. However, tables have a unique context-passing mechanism when it comes to navigation that is important to cover. You'll learn more about tables in Chapter 6, "Tables".

Open **RecipeRowController.swift** and replace the boilerplate code with the following:

```
import WatchKit

class RecipeRowController: NSObject {
  @IBOutlet weak var textLabel: WKInterfaceLabel!
}
```

Reopen **SousChef Watch App\Interface.storyboard** and select the empty **Table Row**. In the **document outline**, select the **Table Row Controller**.

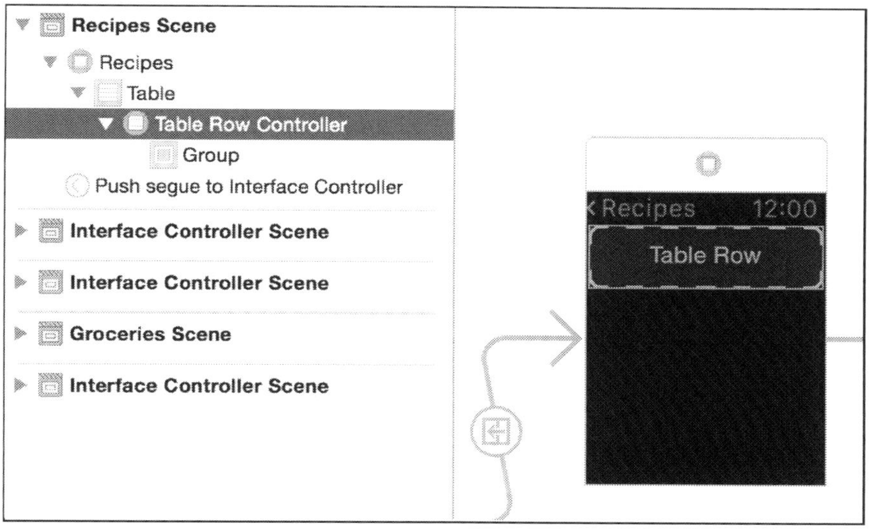

Open the **Identity Inspector** and change the **Class** to **RecipeRowController**. Xcode will automatically fill in the module to which the `RecipeRowController` class belongs.

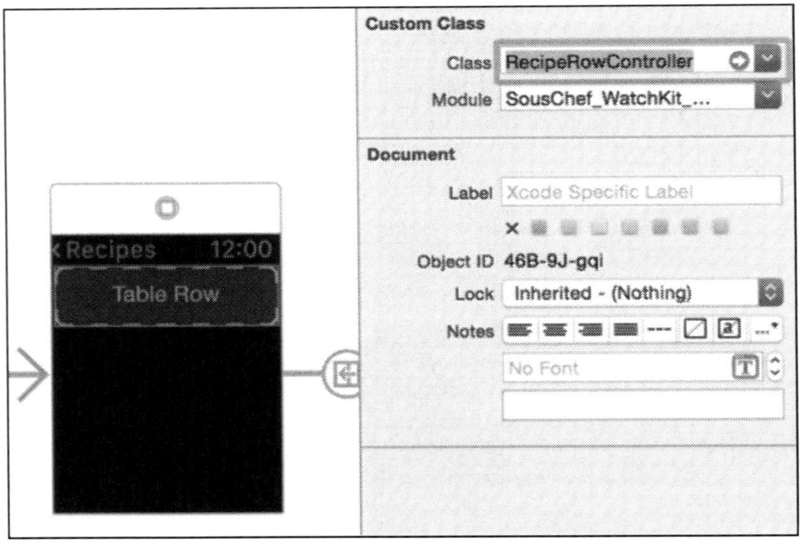

Open the **Attributes Inspector** and change the **Identifier** to **RecipeRowType,** so that you can fetch the right row controller class in code.

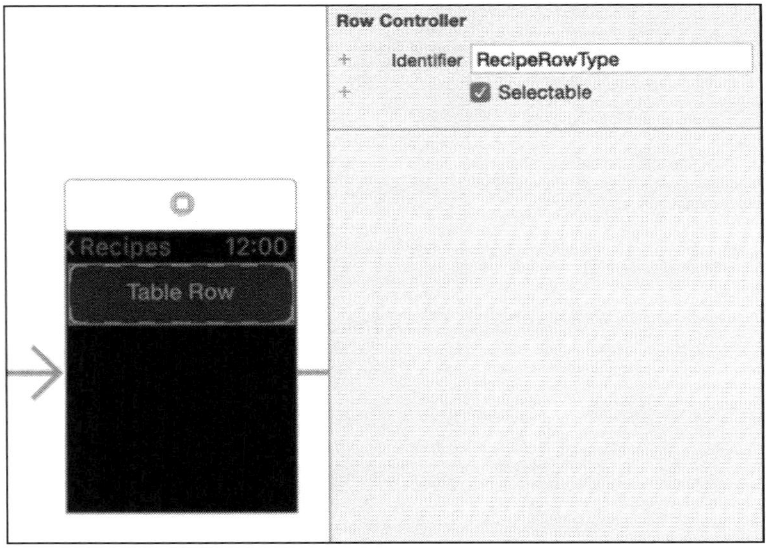

Drag a **label** into the **Table Row**. You'll use this label simply as a placeholder for now, and will make the design much better in the next chapter, where you'll focus on tables.

While pressing the **Option** key, click on **RecipeRowController.swift** to bring it up in the **assistant editor** so you can see both **Interface.storyboard** and **RecipeRowController.swift** in one screen.

There will be a little circle next to the `@IBOutlet` code in **RecipeRowController.swift**. To connect the row controller outlet, click and drag from that circle to the label you just created in the table row. This outlet will allow you to easily set the text for the label in the table row.

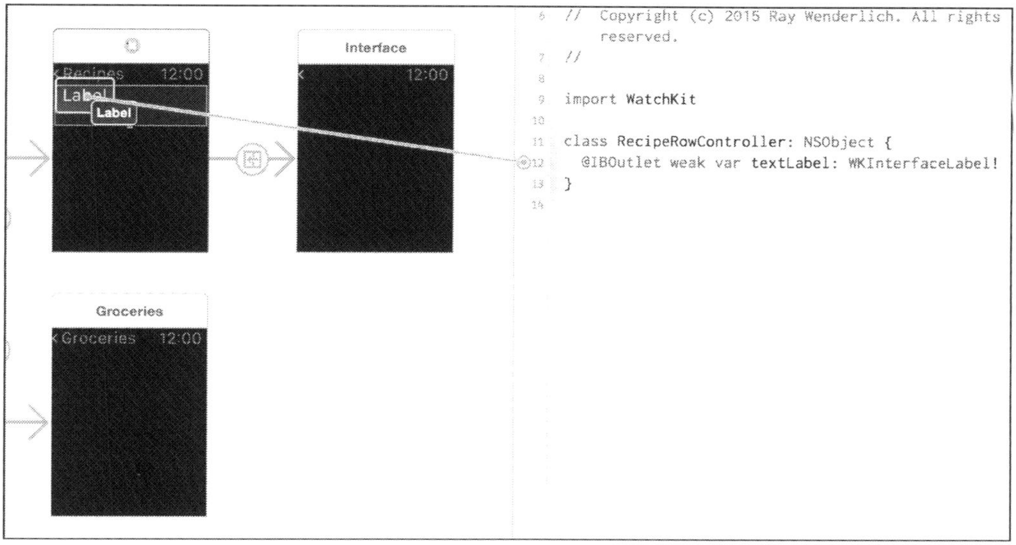

Wiring up an outlet to a row controller

Now that you have your table row set up, it's time to populate it with some dummy data. But before you do that, you need to create a subclass of `WKInterfaceController` for the Recipes controller.

Right-click the **SousChef WatchKit Extension\Interface Controllers** group and select **New File...**. Select **iOS\Source\Swift File** and click **Next**. Name the new class **RecipesInterfaceController.swift**, and make sure you add the file to the **SousChef WatchKit Extension** directory and target.

Click **Create** to make the file.

Open **RecipesInterfaceController.swift** and replace its contents with the following code:

```
import WatchKit

class RecipesInterfaceController: WKInterfaceController {
  // 1
  @IBOutlet weak var table: WKInterfaceTable!
  let recipes = ["Cheeseburger", "Pizza", "Salad"];

  // 2
  override func awakeWithContext(context: AnyObject?) {
    super.awakeWithContext(context)

    // 3
    table.setNumberOfRows(recipes.count,
      withRowType: "RecipeRowType")

    // 4
    for (index, recipe) in enumerate(recipes) {
      let controller = table.rowControllerAtIndex(index)
        as RecipeRowController
      controller.textLabel.setText(recipe)
    }
  }
}
```

Here's how you're populating the table:

1. You create an `IBOutlet` for the table that you added to the Recipes controller. You also create a list of fake recipes that you can use to wire things up without requiring a real data set.
2. You override the `awakeWithContext(_:)` method that's called just before the `WKInterfaceController` object is displayed onscreen.
3. Next, you set the number of rows in the table and the identifier to use for the row controllers, which you set in the storyboard.
4. Finally, you iterate through the recipes and set the text label of each row.

> **Note:** Again, this WatchKit table code probably looks foreign. You'll get much more exposure to what all is going on in Chapter 6, "Tables".

Open **SousChef Watch App\Interface.storyboard** and select the **Recipes** controller. In the **Identity Inspector**, change the **Class** to **RecipesInterfaceController**.

Option-click on **RecipesInterfaceController.swift** to open the file in the **assistant editor**. Just like you did with the row controller, click the small circle next to the `table` outlet and drag it to the **Table** in the **Recipes** controller.

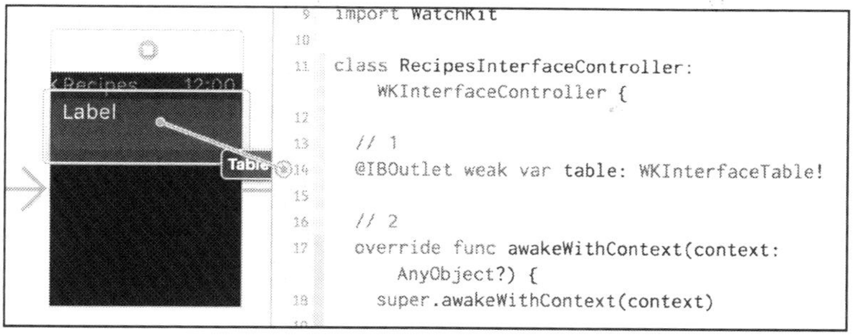

Build and run. Tap on the Recipes button, and you'll see your tiny list of recipes. Tapping any of these recipes will then push a blank interface controller onto the navigation stack as well.

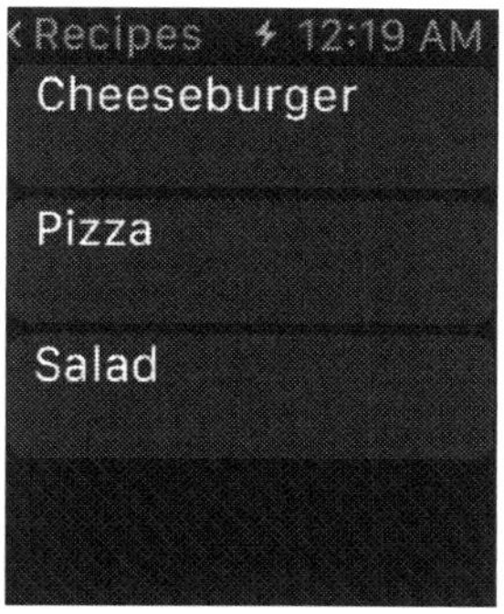

A really simple recipes table

Context passing

Building this table and wiring up cell selection isn't very useful if the controller you're pushing onto the stack doesn't know what it's supposed to be displaying.

To fix this, open **RecipesInterfaceController.swift** and implement the following method:

```
override func contextForSegueWithIdentifier(segueIdentifier:
  String, inTable table: WKInterfaceTable, rowIndex: Int)
    -> AnyObject? {
  return recipes[rowIndex]
}
```

This is the context-passing method you use when using both hierarchical navigation and a `WKInterfaceTable`. You can quickly figure out which data item the user selected and return it from this method. Then, that object is then passed along to whatever controller the app is going to present next.

> **Note:** This method isn't restricted for use with hierarchical navigation. If you were going to present a modal controller from a `WKInterfaceTable`, you would use the same method to pass a context object. If you have a more dynamic navigation, make use of the `segueIdentifier` parameter to determine which segue the app is about to perform.

Your Recipes controller now passes along a context object that the next controller can use. But it's not of much use without a way to display the data it contains.

Open **Interface.storyboard** and select the controller that the Recipes controller pushes to. Drag a **label** into it. In the Attributes Inspector change the **Horizontal** position to **Center**, the **Alignment** to **Center**, and **Lines** to **0**. Your interface controller should then look like this:

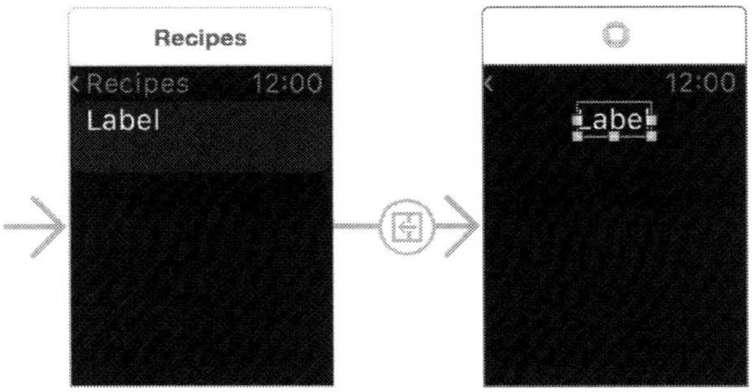

Right-click the **SousChef WatchKit Extension\Interface Controllers** group and create a new **Swift File** called **RecipeDetailInterfaceController**, just as you've done before.

Open **RecipeDetailInterfaceController.swift** and replace its contents with the following:

```
import WatchKit

class RecipeDetailInterfaceController: WKInterfaceController {
  @IBOutlet weak var nameLabel: WKInterfaceLabel!
}
```

Reopen **Interface.storyboard** and, using the **Identity Inspector**, set the class of the controller containing the new label to **RecipeDetailInterfaceController**.

Then, using the assistant editor connect the `nameLabel` outlet to the label in the appropriate interface controller in the storyboard:

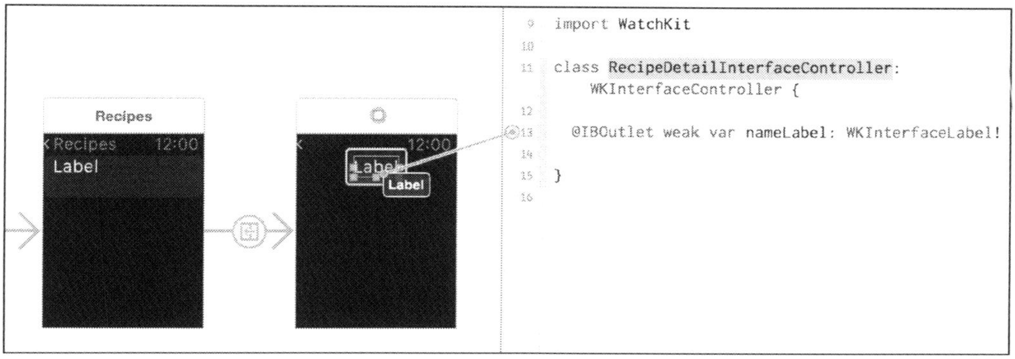

To actually *use* the context object that `RecipesInterfaceController` is passing to `RecipeDetailInterfaceController`, you need to take advantage of the `context` parameter passed to `awakeWithContext(_:)`.

Open **RecipeDetailInterfaceController.swift** and add the following method to the class:

```
override func awakeWithContext(context: AnyObject?) {
  super.awakeWithContext(context)

  if let name = context as? String {
    nameLabel.setText(name)
  }
}
```

This method attempts to cast the `context` parameter to a `String` using optional binding, and if it's successful, sets it as the text of the label.

Build and run. Tap Recipes, then tap on a recipe in the list and check out the label on the new interface controller that gets pushed on to the stack.

Mmmmmm, pizza

Completing the hierarchy

You might remember that you added a couple of other controllers that have just been hanging out doing nothing all this time. Those controllers will eventually display the directions and ingredients for whatever recipe the user might be perusing.

Open **Interface.storyboard** and change the **Title** attribute of both of the empty interface controllers to **Directions** and **Ingredients**, respectively.

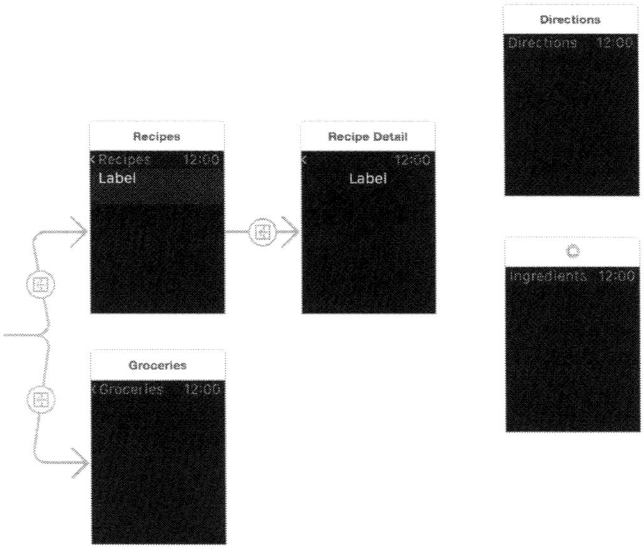

Select the **Initial Interface** controller, open the **document outline** and select the **group** that contains both the Recipes and Groceries buttons. Use **Edit\Copy** to copy the group to your clipboard.

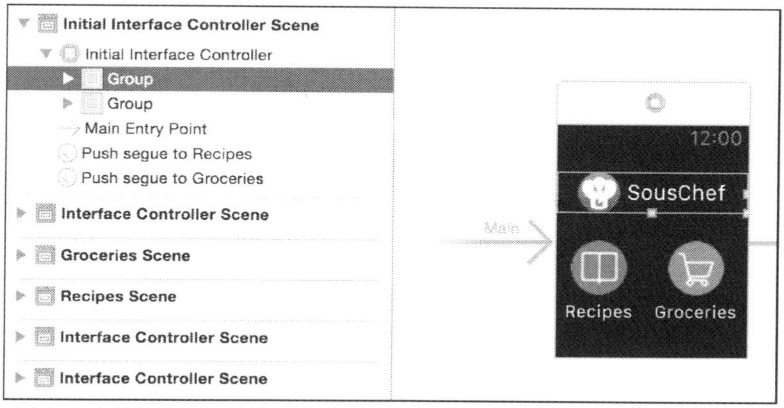

Selecting the button group

Go back to the **Recipe Detail** controller, click anywhere under the label and use **Edit\Paste** to paste in the copied button group.

Open the **Attributes Inspector** and change the first button's **image** to **ingredients** and the label's text to **Ingredients**. Change the second button's image to **directions** and the label's text to **Directions**.

The Recipes detail controller will now look like the following:

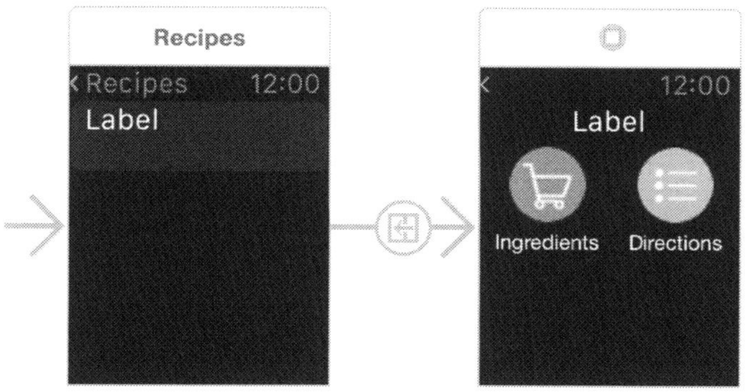

Control-drag from both buttons to their respective controllers and choose the **push** segue when prompted. Make sure you match the titles of the buttons with the titles of the controllers.

Once you have everything wired up, your storyboard will look like this:

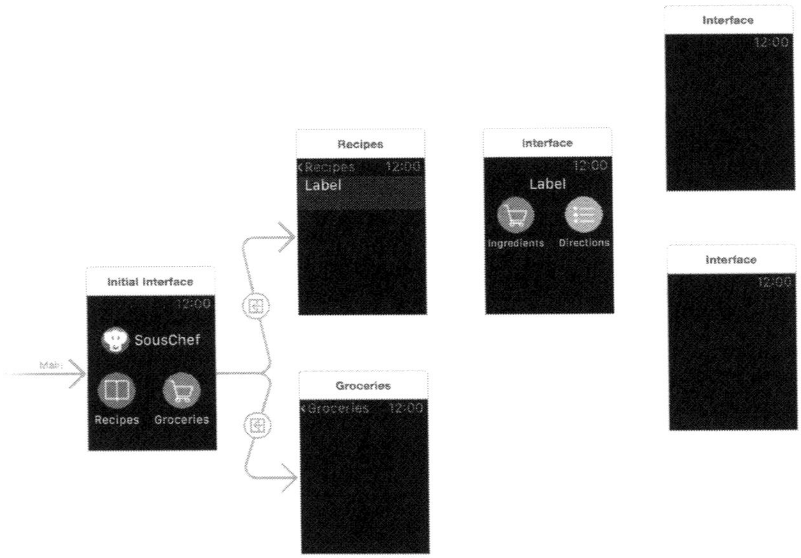

Build and run. Tap around. You might now feel more like you're navigating around a real app!

Where to go from here?

Take a moment to reflect on all of the different ways you learned to get around in WatchKit: modal, page-based, and hierarchical navigation. Remember you need to stick to either page-based or hierarchical throughout your app, but you can intermix by leveraging modals.

The next step will be to start populating the app with data in tables using context menus, so that you can take actions in different views, and of course, use your advanced WatchKit layout skills to make things look beautiful!

You've gotten a little exposure to tables in this chapter. The next chapter will cover tables in much greater depth. Keep reading to learn just how WatchKit tables work, what all you can do with them and how they differ from their iOS counterparts.

Chapter 6: Tables

By Ryan Nystrom

When building any type of software application, you'll almost always find yourself needing to handle a dynamic amount of data. Typically, data sets are structured into arrays, sets or dictionaries—the last of which are also known as *tables*.

Ever since the first proto-developer created the first program, we've had to build tools to abstract the handling and display of these data sets. UIKit's `UITableView` in iOS is no different: a dynamic view that Apple has optimized to display an infinite amount of data in an efficient manner.

When creating apps for the Apple Watch, you'll undoubtedly run into the same scenario: You've got a dynamic array of data and you need to display it on the tiny 38mm screen. This chapter will show you how to do just that.

In the SousChef app, you have sets of data like ingredients and recipes. This is a perfect example of when to use tables!

Tables in WatchKit

Even if you've never built an app for iOS, as long as you're an iPhone user, you've experienced table views… *everywhere*. From the Settings to Mail, `UITableView` is one of the staple views in iOS.

A UITableView in Mail.app

One of the oldest features of the `UITableView` is its **multidimensionality**, which means you can have data structures more complex than a single dimension. You can group data with sections, and even nest them within other sections.

For example with a list of grocery items, you can have "Produce", "Meats", "Baking", and within each section have the individual items. That will make your data both easier to organize and simpler to browse.

WatchKit's table class

WatchKit provides a new class to handle tables, called `WKInterfaceTable`. This class is similar to `UITableView` in that it manages the display of a set of data, but the similarities with `UITableView` pretty much end there.

For starters, `WKInterfaceTable` can only display a single dimension of data; no sections, and definitely no nested sections. This forces your interfaces to use a simple data structure.

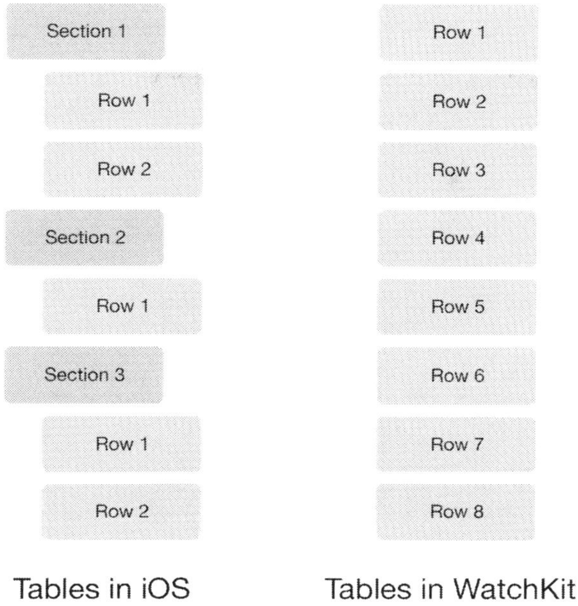

Just like other `WKInterfaceController` and `WKInterfaceObject` classes, `WKInterfaceTable` works perfectly with storyboards. Once you've connected a Table from your storyboard to an `IBOutlet`, you simply set the number of rows to display and their type, like this:

```
table.setNumberOfRows(10, withRowType: "IngredientRow")
```

This single line sets up a table with 10 rows. There's no data source or delegate protocols that you need to implement, or methods that you need to override. Pretty sweet, right?

You probably noticed the **row type** in the code above: that's an identifier, which behaves just like a `UITableViewCell` reuse identifier. At this point you may be thinking, "But it's a single-dimensional table—why do I need an identifier?" If so, keep reading.

> **Note:** If you completed the previous chapter on navigation, you implemented a basic table. This chapter builds on that previous implementation, and if you did complete the navigation chapter, then you've already gotten good exposure to wiring up a `WKInterfaceTable`.

At first glance, WatchKit's table architecture seems pretty simple: you don't need to muck around with any stringly-typed dictionary structures or other homegrown architecture in order to support the section-row and data source patterns of `UITableView`.

But maybe you've also seen some really cool Apple Watch designs like this:

The data is dynamic, and the headers act to create sections. Now you're probably thinking, "Wait a minute—you just told me I had to have a single list! What's with the different sections and rows?"

Row controllers

There's no way we developers would be satisfied with displaying only a single type of row in a table. Users would quickly become confused about where they were in large tables. Sorting a list of ingredients alphabetically certainly *works*, but when you're dealing with hundreds of items, it can quickly become unwieldy.

And who wants to shop in different aisles using an alphabetical list?

In WatchKit, Apple has introduced a new, yet eerily familiar concept called the **row controller**. This is an `NSObject` subclass that houses outlets to the different interface elements displayed by the row.

In the storyboard, you create different table rows, assigning their class to your custom row controller classes and then give them a unique **identifier**, so that the table knows how to instantiate the correct row type.

> **Note:** There's no default row controller class for `WKInterfaceTable`. If you're going to implement a table, you'll have to create a custom class, even if it contains just a single `IBOutlet`.

You might be a little confused as to why there are identifiers and row controllers for a single-dimensional table. The odd thing about the architecture of `WKInterfaceTable` is that even though it's a single-dimensional table, *your row controllers don't all need to have the same class.*

Using the grocery list example image above, you could create a list of eight items that are a mix of section headers and rows. You would then create two different row controllers; one to represent the header and one to represent the row.

You just have to make sure you can easily access your data. Best practices recommend turning any complex section-row architecture into a single `Array` object.

The following image is an example of a single `Array` of section titles and `Recipe` objects alongside the actual interface:

As an example, to implement a list like that shown in the previous image, you would need:

- An object representing the section items like produce, meats and drinks;
- An object representing the ingredient items like carrots, lettuce, steak, milk and coke;
- A row controller object with outlets for the section label and image;
- A row controller object with outlets for the ingredient and quantity labels.

If this is all a little confusing, don't worry; you're about to build both simple and complex tables. Things should make more sense once you've gotten your hands dirty.

Building a table

Open the **SousChef.xcodeproj** app from either the previous chapter, or the starter project for this chapter.

Open **Interface.storyboard** and find the **Recipes** controller. If you recall from the previous chapter, this controller already has a `WKInterfaceTable` wired up with a row controller.

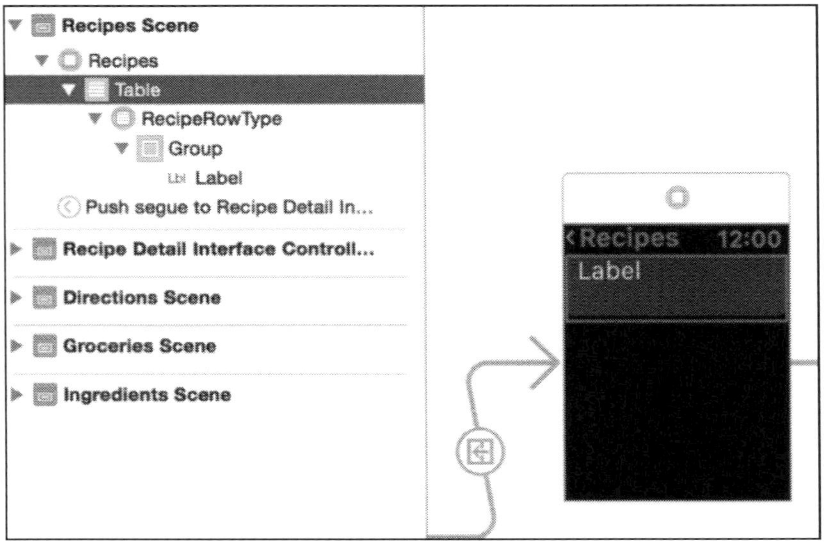

The existing Recipes table

You can also see the lone outlet set up in **RecipeRowController.swift**:

```
class RecipeRowController: NSObject {
  @IBOutlet weak var textLabel: WKInterfaceLabel!
}
```

Build and run. Navigate to the Recipes interface controller; you'll see a very simple table populated with dummy data.

It's nice that this table is already set up; you can thank yourself if you completed the previous chapter. The interface is a touch boring, though. It's time to spice it up!

Building a better interface

Open **Interface.storyboard** and find the **Recipes controller**. Select the **row controller** with the identifier `RecipeRowType`.

Now, select the **label** and change its **Lines** attribute to **0** so that if the recipe has a long name, the words will wrap and the row will size itself accordingly—that way, you can read it all.

> **Note:** If a recipe has a long name, WatchKit's amazing layout system will automatically push any subsequent objects down and make the containing group larger. If you've ever dealt with the complexities of `tableView(_:heightForRowAtIndexPath:)`, you're probably jumping for joy right now. :]

Drag another **label** from the Object Library into the group, just beneath the existing label. By default, row controller groups have a *horizontal* layout. This will quickly become cramped with long recipe names.

Select the row controller group containing the labels and in the **Attributes Inspector**, change the **Layout** to **Vertical**. While you're in there, also change the **Height** to **Size To Fit Content**.

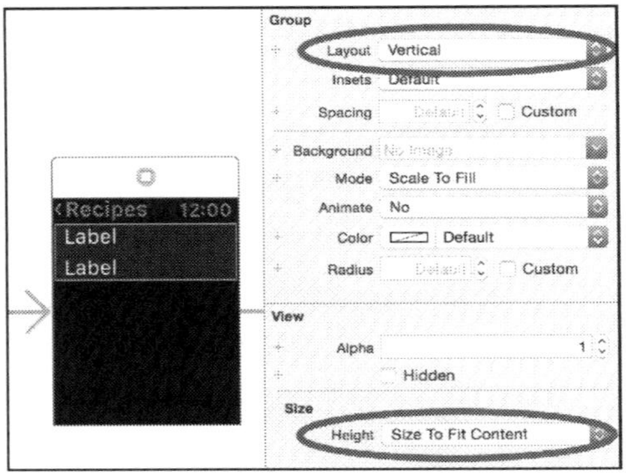

Select the **bottom label** and change the **Text Color** to a **Light Gray Color**. Next, change the **Font** to **Footnote**. This will shrink the label to a predetermined size for footnotes.

The top label will display the recipe name while the bottom label will display how many ingredients are in the recipe. This will help users determine which recipes are likely more complicated.

Option-click on **RecipeRowController.swift** to open it in the assistant editor. **Control-drag** from the **bottom label** to `RecipeRowController` and create a new outlet with the type `WKInterfaceLabel` and a name of `ingredientsLabel`.

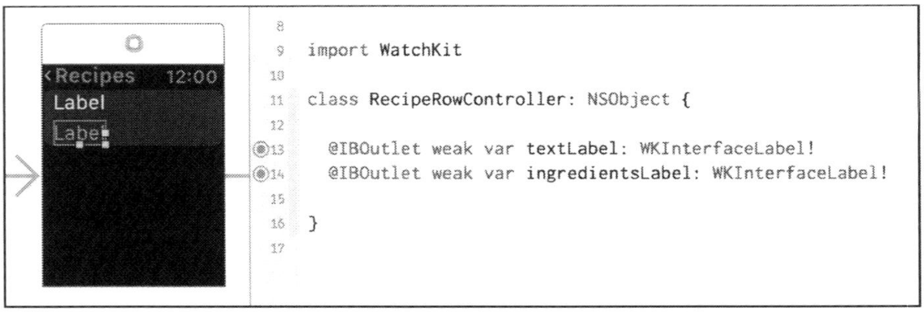

Your newly created ingredients label outlet

The dummy data was useful to get up and running, but it's time to use something a bit closer to reality. Recall that the iPhone companion app has a mechanism for fetching a list of recipes.

Take a look at **SousChefKit\Storage\RecipeStore.swift**. This class is stored in the framework that's shared with both the containing iPhone app and the WatchKit extension. This means that to fetch a list of recipes for the Watch, you can use the exact same classes and methods that the iOS app uses!

Open **RecipesInterfaceController.swift** and import `SousChefKit` under the import for `WatchKit`:

```
import SousChefKit
```

Replace the existing `recipes` variable with a constant that'll store your recipes:

```
let recipeStore = RecipeStore()
```

This will trigger some compiler errors because `recipes` is now gone. To fix some of the errors, replace everything after the call to `super` in `awakeWithContext(_:)` with the following:

```
// 1
let recipes = recipeStore.recipes
// 2
table.setNumberOfRows(recipes.count,
  withRowType: "RecipeRowType")

// 3
for (index, recipe) in enumerate(recipes) {
  // 4
  let controller = table.rowControllerAtIndex(index)
    as RecipeRowController
  // 5
  controller.textLabel.setText(recipe.name)
  // 6
  controller.ingredientsLabel.setText(
    "\(recipe.ingredients.count) ingredients")
}
```

Let's go through this step by step:

1. You use the array of `Recipe` objects as the data source for the table.
2. You tell the table how many rows it will need, and their type. Since there's just one type of row controller in this table, you simply pass the identifier along with the number of rows.
3. Now you iterate over each recipe using the convenient Swift function `enumerate` so that you get handed both the object and the index.

4. Then you get the row controller at the current index. Since you previously set the number of rows and the identifier corresponds to the `RecipeRowController` class in your storyboard, you can cast the controller to `RecipeRowController`.
5. You set the `textLabel` to the recipe's name. This isn't much different from what you were doing with the dummy data before.
6. Swift makes string formatting so much simpler than Objective-C. You set the text of your new `ingredientsLabel` outlet to the number of ingredients in the recipe.

> **Note:** If you're curious about how the containing iPhone app makes use of `RecipeStore`, check out **RecipesController.swift** in the SousChef group, which uses a table view. It's interesting to compare the `UITableView` and `WKInterfaceTable` implementations.

You should have one more compiler error left where you return a context object for use when the table's selection segue is triggered. Change that method now to instead return a recipe from `recipeStore`:

```
override func contextForSegueWithIdentifier(
  segueIdentifier: String,
  inTable table: WKInterfaceTable,
  rowIndex: Int) -> AnyObject? {
  return recipeStore.recipes[rowIndex]
}
```

Build and run. Navigate to the Recipes controller to see your updated table, now with real data!

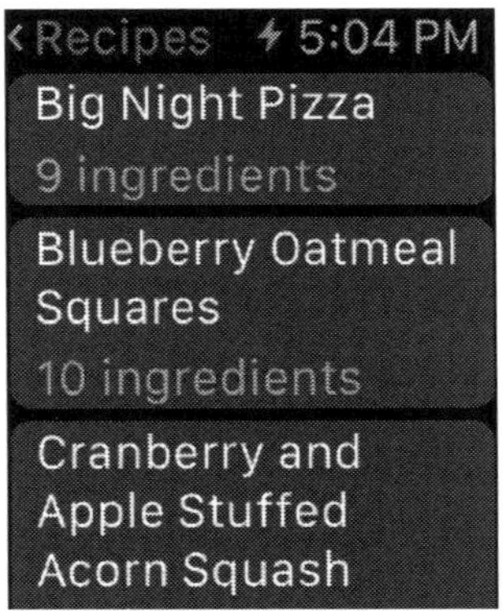

Tap on a recipe item to push the `RecipeDetailInterfaceController` onto the navigation stack, but notice that instead of displaying the recipe's name, the interface controller simply shows "Label". Have you got any idea why?

Remember that you just changed the type of object being passed between controllers during the table selection segue. Open **RecipeDetailInterfaceController.swift** and import SousChefKit just as you did previously:

```
import SousChefKit
```

Then add a new optional to `RecipeDetailInterfaceController`:

```
var recipe: Recipe?
```

Why is this variable an optional? Passing context objects between controllers is entirely optional, and the object isn't received until `awakeWithContext(_:)`, which occurs *after* any `init` methods. There isn't really an elegant away around making a passed context object non-optional.

> **Note:** Swift requires you to initialize all variables, whether immutable or not, by the end of the class' `init`. This is a form of type safety and also allows your code is more declarative, but seasoned Objective-C developers can have a hard time adjusting.

Replace `awakeWithContext(_:)` with the following:

```
override func awakeWithContext(context: AnyObject!) {
  super.awakeWithContext(context)
  recipe = context as? Recipe
  nameLabel.setText(recipe?.name)
}
```

Because the variable is an optional, you can remove the previous `if-let` statement and simply cast the variable as such with the `as?` operator. Then you simply set the label's text with the recipe's name.

Still in **RecipeDetailInterfaceController.swift**, add the following:

```
override func contextForSegueWithIdentifier(
  segueIdentifier: String) -> AnyObject? {
  return recipe
}
```

Remember that there are two segues coming from this controller, one that pushes the Ingredients controller and one that pushes the Directions controller. Both of the new controllers will need to know which recipe they are serving (pun very much intended!), so instead of checking the segue identifier, you can simply pass the current recipe.

Build and run. Navigate to the Recipes controller. Tap on a recipe. You'll see the label is now populated with whatever recipe you tapped on.

Now you're getting somewhere! And I bet you can see where to go from here: you've got two more tables to build.

> **Challenge**: The vertical spacing on the `RecipeDetailInterfaceController` is a little tight. Use your knowledge about WatchKit layout and adjust the spacing. Refer back to Chapter 4, "Layout" if you need help.

Two simple tables from scratch

Both the Ingredients and Directions controllers will be simple tables that display a list of ingredients and directions for the selected recipe respectively. The setup and wiring of these tables will be very similar to what you did for `RecipesInterfaceController`.

Open **Interface.storyboard**, find the **Ingredients** controller and drag a **Table** onto it. Change the new row controller group's **Layout** to be a **Vertical** and its **Height** to **Size To Fit Content**.

Drag two **labels** into the layout group in the row and stack one on top of the other. The **top label** will display the ingredient name, so set its number of **Lines** to 0 to ensure all the text is displayed.

Change the **bottom label** so that it's a **Light Gray Color** with a **Font** of **Caption 1**. This will make the label smaller, but not quite as small as if it were a footnote.

Select the containing **row controller** and in the **Attributes Inspector**, change the **Identifier** to **IngredientRow**. Use the document outline if you have any trouble selecting the row controller.

Your Ingredients controller should now look something like this:

The configured Ingredients controller

You'll use the first label for the name of the ingredient and the second for the quantity. For organizational purposes, it's sometimes helpful to change the default text of labels to something that represents what that will eventually be displayed there. In this case, change the top label's text to **Fresh Pepper** and the second label's text to **1 tsp**.

Now follow a similar process to set up the **Directions** interface controller:

1. Add a **Table** to the controller.
2. Change the row controller's group **Layout** to **Vertical** and its **Height** to **Sized To Fit Content**.
3. Add two **labels** to the controller.
4. Change the top label's **Font** to **Headline**.
5. Change the bottom label's **Lines** to **0** so it will have as many lines as is required to properly layout the text.
6. Set the row controller's **Identifier** to **StepRow**.

You're going to use the top label to name each step, such as "Step 1", "Step 2" and so forth, and the bottom label to display the instructions that accompany that step. You might want to change the default text of the labels to make that a little more obvious.

When you're done adding the interface elements and configuring your tables, the recipe section of your storyboard should look like this:

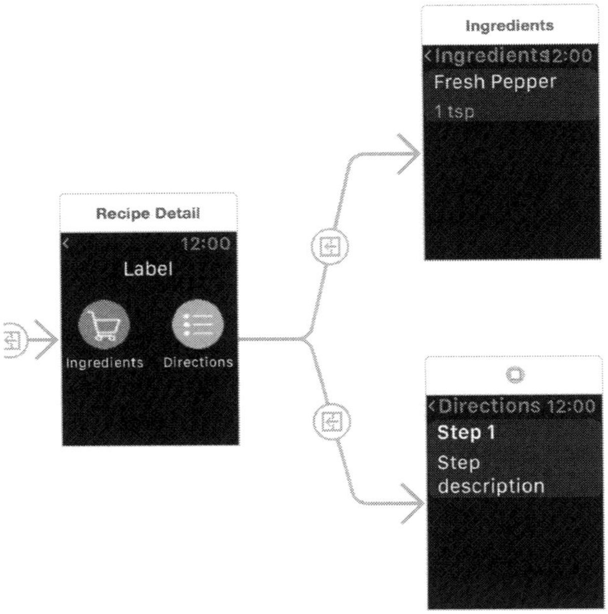

Storyboard set up to display Ingredients and Directions

Now that you've configured your storyboard, it's time to hook up your row controllers in code.

Right-click the **SousChef WatchKit Extension\Row Controllers** group and select **New File...**. Create a new **Cocoa Touch Class** that's a subclass of `NSObject` and name it **IngredientRowController.swift**. Before you click **Create**, make sure you have the **SousChef WatchKit Extension** target selected.

Before you go any further, open **IngredientRowController.swift** and make sure the import statement at the top of the file is for WatchKit. Even though your row controller classes extend `NSObject`, they're still going to access WatchKit-specific classes like `WKInterfaceLabel`:

```
import WatchKit
```

Open **Interface.storyboard** once again and select the **row controller** in the **Ingredients** interface controller. You'll likely need to use the document outline to do this. It should be labeled **IngredientRow**, the same as the identifier:

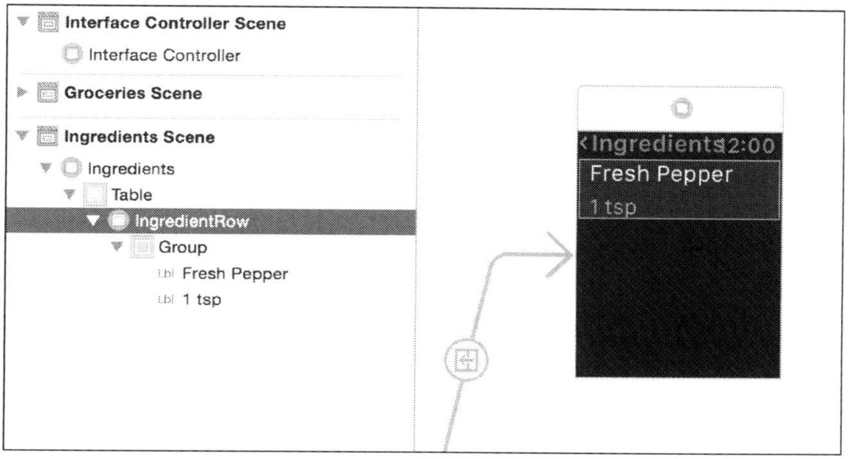

Selecting the row controller for Ingredients

In the **Identity Inspector**, change the class of the row controller to **IngredientRowController**.

Open **IngredientRowController.swift** in the assistant editor. Right-click and drag from the top label into the class to create an outlet called `nameLabel`.

Repeat the process for the bottom label but this time name the outlet `measurementLabel`. When you're done, **IngredientRowController.swift** will look like this:

```
import WatchKit

class IngredientRowController: NSObject {

  @IBOutlet weak var nameLabel: WKInterfaceLabel!
  @IBOutlet weak var measurementLabel: WKInterfaceLabel!

}
```

Now for your **Directions** interface controller, simply repeat all the steps you followed above:

1. Name your new class **StepRowController**. Remember to make it a subclass of `NSObject`.
2. In **StepRowController.swift**, make sure to update the import statement to `WatchKit`.
3. In **Interface.storyboard**, change the class of the appropriate row controller to `StepRowController`.
4. Create an outlet for the top label and call it `stepLabel`.
5. Create an outlet for the bottom label and call it `directionsLabel`.

Your completed `StepRowController` class will look like this:

```
import WatchKit

class StepRowController: NSObject {

  @IBOutlet weak var stepLabel: WKInterfaceLabel!
  @IBOutlet weak var directionsLabel: WKInterfaceLabel!

}
```

The next phase is to create subclasses of `WKInterfaceController` for the Ingredients and Directions interface controllers, set up their `WKInterfaceTable`s and then configure each individual row.

Right-click the **SousChef WatchKit Extension\Interface Controllers** group and select **New File...**. Create a new **Cocoa Touch Class** that subclasses `WKInterfaceController` and name it **RecipeIngredientsInterfaceController.swift**.

First you need to add an `IBOutlet` for the table in the Ingredients interface controller. To do that, you need to make sure the correct class is being used in the storyboard.

Open **Interface.storyboard**, select the **Ingredients** interface controller and in the **Identity Inspector**, change its class to `RecipeIngredientsInterfaceController`.

With the Ingredients interface controller still selected, open **RecipeIngredientsInterfaceController.swift** in the assistant editor. Select the **table** in the Ingredients interface controller (remember to use the document outline if you need to), **ctrl+drag** into `RecipeIngredientsInterfaceController` to create an outlet and name it simply `table`.

`RecipeIngredientsInterfaceController` will now look like this:

```
import WatchKit
```

```
class RecipeIngredientsInterfaceController:
  WKInterfaceController {

  @IBOutlet weak var table: WKInterfaceTable!

  override func awakeWithContext(context: AnyObject?) {
    super.awakeWithContext(context)
  }

}
```

Note: You might notice that you have some boilerplate methods in the class that come from Apple's template. You can remove those, or leave them in there if you'd prefer.

Take a look back in **RecipeDetailInterfaceController.swift** and find `contextForSegueWithIdentifier(_:)`. Recall from the previous chapter on navigation that instances of `WKInterfaceController` can pass context objects between themselves. This alleviates the pain of having to intercept the segue or create special initializers for controllers like you have to in UIKit.

In `RecipeDetailInterfaceController`, you're passing along a `Recipe` to the receiving controller. In this case, there are two segues; one to the Ingredients interface controller and one to the Directions interface controller.

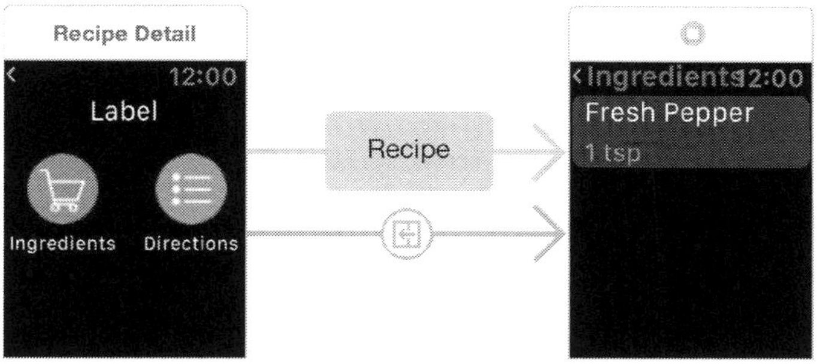

Passing a Recipe object between controllers during a segue

To do anything with the `Recipe`, the Ingredients interface controller must *catch* it. Open **RecipeIngredientsInterfaceController.swift** and import **SousChefKit** at the top of the file:

```
import SousChefKit
```

Next, in the class add an optional for the `Recipe` that you'll be receiving:

```
var recipe: Recipe?
```

In `awakeWithContext(_:)`, capture the context object and cast it to a `Recipe`:

```
recipe = context as? Recipe
```

Well done! Now all you need to do is use this `recipe` variable to figure out how many rows there are in the table, and configure each row controller appropriatley.

Still in `awakeWithContext(_:)`, add the following:

```
// 1
if let ingredients = recipe?.ingredients {
  // 2
  table.setNumberOfRows(
    ingredients.count, withRowType: "IngredientRow")

  for (index, ingredient) in enumerate(ingredients) {
    // 3
    let controller = table.rowControllerAtIndex(index) as!
                       IngredientRowController
    // 4
    controller.nameLabel.setText(
      ingredient.name.capitalizedString)
    controller.measurementLabel.setText(ingredient.quantity)
  }
}
```

Step by step, here's what you're doing:

1. Remember that your `recipe` object is optional, so you want to configure your table only if the object exists. The `ingredients` array is *not* optional, so if `recipe` exists, then transitively, `ingredients` exists.
2. You set the number of rows in your table using the `ingredients` array. The row identifier `IngredientRow` corresponds to the identifier that you set up in on the Ingredients controller in Interface.storyboard.
3. You get the row controller for the ingredient on which you're iterating. You're only using a single identifier (see #2), the one you set up for `IngredientRowController` in Interface.storyboard.
4. You configure the row controller outlets with the ingredient `name` and `quantity`.

Build and run. Tap the Recipes button and select any recipe from the table. When you arrive at the detail screen for the recipe, tap the Ingredients button. You'll see a table of ingredients for the recipe you selected two controllers ago!

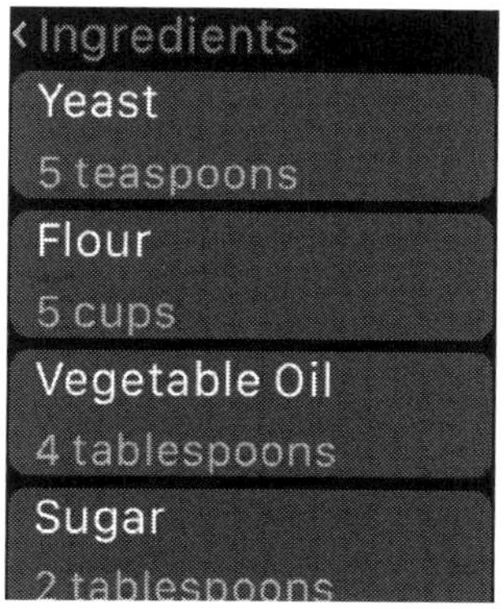

A sharp-looking Ingredients table

Next, you need to get the Directions interface controller wired up in the same manner in which you did for the Ingredients interface controller. Complete the steps below, and refer back to the previous section if you get stuck:

1. Create a new `WKInterfaceController` subclass named **RecipeDirectionsInterfaceController**.
2. In **Interface.storyboard**, set the class of the Directions interface controller to `RecipeDirectionsInterfaceController`.
3. Create an `IBOutlet` for the table in the Directions interface controller and name it `table`.
4. Import **SousChefKit** into **RecipeDirectionsInterfaceController.swift**.
5. Create a `Recipe` optional and set it to the context object in `awakeWithContext(_:)`.
6. Call `setNumberOfRows(_:withRowType:)` on the table using the number of steps in the recipe. Use `StepRow` as the type. Make sure you only set the number of rows if the `recipe` object exists.

If you followed all of the steps correctly, your `RecipeDirectionsInterfaceController` class implementation will look like this:

```
import WatchKit
import SousChefKit

class RecipeDirectionsInterfaceController:
```

```
  WKInterfaceController {
  @IBOutlet weak var table: WKInterfaceTable!
  var recipe: Recipe?

  override func awakeWithContext(context: AnyObject?) {
    super.awakeWithContext(context)
    recipe = context as? Recipe
    if let steps = recipe?.steps {
      table.setNumberOfRows(steps.count, withRowType: "StepRow")
    }
  }
}
```

Beneath the line in `awakeWithContext(_:)` where you call `setNumberOfRows(_:withRowType:)` on the table, add the following:

```
for (index, step) in enumerate(steps) {
  // 1
  let controller = table.rowControllerAtIndex(index) as!
                     StepRowController
  // 2
  controller.stepLabel.setText("Step \(index + 1)")
  controller.directionsLabel.setText(step)
}
```

Here's what you're doing:

1. Row controllers used by the Directions interface controller are instances of `StepRowController`. This matches up with the `StepRow` identifier that you set in the previous chapter.
2. You set the `stepLabel` text to a string containing the current step, such as "Step 2", and set the `directionsLabel` text to the contents of the actual step.

Build and run. Navigate to the Directions interface controller for a recipe. You'll see a nice-looking list of all the steps for each recipe!

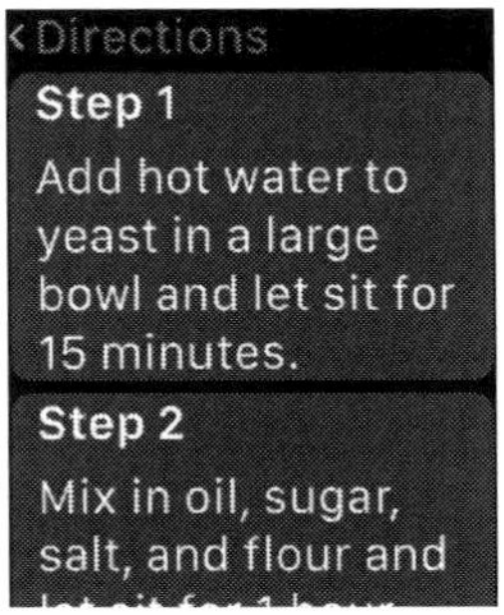

Building a more complex table

The last table you're going to build will be more complicated than the Ingredients or Directions tables. Why is that? Well, take a look at what the final table will look like:

The table from the Grocery list

Notice that there are *two* different types of rows here. If you dig into the `WKInterfaceTable` documentation, you'll find that there are *no headers* in tables whatsoever.

So what are you supposed to do?

Remember how you've been using `setNumberOfRows(_:withRowType:)` to set the number of rows using a particular identifier? Well, there's *another* method you can use to conveniently tell the table how many rows it has and what each row type is!

That method is `setRowTypes(_:)`, and it takes an array of strings, each one corresponding to a row controller identifier that you've set up in your storyboard.

Open **Interface.storyboard** and locate the only empty interface controller. It should have a segue from the initial interface controller.

Drag a **Table** onto this interface controller from the Object Library. Select the new table, and in the Attributes Inspector, change the **Rows** attribute to **2**.

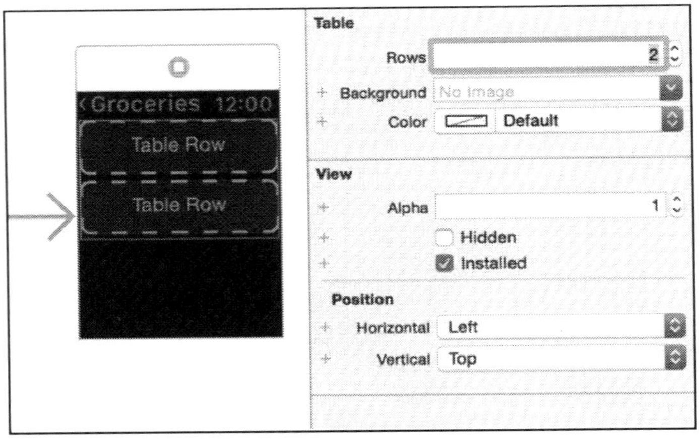

> **Note:** In the rest of this chapter, you'll be manipulating layouts a lot. If you need a refresher, be sure to re-read Chapter 4, "Layout" to get up to speed.

Select the **top row** and in the Attributes Inspector, change the **Identifier** to **GroceryTypeRow**. Select the **bottom row** and change its **Identifier** to **GroceryRow**.

A good way to confirm that your row controllers have identifiers is to check that the document outline has been updated; their names should now match the identifiers, like in the image below:

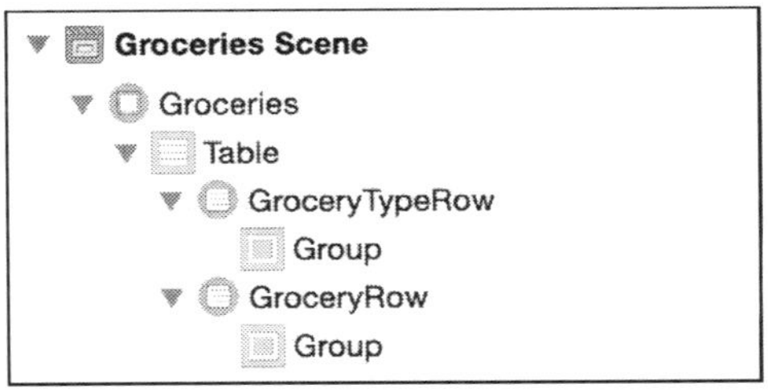

The header row

The top row is going to serve as the header for each type of grocery—meat, produce and so forth. Remember that tables in WatchKit are single-dimensional, so you don't have a section-row data structure.

Drag an **Image** into the top row. Select the image and in the Attributes Inspector, change the **Image** to **meat**—or change it to **produce** if you'd rather! This is just a placeholder image that you'll change at runtime.

Drag in a **label** and change its **Font** to **Headline**.

The image and label are stuck to the top of the group, which looks a little awkward. Change the **Vertical** position of both the image and label to **Center**.

To make the header row stand out when there will likely be a bunch of grocery rows, select the **group** in the **top row** and change the **Color** to **Clear Color**. Since the default color of the row is a dark grey, making the header background clear will make it stand out.

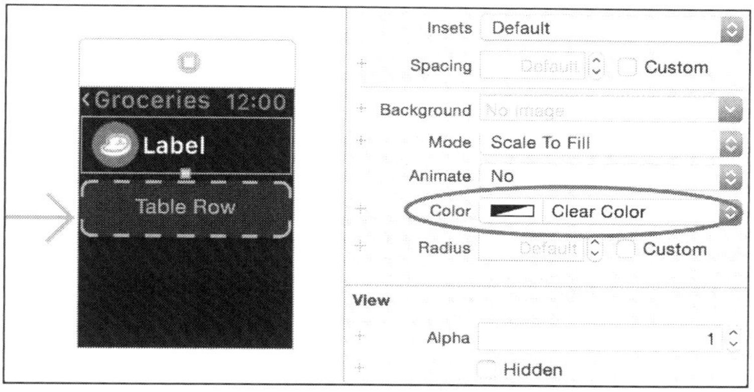

The item row

The bottom row controller in the Grocery table is what displays data about an individual item on the grocery list. It consists of the name of the item, the measurement and the quantity (in case you need to buy more than one).

Select the **bottom row** group and in the Attributes Inspector, change its **Height** to **Size To Fit Content**. This will let the row grow appropriately if the ingredient has a long name. Also, change the **Layout** to **Vertical** so that you can stack interface elements on top of each other.

Drag a **label** into the bottom row and change its **Lines** attribute to **0** so that the label will display all the text, no matter how many times it needs to wrap.

Drag in another **group**. Make sure it lands *beneath* the label you just added, but still inside the table row. This group will hold the labels for the measurement and quantity.

At this point, your Grocery interface controller will look like this:

In the **bottom row**, select the **group** you just added. Add a **label**. Change the **Text Color** to **Light Gray Color** and the **Font** to **Caption 1**. This label will display the *measurement*.

With the new label selected, **Copy** and immediately **Paste** to add an identical label to the group aside the first label.

Change the **Horizontal** position of the **second label** to **Right** in order to pin the label to the right of its containing group. This label will display the *quantity*.

At this point, change the default text of your labels to something a little more representative so you can easily identify what they are.

With more helpful labels, your Grocery interface controller will look like this:

Adding controllers and wiring

With the entire interface constructed, it's time to create some row and interface controllers and connect the necessary outlets so you can display your data.

In the **SousChef WatchKit Extension\Row Controllers** group, create a new **Cocoa Touch Class** that is a subclass of `NSObject` and call it **GroceryTypeRowController**. Open **GroceryTypeRowController.swift** and add an import for WatchKit:

```
import WatchKit
```

Go back to **Interface.storyboard** and select the **row controller** object for the **top row**, the row that will act as the grocery header. Use the **Identity Inspector** to change the row controller's **class** to `GroceryTypeRowController`.

Open **GroceryTypeRowController.swift** in the assistant editor, and create outlets for the `WKInterfaceImage` and `WKInterfaceLabel` in the headers. Name these labels `image` and `textLabel`, respectively.

Once you're done, `GroceryTypeRowController` will look like this:

```
import WatchKit

class GroceryTypeRowController: NSObject {
  @IBOutlet weak var textLabel: WKInterfaceLabel!
  @IBOutlet weak var image: WKInterfaceImage!
}
```

Follow the same steps to create a row controller for the bottom row:

1. Create a new `NSObject` subclass called **GroceryRowController** in the **Row Controllers** group.
2. Change the **Class** of the **bottom row** to `GroceryRowController`.
3. Create outlets for all three labels in the row and name them `textLabel`, `measurementLabel`, and `quantityLabel`.

`GroceryRowController` will then look like the following:

```
import WatchKit

class GroceryRowController: NSObject {
  @IBOutlet weak var textLabel: WKInterfaceLabel!
  @IBOutlet weak var measurementLabel: WKInterfaceLabel!
  @IBOutlet weak var quantityLabel: WKInterfaceLabel!
}
```

Now that each of the rows has a row controller subclass, you can create a `WKInterfaceController` subclass that will connect the data, table and rows together.

In the **SousChef WatchKit Extension\Interface Controllers** group, create another file that is a subclass of `WKInterfaceController`. Name this new file

GroceryInterfaceController, make sure that you have the **SousChef WatchKit Extension** target selected and click **Create**.

Open **Interface.storyboard**, select the Grocery interface controller and change its **Class** to `GroceryInterfaceController` using the Identity Inspector.

Next, open **GroceryInterfaceController.swift** in the assistant editor and, from the **table** in the Grocery interface controller, **ctrl+drag** to create a new outlet named `table`.

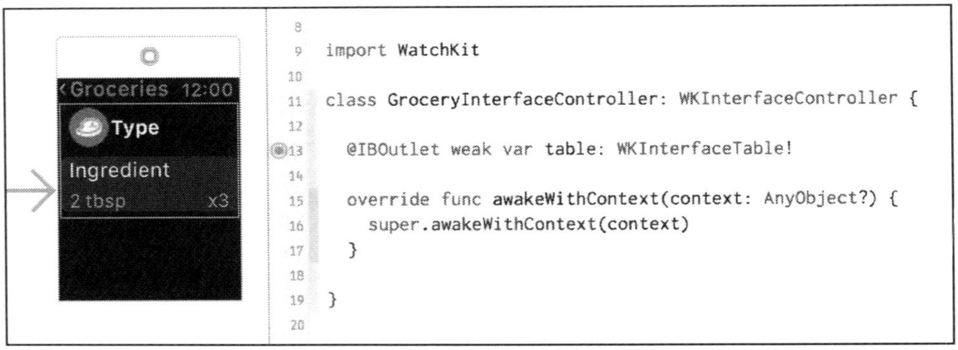

Creating the table outlet for the Grocery controller

To get the groceries data into the table, you need to use the `GroceryList` object found in **SousChefKit\Storage**. Import **SousChefKit** near the top of **GroceryInterfaceController.swift**:

```
import SousChefKit
```

Then inside the `GroceryInterfaceController` class, add a constant for the `GroceryList`:

```
let groceryList = GroceryList(useSample: true)
```

The `useSample` parameter is a convenient way to populate the grocery list with seed data. Without this there wouldn't be a way to populate the list with any items, because you haven't yet built the features to add recipes to your list. You'll remove this in Chapter 7, "Menus" when you start using real data.

`GroceryList` has a bunch of public methods for getting ingredients in a grocery list. The SousChef iPhone app uses section and row architecture because it pairs well with `UITableView`.

Luckily, the developers saw a use-case for a single-dimension list and created a convenience method that flattens all of the data into a single `Array`. If the developers can predict the need for a single-dimensional list, they'd better be buying lottery tickets too!

To access this method, create a lazily-evaluated variable below the `groceryList` constant you just added:

```
lazy var flatList: [FlatGroceryItem] = {
  return self.groceryList.flattenedGroceries()
}()
```

Since this method is generating your data, it's best to use the `lazy` modifier to defer initialization until you actually use the variable.

> **Note:** `flattenedGroceries` in `GroceryList` is not the most efficient algorithm. Using `lazy` in this instance could potentially save time initializing the Grocery interface controller. Even if the iPhone is executing the code, it's always a good idea to use efficient code and data structures!

In `awakeWithContext(_:)`, add a call to a method you haven't yet implemented:

```
override func awakeWithContext(context: AnyObject?) {
  super.awakeWithContext(context)

  updateTable()
}
```

You'll get a compiler error now because `updateTable()` doesn't exist. To make the warning go away, add the following to `GroceryInterfaceController`:

```
func updateTable() {
  table.setRowTypes(flatList.map({ $0.id }))

  for i in 0..<table.numberOfRows {
    // TODO
  }
}
```

The first line sets up the row types and the total number of rows for the table. You're using `map()` to turn the flattened list of `FlatGroceryItem`s into an array of `String`s that represent the type of row.

Remember that your rows are a single-dimensional list of grocery items mixed with header rows. You need different identifiers to distinguish between row types.

Inside `updateTable()`, add the following inside the `for` loop:

```
// 1
let controller: AnyObject! = table.rowControllerAtIndex(i)
let context = flatList[i]

// 2
if let row = controller as? GroceryTypeRowController {
  let type = context.item as! String
  row.textLabel.setText(type)
  row.image.setImageNamed(type.lowercaseString)
// 3
} else if let row = controller as? GroceryRowController {
  let item = context.item as! Ingredient

  row.textLabel.setText(item.name.capitalizedString)
  row.measurementLabel.setText(item.quantity)

  // 4
  let quantity = groceryList.quantityForItem(item)
  let quantityText = quantity > 1 ? "x\(quantity)" : ""
  row.quantityLabel.setText(quantityText)
}
```

Let's break this down:

1. The controller for the current row is declared as `AnyObject`, because you aren't sure yet whether it's a `GroceryTypeRowController` or a `GroceryRowController`.
2. Swift's conditional casting makes it super easy to depend on the row controller's class to decide what to do. In the first branch, if the row is a `GroceryTypeRowController`, you get the type of item from the row tuple and set up the row's text and image. The food icons are already included in the app bundle.
3. In the second branch, the row is a `GroceryRowController`, which is your grocery item row. You need to set up the name of the item, the quantity and then the total number of items that are added.
4. You only set the quantity text if you have more than one, so it's more noticeable when you have to purchase multiple quantities. Plus, saying "1x" when you just need a single item is a little redundant!

> **Note:** You could be cooking four servings of one of your famous recipes, so that would mean you'd have 4x of each quantity (for example, 4x ½ cup milk). Hope you were hungry!

Build and run. Tap on the Groceries button. You'll see an awesome-looking table with different kinds of rows!

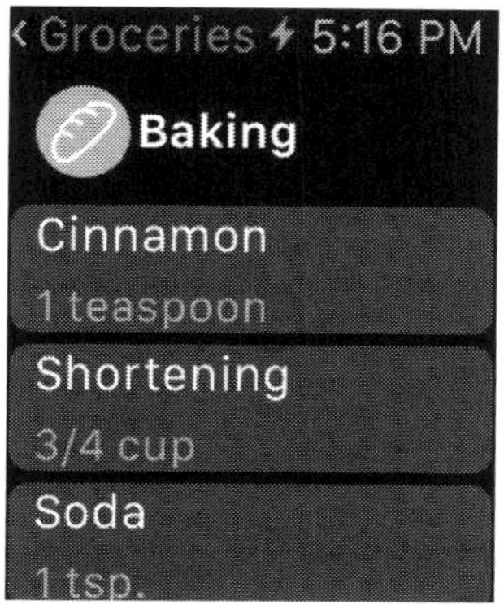

A WKInterfaceTable with headers and rows!

Row selection handling

A grocery list isn't much help if you can't check things off! `WKInterfaceTable` has an API for handling row selection that's very similar to `UITableView`.

The nice thing about WatchKit is that you don't have to inherit from other controllers or conform to protocols in order to respond to touch events. In UIKit, you'd have to inherit from `UITableViewController` or conform to the delegate protocol and implement the necessary methods, but WatchKit does away with all that.

Open **GroceryInterfaceController.swift** and add two computed variables at the top of the class:

```
var cellTextAttributes: [NSObject: AnyObject] {
  return [
    NSFontAttributeName: UIFont.systemFontOfSize(16),
    NSForegroundColorAttributeName: UIColor.whiteColor()
  ]
}

var strikethroughCellTextAttributes: [NSObject: AnyObject] {
  return [
    NSFontAttributeName: UIFont.systemFontOfSize(16),
    NSForegroundColorAttributeName: UIColor.lightGrayColor(),
    NSStrikethroughStyleAttributeName:
      NSUnderlineStyle.StyleSingle.rawValue
  ]
}
```

Both of these computed variables are options for `NSAttributedString`. The `cellTextAttributes` variable represents the normal font attributes for grocery rows. The `strikethroughCellTextAttributes` variable represents a strike-through style for items that have been checked off the list.

At the bottom of the class, add this code to handle row selection:

```
override func table(table: WKInterfaceTable,
  didSelectRowAtIndex rowIndex: Int) {
  // 1
  if let row = table.rowControllerAtIndex(rowIndex)
  as? GroceryRowController {
    let item = flatList[rowIndex].item as! Ingredient
    let text = item.name.capitalizedString

    // 2
    var attributes: [NSObject: AnyObject]?

    // attributes code will go here

    // 3
    let attributedText = NSAttributedString(string: text,
      attributes: attributes)
    row.textLabel.setAttributedText(attributedText)
  }
}
```

Here's how this works:

1. You only respond to tap events if the row is a `GroceryRowController`. You don't want to do anything if the user taps a header row. Then you get the corresponding `Ingredient` and capitalize the text for the row. You capitalize to make a uniform interface no matter how the data is originally formatted.

2. In the next step, you set the attributes variable to one of the computed variables you added earlier.

3. Finally, you create an `NSAttributedString` and set it on the row's `textLabel`.

In the commented area just below where you define the `attributes` variable, add the following code to select the appropriate set of attributes:

```
// 1
if item.purchased {
  attributes = cellTextAttributes
} else {
  attributes = strikethroughCellTextAttributes
}
```

```
// 2
groceryList.setIngredient(item, purchased: !item.purchased)
groceryList.sync()
```

Just two steps here:

1. If the item is already purchased, then it's being removed from the list, so you remove the strikethrough. If the item has *not* been purchased, then you need to apply a strikethrough to purchase it.
2. Make sure to update the data store. Use the `groceryList` object you created earlier and set the item as purchased. The sync function internally saves the grocery data with `NSKeyedArchiver` to make sure your list persists through sessions.

> **Note:** Since WatchKit apps run as an extension, you can use a shared version of `NSUserDefaults` to persist your grocery items between the Watch app and the containing iPhone app! You'll learn more about this in Chapter 8, "Sharing Data".

Build and run. Tap on some items in your grocery list. The rows should toggle between struck-through and normal text when you tap on them.

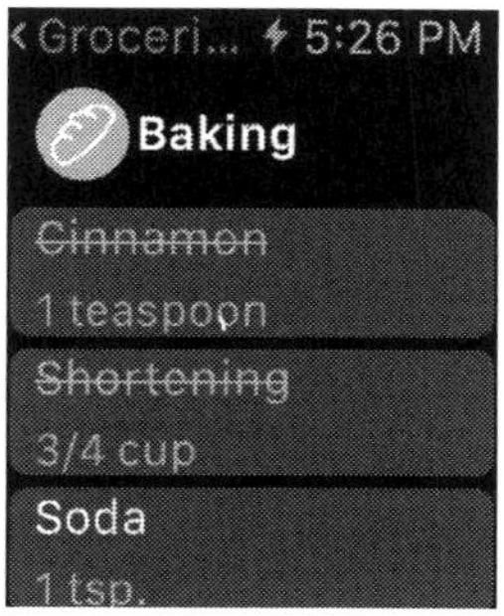

Select a few items, tap the back button and then go back to your grocery list. Notice how none of the items retain their state! The `GroceryList` store knows what items you've purchased, but the UI isn't reflecting it.

This is because when the app initially loads and populates the table, it simply uses the ingredient names and not their purchased state.

To change this, locate `updateTable()` in **GroceryInterfaceController.swift**. In the `if`-statement where you check the class type of the row controller, find the second branch where you check if the controller is a `GroceryRowController`.

Replace the following line in the `if`-statement:

```
row.textLabel.setText(item.name.capitalizedString)
```

With this:

```
if item.purchased {
  // 1
  let attributes = strikethroughCellTextAttributes
  let attributedText = NSAttributedString(string:
    item.name.capitalizedString, attributes: attributes)
  row.textLabel.setAttributedText(attributedText)
} else {
  // 2
  row.textLabel.setText(item.name.capitalizedString)
}
```

And now for your final breakdown:

1. If the Ingredients item has been purchased, you use `strikethroughCellTextAttributes` to format the text just like you did when the user taps the row.
2. If the item hasn't been purchased, you simply set the text of the label.

Notice how the control flow in `updateTable()` is the opposite of `table(_:didSelectRowAtIndex:)`. That is because in `updateTable()` you are **applying** the style, but when you tap a row you are **changing** the style.

Build and run. Check off a couple of items on your grocery list, go back and then revisit your list again. All of your selections will still be there!

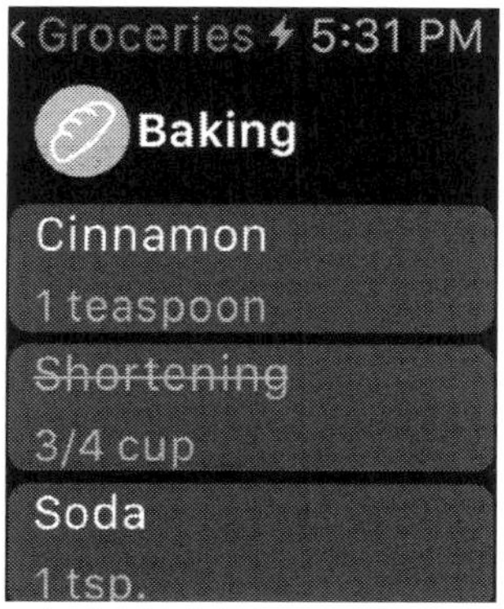

The SousChef app is now what is called in the Software Engineering world as *stateful*. That is, your data and controllers are saved when you navigate elsewhere or the app is killed.

Where to go from here?

The SousChef Watch app is now fully useable! You can browse ingredients, recipes, and even cooking directions. Your tables respond to taps, and they even retain their selection state. Pretty cool!

As things stand, your `GroceryList` is using sample data. In the next chapter, you're going to wire up a context menu so you can add ingredients from recipes to your list.

Even then, SousChef will only be working with local data. In coming chapters, though, you're going to be syncing recipes from the web, sharing data between the watch and phone and exploring some of the more unique features of WatchKit, like notifications and glances. You've got a rich banquet ahead of you!

Chapter 7: Menus

By Ryan Nystrom

When building iOS applications, if you ever wanted to present a context menu or alert view for a particular action, you had to create a `UIAlertView` or `UIActionSheet` (iOS 7 or earlier), or create a `UIActionController` (iOS 8 and later). Whether picking an action from a menu or confirming a more permanent action like deletion, creating menus in iOS has always taken some time.

For WatchKit, Apple introduced a brand new and simple API for creating context menus. Instead of creating menus from scratch and wiring up delegates or blocks, you simply create menu items in Interface Builder and wire up their actions just like you would with buttons or other interface objects.

Wiring up outlets and code can sometimes be confusing when you don't know where the action is initiated from. With WatchKit's menu system, you can create your button actions and menu actions in the same way.

The one pitfall is that if your interfaces are generally dynamic, creating static context menu items in Interface Builder does limit the functionality of your application, as they can't be changed at runtime.

In this chapter, you will learn how to create simple-yet-powerful menu items. You'll also learn how to wire up menus, create their icons, and respond to different actions.

Understanding WatchKit menus

Before diving into creating your first menu, let's take a few minutes to understand how menus work in WatchKit and how you go about creating them.

Gestures

With WatchKit, Apple has introduced a new way to present menus. iOS has a gesture called a "long press" that can be represented in code by using a `UILongPressGestureRecognizer`. WatchKit has a similar gesture, but its semantics are hidden from the developer.

Instead, you have what is called a "force touch" gesture. When the user presses firmly on the screen, it's considered a force touch. The Apple Watch hardware takes care of determining the difference between the hard force touch to bring up a menu, and a lighter tap. You can't change the behavior of a force touch; it will always bring up the context menu, if one exists.

Menu interface

To create a menu, you first need to set up what are called menu items. Each menu item has a title that is displayed as text in the interface and an image that is displayed as a vibrant image over a blurred background.

A menu with action and a cancel buttons

The Apple Watch comes with a selection of stock icons you can use, as shown here:

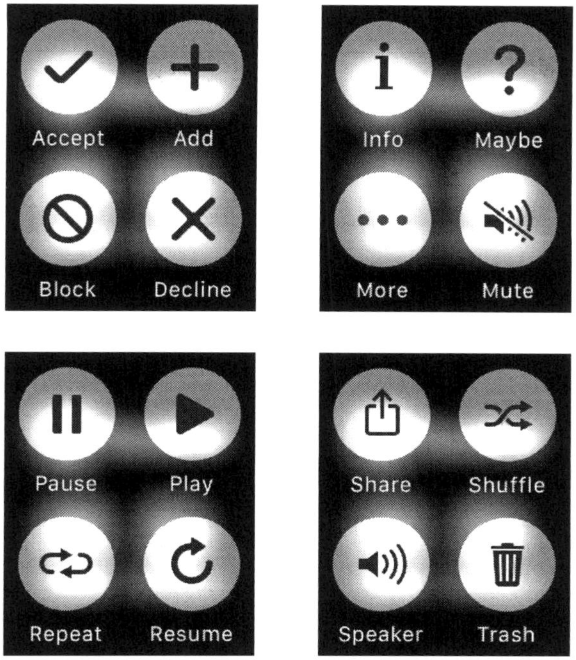

Since the 38mm and 42mm Watches have different screen densities, if you want to create a custom icon, you'll need to create differently sized icons for each device. The Apple Watch Human Interface Guidelines include specifics for how you should design your custom icons:

- For 38mm icons, you'll want to make your icon canvas size 70 pixels and the content size 46 pixels. When you're making lines for glyphs, keep them between 4 and 8 pixels.
- When making icons for the 42mm Apple Watch, make your icon canvas size 80 pixels and the content size 54 pixels. When you're making lines for glyphs, keep them between 5 and 9 pixels.

> **Note**: The **canvas size** of an icon is the entire size that it occupies. The **content size** is the actual bounds of the icon; the height and the width. When creating WatchKit icons, you can simply fit your icons into the content size and the system will scale the image appropriately.

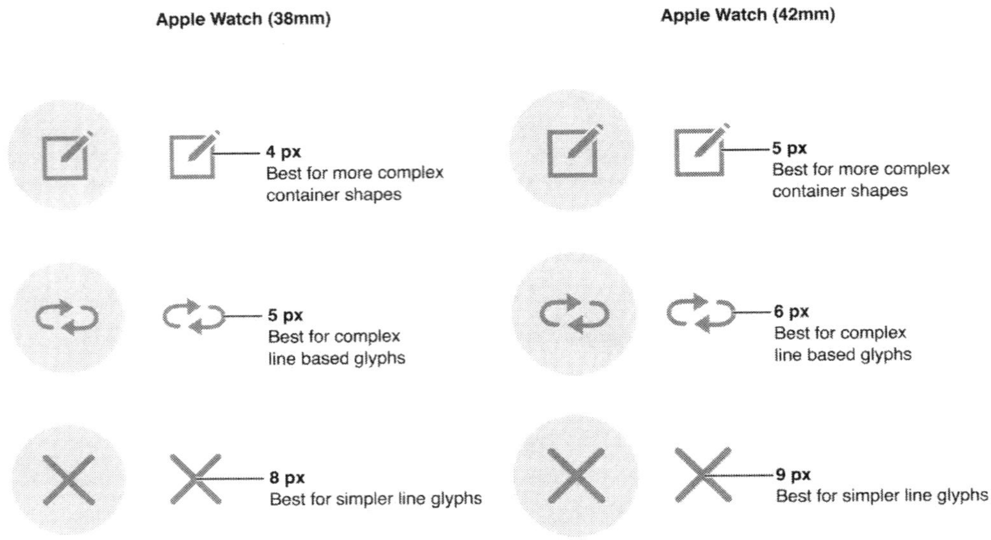

Apple's graphic for 38mm and 42mm line icons

At most, you can only fit four menu icons onto the screen at once. Usually, one icon is reserved for a "cancel" button, leaving you only three icons for your custom actions. Be very careful to choose only actions and icons that pertain to the interface controller that the user is currently viewing.

> **Note:** Menu interfaces don't scroll or allow you to add arbitrary interface objects. If you add more than four objects, WatchKit will only show the first four and ignore the rest.

Default actions

Unlike `UIActionSheet` or `UIAlertView`, you don't have to conform to any protocols or wire up any delegates to get WatchKit menus working. Instead, you simply create menu items in Interface Builder or in code and then simply connect the items to actions in your `WKInterfaceController` using the familiar target-action pattern.

This allows for a much cleaner and simpler API, allowing you to focus on your app's features instead of creating stringly-typed delegates like you would in UIKit.

By default, menu items are "cancel" actions. If you don't connect an action, either through Interface Builder or through code, tapping on a menu item will simply dismiss the context menu. This makes creating "cancel" buttons a breeze!

Working with menus

The SousChef app you've been creating thus far is pretty robust. You can browse recipes, view their ingredients and directions and even browse your own grocery list.

But one major flaw of the application is that you can't add ingredients from the recipes to your grocery list. This kind of defeats the purpose of having both a recipe browser and a grocery list in the same app!

Completing your grocery list

Open **Interface.storyboard** and find the **Ingredients** interface controller. From the Object Library, drag a **menu** onto the **Ingredients** interface controller.

Open the **document outline** and you'll see how Xcode has created the menu in the controller alongside the table, even though there's no visual indication of the menu on the interface controller itself.

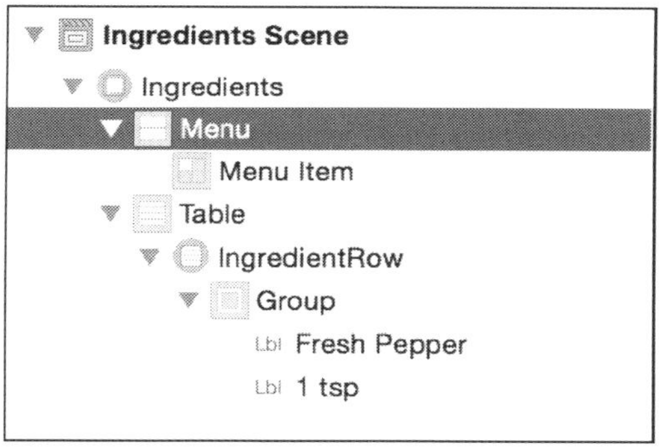

Select the **menu** in the document outline and open the Attributes Inspector. Change **Items** to **2**. You should see another "Menu Item" appear in the document outline.

Select the first **menu item** in the document outline, change the **Title** attribute to **Add to List** and change the **Image** to **Add**. This will be the menu item that you select to add the current ingredients to your grocery list.

Next, select the second **menu item** and change the **Title** to **Cancel** and the **Image** to **Decline**. This will use a system provided "X" image.

Build and run the Watch app. Tap Recipes, pick a recipe, tap Ingredients, and then perform a force touch on the interface. To force touch in the simulator, simply tap and hold as if you were doing a long press. You should see your new context menu appear:

Tap a menu item. The menu will simply be dismissed because you haven't wired up any actions to the menu items yet.

With **Interface.storyboard** open in the main editor window, open **RecipeIngredientsInterfaceController.swift** in the assistant editor. Drag from the **Add to List** menu item in the document outline to the class to create a new action. Name it `onAddToGrocery`:

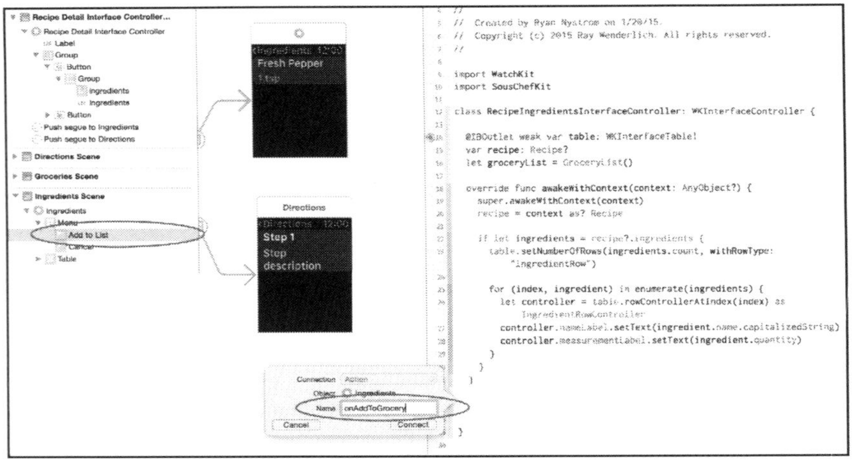

Creating an IBAction for the Add to Grocery menu item

In **RecipeIngredientsInterfaceController.swift**, create a constant that references the `GroceryList` near the top of `RecipeIngredientsInterfaceController`:

```
let groceryList = GroceryList()
```

This will serve as the gateway to the shared storage for items on your grocery list.

Update `onAddToGrocery()` so it looks like the following:

```
@IBAction func onAddToGrocery() {
```

```
    if let items = self.recipe?.ingredients {
      for item in items {
        groceryList.addItemToList(item)
      }
      groceryList.sync()
    }
  }
```

Here you use optional unwrapping to get the list of items, and then iterate over the items in the current recipe adding each one to the current grocery list. At the very end, you synchronize the grocery list so that any changes you made are persisted throughout the rest of the app.

Build and run. This time, navigate to the ingredients for a particular recipe and then perform a force touch. When the context menu appears, tap the **Add to List** button. Try this for a couple of different recipes.

Once you're done adding recipes to your grocery list, navigate back to the initial interface controller and select **Groceries**. You should see all of the grocery items that you selected with their appropriate quantities!

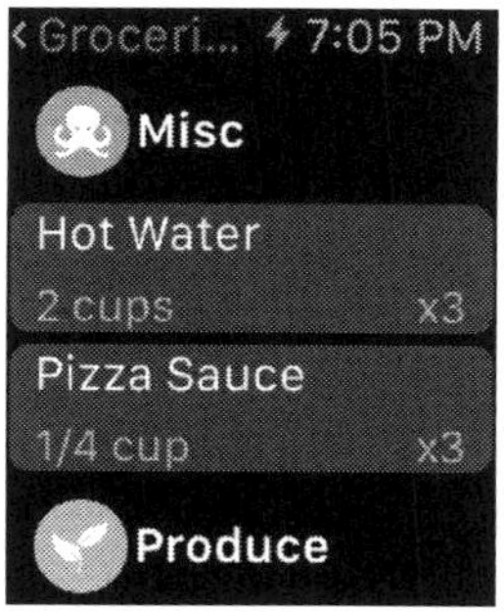

A grocery list with a couple of pizzas added to it

Clearing items from the list

A grocery list is no good without a way to clear it. You'll be creating tons of delicious recipes after completing the chapters in this book, so you'll need a way to keep your lists clear of unnecessary ingredient clutter.

Open **Interface.storyboard** and find the **Groceries** interface controller. Add a **menu** to it, just as you did for the Ingredients interface controller.

Select the new **menu** in the **document outline** and in the Attributes Inspector, change **Items** to **3**. Change their titles and images to the following:

- Title the first item **Clear All** and assign it the **Trash** image.
- Title the second item **Purchased** and assign it the custom image **clear-purchased**.
- Title the third item **Cancel** and assign it the **Decline** image.

Notice that the middle menu item uses a custom image called **clear-purchased**. This image is simply a 54x54-pixel icon. WatchKit prefers that you create solid-line icons and let it handle applying the vibrancy effect and blurred background.

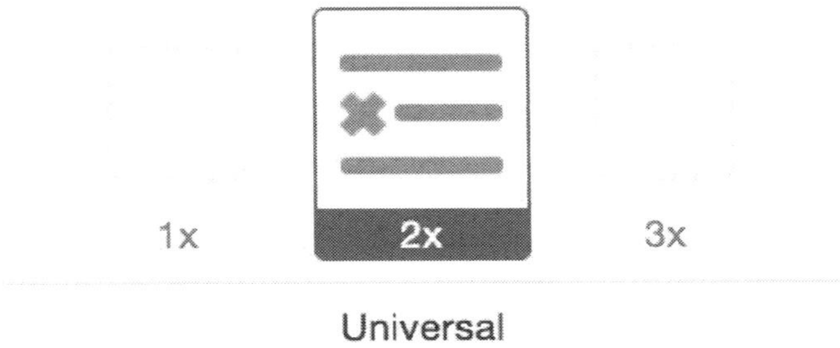

The clear-purchased icon in the Image.xcassets

Build and run. Navigate to the Groceries interface controller and perform a force touch to invoke your new context menu. You'll see all three items appear. WatchKit handles the display and layout on your behalf!

With **Interface.storyboard** open in the main editor, open **GroceryInterfaceController.swift** in the assistant editor. Create an action by dragging from the **Clear All** menu item in the document outline to the class and name it `onClearAll`. Create a second action by this time dragging from the Purchased menu item, and name it called `onRemovePurchased`.

You'll be using these items to prune your grocery lists of either all items or just the ones that have already been purchased.

> **Note:** Remember, you don't have to make actions for cancel buttons because the default action for menu items is to dismiss the menu.

Open **GroceryInterfaceController.swift** and find the property and variable declarations near the top of the class. Change `groceryList` to the following:

```
let groceryList = GroceryList()
```

This tells the `GroceryList` to initialize without the sample data you were using in the previous chapters. Now that you can add ingredients from recipes, you don't need to use dummy data.

Find the `onClearAll()` method you just created and change it so it looks like the following:

```
@IBAction func onClearAll() {
  // 1
  let indices = NSIndexSet(indexesInRange:
    NSRange(location: 0, length: table.numberOfRows))
  table.removeRowsAtIndexes(indices)

  // 2
  groceryList.removeAllItems()
  groceryList.sync()

  // 3
  for (index, listItem) in enumerate(flatList) {
    if let item = listItem.item as? Ingredient {
      item.purchased = false
    }
  }

  // 4
  flatList = self.groceryList.flattenedGroceries()
}
```

Here's what you're doing in the code above:

1. You create a list of all of the indices in the `WKInterfaceTable` and remove them. Remember that this includes both rows and headers like "Produce" and "Dairy".

2. You tell the `GroceryList` store to remove all of its items and synchronize the changes.
3. You iterate over all of the items currently in your stored list of ingredients and set their purchased state to `false`.
4. Finally, you reset the current list of grocery items to what the `GroceryList` has synced. This will keep your UI and data store in sync in case something goes wrong.

Next, find `onRemovePurchased()` and update it to reflect the following:

```
@IBAction func onRemovePurchased() {
  // 1
  var indexSet = NSMutableIndexSet()

  // 2
  for (index, listItem) in enumerate(flatList) {
    if let item = flatList[index].item as? Ingredient {
      if item.purchased {
        indexSet.addIndex(index)
        groceryList.removeItem(item)
      }
    }
  }
  groceryList.sync()

  // 3
  table.removeRowsAtIndexes(indexSet)
  flatList = self.groceryList.flattenedGroceries()
}
```

Let's break this down:

1. Before clearing the list, you need to iterate over all of the Ingredient items. The `indexSet` variable will keep track of the rows that need to be removed.
2. You iterate over each item and if it's both an Ingredient and marked as purchased, you add its index to the `indexSet` and remove the item from the `groceryList`. Make sure to synchronize the data store at the end.
3. `removeRowsAtIndexes(_:)` will animate the removal of table rows at the given indexes. Also, you recreate the `flatList` since you've removed items from the data store.

Build and run. Add some ingredients to your grocery list, and then remove some SousChef now can now track the ingredients you need to purchase, and it should be easy to use while shopping!

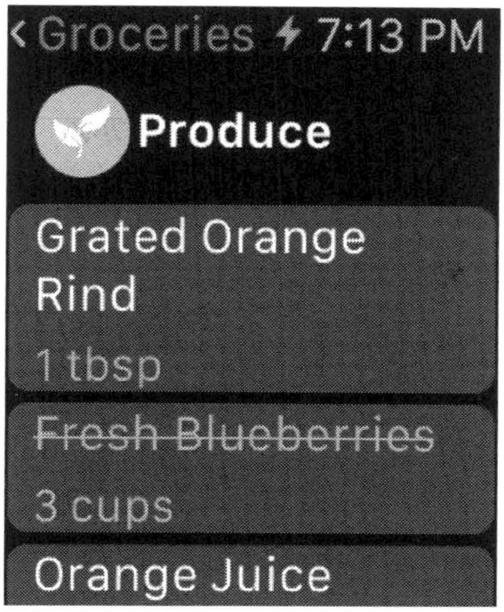

Time to go shopping!

Where to go from here?

Your cooking companion is finally ready to use! You can browse recipes, add their ingredients to a grocery list, shop, and cook all from your wrist!

But there are many more things you can do. In the next chapter you'll learn how to sync data on your iPhone with the Apple Watch so that your shopping and browsing data match.

After that you'll learn how to add timers and alerts to the Watch app so that you can remember to take the roast out of the oven!

You've learned a lot about building WatchKit apps so far—enough to be considered dangerous. Keep on reading to become a WatchKit wizard!

Section II: Intermediate WatchKit

It's paramount that your Watch app and containing iPhone app share data; what use is the convenience of the Watch if it doesn't display the same up-to-date data as your iPhone? In this section, you'll start by learning exactly that—how to share data between the phone and the watch—and update the SousChef app to share its recipes between both devices.

After that, you'll create a glance, which is the WatchKit equivalent of a Today extension, before getting your glance and Watch app talking via Handoff. You'll finish off the section by taking a look at how to handle incoming notifications, both local and remote.

Chapter 8: Sharing Data

By Soheil Moayedi Azarpour

At this point, you're familiar with the overall architecture of WatchKit. In this chapter, you'll learn how to share data between the containing iPhone application and its WatchKit extension.

Even though the WatchKit extension is bundled and shipped with the iPhone app, from a security domains standpoint, each resides within its own sandbox. That means that, by default, neither of them has access to the other's container.

To share data between a companion app and its extensions, including its WatchKit extension, you need to enable app groups. An app group refers to a container on the local file system that both an extension and its containing app can access.

You aren't limited to just a single app group. You can define multiple app groups and enable them for different extensions. For example, if you have both a Today extension and a WatchKit extension, you may decide to use different app groups to keep each container distinct and uncluttered, reserved exclusively for its individual purpose.

In this chapter, you'll continue to work with the SousChef project. It's the freshest take on the standard "cooking and recipes" style of app! Here's what you have in store:

- You'll learn about different approaches to accessing data in a shared container;
- You'll enable app groups so that both the Watch app and its containing iOS app share the same recipes file;
- You'll hook up the recipes store inside the app to a remote server so that you can update recipes periodically;
- You'll learn about shared documents best practices, such as how to coordinate reads and writes to avoid file corruption.

So, without further ado, let's dive into app groups!

Accessing data in a shared container

Once you've enabled an app group, the OS creates a specific folder on the local file system. Anything that you create or reference by the app group identifier resides in this folder. There are a few ways to interact with this container:

- Read or write flat files directly;
- Use Core Data or SQLite;
- Use `NSUserDefaults`.

The rest of this section covers the basics of these approaches. You'll learn more about some of these approaches a little later, and you'll implement reading and writing files and using `NSUserDefaults` in this chapter.

Reading and writing flat files

To directly read and write files to and from the shared container, you have to use `NSFileManager`. There is a single API for this:

```
let identifier = "group.com.raywenderlich.souschef.documents"
var sharedContainerURL = NSFileManager.defaultManager().
  containerURLForSecurityApplicationGroupIdentifier(identifier)
```

If you've correctly set up app groups for the specified group identifier, the API returns a non-`nil` URL pointing to the shared container; otherwise, it returns `nil`.

From this point on, you can use the URL as you would normally use URLs for the local file system to read and write, as shown in the following code snippets:

```
let identifier = "group.com.raywenderlich.souschef.documents"
var sharedContainerURL = NSFileManager.defaultManager().
  containerURLForSecurityApplicationGroupIdentifier(identifier)
if let sharedContainerURL = sharedContainerURL {
  let documentURL = sharedContainerURL.
    URLByAppendingPathComponent("UserData.json")
  let data = ... // Some JSON data.
  // Write data to disk
}
```

In a bit, you'll add support for shared data to the SousChef project using `containerURLForSecurityApplicationGroupIdentifier(_:)`. Check out the "Shared documents best practices" section at the end of this chapter to learn about using file coordinators and migration.

Sharing's good!

Core Data and SQLite

To share a Core Data persistent store file or SQLite database file, you essentially use the same mechanism as discussed above. You obtain a URL that points to a shared container using `NSFileManager`, and you set your store path accordingly.

The following code snippet shows how to set up a Core Data persistent store in a shared container:

```
let identifier = "group.com.raywenderlich.souschef.documents"
var sharedContainerURL = NSFileManager.defaultManager().
  containerURLForSecurityApplicationGroupIdentifier(identifier)
if let sharedContainerURL = sharedContainerURL {
  let storeURL = sharedContainerURL.
    URLByAppendingPathComponent("MyCoreData.sqlite")
  var coordinator: NSPersistentStoreCoordinator? =
    NSPersistentStoreCoordinator(managedObjectModel:
     self.managedObjectModel)
  coordinator?.addPersistentStoreWithType(NSSQLiteStoreType,
    configuration: nil,
    URL: storeURL,
    options: nil,
    error: nil)
}
```

This next code snippet shows how to access a SQLite database in a shared container:

```
let identifier = "group.com.raywenderlich.souschef.documents"
var sharedContainerURL: NSURL? = NSFileManager.defaultManager().
  containerURLForSecurityApplicationGroupIdentifier(identifier)
if let sharedContainerURL = sharedContainerURL {
```

```
    let SQLiteDB = sharedContainerURL.
      URLByAppendingPathComponent("MyDatabase.sqlite3")
      // Use database...
  }
```

Shared user defaults

You're probably familiar with, or have heard of, `NSUserDefaults`. It's a lightweight persistent storage mechanism backed by a property list that the iOS SDK provides out of the box.

`NSUserDefaults` is a good choice for storing your app-specific configuration or user preferences. `NSUserDefaults` is *not* a good choice for storing large blobs of data like image files, documents, music and so forth.

You usually access the standard user defaults by calling `NSUserDefaults.standardUserDefaults()`. The standard user defaults are stored in the sandbox folder, meaning user defaults for the companion app aren't accessible to the WatchKit extension and vice versa.

To create user defaults storage in the shared container of an app group, you need to initialize a new `NSUserDefaults` object using `NSUserDefaults(suiteName:)` and pass in the unique identifier of the app group, like so:

```
let sharedUserDefaults = NSUserDefaults(suiteName:
  "group.com.raywenderlich.souschef.documents")
```

Unlike standard user defaults, this is not a singleton, and you have to keep a reference to the returned value around for as long as you want to use it. However, you don't need to re-initialize it every time there's a change in the store. If you're going to use `NSUserDefaults` with app groups in a large project, you may want to abstract this out into a custom class and provide a singleton shared user defaults for your entire app.

From this point on, you can interact with the `sharedUserDefaults` the same way you would interact with `standardUserDefaults`, except that other processes with access to your app group container can also access everything you save in `sharedUserDefaults`.

For example, this is how the iPhone app and WatchKit extension can read and write to the same set of user defaults:

```
// In the companion app, i.e. iPhone user prefers using
Fahrenheit.
let identifier = "group.com.raywenderlich.souschef.documents"
var sharedUserDefaults = NSUserDefaults(suiteName: identifier)
if let sharedUserDefaults = sharedUserDefaults {
```

```
    sharedUserDefaults.setObject("F", forKey: "temperatureUnit")
  }

  // In the WatchKit extension.
  let identifier = "group.com.raywenderlich.souschef.documents"
  var sharedUserDefaults = NSUserDefaults(suiteName: identifier)
  if let sharedUserDefaults = sharedUserDefaults {
    var unit = sharedUserDefaults.objectForKey("temperatureUnit")
  }
```

You can see in the first code block how the iPhone companion app writes the user's preference for the Fahrenheit temperature scale. In the second code block, the WatchKit extension reads that preference and can then use it to update its interface accordingly.

A toast to shared preferences!

Sweet! There's just one more thing to keep in mind: When you make a change to `standardUserDefaults`, the OS sends a free notification named `NSUserDefaultsDidChangeNotification`. However, this doesn't apply to `sharedUserDefaults`. The best method for ensuring you have the most up-to-date shared object or value is to retrieve it from the shared store as late as possible—essentially, right before you need it.

Setting up app groups

It's easy to set up an app group, but there is a little bit of housekeeping that you're better off doing now rather than later. It'll save you both time and headaches!

"What could possibly go wrong?!"

First, you need to make sure you've selected a valid team ID and that it matches your bundle identifier in Xcode. This is because app groups require entitlements to work. Open the SousChef project in Xcode and make sure the project is selected in the project navigator.

Make sure all the targets in the SousChef project have the same team selected. You can see in the following screenshots that I've selected my team for each target:

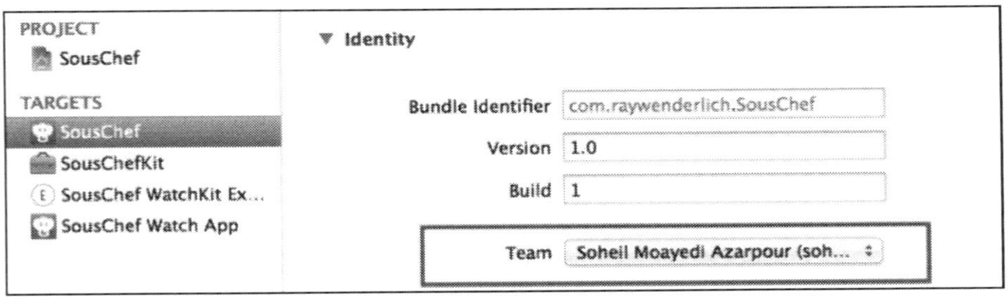

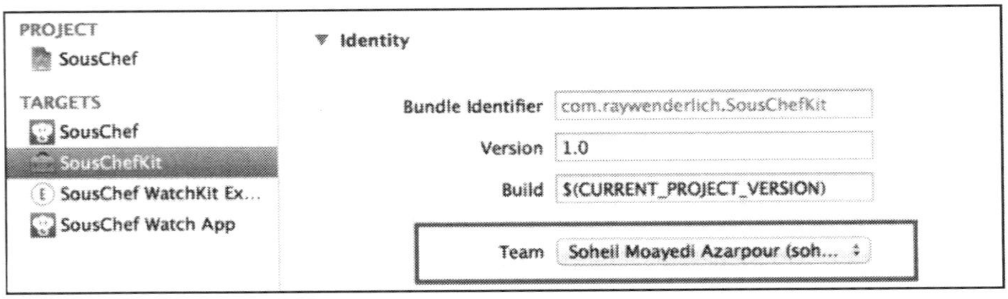

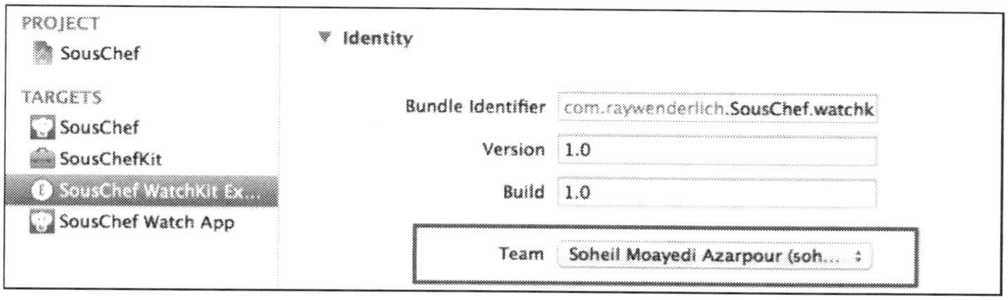

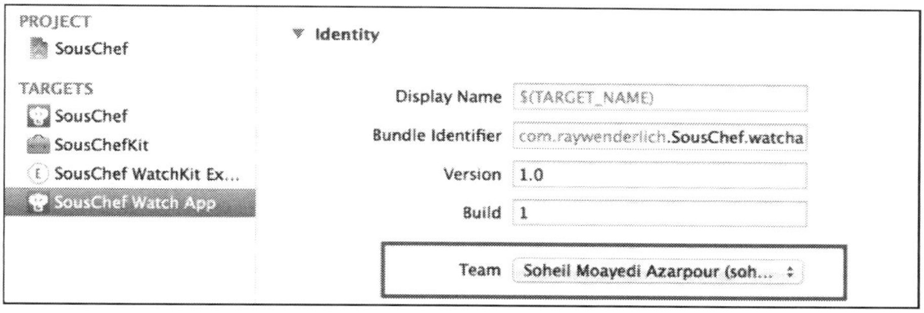

If you don't have any teams in the drop-down menu, make sure you've added a developer account in Xcode's preferences:

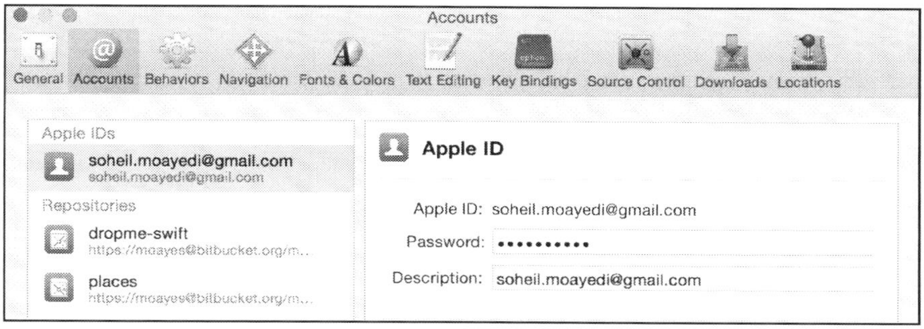

> **Note**: To enable app groups, you'll need admin privileges on an active developer account. If you don't have admin privileges or an active developer account, you won't be able to complete the steps outlined in this chapter.

You now have to change the **bundle identifier** of the project to one that is associated with your developer account. For example, it should begin with `com.yourdomain` instead of `com.raywenderlich`.

It's an easy thing to change, but unfortunately there are far too many places that you need to make this change, as is always the case with projects with many targets. It could be cumbersome, and things could go wrong quickly! Therefore, we've done the heavy lifting and provided you with a nice and easy shortcut!

A user-defined setting has been created for you in the SousChef project build settings called **SOUSCHEF_BUNDLE_PREFIX**. As this is defined at the project level, all targets inherit it by default. You're going to update this setting in just one place, and it will automatically propagate to everywhere it's needed.

Make sure the SousChef project is selected in the project navigator and then select **SousChef** under the **Project** heading in the middle pane. Select the **Build Settings** tab and scroll all the way down until you reach the **User-Defined** section, as shown in the following screenshot:

Here you'll find the `SOUSCHEF_BUNDLE_PREFIX` entry. Update the value to match your domain; that is, something like `com.raywenderlich`.

You've finished your *mise en place*, so you're all ready to cook up an app group in SousChef.

Enabling app groups

Now switch to the **SousChef** target and select the **Capabilities** tab. Enable **App Groups** by flicking the switch to **On**:

Make sure the **App Groups** section is expanded, and tap the **+** button to add a new group.

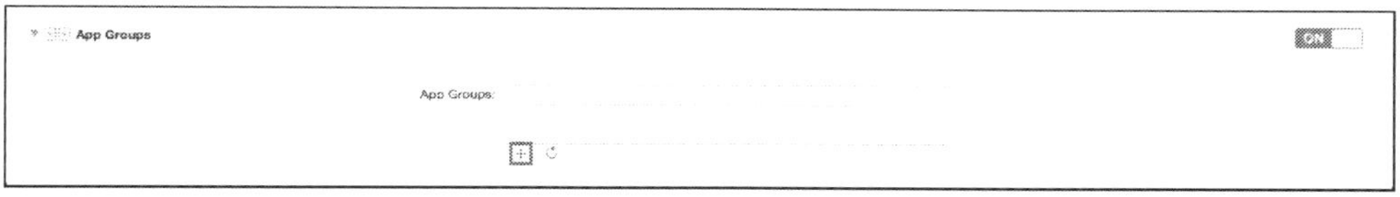

Xcode then prompts you to enter a name for the new app group. Name it group.com.<YOUR_DOMAIN>.<GROUP_NAME>. Replace <YOUR_DOMAIN> with your actual domain, as in `raywenderlich`, and replace <GROUP_NAME> with a meaningful name for your project, like `souschef.documents`.

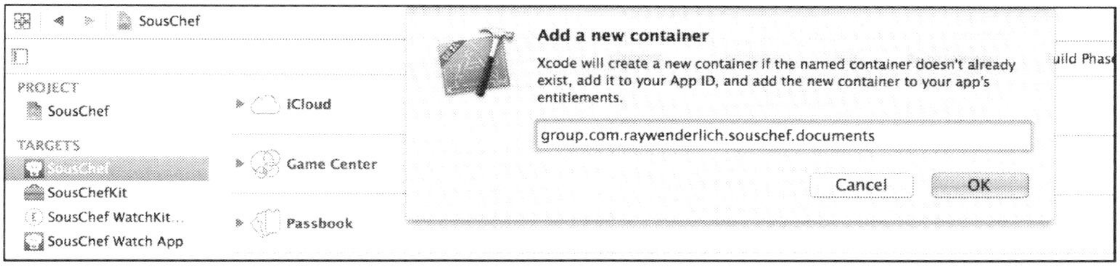

You must prefix all app groups with the word "group" followed by a period.

If you're a member of more than one development team, you'll likely see a modal dialog appear asking you to select a team. Choose the one that's most appropriate for the SousChef project (usually your personal one) and click **Choose** to continue.

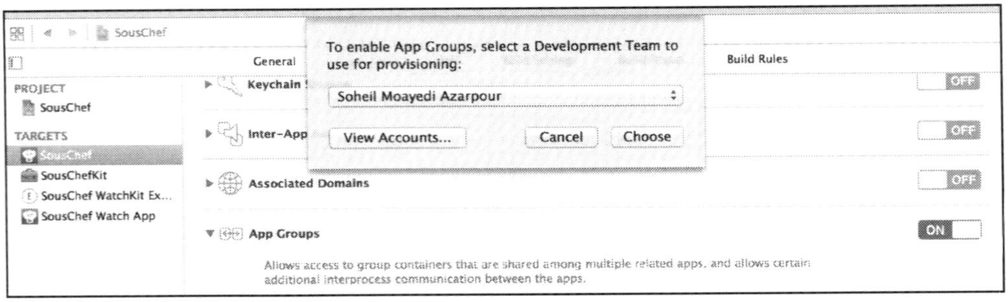

Xcode will automatically add any required entitlements to your project. If you don't have an existing entitlements file, Xcode will create one:

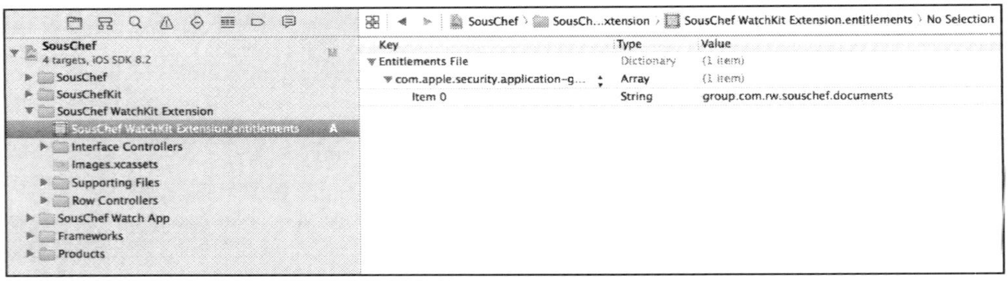

If everything goes well, you'll see the app group selected. However, if for any reason it fails, the app group name will appear in red.

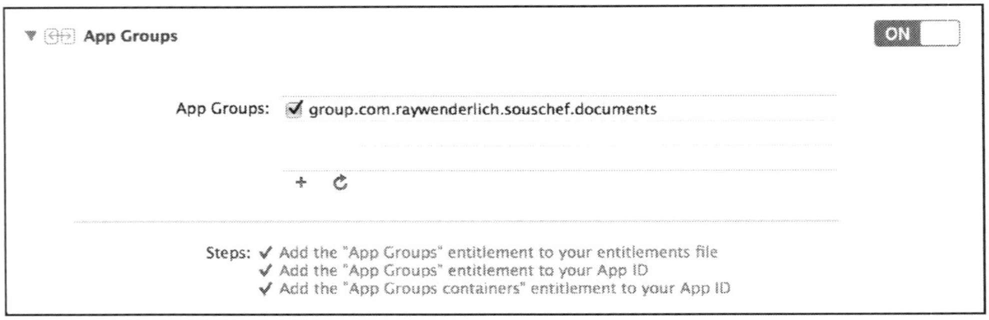

> **Note**: It's unlikely that adding a new app group will fail, but in cases where it does, the following list will give you an idea of what might have gone wrong:
>
> - You don't have admin privileges on your developer account, or you don't have an active developer account.
> - You used a name for the group that is already in use by you or another developer.
> - You added and removed similar app groups with different casing (for example, `group.rw` versus `group.RW`). This can confuse Xcode because it usually takes a few minutes for the changes to propagate from Xcode to Apple's servers.

If Xcode fails to automatically create the app group, you may have to go to http://developer.apple.com and create an app group manually.

To manually add an app group, open your favorite web browser and navigate to http://developer.apple.com. Click on **Member Center** and log in. Then choose **Certificates, Identifiers & Profiles**:

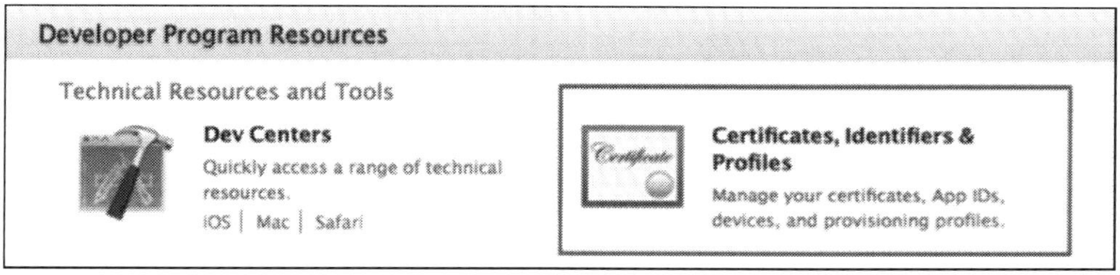

From the list presented, select **Identifiers**. Then, near the bottom of the list on the left-hand side, select **App Groups**:

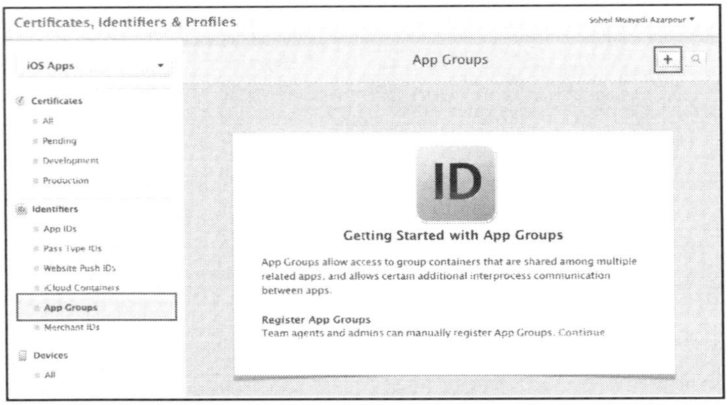

Click the **+** button in the upper right and follow the instructions to add a new app group. When you're finished, go back to Xcode and click the refresh button in the App Groups section:

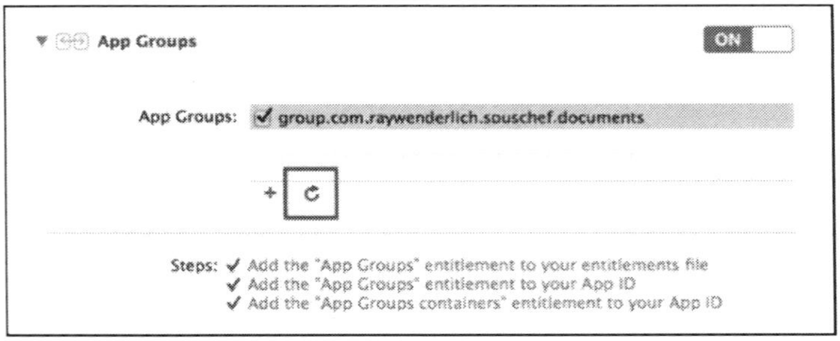

The app group you just created will appear in the list, and you can select it by checking the appropriate box.

Next, enable app groups by repeating the same steps for the **SousChef WatchKit Extension** target. This time, Xcode will show you a list of available app groups once you've flicked the switch. All you have to do is select the app group you just created:

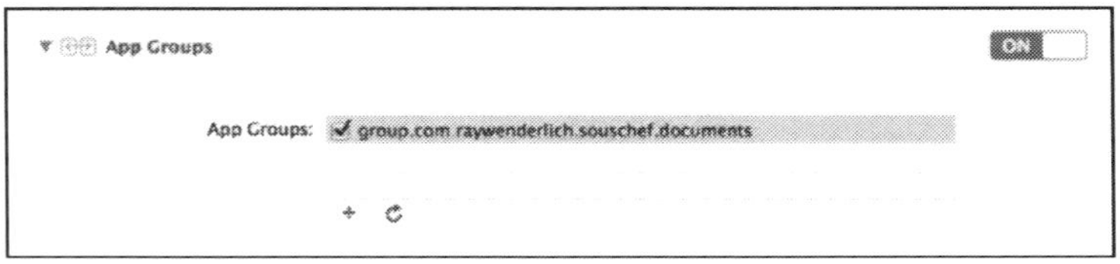

Now go to the developer portal, and you'll see a new app group in your developer account, located in **Certificates, Identifiers & Profiles\Identifiers\App Groups**.

You can also manage or edit app groups from the same page:

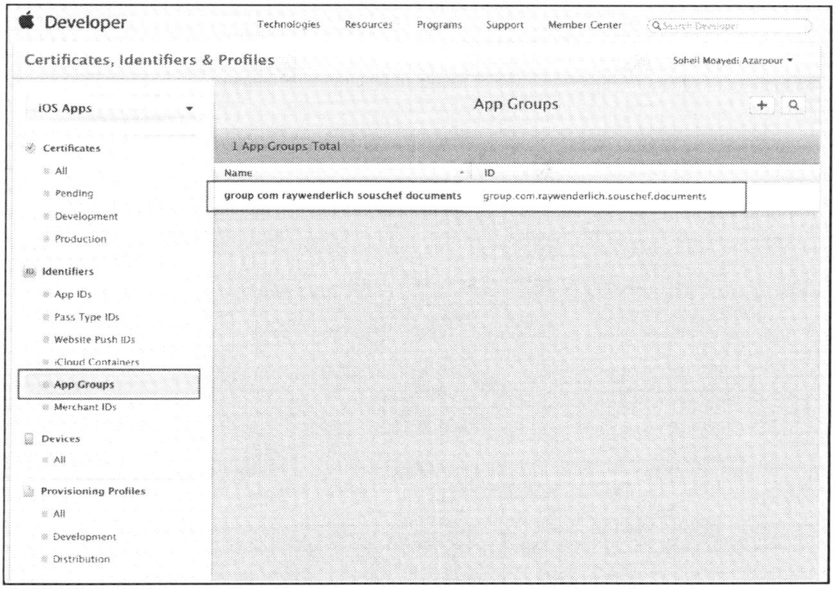

You may have noticed that app groups are similar to bundle identifiers, in that each app group has its own unique identifier. You'll use exactly the same identifiers in code to refer to each respective app group.

Updating a shared file from a remote server

With your solid understanding of app groups and how they work, it's time to do a little hacking on SousChef.

There's an important feature you need to implement in SousChef. Right now, the app reads the list of recipes from **Recipes.json**, a JSON file in the app bundle. You want to be able to update this file periodically from a remote server, as well as whenever there is a push notification about new recipes being available.

Both the containing iPhone app and the WatchKit extension should be able to trigger an update, and if one updates the recipes, the other should be able to see those changes.

Migrating data to a shared container

Find and open **RecipeStore.swift** in the SousChefKit group. This is the class responsible for managing the list of recipes. Take a look at it to get familiar with its implementation—this is where most of your update will happen.

`RecipeStore` will consolidate read and write tasks to the recipes JSON file on disk. But you must take some precautions first.

Avoiding data corruption

When you want to read from or write to a shared container, you must do so in a coordinated manner to avoid data corruption. This is because separate processes can access a shared container at the same time.

To avoid data corruption, Apple advises that you should use both NSFilePresenter and `NSFileCoordinator` to coordinate read and write operations, or use individual atomic save and serial read operations.

Note: We chose to use atomic save and serial read operations due of the following reasons:

- The recipes are stored in flat file which has a small size, so read and write operations don't take long.

- The Watch app has read-only access, while the iPhone app is responsible for writing, so there won' t be more than one writing process at any given time.

First, make sure you're still in **RecipeStore.swift**. Then add the following private constants to the beginning of the file:

```
private let kAppGroupIdentifier =
  "group.com.<YOUR_DOMAIN>.souschef.documents"
private let kInitialRecipesCopiedKey =
  "com.rw.souschef.recipesCopied"
```

Remember to change `<YOUR_DOMAIN>` to match the one you set up for the app group.

In a bit, you'll use these constants to move the recipes file that is bundled with the project into the shared container.

Next, update the definition of `savedRecipesURL` inside the `RecipeStore` class definition:

```
private let savedRecipesURL: NSURL = {
  var sharedContainerURL: NSURL? =
    NSFileManager.defaultManager().
      containerURLForSecurityApplicationGroupIdentifier(
        kAppGroupIdentifier)

  var docURL = NSURL()
  if let sharedContainerURL = sharedContainerURL {
    docURL = sharedContainerURL.URLByAppendingPathComponent(
      "\(kRecipesFileName).\(kRecipesFileExtension)")
  }
  return docURL
}()
```

Here, you update the implementation to return a URL for the recipes file that points to the shared container instead of the bundle.

Next, update the implementation of `init()` as follows:

```
public init() {
  // 1.
  if let sharedUserDefaults =
    NSUserDefaults(suiteName: kAppGroupIdentifier) {
    let isRecipesCopied = sharedUserDefaults.
      boolForKey(kInitialRecipesCopiedKey)
    if isRecipesCopied == true {
      return
    }

    // 2.
    var bundledRecipesURL =
      NSBundle(forClass: RecipeStore.self).
        URLForResource(kRecipesFileName, withExtension:
          kRecipesFileExtension)
    if (bundledRecipesURL == nil) {
      return
    }

    // 3.
    var data = NSData(contentsOfURL: bundledRecipesURL!)
    if (data == nil) {
      return
    }

    // 4.
    let success = data?.writeToURL(self.savedRecipesURL,
      atomically: true)
    if (success == true) {
      sharedUserDefaults.setBool(true,
        forKey: kInitialRecipesCopiedKey)
    } else {
      println("Failed to copy Recipes from bundled into
        the shared container.")
    }
  }
}
```

This is the migration code that copies the recipes file from the bundle to the shared container. Does it look scary? It's not! Here's the explanation step by step:

1. You create an instance of `NSUserDefaults` that's instantiated with your registered app group; these user defaults are shared between the WatchKit extension and iPhone app. If the migration flag, `kInitialRecipesCopiedKey`, is already `true`, you know the migration has already been performed and simply return.

You use shared user defaults here because `RecipeStore` is in a framework, so it may be accessed from either the iPhone app or the WatchKit extension. No matter which side initiates the migration process, you only want to do the migration once and set a flag that you can easily access again.

2. If you haven't performed the migration yet, you read the content of the recipes file from the bundle.
3. Here you simply unwrap the optional value to proceed safely.
4. You try to write the data to the shared container. If you succeed, you set the migration flag in the shared user defaults to `true`.

It's not complete yet, but now is a good time to **build and run** to ensure everything compiles. You should be able to see the recipes in the app as if nothing has changed. But behind the scenes, you've migrated the recipes to the shared container.

> **Note**: If your app crashes or you don't see any recipes, check if `savedRecipesURL` is `nil`. If you aren't being handed a valid URL, it's likely there was a problem setting up provisioning for app groups. Try repeating the steps from the previous section. To ensure you've downloaded your most up-to-date provisioning profiles in Xcode, click **Xcode\Preferences\Accounts** and select your Apple ID. Then double-click your name, and finally click the refresh button.

Excellent! Now that you've verified everything is in good shape, you can move on to the next step.

Updating a file from a remote server

You want to be able to update the recipes file from a remote server. A public repository is already set up for remote recipes on GitHub, available here:
https://github.com/raywenderlich/recipes.

We highly recommend that you make a fork from this repository for yourself, so you can update the recipes file on GitHub and see how the app uses that to update the available recipes.

> **Note:** You need a free GitHub account to fork the above-mentioned repository. If you aren't familiar with forking a git repository, you can learn about it here:
>
> https://help.github.com/articles/fork-a-repo

Once your forked repository is ready, go to **your** recipes repository on GitHub and click on **Recipes.json**:

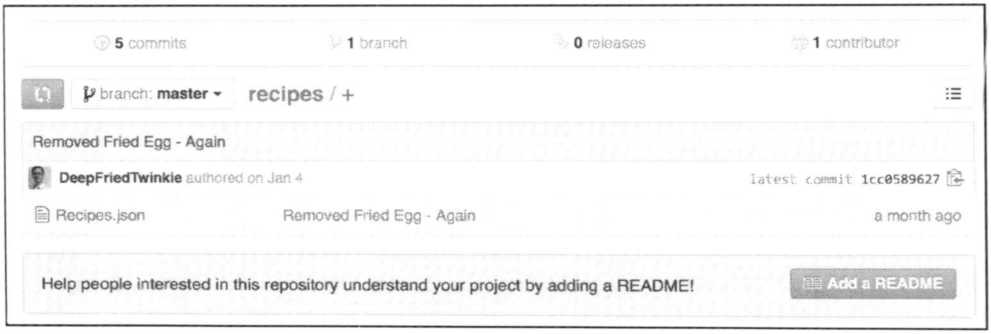

You'll be redirected to a page where you can see the file contents. On that page, click the **Raw** button:

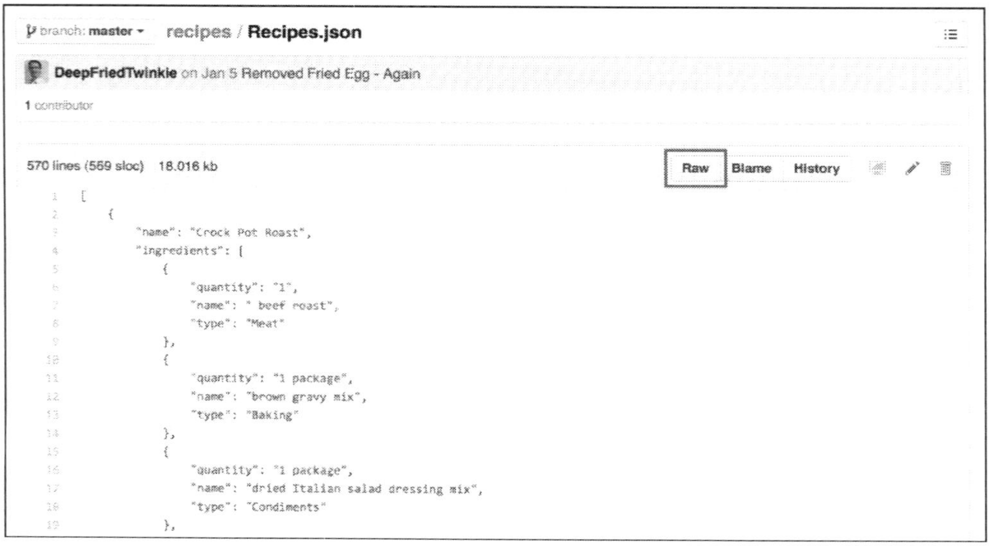

GitHub will redirect you to a URL that displays the raw contents of the file without all the formatting GitHub applies:

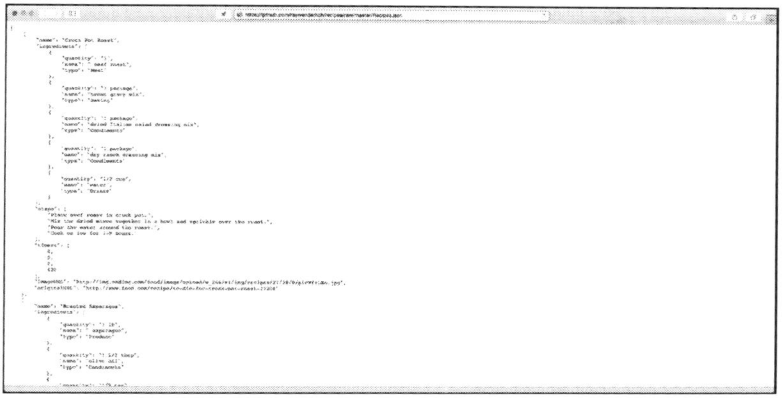

On this page, copy the URL from the address bar. Go back to Xcode and open **RecipeStore.swift**. Add the URL you just copied as a constant to the top of the file:

```
private let kRemoteRecipesURLString =
"https://raw.githubusercontent.com/raywenderlich/recipes/master/
Recipes.json"
```

Your URL will be different from the one here, and should have your username in there somewhere.

Now add the following method to **RecipeStore.swift**:

```
// 1.
public func refresh(#completion:((recipes: [Recipe],
  error: NSError?) -> Void)?) {
  // 2.
  let session = NSURLSession.sharedSession()
  session.configuration.requestCachePolicy =
    NSURLRequestCachePolicy.ReloadIgnoringLocalCacheData
  if let remoteRecipesURL =
    NSURL(string: kRemoteRecipesURLString) {
    let task = session.dataTaskWithURL(remoteRecipesURL,
      completionHandler: { (data: NSData?,
        response: NSURLResponse?,
          error: NSError?) -> Void in
      // 3.
      if let data = data {
        if data.writeToURL(self.savedRecipesURL,
          atomically: true) {
          self.recipes =  self.recipesFromData(data)
        }
```

```
      }
      // 4.
      if let completion = completion {
        dispatch_async(dispatch_get_main_queue(), {
          () -> Void in
          completion(recipes: self.recipes, error: error)
        })
      }
    })
    task.resume()
  }
}
```

That's quite the code block! Here's what's going on:

1. You declare a `refresh(completion:)` method with an optional completion block.
2. You use the shared session of `NSURLSession` to download the JSON file from the remote server.
3. If the download succeeds, you save the file to the shared container and update `recipes`.
4. At the end, you call the completion block, if one was provided, on the main thread and pass in the updated recipes.

At a minimum, you want to download the recipes file every time the containing iOS app is launched. Open **AppDelegate.swift** and add the following helper methods:

```
// 1.
func updateRecipesWithRemoteServerWithCompletionBlock(
  block:((Void) -> Void)?) {
    recipeStore.refresh(completion: {
      (recipes, error) -> Void in
        if let block = block {
          block()
      }
  })
}
// 2.
func updateRecipesController() {
  updateRecipesWithRemoteServerWithCompletionBlock {
    (Void) -> Void in
    if let tabBarController =
      self.window?.rootViewController as? UITabBarController {
      if let navigationController =
        tabBarController.viewControllers?.first as?
          UINavigationController {
        if let recipesController =
```

```
            navigationController.viewControllers?.first as?
              RecipesController {
            recipesController.reloadContent()
          }
        }
      }
    }
  }
```

Here is what's going on:

1. You add a helper method named `updateRecipesWithRemoteServerWithCompletionBlock(_:)` whose job is simply updating the recipe store by calling `refresh(completion:)` on the `RecipeStore` property. You'll use this helper function in a couple of places.
2. You add a second helper method named `updateRecipesController()`. Here, you update the recipe store by calling `updateRecipesWithRemoteServerWithCompletionBlock(_:)`. Then in its completion block, you notify the view controller that displays recipes, `RecipesController`, to update its content.

Still in **AppDelegate.swift**, add the following to the bottom of `application(_:didFinishLaunchingWithOptions:)`, just before the `return` statement:

```
updateRecipesController()
```

Then, add the following to `AppDelegate`:

```
func applicationWillEnterForeground(application: UIApplication)
{
  updateRecipesController()
}
```

Here you make sure `updateRecipesController()` is called every time the iOS app is launched or brought to the foreground.

Build and run. Everything should work just as before. From the user's standpoint, nothing has changed, but under the hood you're now able to update the recipes file from a remote server.

It's time to see updating the recipes remotely in action. Head back to your recipes repository on GitHub, to the same page that had the **Raw** button. This time around, click the **Edit** button:

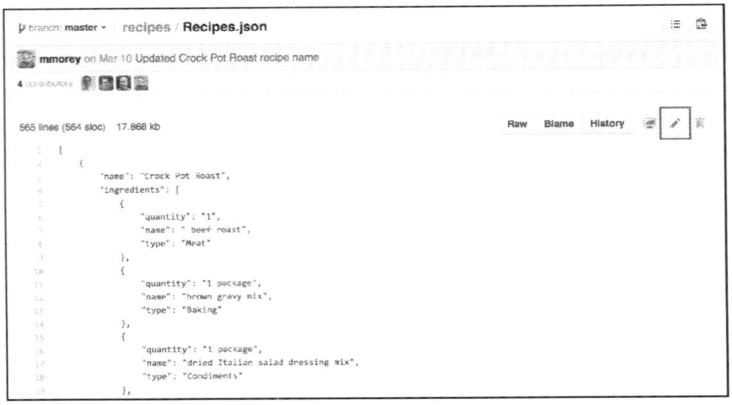

Find "Curried Lentils and Rice" and change its title to "World's Greatest Curried Lentils and Rice" as per the following screenshot. Be careful to not change the structure of the JSON file, otherwise the app will fail to parse it.

Once you're done, enter a commit message and click **Commit changes**:

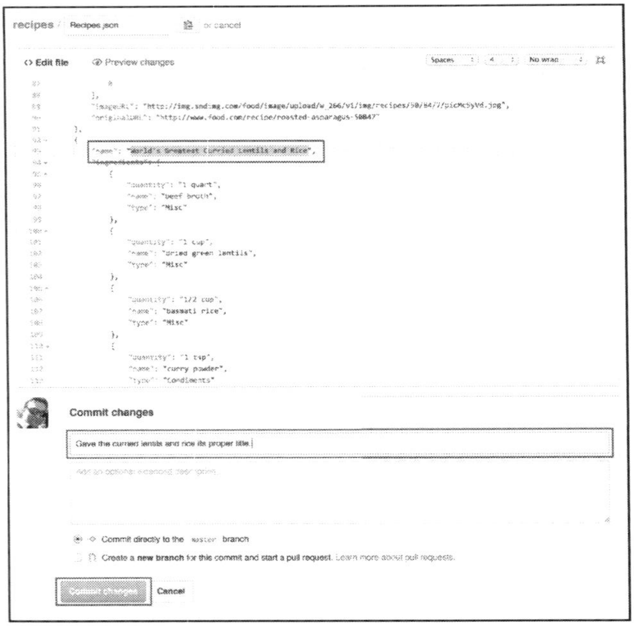

Now go back to Xcode, select the **SousChef** scheme and **build and run**. You should see the updated roast recipe in the app:

Updating the WatchKit extension

Perfect! But wait! What about the WatchKit extension? How does that get updated and notified? This is the final piece of the puzzle and you'll be doing it next.

Open **RecipesInterfaceController.swift** and add the following helper method to the class:

```
func updateTable() {
  let recipes = recipeStore.recipes
  if table.numberOfRows != recipes.count {
    table.setNumberOfRows(recipes.count,
      withRowType: "RecipeRowType")
  }

  for (index, recipe) in enumerate(recipes) {
    let controller = table.rowControllerAtIndex(index)
      as RecipeRowController
    controller.textLabel.setText(recipe.name)
    controller.ingredientsLabel.setText(
      "\(recipe.ingredients.count) ingredients")
  }
}
```

This is the same code as in `awakeWithContext(_:)` but refactored out into a separate method. That means you'll be able to call this method whenever the data changes.

Next, update awakeWithContext(_:) as follows:

```
override func awakeWithContext(context: AnyObject?) {
  super.awakeWithContext(context)
  updateTable()
}
```

The method is much shorter now that it just calls the helper method!

Finally, add the following method to the class:

```
override func willActivate() {
  super.willActivate()
  // 1.
  let kGroceryUpdateRequest =
    "com.raywenderlich.update-recipes"
  let requestInfo: [NSObject: AnyObject] =
    [kGroceryUpdateRequest: true]
  WKInterfaceController.openParentApplication(requestInfo) {
    (replyInfo: [NSObject : AnyObject]!, error: NSError!) ->
      Void in
    // 2.
    self.updateTable()
  }
}
```

Here's what's going on:

1. Every time RecipesInterfaceController is activated, you send a request to the containing iOS app by calling the WKInterfaceController class method, openParentApplication(_:reply:). You package the request in a userInfo dictionary. The key-value pairs in this dictionary must conform to a property list format. Here you pass a key and value that instructs the containing iPhone app to perform a refresh. You'll learn about the other side of this communication line in a moment.

2. In the reply block, you simply update the interface.

You may ask, why are you doing this? There are two ways that you can choose to refresh the recipes store:

- Call refresh(completion:) on RecipeStore directly;
- Ask the containing iPhone app to initiate this and notify you once it's complete.

iOS extensions, including WatchKit extensions, don't have a background state. They are either (a) running in the foreground, (b) suspended or (c) terminated. iOS extensions also don't have the ability to run background tasks. This means they can't ask the system for extra processing time before being suspended, nor will the system do anything on their behalf.

If you're going to do network operations that don't require you to persist the response, it's OK to dispatch them from the WatchKit extension.

For example, if you want to check the status of a flight, you always want to get the most up-to-date data from a server. You don't want to persist the response because, once it's stale, it's no longer useful. In such cases, you should cancel any in-flight operations when the extension is suspended—that is, when `didDeactivate()` is called. Then the next time the user comes to your app, you'll dispatch a new request. However, this is not the most common use case.

Usually, you want to persist the response. If for any reason your future update calls fail, you can always use the cached data and it will still be useful to the user. In such cases, you want to delegate the task of updating and persisting to something that can handle background tasks; in this case the containing iOS app.

Back in the iPhone app target, open **AppDelegate.swift** and add the following:

```
func application(application: UIApplication,
  handleWatchKitExtensionRequest userInfo:
    [NSObject : AnyObject]?,
      reply: (([NSObject : AnyObject]!) -> Void)!) {
  let kGroceryUpdateRequest =
    "com.raywenderlich.update-recipes"
  if let updateRecipesRequest =
    userInfo?[kGroceryUpdateRequest] as? Bool {
    updateRecipesWithRemoteServerWithCompletionBlock {
      (Void) -> Void in
      reply(nil)
    }
  }
}
```

This is the other end of the communication line! The system will automatically call `application(_:handleWatchKitExtensionRequest:reply:)` in the app delegate in response to your request. If the containing iPhone app is suspended or terminated, the system will launch it in the background first.

Inside `application(_:handleWatchKitExtensionRequest:reply:)`, you simply introspect the `userInfo` dictionary. If you find the key that indicates a refresh of the recipes is required, you perform one.

Once you've updated the recipes, you reply to the WatchKit extension by executing the `reply` block your handed. The dictionary you pass in may contain data that you want to return to the WatchKit extension. However, this parameter is completely optional and therefore you may pass `nil`.

> **Note**: As of the writing of this chapter, you can't call a reply block multiple times; this is a one-time shot. Each request maps to exactly one reply block. You don't have to call the reply block, but you can't call it more than once, either.
>
> Communication between the WatchKit extension and the containing iPhone app via this approach is executed asynchronously.

Recipes updated! Mission accomplished!

Follow the earlier steps to update the remote recipes.json file a second time, and then select the **SousChef Watch App** scheme and **build and run**. Navigate to Recipes, and this time you'll see the recipes update on the Watch app—great job!

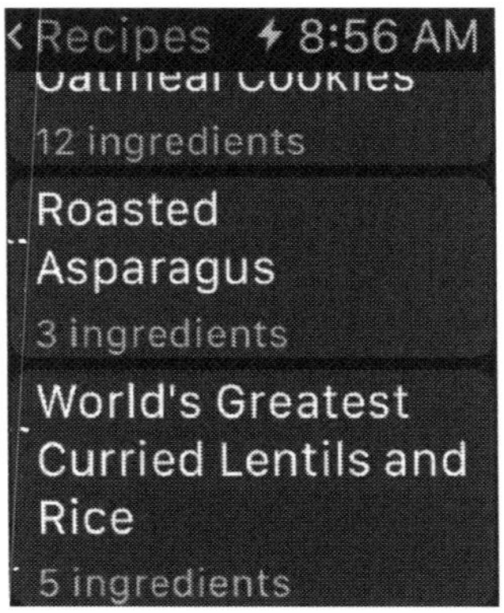

Shared documents best practices

Before you go, I thought I'd leave you with a few best practices for sharing documents between processes.

- **Share responsibly**: Pay particular attention to the method you choose to read and write data in a shared container. The best practice is to read and write in a coordinated manner to avoid data corruption.

  You can access a shared container from separate processes at the same time. The recommended way to coordinate reads and writes is using `NSFilePresenter` and `NSFileCoordinator`. However, you must not use file coordination APIs directly in an app extension, or you might end up with deadlocks.

> To learn more about file presenters and coordinators, see Apple's File System Programming Guide:
>
> https://developer.apple.com/library/prerelease/ios/documentation/FileManagement/Conceptual/FileSystemProgrammingGuide/Introduction/Introduction.html
>
> To learn more about the "gotchas" of using file presenter and file coordinator in app extensions, see Apple's Technical Note TN2408: "Accessing Shared Data from an App Extension and its Containing App":
>
> https://developer.apple.com/library/prerelease/ios/technotes/tn2408/_index.html

- **Migration**: Whether you're adding shared `NSUserDefaults` or a shared container for documents to an existing project, you'll need to think about migration. Migration can be as simple as copying the existing `NSUserDefaults` from `standardUserDefaults` to `sharedUserDefaults`, or it may involve some ad hoc process to move files to the shared container. Create a cast-iron migration plan that provides a seamless upgrade path for your app's users and mitigates the risk of losing or corrupting your users' data.

Where to go from here?

In this chapter, you've developed keen insight into the basics of app groups and sharing data between the WatchKit extension and its containing iPhone app. You've also learned how to communicate with the containing iPhone app directly from the WatchKit extension.

Now that you have your shared documents working, move on to the next chapter, where you'll add a glance to the SousChef Watch app that displays the items on your grocery list you haven't yet purchased. This SousChef app has got every base covered, from shopping to cooking!

Chapter 9: Glances

By Ben Morrow

A glance is an extension of your Watch app that lets you present important information the user needs right away, information they can consume immediately without first having to launch your Watch app. Glances are the WatchKit equivalent of Today extensions in iOS 8.

To help you understand and make the most of glances, this chapter will walk you through creating a glance for the SousChef Watch app you've been building in the previous chapters.

This glance will show the user's progress on their grocery list—that is, how many items the user has purchased, such as "3/7", as well as the two items next on the list.

The glance will automatically update as the user crosses items off their grocery list in the Watch app, perhaps making it easier to shop quickly and make it home with everything from the store!

Here's what the glance will look like by the time you've finished this chapter:

Getting started

To access glances, users swipe up from the bottom of their Watch screens—the same gesture used to access Control Center on the iPhone and iPad. The glances provided by the Watch apps installed on the Watch will be queued up with page indicator dots at the bottom of the screen; the user can swipe horizontally to navigate between them. Tapping anywhere on a glance will launch the corresponding Watch app.

Glances can make use of Handoff to inform the Watch app what was being displayed when the user tapped the glance. The Watch app can then use this information to update its interface accordingly. You'll be taking a look at Handoff in the very next chapter.

Designing a glance

Apple intends for users to experience glances with just a quick glance—hence the name! That means there are some restrictions as to what you can do with a glance:

- Each Watch app can only contain a single glance.
- The content is read-only; interactive components like buttons or switches aren't allowed.
- A glance isn't scrollable, so you need to make sure all your content fits within a single screen. This means you must be selective about the information you choose to display, making sure it's absolutely relevant in the current context.

Don't despair, though! These limitations actually make it much easier to design glances for their intended purpose—to enhance your app and provide a rich user experience measured in fractions of a second.

You can use Interface Builder to construct your glance. In this chapter, you'll lay out your glance in the storyboard and connect it to the data provided by your WatchKit extension.

Creating the glance interface controller

There are two different ways you can add a glance to your Watch app:

1. When you first add the Watch app target to your Xcode project, there's an option you can check called **Include Glance Scene**. Checking this will add a glance interface controller to your storyboard and a suitably-named `WKinterfaceController` subclass to your WatchKit extension:

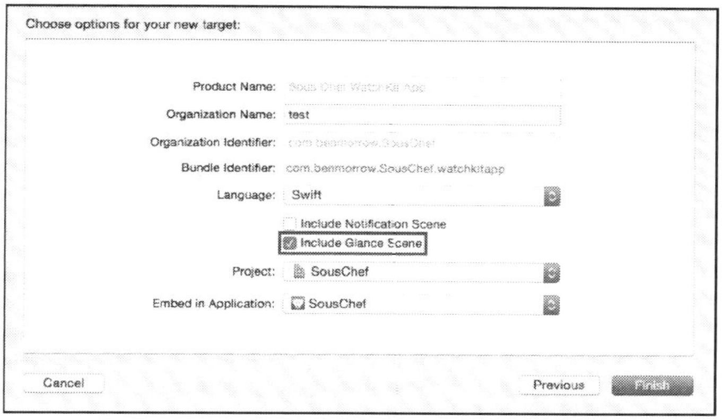

2. Or, you can choose to add a glance manually, which is what you'll do here.

Fire up Xcode and open the SousChef Project.

> **Note**: As with the rest of this book, this chapter builds on the chapters that precede it. If you're beginning with the starter project for this chapter because you've skipped previous chapters or simply want to start with a clean slate, you'll need to set up the necessary provisioning profiles and enable App Groups in order to share recipes between the containing iPhone app and the Watch app. For more information on what's required, see Chapter 8, "Sharing Data".

The first thing you need to do is subclass `WKinterfaceController`. So right-click on the **SousChef WatchKit Extension\Interface Controllers** group in the **project navigator** and choose **New File...** Then select the **iOS\Source\Swift File** and click **Next**.

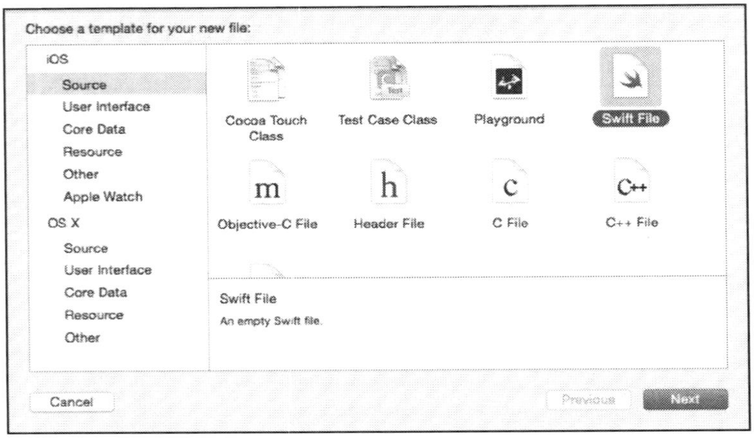

Name this file **GlanceController**, ensure that it is created in the **SousChef WatchKit Extension**, and click **Create**.

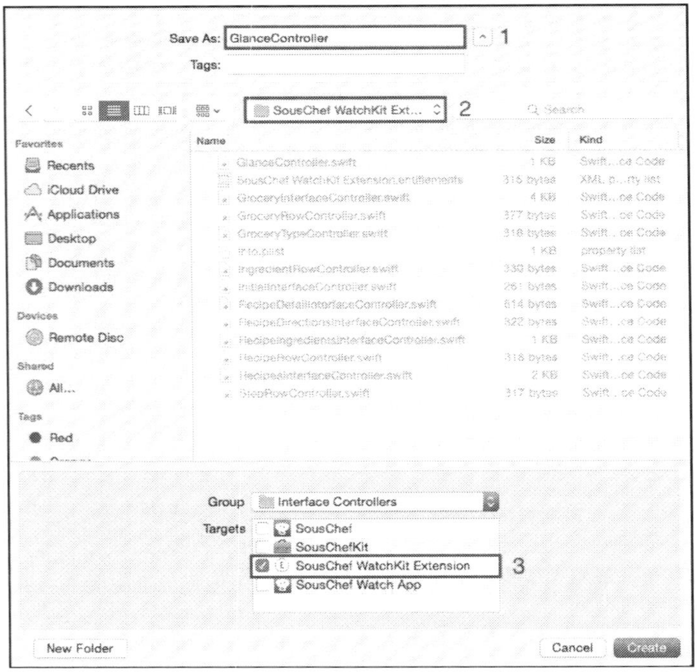

Open the new file and replace the contents with the following:

```
import WatchKit
import SousChefKit

class GlanceController: WKInterfaceController {

}
```

Adding the glance to the storyboard

Open **Interface.storyboard** and drag a **glance interface controller** from the **Object Library** onto the storyboard canvas.

You'll immediately notice the two layout groups:

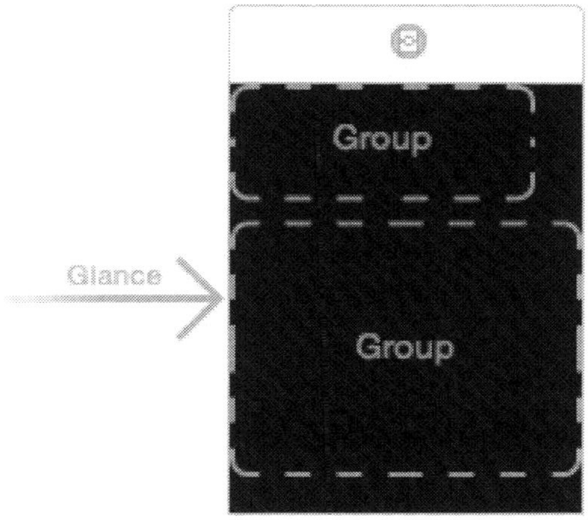

Glances are template-based, meaning you don't have *total* control over their appearance. Their interface is split into **upper** and **lower** layout groups.

Select the **Glance interface controller** in the Document Outline and then take a look at the **Attributes Inspector**. Click on the **Upper** section and choose the bottom-left template.

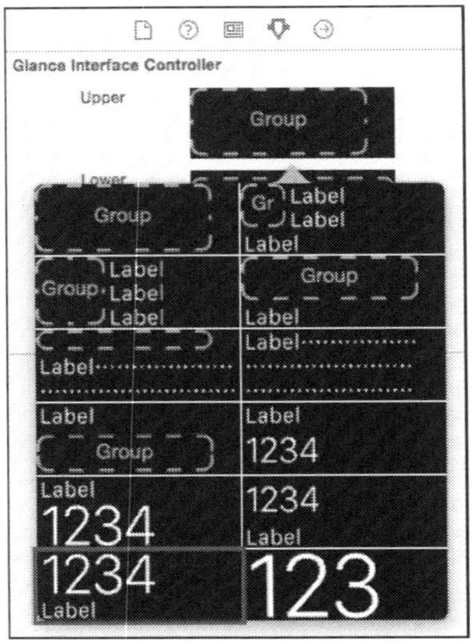

By choosing the appropriate the templates, you can create glances for a variety of content to best match the data in your app.

Now you need to set the **Custom Class** for your **Glance interface controller** so it uses the Swift file you just created. Open the **Identity Inspector** and set **Class** to `GlanceController`:

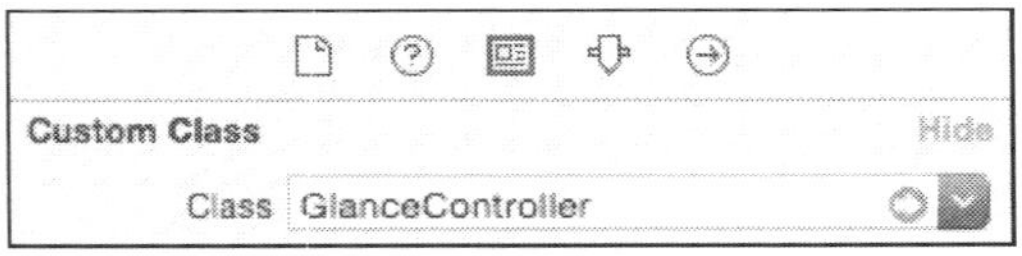

Creating the glance build scheme

To run your glance in the Watch simulator, you'll need to create a custom build scheme.

Open the **Scheme** menu and choose **Manage Schemes…**.

Next, select the **SousChef Watch App** scheme and then click the **gear** icon at the bottom of the pane. Choose **Duplicate** from the pop-up menu:

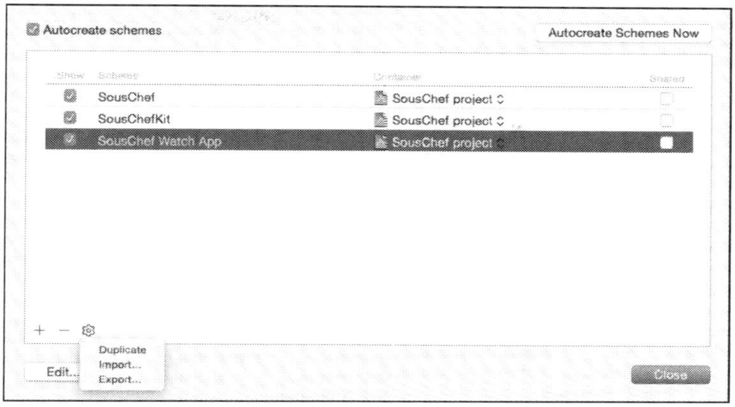

You need to give the new scheme a name, so call it **Glance**.

Then select the **Run** build option in the left-hand pane and in the center pane, change **Watch Interface** to **Glance**:

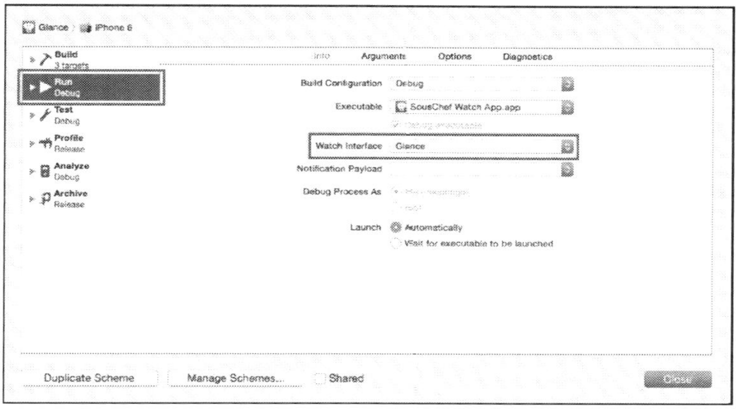

Click **Close**, and **Close** again to save the changes.

Now, before you're able to run your glance on the Watch simulator, there's one final step you need to complete, and you only have to do it once. As the glance is bundled with the Watch app, and the Watch app is bundled with the containing iOS app, you need to run the iOS app to install the Watch app, which in turn installs the glance. Phew, what a mouthful!

Do that now. Change the scheme to **SousChef** and then **build and run**. Once you see the launch screen, you can stop the app.

Change the scheme to **Glance** and **build and run**. You'll see your glance in the simulator, using the template you selected earlier:

The Watch simulator is looking pretty empty, but the two labels demonstrate that everything is working as expected at this point.

Tap anywhere on the glance in the Watch simulator and you'll be launched into the SousChef Watch app.

After you've confirmed everything is working, jump back to Xcode and get ready to build out the rest of your interface.

Designing the glance in the storyboard

Start with the **Upper** layout group. In the **Attributes Inspector** set the **Text** attribute of the two labels to **3/7** and **Groceries**, respectively.

Your glance will now look like the following:

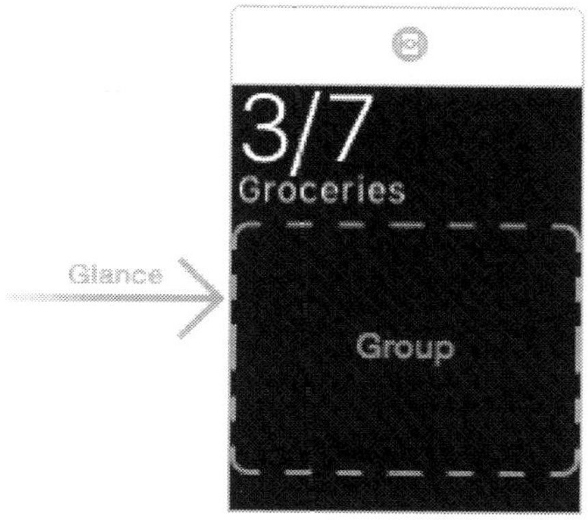

For the **Lower** group, let's get a bit fancy. Set the **Background Image** to **blur** and the **Mode** to **Aspect Fit**:

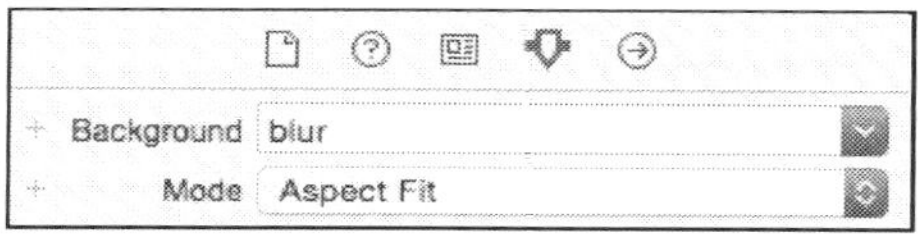

Behind the curtain, the **blur** image is simply a pre-processed PNG image. You *could* use Photoshop or Sketch to add a Gaussian blur to the SousChef logo, but fortunately for you, I have your back and have already prepared an image for you—you can find it in the chapter's resources.

To add the background image, open **Images.xcasssets** from the **SousChef Watch App** group. Then, using **Finder**, navigate to this chapter's resources folder and drag **blur@2x.png** into the sidebar of the asset catalog, where the other image names are listed:

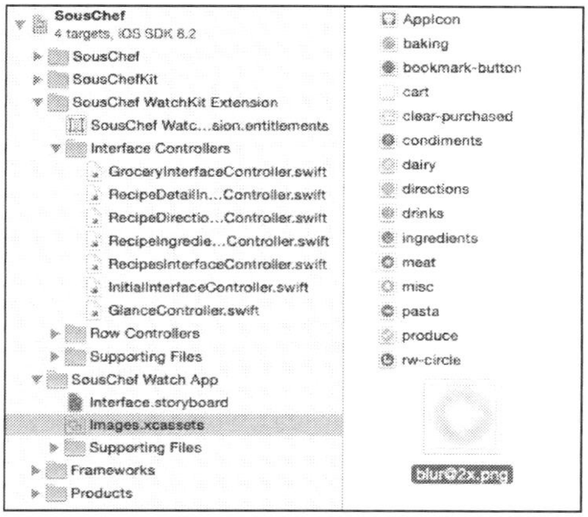

Now jump back to **Interface.storyboard**. Awesome! Notice how, with just a small amount of work up front, you can make an aesthetically pleasing interface.

Your glance should now look like this:

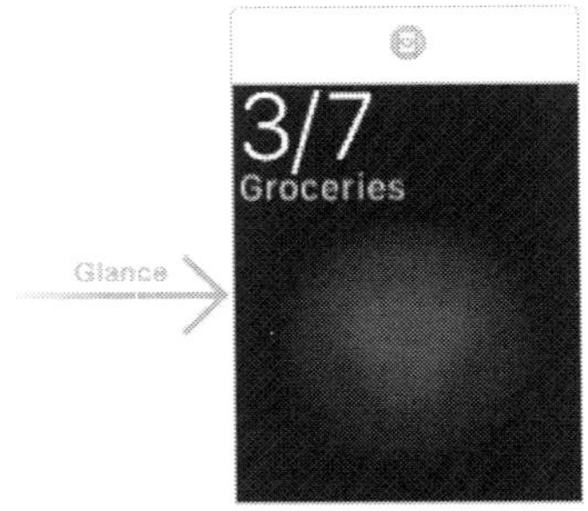

With the SousChef icon present, there will be no confusing this glance with another. The interaction can be *that much quicker*—and you have yet another opportunity to display the app's style and branding and build a connection with your users.

Now you need a way to display the next couple of grocery items on your list. Drag two **labels** from the **Object Library** into the **Lower** group. Change their **Text** attribute to **Bread** and **Milk**, respectively:

Notice how the labels are side by side, rather than being stacked on top of each other? Well, that just won't do!

Select the **Lower** layout group, and in the **Attributes Inspector**, change its **Layout** to **Vertical**:

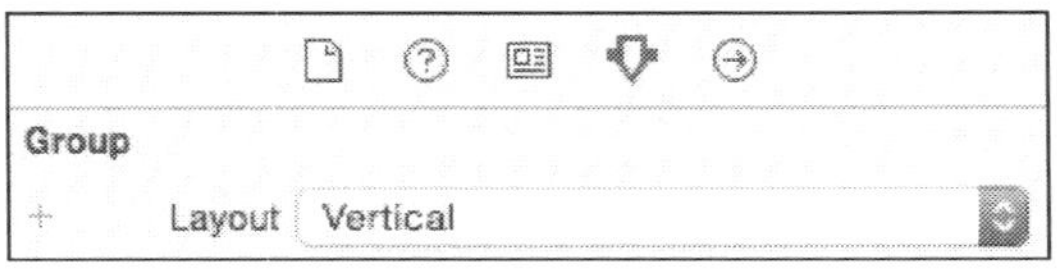

Much better! Now change the **Horizontal** position of both labels to **Right**:

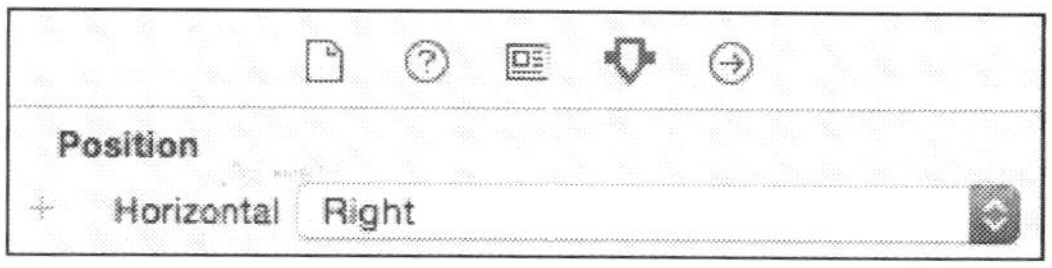

One last thing—you need to demonstrate some visual hierarchy. Since the grocery item *on deck* is further in the future, and therefore slightly less important than the one that is *up next*, you can indicate that visually using a different font style.

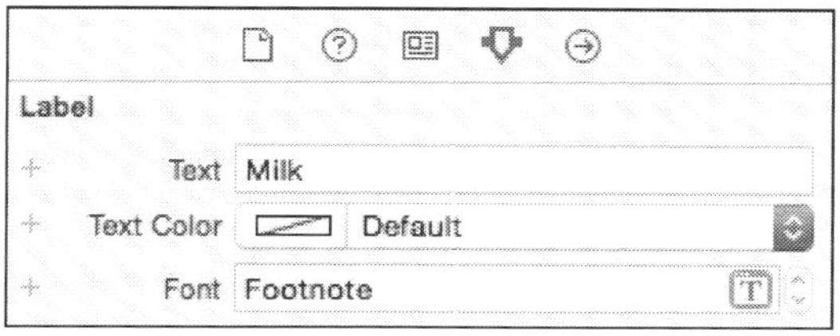

Change the **Font** of the **Milk** label to **Footnote**.

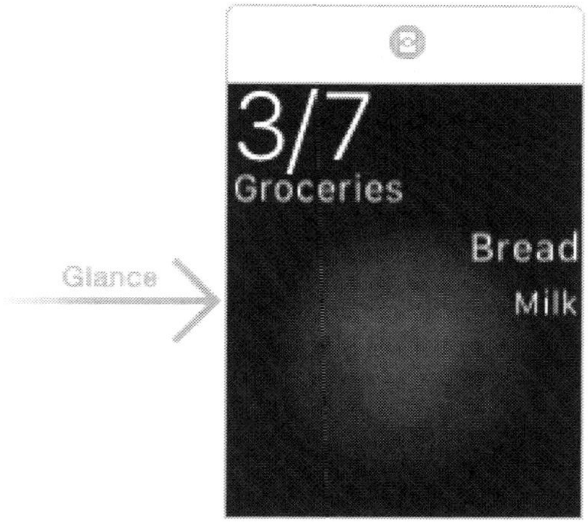

And that's it. Your completed glance layout looks fantastic! Good work.

In the next section, you'll make allowances for those pesky grocery items that have long and unusual names.

Fitting text into a glance

So, what happens if a grocery item has a really long name?

Try changing the text of both items to **Fresh-trimmed organic celery heart bundle**:

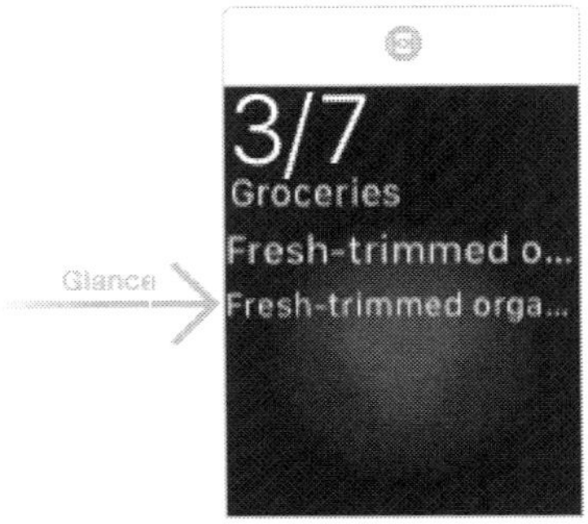

Well, that just looks awful! You certainly won't be building any connections with your users with an interface like that.

The first problem is that the text is truncated. If you kept the glance like this, you'd find yourself wandering aimlessly through the grocery store thinking, "Fresh-trimmed… what?"

To ensure that a grocery item will be properly displayed, change the **Lines** attribute to **0**. This is a special setting that really means "no limit"—the label will resize automatically to fit all the text it holds:

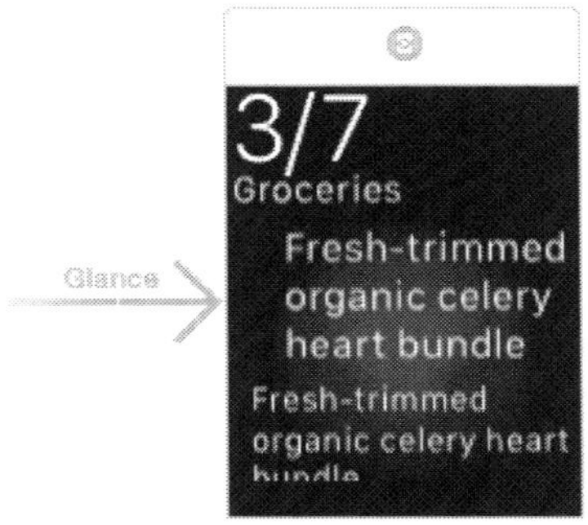

All right! You got the glance to display the full item name. But now you'll notice that the *on deck* label doesn't have enough room to display its text—what to do?

Remember, a glance can only take up a single screen—there is no scrolling. You need to make sure that when there's a long grocery item name, your interface elements don't get too big to fit on the screen.

So, on second thought, it's probably best to constrain the multiple lines of text to a fixed number to stay within the height of the glance interface.

To do that, simply set the **Lines** attribute to **2** for both labels in the lower layout group:

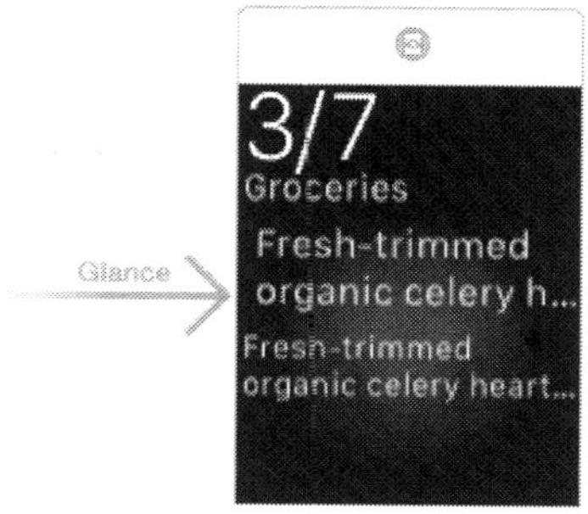

And with that, you're a shopping machine!

Oh, wait. The text isn't right-aligned. What happened? Setting the **Horizontal** position to **Right** is simply a hack that relies on the label being narrower than the width of the interface.

If you have long text in a label, as you do here, you'll need to align it the proper way.

With the first label selected, set the **Width** attribute to **Relative to Container**:

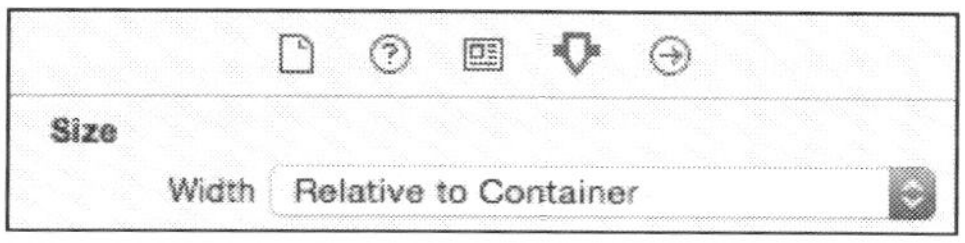

Then set the **Alignment** to **Right**:

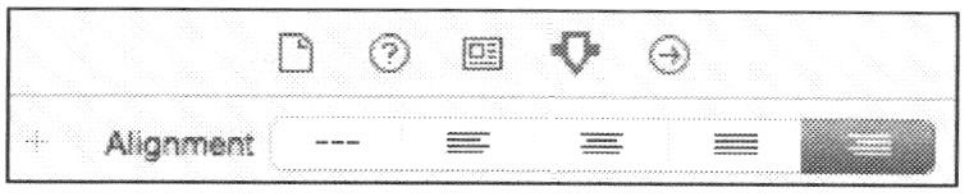

Make the same changes to the second label. Your glance interface will now look like the following:

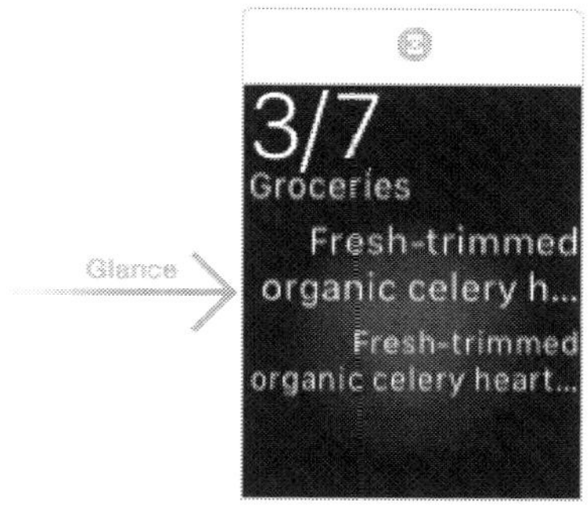

Now, wouldn't it be great if there were a bit of whitespace between the two grocery item labels? To do that, select the **Lower** group and in the **Attributes Inspector**, change **Spacing** to **20**:

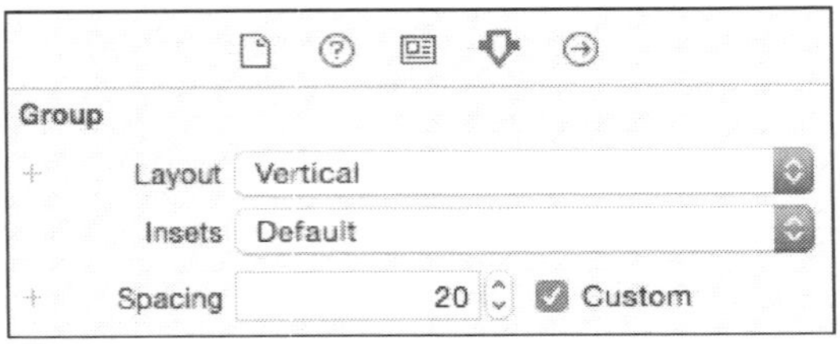

Finally, change the text of the two labels back to **Bread** and **Milk**, respectively. Your finished glance interface will now look like the following:

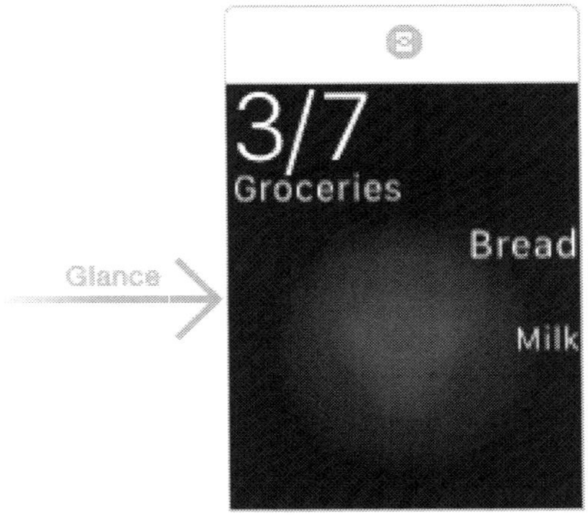

Great work! It's time to populate the glance with some real data.

Hooking up the controller

To populate those labels with real data, you need to create some outlets. With the storyboard still open, open the **assistant editor** and make sure it is displaying the `GlanceController` class. Then **Control-drag** from the first label in the glance into `GlanceController`:

In the pop-up dialog, name the outlet `statusLabel`.

Repeat the process for the **Bread** and **Milk** labels, naming them `upNextLabel` and `onDeckLabel`, respectively. Your class will now have the following outlets defined:

```
@IBOutlet weak var statusLabel: WKInterfaceLabel! // 3/7
@IBOutlet weak var upNextLabel: WKInterfaceLabel! // Bread
@IBOutlet weak var onDeckLabel: WKInterfaceLabel! // Milk
```

With those in place, it's time to figure out what data to display.

Running the calculations

Close the assistant editor, and in the standard editor open **GlanceController.swift**.

Each time the user invokes your glance you want to show them current data and update the interface accordingly. In order for the code to run each time, you'll want the logic inside `willActivate()`. Remember that any code outside of this method, like the code inside `activateWithContext(_:)` or any class properties will only be evaluated the first time, and will not update on subsequent launches.

Add the `willActivate()` function below the IBOutlet definitions:

```
override func willActivate() {
  super.willActivate()

  // 1
  let groceryList = GroceryList().flattenedGroceries()

  // 2
  let items = groceryList.filter {
    $0.item is Ingredient
  }.map {
```

```
      $0.item as! Ingredient
    }

    // 3
    let notPurchased = items.filter {
      return $0.purchased == false
    }

    // 4
    let purchasedCount = items.count - notPurchased.count
    statusLabel.setText("\(purchasedCount)/\(items.count)")

    // 5
    if notPurchased.count > 0 {
      upNextLabel.setText(notPurchased[0].name.capitalizedString)
    }
    if notPurchased.count > 1 {
      onDeckLabel.setText(notPurchased[1].name.capitalizedString)
    }
  }
```

Here's what you're doing, one step at a time:

1. The SousChefKit `GroceryList` class provides a method called `flattenedGroceries()` that conveniently returns an array of the groceries for you.
2. As the `flattenedGroceries()` method is primarily designed for use with tables, the array it returns contains section names. So you `filter` down to only the indices that contain `Ingredient` items, therefore excluding the section names. Then you use `map` to create a new array that has the correct type: `Ingredient`.
3. The `items` array contains both groceries that are already purchased and those that are still remaining. In this step, you single out only those that are yet to be purchased.
4. At this point, you can calculate how many groceries have been purchased and set the corresponding label text.
5. As long as there are items remaining in the grocery list, you can populate `upNextLabel` and `onDeckLabel` with the correct text. Using `capitalizedString` ensures that the first letter is uppercase.

Before you test the glance, make sure you have some items in the grocery list by launching the Watch app and adding ingredients to the list. Now **build and run** the **Glance** scheme. You'll see the labels populated with the correct data:

Your glance is looking great!

Once again, tapping on the glance will launch you into the Watch app itself:

Great work on building a glance that not only performs a very useful function, but also does so in an aesthetically pleasing way, promoting the style and design of the rest of the SousChef app. No more forgotten ingredients.

Where to go from here?

You now have a solid understanding of how to set up a glance, as well as a firm grasp on how to manipulate the glance interface.

Remember, you can configure the glance interface in much the same way as a Watch app. The only differences are these: You can't use any interactive elements like buttons or switches, and you have to keep all the objects within a single screen since scrolling isn't supported.

Now that you have your glance looking polished, consider this: As things stand, tapping on your glance takes you to the first page of the SousChef Watch app. To see or update your grocery list, you have to tap through to it again, wasting precious seconds that you could spend shopping!

In the next chapter, "Deep Linking with Handoff", you'll learn how to make your glance and your Watch app communicate with each other. Working with Handoff, you'll make it so that tapping on the glance takes the user directly to the grocery list in the SousChef Watch app and marks the *next* item as purchased.

Chapter 10: Handoff

By Soheil Moayedi Azarpour

You've probably heard of Handoff before, but you may not yet understand how it applies to the Apple Watch. Apple introduced Handoff as a way to facilitate the seamless transfer of tasks between two devices. Handoff lets you instantly continue an activity you start on one device on another, without the need to launch the same app on that second device and load a file, or wait for iCloud to sync and so forth—it was designed to appear almost magical, and it certainly feels that way the first few times you use it. :]

For example, Handoff allows you to start writing an email on your iPhone and then continue writing from exactly the same spot on your Mac.

In the previous chapter you added a glance in which you displayed items from the user's grocery list that were yet to be purchased. In this chapter, you'll continue working on SousChef project; specifically you'll add support for Handoff between the glance and the Watch app. When the user taps the glance, WatchKit launches your Watch app, and informs it that it was launched in response to the user tapping the glance. Once you're finished, the Watch app will magically navigate to the grocery list, and the item that was shown as being "next" in the glance is crossed off automagically!

It's time to implement some magic!

The Handoff API: A quick look

Handoff is based around the concept of **user activities**. These are stand-alone collective units of information that you can hand off without any dependencies on other information.

A user can only hand off tasks from one device to another device if the user is logged into the same iCloud account on both devices and the devices have already been paired via iCloud.

In the context of the Apple Watch, you use Handoff to seamlessly transition from a glance to either your main Watch app interface or another app on the iPhone.

The user activity that you pass from a glance is a dictionary in which you can store information about what the glance is currently displaying. If the user taps the glance, that contextual information is passed to the initial interface controller of the Watch app, which you can then use to configure the interface appropriately. Keys and values in the dictionary must be one of the following classes:

- `NSArray`
- `NSData`
- `NSDate`
- `NSDictionary`
- `NSNull`
- `NSNumber`
- `NSSet`
- `NSString`
- `NSURL`

These are the only classes compatible with the plist format, which is what Handoff uses under the hood.

Passing `NSURL` can be a bit tricky; make sure to check out the "Best Practices" section of this chapter before using `NSURL` with Handoff.

Handoff nuts and bolts

Before you dive into the code, let's take a quick look at the nuts of bolts of the API.

`WKInterfaceController` has a method, `updateUserActivity(_:userInfo:)`, that updates and broadcasts a user activity ready for use with Handoff:

```
override func willActivate() {
  updateUserActivity("com.rw.souschef.glance",
    userInfo: ["someKey": "someValue"], webpageURL: nil)
    // Some code...
}
```

To start broadcasting, you can call this method at any time during the execution of the interface controller's code. The system stores the `userInfo` dictionary and will transfer it to the target when appropriate.

You may also pass in a webpage URL. The URL must have an `http` or `https` scheme; otherwise the system throws an exception. The system will use the URL to load the webpage in a browser when the user continues the activity.

> **Note**: You can learn more about native App -> Web Browser Handoff and vice versa in Apple's Handoff Programming Guide, which can be found here:
>
> https://developer.apple.com/library/ios/documentation/UserExperience/Conceptual/Handoff/HandoffFundamentals/HandoffFundamentals.html

You must pass in either a valid `userInfo` dictionary or a valid webpage URL, or both.

> **Note**: Keep in mind that if the device suspends execution of your code, you need to start broadcasting again. For example, if the Watch puts your app in the background then it will be suspended for at least a short time. If your Handoff code were in `awakeWithContext(_:)`, the Watch wouldn't execute it when the app returned to the foreground. This typically makes `willActivate()` a much better place to start broadcasting the current user activity for use with Handoff.
>
> To simulate this behavior, you can lock the simulator by pressing **CMD+L** or by selecting **Hardware\Lock** from the menu. Then press **CMD+L** again and swipe on unlock.

To stop broadcasting Handoff, you call `invalidateUserActivity()` in your `WKInterfaceController` subclass:

```
override func didDeactivate() {
  super.didDeactivate()
  invalidateUserActivity()
}
```

You may call `invalidateUserActivity()` anytime during the execution of the interface controller, but the most common place to do so is in `didDeactivate()`. If you don't, the system will automatically stop broadcasting on your behalf based on some internal heuristics, after the controller becomes deactivated.

From a glance, the user has two options:

1. Tap the glance and launch the Watch app;

2. Pick up the broadcasted activity on another device. For this option to work, you need to configure the companion app properly, which is out of scope for this chapter.

When the user taps on your glance, the system launches your Watch app and passes the `userInfo` dictionary to the initial interface controller:

```
override func handleUserActivity(userInfo:
  [NSObject : AnyObject]!) {
  if let someValue = userInfo["someKey"] as? String {
    // The app is launched via Glance.
    // Some code...
  }
}
```

The `handleUserActivity(userInfo:)` method is the sole point of entry for Handoff in a Watch app. The system calls it in your app's initial interface controller. If you're using a page-based interface as opposed to a hierarchical interface, the system calls this method for each interface controller that's part of the initial interface. Each interface controller should look at the `userInfo` dictionary and decide what action it needs to take.

> **Note**: The documentation for `WKInterfaceController` explicitly states that the default implementation of this method does nothing and that you shouldn't call `super`. The documentation doesn't give any real explanation as to why this is the case, but sometimes it's just best to do as you're told. ;]

That's it! You've gotten a taste of how to work with Handoff. To experience it for yourself, let's get coding!

Bring it on!

Working with Handoff

You're going to implement Handoff in SousChef in two steps: first you'll create a user activity and broadcast it when the glance is displayed, and then you'll receive and handle that user activity in the Watch app itself.

Creating a user activity

Fire up Xcode and open the SousChef project.

> **Note**: As with the rest of this book, this chapter builds on the chapters that precede it. If you're beginning with the starter project for this chapter because you've skipped previous chapters or simply want to start with a clean slate, you'll need to set up the necessary provisioning profiles and enable App Groups in order to share recipes between the containing iPhone app and the Watch app. For more information on what's required, see Chapter 8, "Sharing Data".

You'll use some constant values with Handoff and refer to them from multiple places within the app. It's good practice to add constants to a separate file.

Right-click on the **Interface Controllers** group in the project navigator and select **New File...**. Then choose **iOS\Source\Swift File**. Name the class **HandoffConstants.swift** and ensure you add your new class to the **SousChef WatchKit Extension** target:

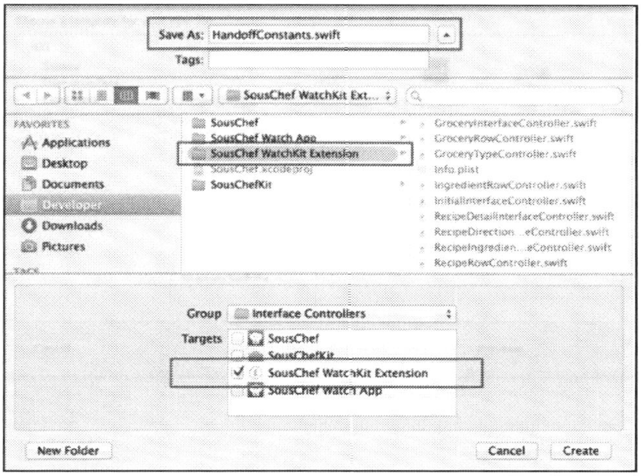

Add the following to your new file:

```
let kHandoffVersionKey = "version"
let kHandoffVersionNumber = "1.0"
let kGlanceHandoffActivityName = "com.rw.souschef.glance"
let kGlanceHandoffNextItemKey = "nextItem"
```

Now open **GlanceController.swift** and edit the following section near the end of `willActivate()`:

```
if notPurchased.count > 0 {
  upNextLabel.setText(notPurchased[0].name.capitalizedString)

  updateUserActivity(kGlanceHandoffActivityName,
    userInfo: [kHandoffVersionKey: kHandoffVersionNumber,
      kGlanceHandoffNextItemKey: notPurchased[0].name],
    webpageURL: nil)
}
```

Each time the glance is activated, you update the user activity with an activity type named `com.rw.souschef.glance`, as defined in **HandoffConstants.swift**. It denotes that the handoff is coming from the glance. You store the name of the next item in the grocery list in the `userInfo` dictionary. On the receiving side, you'll cross the passed-in item off the grocery list. You pass in `nil` for `webpageURL`, as this handoff won't be navigating to a web page.

You also store a version key-value. This is a simple way of future-proofing your app. Check out the "Best Practices" section of this chapter about versioning for Handoff.

Still in **GlanceController.swift**, add the following code to the end of `GlanceController`:

```
override func didDeactivate() {
  super.didDeactivate()
  invalidateUserActivity()
}
```

Here you simply stop broadcasting the user activity when the glance is dismissed.

Next, open **InitialInterfaceController.swift** and implement `handleUserActivity(userInfo:)` as follows:

```
override func handleUserActivity(userInfo:
  [NSObject : AnyObject]!) {
  println("Received a Handoff payload: \(userInfo)")
}
```

Here, you override the necessary method for responding to Handoff, simply printing the payload to the console.

It's time to verify everything is working as expected. Launch the Watch app and add some ingredients to the grocery list using the context menu you implemented in Chapter 7, "Menus". Then stop the app go back to Xcode and make sure **Glance** scheme is selected:

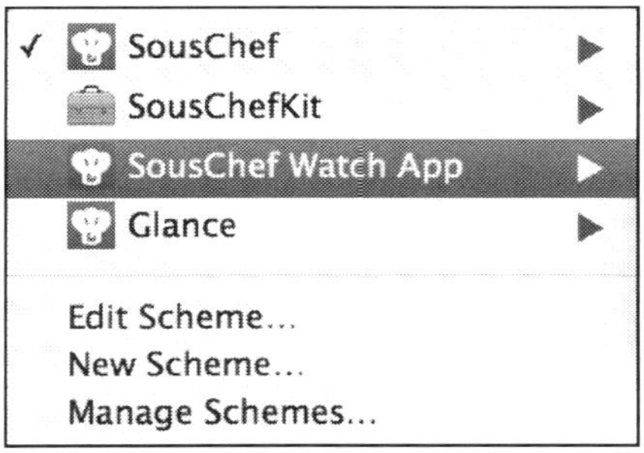

Then **build and run**:

Once the glance appears, tap it to launch the Watch app. Then check the console and verify you see a message similar to the following:

```
Received a handoff payload: [version: 1.0, nextItem: fresh
blueberries]
```

Awe yeah—hands-on with Handoff!

Receiving a user activity

When you receive a user activity via Handoff, you're responsible for handling it, and if necessary passing it on to the appropriate interface controllers for further processing.

Open **InitialInterfaceController.swift** and update `handleUserActivity(userInfo:)` so it matches the following:

```
override func handleUserActivity(userInfo: [NSObject :
  AnyObject]!) {
  println("Received a Handoff payload: \(userInfo)")
  if let version = userInfo[kHandoffVersionKey] as? String {
    if version == kHandoffVersionNumber {
      if let nextItem = userInfo[kGlanceHandoffNextItemKey]
        as? String {
        self.pushControllerWithName(
         "GroceryController", context: nextItem)
      }
    }
  }
}
```

Here's what's happening:

1. You inspect the `userInfo` dictionary. If it's a version that you know how to handle, like version `1.0`, you continue.
2. If you find a valid value for `kGlanceHandoffNextItemKey` in the dictionary, you know it's been handed off by the glance. So you route the user to a `GroceryInterfaceController` by pushing it onto the navigation stack.

3. You also pass on the `nextItem` value as the `context` to `GroceryInterfaceController` so it can be handled appropriately.

Open **GroceryInterfaceController.swift**. Find and update `awakeWithContext(_:)` as follows:

```
override func awakeWithContext(context: AnyObject?) {
  super.awakeWithContext(context)
  println("Received context: \(context)")
  updateTable()
}
```

Finally, make sure the interface controller has its identifier set. Open **Interface.storyboard** and select the Groceries interface. In the Attributes Inspector, set the **Identifier** to "GroceryController":

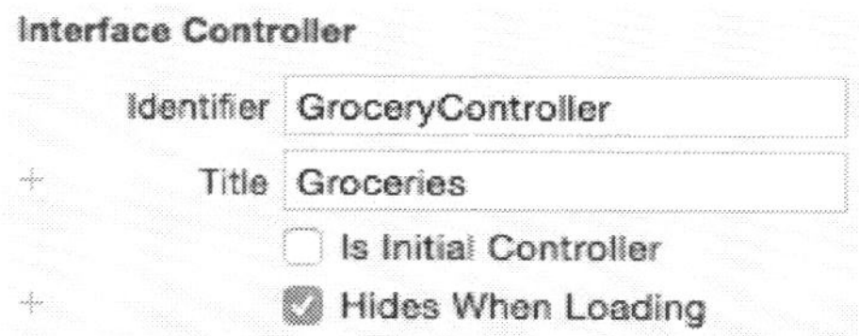

Now you need to verify everything is working as expected. Once again, make sure the **Glance** scheme is selected—then **build and run**. Once the glance appears, tap it to launch the Watch app. Check the console and verify that you see a message similar to the following:

```
Received a handoff payload: [version: 1.0, nextItem: eggs]
Received context: Optional(eggs)
```

You'll also be presented with the appropriate `GroceryInterfaceController` in the Watch simulator rather than the initial interface:

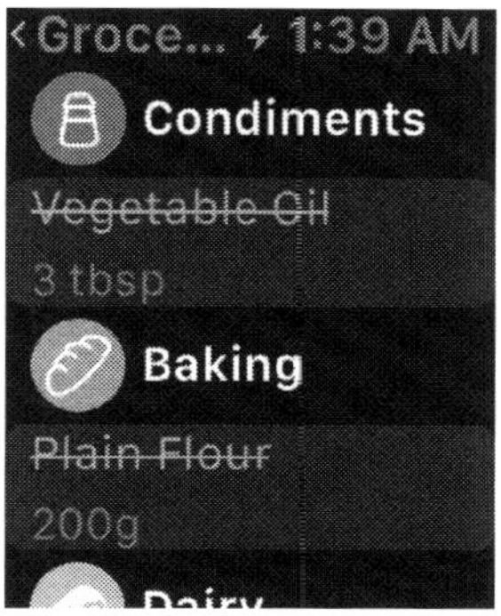

Sweet! You're now successfully passing along the relevant parts of the Handoff payload from `InitialInterfaceController` to `GroceryInterfaceController`. Now it's time to update `GroceryInterfaceController` so it actually does something meaningful with what it's receiving.

Open **GroceryInterfaceController.swift** and update `awakeWithContext(_:)` so it matches the following:

```
override func awakeWithContext(context: AnyObject?) {
  super.awakeWithContext(context)
  println("Received context: \(context)")
  if let context = context as? String {
    for (index, value) in enumerate(flatList) {
      if let ingredient = value.item as? Ingredient {
        if context == ingredient.name {
          groceryList.setIngredient(ingredient, purchased: true)
          groceryList.sync()
          break
        }
      }
    }
  }
  updateTable()
}
```

Make sure you add the above code before the call to `updateTable()`.

Here's what's happening:

1. If there's a valid `context` and it's a `String`, you try to find an ingredient in the grocery list whose name matches the `context`.
2. If you find one, you set that ingredient as purchased, and then sync the grocery list.
3. Finally, you update the table.

And that's it! Make sure the **Glance** scheme is selected, then **build and run**. Once the glance appears, tap it to launch the Watch app. You're now automatically routed to `GroceryInterfaceController` and the "up next" item that was displayed by the glance is now crossed off:

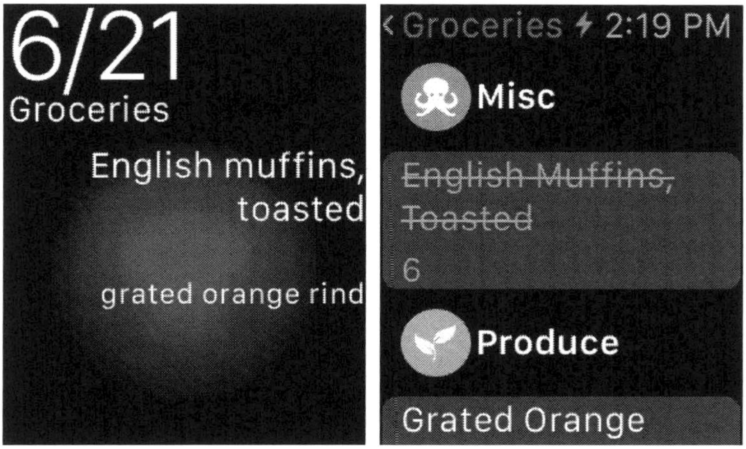

Great work!

I'm sure you'll agree that Apple has done a fantastic job of abstracting away the complexities of Handoff so you can implement it using *just* two methods—*cheers Apple!*

Next, you'll look at some of the best practices to think about when implementing Handoff in your own apps.

Handoff best practices

Before you go, consider these few thoughts on Handoff best practices.

- **NSURL**: Using NSURL in the `userInfo` dictionary can be tricky. The only URLs you can pass safely in Handoff are those that point to iCloud documents, as well as website URLs that use either HTTP or HTTPS. You can't pass local file URLs, as the receiver won't translate and map the URL properly on their end. The best way to achieve file links is to pass a relative path and re-construct the URL manually on the receiving side.

- **Platform-specific values**: Avoid using platform-specific values like the content offset of a scroll view; it's always better to use relative landmarks. For example, if your user is viewing some items in a table view, pass the index path of the top, most visible item in the table view instead of passing the content offset or visible rect of the table view.

- **Versioning**: Think about using versioning so you can future-proof updates of your app. It's entirely plausible that you could add new data formats or remove values entirely from your `userInfo` dictionary in future versions of the app. Versioning gives you more control over how your app handles user activities in current and future versions.

Where to go from here?

This chapter has given you insight into using Handoff between a glance and its containing Watch app. Handoff makes it easier than ever to provide a rich, seamless user experience between your apps in multiple contexts, and on multiple devices.

If you'd like to learn more about Handoff between multiple devices, check out Chapter 23, "Handoff" in *iOS 8 By Tutorials*, which you can find here:

- http://www.raywenderlich.com/store/ios-8-by-tutorials

If you'd like to learn more about streaming and document-based Handoff, be sure to check out Apple's Handoff Programming Guide:

- https://developer.apple.com/library/prerelease/ios/documentation/UserExperience/Conceptual/Handoff/HandoffFundamentals/HandoffFundamentals.html

In the next chapter you'll learn all about handling local and remote notifications for your Watch app.

Chapter 11: Notifications

By Matthew Morey

Local and remote notifications enable an app that isn't running in the foreground to inform users about new, relevant information that's available.

iOS has had notification support since iOS 3, and its abilities have steadily increased over the years. With iOS 7, Apple added silent remote notifications support, allowing apps to wake up in the background and perform important tasks. Actionable notifications, added in iOS 8, allow users to take an action on a notification without first opening the app.

Existing iPhone apps that currently support notifications will work on the Apple Watch without any changes. WatchKit uses a default system interface to show notifications.

However, with a little work, you can build beautiful, custom Watch notifications. WatchKit introduces two new types: short look and long look notifications.

The SousChef phone app already supports two notifications: a local one that allows the user to create a kitchen timer for recipe directions, and a remote one that informs the user when a new recipe is available.

In this chapter, you'll add custom interfaces for the local and remote notifications to the SousChef Watch app—one during the bulk of this chapter and another on your own, with a little guidance.

> **Note:** If you're not that familiar with how notifications work in iOS or you find this chapter a little difficult, I recommend you read our Apple Push Notification Services tutorial:
>
> http://www.raywenderlich.com/32960/apple-push-notification-services-in-ios-6-tutorial-part-1

Getting started

In this section, you'll learn how to test notifications with the Watch simulator and what they look like.

This chapter's starter project is a continuation of the SousChef project from the last chapter. You can use either your final project from that chapter, or the starter project for this chapter.

> **Note**: As with the rest of this book, this chapter builds on the chapters that precede it. If you're beginning with the starter project for this chapter because you've skipped previous chapters or simply want to start with a clean slate, you'll need to set up the necessary provisioning profiles and enable App Groups in order to share recipes between the containing iPhone app and the Watch app. For more information on what's required, see Chapter 8, "Sharing Data".

Testing with the Watch simulator

New to Xcode 6.2 is the ability to test remote notifications on the Watch simulator using a local file to mimic the JSON payload file that's sent by Apple's Push Notification Service.

To use this new feature, you simply need to add a new file with the extension ".apns" to your project.

Open the SousChef project in Xcode and then show the project navigator. **Right-click** on the **Supporting Files** group in the **SousChef WatchKit Extension** group and select **New File…**. Select the **iOS\Apple Watch\Notification Simulation File** template and click **Next**.

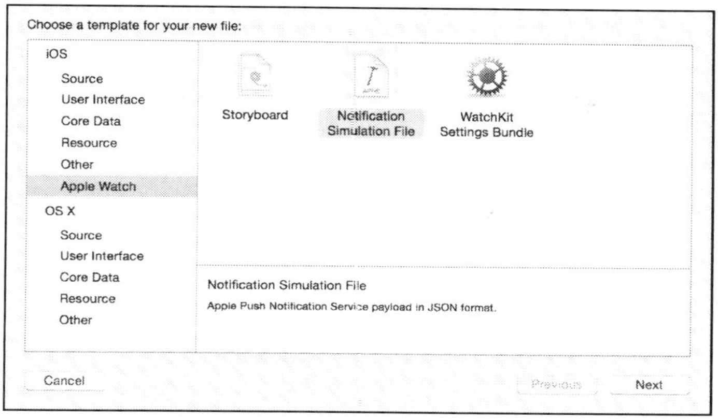

Name the file **KitchenTimerNotificationPayload.apns**, as this will be the file you use later to test the kitchen timer local notification. Ensure no Targets are checked and click **Create**.

The **KitchenTimerNotificationPayload.apns** file you just created is a plain text file with an example JSON payload:

```
{
  "aps": {
    "alert": {
      "body": "Test message",
      "title": "Optional title"
    },
    "category": "myCategory"
  },
  "WatchKit Simulator Actions": [
     {
     "title": "First Button",
     "identifier": "firstButtonAction"
     }
   ],
  "customKey": "Use this file to ..."
}
```

If you've implemented remote notifications before, you know that the **aps** dictionary includes the notification title, message and optionally, a category. When the iPhone or iPad receives a notification and the app is in the background, the device displays a system dialog or banner showing the title and message.

Because the Watch simulator doesn't have access to the iPhone app's registered notification actions, the JSON payload includes a special key, `WatchKit Simulator Actions`, for testing. The value of this key is an array of items, with each item representing a single action button that will be appended to the Watch's notification interface.

Even though the kitchen timer you're building is a local notification, you can pretend it's a remote notification for testing purposes. To WatchKit, there is no fundamental difference between a local and a remote notification, as it shows both to the user in the same manner.

Now that you have a sample JSON payload for testing notifications on the Watch, you need to create a new scheme.

To add a new scheme, you'll first duplicate the current Watch App scheme. Choose **Product\Scheme\Manage Schemes**, select the **SousChef Watch App** scheme, click on the gear icon and then click on **Duplicate**.

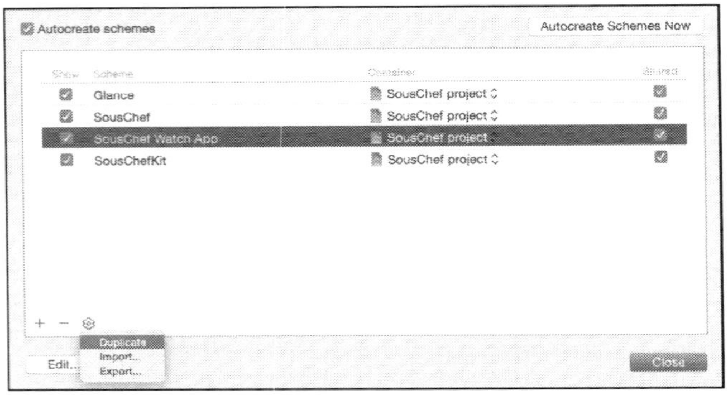

Name the scheme **Kitchen Timer Notification for Watch App**. Select the **Run** option in the left-hand column of the scheme editor. In the **Info** pane, select the **Dynamic Notification** Watch Interface. The Notification Payload should automatically be set to the **KitchenTimerNotificationPayload.apns** file.

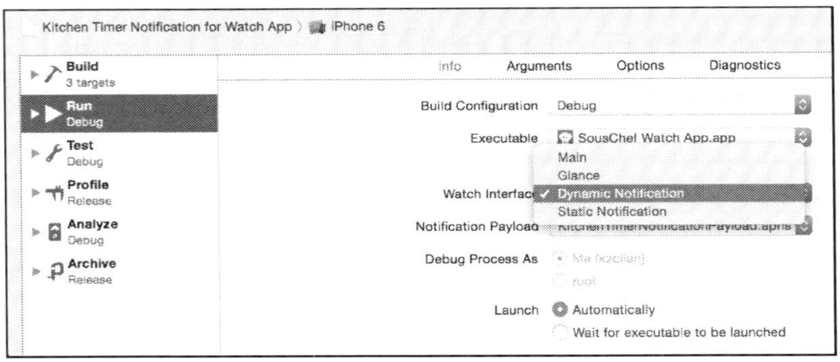

> **Note:** If your app supports more than one notification, you can add multiple APNS files and multiple schemes to make it easy to test each one.
>
> You can also select the Static Notification option to test the static version of a notification. Keep reading to find out what a static interface is.

Close both windows to return to the main Xcode interface, and **build and run** the new notification scheme. You'll see the following message displayed on the Watch simulator:

As the message indicates, the simulator doesn't know how to handle the notification because you haven't set up a notification scene in the Watch app's storyboard.

To fix this, simply open **Interface.storyboard** from the SousChef Watch App group and drag a **notification interface controller** from the Object Library onto the storyboard.

In your storyboard, notification categories are shown as arrows, or entry points, pointing to a notification scene. Since apps can have multiple notification types, categories are used to differentiate one notification scene from another.

> **Note:** Notification categories are typically registered in the app delegate of the containing iOS app. Check out "Setting Up Notifications in the iPhone App" in the appendix of this book to learn how and where SousChef configures the various notification categories.

For now you don't have to do anything else, since the category for a new notification scene is set to default, meaning it can show any notification regardless of the category specified in the payload.

Build and run. This time the notification works.

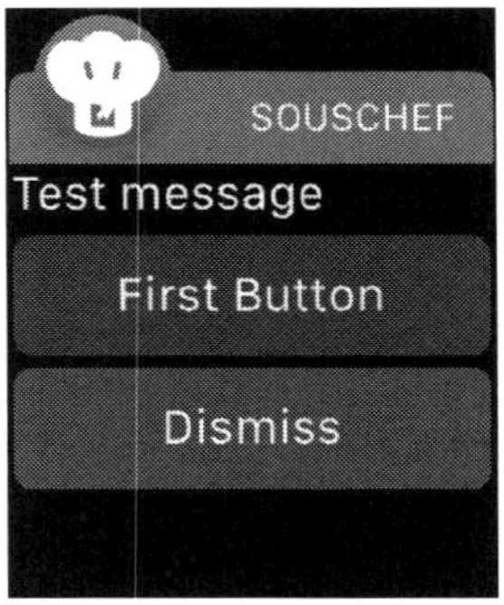

Delicious! You just received your first notification on the Apple Watch simulator.

Xcode used the "Test message" string from **KitchenTimerNotificationPayload.apns** to populate the notification interface.

This new feature in Xcode allows you to focus on the notification user interface without having to worry about servers, device tokens and the other complexities related to testing remote notifications.

Short looks vs. long looks

When the iPhone app receives a remote or local notification, iOS decides whether to display the notification on the iPhone or the Apple Watch.

If the Watch receives the notification, it will notify the user via a subtle vibration. If the user chooses to view the notification, which she'll do by raising her wrist, the Watch will show an abbreviated version called a short look. If the user continues to view the notification, the Watch will show a more detailed version, or a long look.

The short look notification is a quick summary for the user. Short looks show the app's icon and name, and the notification title in a predefined layout. The notification title is a very short blurb about the notification, such as "New Bill", "Reminder" or "Score Alert". This allows the user to decide whether or not to stick around for the long look interface.

The text color of the app name is perhaps the only thing customizable about the short look notification interface. You can change it by setting the tint color in the Attributes Inspector for the notification interface controller.

The long look is a scrolling interface that you can customize, with a default static interface or an optional dynamically-created interface. Unlike the short look interface, the long look offers significant customization.

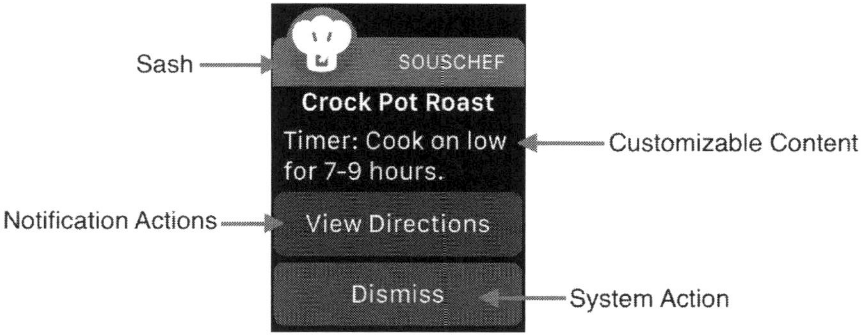

The **sash** is the horizontal bar at the top. It's translucent by default, but you can set it to any color and opacity value.

You can customize the content area as if it were a standard interface, but without any interactive controls such as buttons and switches.

Long look interfaces can show up to four custom notification actions. These actions need to be registered by the iPhone app. If they are, the long look interface displays them automatically, based on the notification's category.

The system-provided Dismiss button is always present at the bottom of the interface. Tapping Dismiss hides the notification without informing the iPhone app or the Watch extension.

You've just learned how to test notifications on the Watch using the special APNS file. You also now know the differences between a short look and a long look notification, and what parts of each you can customize.

In the next section, you'll learn how to create the kitchen timer local notification.

Creating a local timer notification

Now that you've done all the prep work, you get to build the kitchen timer local notification, which will look like this:

The interface consists of two labels, one for the recipe name and a second for the cooking direction. It also contains an action, View Directions, which allows the user to jump straight to the full list of directions for the recipe.

> **Note:** To see how the iPhone app handles notifications, check out "Notifications in the iPhone App" in the appendix of this book.

Testing timer notifications

To build the kitchen timer notification, you first need to update the APNS file with real data.

Open **KitchenTimerNotificationPayload.apns** and replace its contents with the following:

```
{
  "aps": {
    "alert": {
      "body": "Timer: Cook on low for 7-9 hours.",
      "title": "Crock Pot Roast"
    },
    "category": "timer"
  },

  "WatchKit Simulator Actions": [
    {
      "title": "View Directions",
      "identifier": "viewDirectionsButtonAction"
    }
  ],

  "message": "Timer: Cook on low for 7-9 hours.",
  "title": "Crock Pot Roast",
}
```

Here you update the body and title strings inside the aps dictionary with real example content.

You set the category to the timer type to match the category registered in **AppDelegate.swift**. If you accidentally use the wrong category the custom timer notification scene you are about to create will not work.

WatchKit Simulator Actions includes a single button, View Directions, with an identifier of `viewDirectionsButtonAction`.

The last two strings, message and title, are custom strings that you'll use shortly to configure the dynamic long look notification interface.

Now that you've updated the JSON payload with "real" content and set the category, you're ready to update the storyboard.

Open **Interface.storyboard** and select the **notification entry point** for the notification scene you created earlier in this chapter —that's the "Notification" arrow itself. Next, set the **notification category name** to **timer** in the Attributes Inspector, which is the same string you used in **KitchenTimerNotificationPayload.apns**.

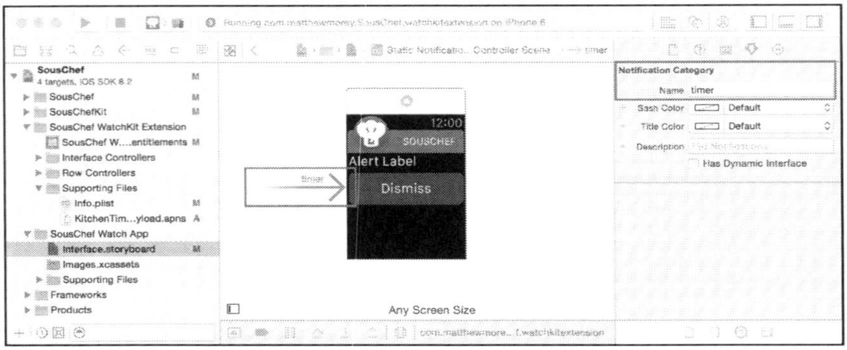

After updating **Interface.storyboard**, **build and run**. You'll see this:

It works! Kind of. The label is truncating the notification message, but don't worry, it's an easy fix. In the next section, you'll learn how to customize the label.

Creating a custom interface

Until this point, you've been using the default static notification interface controller. Default interfaces are so bland! It's time to spice things up by customizing the interface.

First, you'll fix the truncated message. With **Interface.storyboard** open, select the **timer notification scene**, then the **Alert Label**, and then show the **Attributes Inspector**.

Change the **Lines** parameter to **0** so that the label text will automatically wrap without truncating.

Set the **Horizontal** position to **Center**.

Build and run. As you can now see, the label is no longer truncating its text.

Static notification interfaces such as this are important, as they provide a fallback in situations where dynamic interfaces are unavailable or fail to load.

You can only configure a static notification interface in the storyboard. That means you can't run any code to update its contents or configure its interface.

The only content that is dynamically updated in a static notification is the label, which is connected to a special outlet named `notificationAlertLabel`. The system automatically updates the text of this label with the alert message from either a remote or local notification or a test APNS file.

> **Note**: You might be wondering why a dynamic long look notification interface would fail to load. Imagine your dynamic interface receives an image URL from the notification payload and downloads the image for display. If the URL for the image is no longer valid or has been removed, the network request could potentially take a long time to fail.
>
> Instead of making the user wait—or worse, not even showing the notification—WatchKit will automatically fall back to using the static interface.

Now that the static long look interface is complete, it's time to create the dynamic version.

With **Interface.storyboard** still open, select the **timer** notification category. In the Attributes Inspector, enable **Has Dynamic Interface**.

Interface Builder will automatically create a new scene and add a segue from the static interface to the dynamic interface.

Interface.storyboard now looks like this:

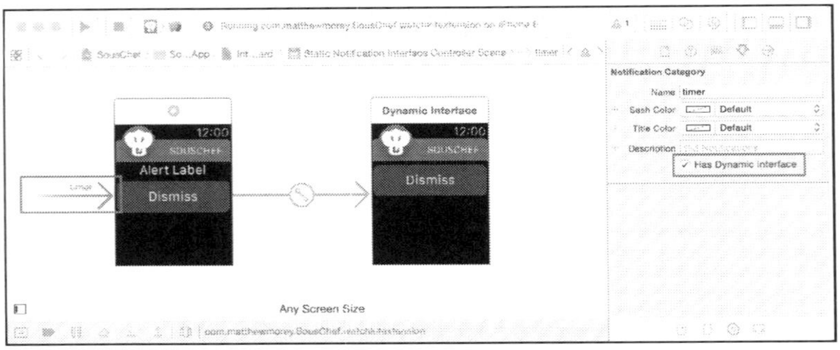

Next, drag two labels from the Object Library onto the new dynamic interface.

The first label will show the recipe name. After selecting the label, open the Attributes Inspector and set the **Text** to **<title>**, the **Font** to **Headline**, the **Lines** to **0,** and the **Horizontal** position to **Center**.

The second label will show the recipe directions associated with the expired timer. Select the label, and then set the **Text** to **<message>**, the **Lines** to **0,** and the **Horizontal** position to **Center**.

You may be tempted to add interactive controls to the long look interface, such as buttons and switches. Don't do it; they won't work! Interactive elements aren't allowed in notification interfaces. You add buttons by setting up related notification actions when registering for notifications in the accompanying iPhone app. WatchKit will always show them at the bottom of the long look interface.

After configuring the two labels, the storyboard file now looks like this:

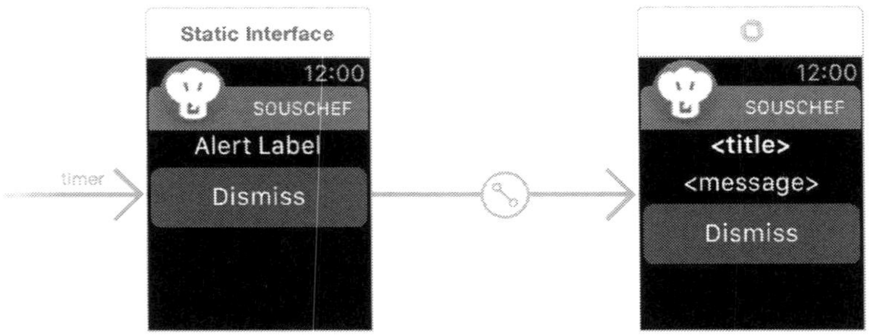

To update the <title> and <message> labels, you need to write some code.

With the project navigator visible, right-click on the **Interface Controllers** group in **SousChef WatchKit Extension** and select **New File**. Select **iOS\Source\Swift File** and click **Next**.

Name the file **KitchenTimerNotificationController.swift** and ensure you're adding it to the **SousChef WatchKit Extension** target.

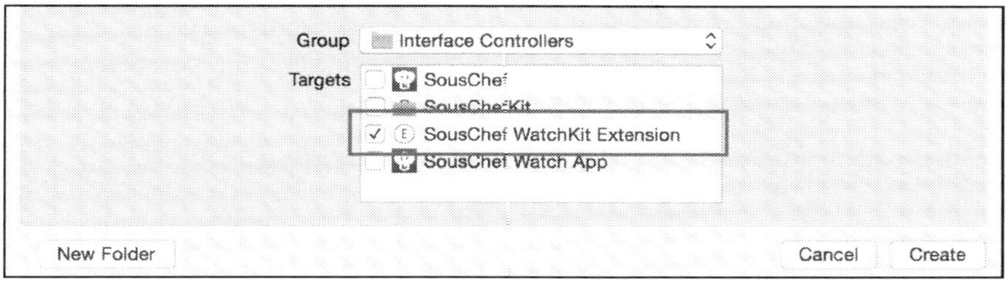

Add the following code to the new file:

```
import WatchKit

// 1
class KitchenTimerNotificationController:
  WKUserNotificationInterfaceController {

  // 2
  @IBOutlet weak var titleLabel: WKInterfaceLabel!
  @IBOutlet weak var messageLabel: WKInterfaceLabel!

  // 3
  override func didReceiveLocalNotification(
    localNotification:UILocalNotification, withCompletion
    completionHandler:(WKUserNotificationInterfaceType)->Void) {
    if let userInfo = localNotification.userInfo {
      processNotificationWithUserInfo(userInfo,
        withCompletion: completionHandler)
    }
  }

  // 4
  override func didReceiveRemoteNotification(
    remoteNotification:[NSObject : AnyObject], withCompletion
    completionHandler:(WKUserNotificationInterfaceType)->Void) {
    processNotificationWithUserInfo(remoteNotification,
      withCompletion: completionHandler)
  }
}
```

This code does the following:

1. It creates the class `KitchenTimerNotificationController`, a subclass of `WKUserNotificationInterfaceController`.
2. It includes an outlet for the title and message labels. The labels are of type `WKInterfaceLabel`.
3. Next, the code overrides `didReceiveLocalNotification(_:withCompletion:)`, which WatchKit calls when it receives a local notification. WatchKit calls the function before displaying the notification interface, allowing you to configure the interface. The code calls the helper function `processNotificationWithUserInfo(_:withCompletion:)`, which you'll implement soon.
4. Finally, the code overrides `didReceiveRemoteNotification(_:withCompletion:)`, which does the same thing as `didReceiveLocalNotification(_:withCompletion:)` but for remote notifications. Because the kitchen timer notification you're building is a local notification, the app you ship will never call this function, but you need it for development and testing. This function also calls the helper function `processNotificationWithUserInfo(_:withCompletion:)`.

Now add the following method to the end of the class:

```
// 1
func processNotificationWithUserInfo(
  userInfo: [NSObject : AnyObject], withCompletion
    completionHandler:(WKUserNotificationInterfaceType)->Void) {

  // 2
  messageLabel.setHidden(true)
  if let message = userInfo["message"] as? String {
    messageLabel.setHidden(false)
    messageLabel.setText(message)
  }

  // 3
  titleLabel.setHidden(true)
  if let title = userInfo["title"] as? String {
    titleLabel.setHidden(false)
    titleLabel.setText(title)
  }

  // 4
  completionHandler(.Custom)
}
```

Let's go through this code step by step:

1. `processNotificationWithUserInfo(_:withCompletion:)` receives a `userInfo` dictionary and a `completionHandler`. The `userInfo` dictionary contains the recipe details. The completion handler is simply passed through from `didReceiveLocalNotification(_:withCompletion:)` and `didReceiveRemoteNotification(_:withCompletion:)`.
2. If the `userInfo` dictionary contains a message string, you show the label and set the text to the message, which is the direction for the expired timer.
3. If the `userInfo` dictionary contains a title string, you show the label and set the text to the title, which is the recipe name.
4. Finally, you call the completion handler with the `Custom` type. By specifying `Custom` for the type, you're telling WatchKit that you want it to use your custom long look interface instead of the static interface. Specifying `Default` would load the static interface.

Now open **Interface.storyboard**, select the dynamic notification interface and in the Identity Inspector set the **Class** to **KitchenTimerNotificationController**.

Time to wire up the outlets for the title and message.

Show the **assistant editor** and Control-drag from the **<title>** label to the `titleLabel` outlet declared in the code.

Do the same thing for the **<message>** label, but drag to the `messageLabel` outlet instead.

With the notification scheme selected, **build and run**. You'll see the following customized, dynamic long look notification.

Great work! Now you know how to add custom notification interfaces to your Watch apps.

Next, you'll get the View Directions button working.

Handling actions

The system automatically adds the View Directions button when it receives a notification with the timer category. When the user taps on an action, the action identifier `viewDirectionsButtonAction`, is passed to the Watch app's initial interface.

Open **InitialInterfaceController.swift** and add the following code to the bottom of the class:

```
// 1
let recipeStore = RecipeStore()

// 2
override func handleActionWithIdentifier(identifier: String?,
  forLocalNotification localNotification: UILocalNotification) {
  if let userInfo = localNotification.userInfo {
    processActionWithIdentifier(identifier,
      withUserInfo: userInfo)
  }
}

// 3
override func handleActionWithIdentifier(identifier: String?,
  forRemoteNotification remoteNotification:
  [NSObject:AnyObject]){
  processActionWithIdentifier(identifier,
    withUserInfo: remoteNotification)
}
```

Here's what you're doing in this code:

1. You create a constant to hold a reference to the `RecipeStore` so that the system can find recipes when users tap on the View Directions button in a kitchen timer notification.
2. You override `handleActionWithIdentifier(_:forLocalNotification:)`, which the system calls when a user taps on an action button in a local notification. You provide the action identifier string and the notification. If a `userInfo` dictionary is present, you call the helper function `processActionWithIdentifier(_:withUserInfo:)`.
3. Just as you did with `handleActionWithIdentifier(_:forLocalNotification:)`, you override `handleActionWithIdentifier(_:forRemoteNotification:)`, which the system calls whenever a user taps on an action button for a remote notification. Because the kitchen timer notification you're building is a local notification, the app you ship will never call this function, but you need it for development and testing. This function also calls the helper function `processActionWithIdentifier(_:withUserInfo:)`.

Now add the following code to the bottom of `InitialInterfaceController`:

```
func processActionWithIdentifier(identifier: String?,
  withUserInfo userInfo: [NSObject : AnyObject]) {
```

```
  // 1
  if identifier == "viewDirectionsButtonAction" {

    // 2
    if let title = userInfo["title"] as? String {
      // 3
      let matchingRecipes =
        recipeStore.recipes.filter({$0.name == title})
      // 4
      pushControllerWithName("RecipeDirections",
        context: matchingRecipes[0])
    }
  }
}
```

Let's go through the code step by step:

1. You check the identifier to see if the user tapped the View Directions button. The `viewDirectionsButtonAction` identifier for the timer category is set up in **AppDelegate.swift**.
2. You check the `userInfo` dictionary for a title string. For the kitchen timer notification, the title string is the recipe name.
3. You retrieve the recipe object with the correct name from `recipeStore`. You use `filter` to remove all recipes that don't have the correct name.
4. Finally, you use the first recipe in the results array `matchingRecipes` to show the Recipe Directions interface.

Now open **Interface.storyboard**, select the Recipe Directions scene, and set the **Identifier** to **RecipeDirections** in the Identity Inspector.

With the notification testing scheme selected, **build and run**. When the notification interface appears, tap on the **View Directions** button. You'll be taken directly to the directions for the recipe associated with the expired timer.

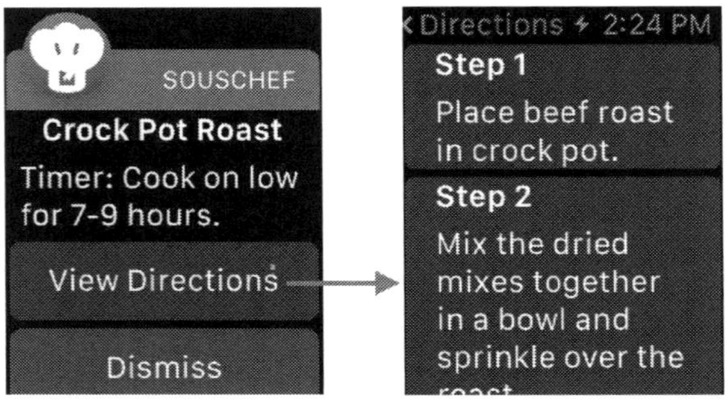

Scheduling local notifications

So far, you've built a custom long look notification interface and you've even implemented action-handling logic. But right now, you can only schedule kitchen timer notifications via the iPhone app. Wouldn't it be helpful if you could schedule kitchen timers from the Watch app?

Now you'll add a modally-presented interface that will appear whenever a user taps on a recipe direction that includes a timer.

Open **Interface.storyboard** and drag an **interface controller** from the Object Library onto the storyboard. Set the **Identifier** to **TimerScheduler** in the Identity Inspector.

Add a label to the interface to ask the user if she wants to start the timer. After adding the label, select it, and then open the Attributes Inspector. Set the **Text** to **<message>**, the **Font** to **Headline**, the **Lines** to **0**, and the **Horizontal** and **Vertical** positions to **Center**.

Next, add two buttons to the interface:

- The first button will start the kitchen timer. Set its **Title** to **Start** and the **Horizontal** and **Vertical** positions to **Center**.
- The second button will cancel the kitchen timer and dismiss the interface. Set its **Title** to **Cancel** and the **Horizontal** and **Vertical** positions to **Center**.

Once you're done adding the label and buttons, the interface will look like this:

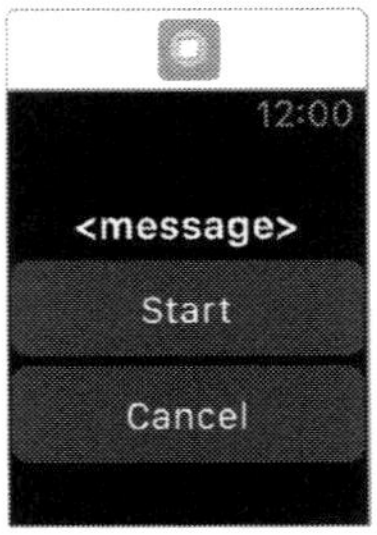

If the label and buttons are in a different order, you can drag them around right on the scene or in the document outline.

Next, you'll write the code for this interface. Don't worry—it's really simple.

With the project navigator visible, right-click on the **Interface Controllers** group in **SousChef WatchKit Extension** and select **New File...**. Select **iOS\Source\Swift File** and click **Next**.

Name the file **TimerSchedulerInterfaceController.swift** and ensure you add it to the **SousChef WatchKit Extension** target.

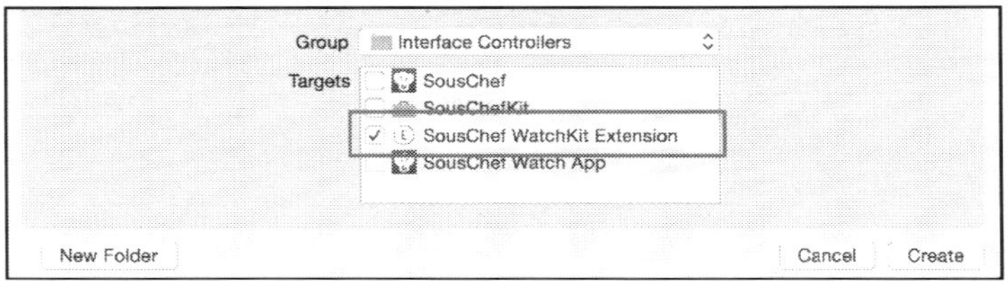

Add the following code to the new file:

```
import WatchKit
import SousChefKit

class TimerSchedulerData {
  let recipe:Recipe
  let stepInstruction: String
  let timer:Int

  init(recipe: Recipe, stepInstruction: String, timer: Int) {
    self.recipe = recipe
    self.stepInstruction = stepInstruction
    self.timer = timer
  }
}
```

This code first imports **WatchKit** and then imports the shared framework **SousChefKit**.

Next, the code creates a small class called `TimerSchedulerData`. `RecipeDirectionsController` will use this class to pass the necessary data to the scheduler. The class includes three constants: `recipe`, `stepInstructions` and `timer`, all of which are necessary to populate the interface.

Now add the following code to the end of the file:

```
// 1
class TimerSchedulerInterfaceController: WKInterfaceController {

  // 2
  @IBOutlet weak var messageLabel: WKInterfaceLabel!

  // 3
  var recipe: Recipe!
  var stepInstruction: String!
  var timer: Int!

  // 4
  override func awakeWithContext(context: AnyObject!) {
    if let timerSchedulerData = context as? TimerSchedulerData {
      recipe = timerSchedulerData.recipe
      stepInstruction = timerSchedulerData.stepInstruction
      timer = timerSchedulerData.timer
      messageLabel.setText("Start \(timer) minute timer?")
    }
  }
}
```

Here's what it does:

1. The code creates the class `TimerSchedulerInterfaceController`, a subclass of `WKInterfaceController`.
2. Then it creates the `messageLabel` outlet. This label will hold a question asking the user if he wants to start the timer.
3. The code then declares the `recipe`, `stepInstruction` and `timer` variables.
4. Finally, the code overrides `awakeWithContext(_:)`. The context parameter will be an instance of the `TimerSchedulerData` class you created earlier. The code sets the `messageLabel` text based on the value of the timer parameter.

Now you simply need to write the code for handling the button taps.

Add the following code to the end of the `TimerSchedulerInterfaceController` class declaration:

```
// 1
@IBAction func startButtonTapped() {
  let userInfo: [NSObject : AnyObject] = [
    "category" : "timer",
    "timer" : timer,
    "message" : "Timer: \(stepInstruction)",
    "title" : recipe.name
  ]
  WKInterfaceController.openParentApplication(userInfo, reply: {
      (userInfo:[NSObject:AnyObject]!, error: NSError!)->Void in
    self.dismissController()
  })
}

// 2
@IBAction func cancelButtonTapped() {
  dismissController()
}
```

This code does the following:

1. The Watch app will call `startButtonTapped()` whenever the user taps Start. This function packages together in the `userInfo` dictionary the information needed to schedule the local notification. Then it passes the `userInfo` dictionary to the `WKInterfaceController` class function `openParentApplication(_:reply:)`, which calls the iPhone app in the background. When it's finished scheduling the local timer, it will call the reply closure to dismiss the interface.

   Don't worry about `openParentApplication(_:reply:)` just yet. You'll learn how it works later in this chapter.

2. `cancelButtonTapped()` dismisses the interface whenever the user taps Cancel.

Because the Watch isn't capable of scheduling local notifications, you have to pass the necessary data to the containing iPhone app so that it can schedule the notification on behalf of the Watch app. It makes the code more complicated, but it's the only way with the current release of WatchKit.

You've now written all the necessary code for `TimerSchedulerInterfaceController`. All that's left is to wire up the outlet and actions in Interface Builder.

Open **Interface.storyboard** and use the Identity Inspector to change the class of your new interface controller to **TimerSchedulerInterfaceController**. Then, using the

assistant editor, Control-drag from the **<message>** label to the `messageLabel` outlet you already declared in the code.

To connect the Start and Cancel buttons, simply Control-drag from the buttons to the `startButtonTapped()` and `cancelButtonTapped()` functions, respectively.

Now you need show the new interface whenever the user taps on a recipe direction that has a timer.

Open **RecipeDirectionsInterfaceController.swift** and add the following method to the class:

```
override func table(table: WKInterfaceTable,
  didSelectRowAtIndex rowIndex: Int) {
  if let timer = recipe?.timers[rowIndex] {
    if timer > 0 {

      let timerSchedulerData = TimerSchedulerData(
        recipe: recipe!,
        stepInstruction: recipe!.steps[rowIndex],
        timer: timer)

      presentControllerWithName("TimerScheduler",
        context: timerSchedulerData)
    }
  }
}
```

As you can see, this code checks if the recipe direction includes a valid timer, then shows the `TimerScheduler` interface with the necessary data. It uses the helper class `TimerSchedulerData` for the context parameter.

You're almost done! The last thing you need to do is add a function to the iOS app's application delegate to handle the watch-to-phone communication.

Open **AppDelegate.swift** in the iPhone app group and find `application(_:handleWatchKitExtensionRequest:reply:)`. Replace the method with the following implementation:

```
func application(application: UIApplication!,
  handleWatchKitExtensionRequest
    userInfo: [NSObject : AnyObject]!,
      reply: (([NSObject : AnyObject]!) -> Void)!) {
  // 1
  if let category = userInfo["category"] as? String {
    // 2
    if ((application.currentUserNotificationSettings().types &
      UIUserNotificationType.Alert) != nil)
```

```
      && category == "timer" {
        scheduleTimerNotificationWithUserInfo(userInfo)
        // 3
        if (reply != nil) {
          reply(nil)
        }
      }
    } else {
      let kGroceryUpdateRequest =
        "com.raywenderlich.update-recipes"
      if let updateRecipesRequest =
       userInfo[kGroceryUpdateRequest] as? Bool {
        updateRecipesWithRemoteServerWithCompletionBlock {
          (Void) -> Void in
          reply(nil)
        }
      }
    }
  }
```

The system executes `application(:handleWatchKitExtensionRequest:reply:)` when the Watch app calls `openParentApplication(_:reply:)`.

1. First, the method checks the `userInfo` dictionary for the category string.
2. Next the method checks the user's notification settings. If the user has disabled notifications, there's no point in scheduling the kitchen timer since it won't be visible. It also checks if it's the `timer` category. Then the method calls `scheduleTimerNotificationWithUserInfo(_:)`, which simply schedules the local notification.
3. Finally, if a `reply` closure exists, the method calls it. This completes the round trip, starting with the Watch, moving to the phone and then back to the Watch.

The rest of the method inside the `else` block is the code that was already there to handle data updates.

Select the Watch app scheme then **build and run**. Tap on a **recipe**, then **directions**, and finally a **direction that has a timer**. You'll see the new kitchen timer scheduler interface.

Tap on **Start**.

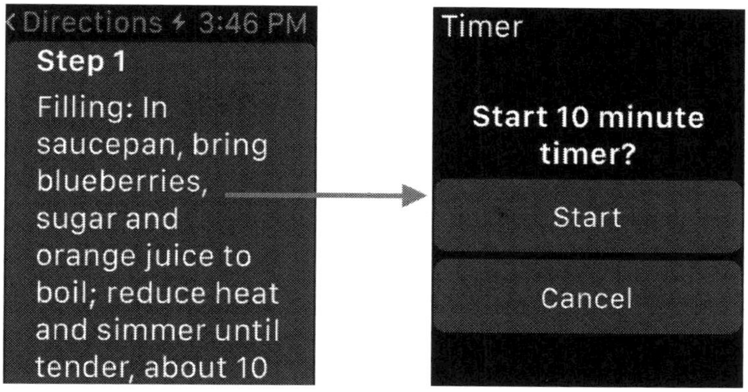

You're really cooking up a storm here! You took the raw ingredients and made a delicious app that supports creating and receiving custom notifications.

> **Note**: You must run the iPhone app at least once before trying to schedule a notification from the Watch app. On first launch, iOS will present a dialog asking the user for permission to present user-facing notifications. Tap OK when you see this dialog.

Where to go from here?

In this chapter, you tested Watch notifications, learned about short look and long look interfaces and how they differ, and most impressively, you built a custom, dynamically updated, long look local notification as a kitchen timer for the Apple Watch.

After all you've done in this chapter, you've probably worked up quite the appetite. Once you've eaten, maybe after testing a recipe for crock pot roast, come back and practice your skills in the challenge below.

Still have an appetite for notifications? Check out the "Setting Up Notifications in the iPhone App" and "Setting Up a Push Notification Server" sections in the appendix.

Then proceed to the next chapter, where you'll learn how to use images and animations to spice up your Watch app interface.

Cooking up a challenge

With your newfound knowledge, create a recipe remote notification interface for the Watch that informs the user when a new recipe is available. When you're finished, it should look like this:

The interface should include an image of the prepared dish, the name of the recipe, a brief message, the number of ingredients required, the number of steps and finally, a button to view the recipe.

Just as with the kitchen timer, you'll need to add a new notification scene to **Interface.storyboard**. Then, you'll need to create a new `WKUserNotificationInterfaceController` subclass and override `didReceiveRemoteNotification(_:withCompletion:)`.

To download the recipe image, you should use the `NSURLSession` method `dataTaskWithRequest(_:completionHandler:)`. In the `completionHandler` closure, be sure to call the `didReceiveRemoteNotification(_:withCompletion:)` completion handler so WatchKit knows you're finished customizing the interface.

Create a second APNS file and use the following JSON payload to test the notification:


```
{
  "aps": {
    "alert": {
      "body": "New Crock Pot Roast recipe is now available.",
      "title": "Crock Pot Roast"
    },
    "category": "new_recipe"
  },

  "WatchKit Simulator Actions": [
    {
      "title": "View Recipe",
      "identifier": "viewRecipeButtonAction"
     }
  ],

  "ingredients": "5",
  "steps": "4",
  "imageURL": "http://img.sndimg.com/food/image/upload/w_266/v1/
     img/recipes/27/20/8/picVfzLZo.jpg",
}
```


If you get stuck, check out the solution found in the resources for this chapter. But no peeking until you've given it your best shot!

Section III: Advanced WatchKit

In this section, you'll approach the more advanced topics of WatchKit, beginning with how WatchKit handles animation—spoiler: there's no Core Animation!—as well as how to cache images on the Watch itself. Then, you'll move on to adding iCloud sync by updating both the iPhone and Watch SousChef apps to use `UIDocument`. Next, you'll take a deeper dive into some of the pitfalls you may stumble upon when creating apps for the Watch, and how to work around them. And finally, you'll see what it takes to increase the international reach of your Watch app by learning all about localization and internationalization.

Chapter 12: Image Caching and Animation

By Jack Wu

By now, you've seen most of what WatchKit has to offer. You've probably also noticed that the Watch app you've been making isn't all that *visual*. Yes, there are tables and buttons with images, but it's just not in the same league as the Health & Fitness app Apple demoed in the keynote announcement:

At first glance, this interface seems impossible to create with the seemingly limited power of the WatchKit layout system, and the lack of a general purpose animation framework like Core Animation.

This chapter will show you that with a clever use of images, it's actually much easier than you think. :]

Don't get too excited just yet; this chapter will first go through the basics of how to both cache images and make use of animated images. These are both important topics to cover since you don't want to be sending images repeatedly over the wire when they can be cached on the Watch; it's terribly inefficient. And to be able to build a delightful interface you're going to need to know about how WatchKit handles animation.

Then, you'll learn ways to automatically generate animation frames that you can use in your Watch app so you don't need to create each frame of the animation manually, by hand.

Once you've covered all that, you'll be fully equipped to tackle the beautiful Fitness app interface.

Images in WatchKit

If you've worked through all of the preceding chapters in this book, then you're likely very familiar with using `WKInterfaceImage` to display images.

If you glance at the API of `WKInterfaceImage`, you'll find there are *three* different methods to display images:

- `setImage(_:)`
- `setImageData(_:)`
- `setImageNamed(_:)`

There's only a small difference between `setImage(_:)` and `setImageData(_:)`. They both send an image from the iPhone to the Watch, but when you have bitmap data, you can use `setImageData(_:)` for a performance boost, as it saves the overhead of creating an instance of `UIImage`.

`setImageNamed(_:)`, on the other hand, *doesn't* send any images from the iPhone to the Watch. Instead, it only sends the name of an image, and the Watch will load that image from either its **bundle** or **on-device cache**.

Thus, `setImageNamed(_:)` is the fastest and most efficient of the three, and you should try to use it whenever possible. You should treat the other two as convenience methods and use them when you're certain the app will display the image only **once**.

> **Note:** These differences also apply to the `setBackgroundImage(_:)`, `addAnnotation(_:withImage:centerOffset:)` and `addMenuItemWithImage(_:title:action:)` methods found in the other interface elements and controllers in WatchKit. Read through the appropriate class documentation for more information.

You've probably heard of the **on-device cache** several times by now—it's time to dig right into it!

Caching images

As with all APIs in WatchKit, the caching API is simple, read-only and optimizes for the least amount of communication between the iPhone and the Watch. Sounds like a divorce is coming their way. :[

That means you're going to have to do a bit more work to make caching work for you.

There are four methods on `WKInterfaceDevice` that deal with the cache:

- `addCachedImage(_:name:)`
- `addCachedImageWithData(_:name:)`
- `removeCachedImageWithName(_:)`
- `removeAllCachedImages()`

The first two methods return a `Bool` that tells you whether or not the caching was successful. A `false` value indicates that the 20MB cache—yes, you read that right, twenty megabytes—is full and you need to evict some images.

The remaining two methods, as their names suggest, remove images from the cache.

WatchKit also provides the `cachedImages` property that tells you which images already exist in the cache. This returns a dictionary with the cached image names as the keys and instances of `NSNumber` containing the size of the image as the values.

Really, *really* simple isn't it? It boils down to just two actions: cache an image and remove an image.

With that in mind, here's a simple two-step guide to follow when using the cache:

1. Only cache an image if it isn't already cached. You can determine this using `cachedImages`.
2. If the cache is full, evict images until the new image is successfully cached.

> **Cache Eviction**—The second step here raises an age-old question in computer science—*which object should I evict from the cache?* The ideal strategy here is to evict the images that are least likely to be used again in the future.
>
> Since you cannot predict the future in most cases, there are a few caching strategies that work pretty well. The most popular ones are "least recently used (LRU)", "least frequently used (LFU)", and "first in first out (FIFO)". You can choose between these on a case-by-case basis.
>
> There is plenty of existing material online about cache eviction so this chapter will avoid diving into this topic and go with an even simpler strategy—random eviction.

Great! Now that you've learned all about images and caching in WatchKit, it's time to put that knowledge to good use!

Displaying recipe images

Let's return to your favorite recipe app—SousChef!

In this section, you'll return to the Watch app you've been building throughout the rest of the book and spice it up a bit by displaying the recipe images in the recipe detail interface. You'll finally be able to see what the resulting dish is *supposed* to look like!

Open up **SousChef** in Xcode and then open **Interface.storyboard** from the SousChef WatchKit App group. You can use the version of SousChef that you've been working on or grab the starter project provided for this chapter.

> **Note**: As with the rest of this book, this chapter builds on the chapters that precede it. If you're beginning with the starter project for this chapter because you've skipped previous chapters or simply want to start with a clean slate, you'll need to set up the necessary provisioning profiles and enable App Groups in order to share recipes between the containing iPhone app and the Watch app. For more information on what's required, see Chapter 8, "Sharing Data".

Find the **RecipeDetail Scene** and add a new **group** to the top of the scene. Change the following attributes in the Attributes Inspector:

- Change **Layout** to **Vertical**
- Change **Mode** to **Aspect Fill**
- Set **Width** to **Relative to Container**
- Set **Height** to **Fixed** with a value of **60**

Now move the label into the new group and change its **Vertical** position attribute to **Bottom**. This label will show the recipe name, so set its text to **Recipe Name** to remind you what it's for.

The scene should now look like this:

You need to set the background image of this new group, so create an IBOutlet for the new group in **RecipeDetailInterfaceController.swift** called **nameGroup** and connect it to the new group.

Now locate the following two files in the resources for this chapter, **OnDeviceCacheHelper.swift** and **UIImage+Helpers.swift**. Import these two files into Xcode, making sure they're added to your **SousChef WatchKit Extension** group and target.

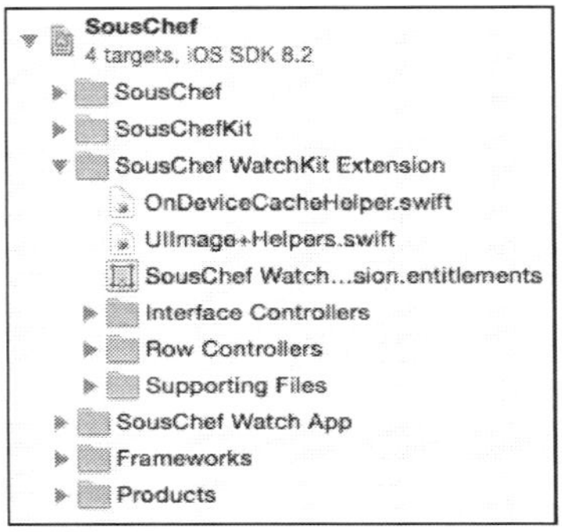

UIImage+Helpers.swift contains a few new methods. The first draws a color overlay onto an image, which will allow you to maintain the dark overlay you have in the main app. The second is a set of methods that resize an image to fill a certain frame, which is perfect for displaying images on the Watch!

OnDeviceCacheHelper.swift helps you with adding and removing images from the cache. Open **OnDeviceCacheHelper.swift** and take a quick look at the methods.

The class is really tiny and helps you add images and evict images from the cache. It also provides a convenience method to check whether or not an image is already cached. Here you only need to implement the most important method: `addImageToCache(_:name:)`.

Add the following code to `addImageToCache(_:name:)`:

```
// 1
let device = WKInterfaceDevice.currentDevice()
// 2
while (device.addCachedImage(image, name: name) == false) {
  // 3
  let removedImage = removeRandomImageFromCache()
  if !removedImage {
    // 4
    // Try one last time
    device.removeAllCachedImages()
    device.addCachedImage(image, name: name)
    break
  }
}
```

Here's the step by step explanation:

1. You get a reference to the current device on which to call the caching methods.
2. You use a `while` loop to evict images from the cache *until* your new one fits in. If `addCachedImage(_:name:)` succeeds the first time, the method won't execute the contents of the loop.
3. If `addCachedImage(_:name:)` fails, then your cache is full, so you remove a random image to try to make enough space. This is part of your random eviction strategy.
4. If you've already removed all the images and the cache *still* can't fit your new image, it probably means your image is too large. Here you make a last-ditch effort by removing all the cached images and trying one final time to cache the new image.

It's time to put `OnDeviceCacheHelper` to use. Open **RecipeDetailInterfaceController.swift** and add the following to the end of `awakeWithContext(_:)`:

```
// 1
if let imageName = recipe?.imageURL?.path?.lastPathComponent {
  // 2
  let cacheHelper = OnDeviceCacheHelper()
  // 3
  if cacheHelper.cacheContainsImageNamed(imageName) == true {
    // 4
    nameGroup.setBackgroundImageNamed(imageName)
  }

  // to be filled in later...
}
```

Here's what's happening:

1. You use `lastPathComponent()` on the URL to determine the name of the image.
2. You create an instance of the `OnDeviceCacheHelper`.
3. You check if the image is already in the cache.
4. If it is, you directly set it as the background image, using `setBackgroundImageNamed(_:)` for maximum performance.

That's all fine and dandy, but if the image hasn't been cached, you'll need to download it from the URL. Add the download code where the "to be filled in later" comment appears:

```
// 1
else if let imageURL = recipe?.imageURL {
  // 2
  dispatch_async(dispatch_get_global_queue(
    DISPATCH_QUEUE_PRIORITY_HIGH, 0)) {
    // 3
    let imageData = NSData(contentsOfURL: imageURL)!
    let recipeImage = UIImage(data: imageData)!
    // 4
    let retinaRect = CGRect(x: 0, y: 0,
      width: self.contentFrame.size.width * 2,
      height: self.contentFrame.size.height * 2)
    let resizedImage =
      recipeImage.resizedImageWithAspectRatioInsideRect(
      retinaRect)
    let overlayedImage = resizedImage.imageWithOverlayedColor(
       UIColor.blackColor().colorWithAlphaComponent(0.3))

    // 5
    dispatch_async(dispatch_get_main_queue()) {
      cacheHelper.addImageToCache(
        overlayedImage, name: imageName)
      self.nameGroup.setBackgroundImageNamed(imageName)
    }
  }
}
```

There's quite a lot happening here:

1. If the image isn't in the cache, you check if it has an `imageURL`.
2. Since you'll be making a network call, you'll need to execute it on a background thread.

3. You download the image data from the URL and use it to create an instance of `UIImage`.

4. Next, you resize the image and add a black overlay to it. It is *very important* that you resize images before you cache them, or you'll be sending a huge image over to the user's Watch. Remember, you only have 20MB of image cache.

5. Now that the image is ready, you dispatch back to the main thread and add it to the cache. Finally, you use `setBackgroundImageNamed(_:)` to set the background image on the group.

And that's it—your app is ready to show the recipe images!

Build and run. Navigate to a recipe page, and you'll see the app display the image after a short delay.

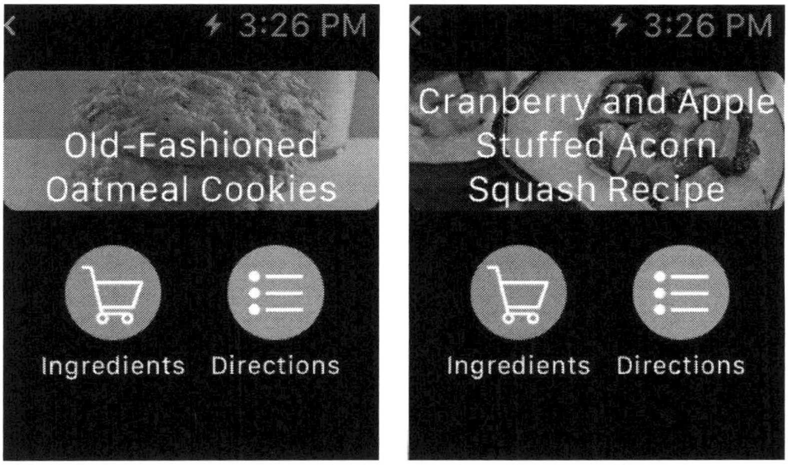

Go back a screen, or restart the app, and then navigate back to the same recipe, and you'll see the image appears immediately. Thanks to you, cache!

Animations in WatchKit

As you've already heard from earlier in this book, creating animations in Watch apps are *nothing* like the animations you know and love in iOS apps.

The only kind of animation WatchKit can perform is displaying a sequence of images, one at a time, to give the illusion of animation. Much like how a GIF works, or an old skool flipbook. Thus, WatchKit refers to these as **animated images**.

This is quite a big change from what you are used to in UIKit. You cannot animate properties, which means no elements zooming, panning, flying, zipping, bouncing or galloping around. WatchKit makes this all very simple—if you want animations, use a series of animated images.

The good news is that animated images are *just images*.

YOU DON'T SAY?

It might sound obvious, but this is important. It means that in most places, you can display an animated image in place of a regular image!

WatchKit even stores animated images just like regular images—using `UIImage`! `UIImage` has actually had this functionality since iOS 5, but it hasn't received much attention until now.

Animated images are created in the following two ways:

1. You can use the `UIImage` method `animatedImageWithImages(_: duration:)` to create an animation from a series of images. This is also how you should cache animations on the Watch. Do *not* send over all the frames individually; it won't work!
2. To create an animated image from images in your Watch app's bundle, you first need to number the frames by appending an integer to them, starting from 0, such as frame0.png, frame1.png and so on. You set the animated image to an interface element by using the `setImageNamed(_:)` set of methods and passing in the filename prefix, in this case "frame".

After you've set the animated image on an interface element, you can control the animation using these methods:

- `startAnimating()` starts the animation with the default values set in the storyboard.
- `startAnimatingWithImagesInRange(_:duration:repeatCount:)` starts the animation with the specified range, duration and repeat count. A repeat count of 0 will make the animation repeat forever.
- `stopAnimating()` stops the animation. No surprises here!

You're almost ready to start using animated images. The final missing pieces are—some actual images to animate!

Creating animations

There's one *major* difference between animated images and regular images: You need many, many images for an animated image. It's a tough ask to draw or source all of those individual frames.

This is definitely a task for the computer!

This section will show you how to use the familiar Core Graphics framework to generate frames to use.

Generating arcs

Generating story arcs *would* be quite awesome, but no, this section is about a different kind of arc, one that has a specific meaning for the Apple Watch.

Circular bars, or **arcs** as this chapter calls them, seem to be Apple's choice of interface on the Apple Watch. The first apps Apple demonstrated all have arcs to indicate progress:

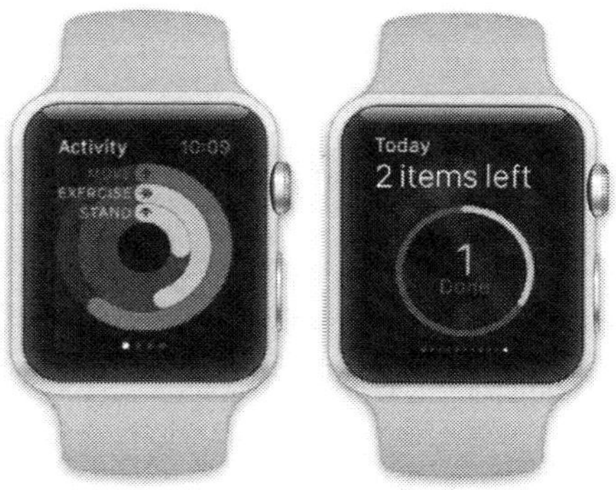

It's safe to say that arcs will be a staple in several Apple Watch interfaces. They definitely look at home on the dark, square screen.

To get started, open the Xcode project in the **ArcGenerator-Starter** folder in the resources for this chapter.

Here's a broad overview of the app's classes:

- `Arc`, as its name suggests, describes a single arc.
- `ArcAnimation` describes how an initial arc animates over time to create a full animation. It does so by specifying the initial arc and a function that generates the next "step" in the animation.
- `ArcGenerator` not only has the coolest name of the three classes—it also takes an `ArcAnimation`, draws its frames, and saves them all to disk. Cool, and useful!

These are a few simple concepts that are already implemented for you such as the implementation of arcs. You'll be making enhancements to them very soon, though!

Lastly, take a look at **ViewController.swift**. Here's the code that currently uses `ArcGenerator`:

```
let generator = ArcGenerator()
let animation = ArcAnimation.spinningArcAnimation()
animation.name = "spinning"
generator.generateArcAnimationFrames(animation)
```

This is just an example that's already implemented. First, it instantiates instances of the generator and animation. Then, it sets the name of the output files and folders, and calls `generateArcAnimationFrames(_:)` to generate the frames. Easy-peasy!

Build and run on the simulator. A few moments after the app launches, the console should print output similar to this:

```
Done generating frames "spinning" to path:
/Users/jackwu/Library/Developer/CoreSimulator/Devices/F5757BEE-
CD7C-4A21-883B-
174DE61DF38E/data/Containers/Data/Application/47F9B7C0-DBD0-
4B91-B1E7-4B7B6DEB842D/Documents/spinning
Done generating frames "progress" to path:
/Users/jackwu/Library/Developer/CoreSimulator/Devices/F5757BEE-
CD7C-4A21-883B-
174DE61DF38E/data/Containers/Data/Application/47F9B7C0-DBD0-
4B91-B1E7-4B7B6DEB842D/Documents/progress
```

That means it's done generating! **Copy** the path and then open your favorite terminal.

Type `open` and **paste** the copied path. Press **Return** and Finder should open, containing all of your animation frames:

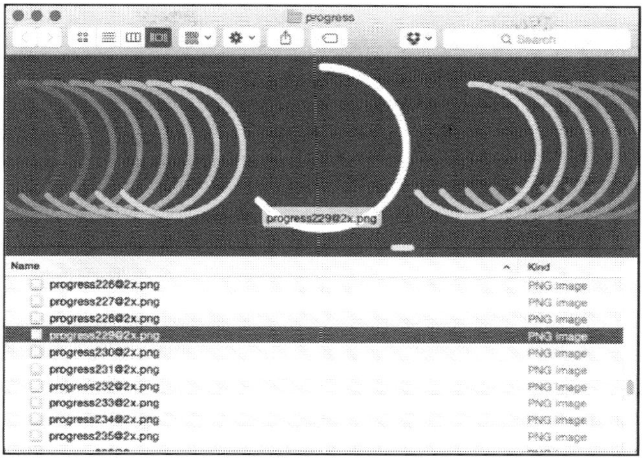

Not bad for default settings! However, it needs a little *oomph*.

Drawing custom arcs

You want something more like akin to this:

That definitely looks more like the arcs in Apple's apps. The current settings in `ArcGenerator` don't allow for drawing the empty arc, though. It looks like you're going to have to dive in and make some changes!

You draw arcs by calling `stroke()` on the `Arc` class. This is where you'll add code to draw the empty path color.

Open **Arc.Swift** and add two new animatable properties after `color:`

```
public var drawsEmptyArc: Bool
public var emptyArcColor: UIColor
```

These properties will define whether the empty arc should be drawn, as well as its color.

They'll need to be initialized, so replace the existing initializer with the following:

```
public init(radius: Int = 100,
  lineWidth: Int = 6,
  padding: Int = 0,
  startAngle: Double = 3.0*M_PI/2.0,
  endAngle: Double = M_PI,
  clockwise: Bool = true,
  color: UIColor = UIColor.whiteColor(),
  drawsEmptyArc: Bool = true,
  emptyArcColor: UIColor =
    UIColor.whiteColor().colorWithAlphaComponent(0.3)
  ) {
    self.radius = radius
    self.lineWidth = lineWidth
    self.padding = padding
    self.startAngle = startAngle
    self.endAngle = endAngle
    self.clockwise = clockwise
    self.color = color
    self.drawsEmptyArc = drawsEmptyArc
    self.emptyArcColor = emptyArcColor
}
```

Here you add the two new properties to the initializer and give them default values. Note the use of `colorWithAlphaComponent(_:)` to make the empty color a little transparent.

Now to draw the empty arc, add the following snippet to the very beginning of `stroke()`:

```
if drawsEmptyArc {
  emptyArcColor.setStroke()
  let fullCircle = UIBezierPath(arcCenter: center,
    radius: CGFloat(compensatedRadius),
    startAngle: CGFloat(0),
    endAngle: CGFloat(2.0 * M_PI),
    clockwise: true)
  fullCircle.lineWidth = CGFloat(lineWidth)
  fullCircle.stroke()
}
```

This code draws a full circle with `emptyArcColor` before the original arc is drawn. This way, the full empty circle is always drawn beneath the filled portion, creating the desired effect.

Lastly, you need to make use of this new code. Go to **ViewController.swift** and replace the code inside `viewDidLoad()` with this:

```
super.viewDidLoad()
let generator = ArcGenerator()
let animation = ArcAnimation.progressArcAnimation()
animation.name = "progress"
animation.initialArc.color = UIColor.magentaColor()
animation.initialArc.emptyArcColor =
  UIColor.magentaColor().colorWithAlphaComponent(0.3)
generator.generateArcAnimationFrames(animation)
```

This is almost the same code as before, except you set the arc's color to magenta.

All right! **Build and run**. Once that's complete, open the folder with the new assets, and you should see your awesome new arcs:

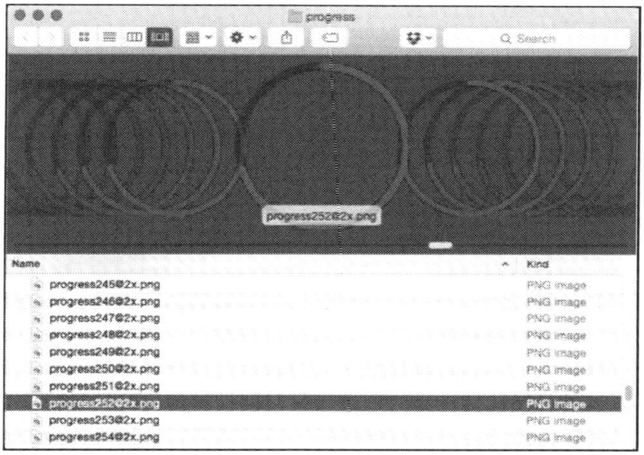

Are you beginning to feel confident about recreating Apple's Health & Fitness app interface? You definitely should be!

The `ArcGenerator` is all you need to recreate the interface. So no more waiting—it's time to put everything together and make something stunning.

Creating Health & Fitness-style arcs

In this section, you'll take these two steps to recreate the beautiful arcs from Apple's Health & Fitness app:

1. You'll generate three different colors of arc frames with the correct sizes.
2. Then, you'll set the arcs to your interface elements and animate them when the app starts.

Generating multi-ring arcs

Before you begin generating new arcs, you need to determine their parameters. This depends on how you plan to display these arcs to create the three-ring effect.

The strategy is quite simple: display images over each other by using nested groups of the same size. By setting the background of these nested groups with arcs of different diameter, you will be able to "stack" arcs to achieve the effect.

With a teensy little bit of math, you will create arcs like this:

Open **ArcGenerator** again in Xcode and go to **ViewController.swift**. Replace the contents of `viewDidLoad()` with this:

```
super.viewDidLoad()
// 1
let generator = ArcGenerator()
let width = 10
let radius = 60
let gap = 2

// 2
var animation = ArcAnimation.progressArcAnimation()
animation.totalFrames = 100
animation.name = "progressRed"
// 3
animation.initialArc = Arc(radius: radius,
  lineWidth: width, padding: 0,
  startAngle: 3.0 * M_PI / 2.0, endAngle: 3.0 * M_PI / 2.0,
  clockwise: true, color: UIColor.magentaColor())
animation.initialArc.emptyArcColor =
  UIColor.magentaColor().colorWithAlphaComponent(0.3)
animation.initialArc.lineWidth = width
// 4
generator.generateArcAnimationFrames(animation)
```

Here's what's going on:

1. You create the `ArcGenerator` and define constants for your arcs. The radius of 60 means the arc frames will be 120 points in width—perfect for the smaller Watch screen of 136 points.
2. You instantiate the default `progressArcAnimation`, set the total frames to 100 and name it "progressRed". Since you're generating three sets of frames, limiting it to 100 frames will prevent the bundle from growing too large.
3. Next, you set the parameters for the first arc, using `magentaColor` for the first, outermost arc.
4. Finally, you pass the animation to the `ArcGenerator`.

This will create the frames for the outermost arc. To create the remaining two, you need a bit of math. Add the following code to the end of `viewDidLoad()`:

```
animation = ArcAnimation.progressArcAnimation()
animation.totalFrames = 100
animation.name = "progressCyan"
animation.initialArc = Arc(radius: radius - (width + gap),
lineWidth: width, padding: width + gap,
  startAngle: 3.0 * M_PI / 2.0, endAngle: 3.0 * M_PI / 2.0,
  clockwise: true, color: UIColor.cyanColor())
animation.initialArc.emptyArcColor =
  UIColor.cyanColor().colorWithAlphaComponent(0.3)
generator.generateArcAnimationFrames(animation)

animation = ArcAnimation.progressArcAnimation()
animation.totalFrames = 100
animation.name = "progressGreen"
animation.initialArc = Arc(radius: radius - (width + gap) * 2,
  lineWidth: width, padding: (width + gap) * 2,
  startAngle: 3.0 * M_PI / 2.0, endAngle: 3.0 * M_PI / 2.0,
  clockwise: true, color: UIColor.greenColor())
animation.initialArc.emptyArcColor =
  UIColor.greenColor().colorWithAlphaComponent(0.3)
generator.generateArcAnimationFrames(animation)
```

The main differences in the two inner arcs, other than name and color, are `radius` and `padding`.

Since each arc is smaller in radius than the previous by `(width + gap)` points, you add that amount to the padding so the size of the frame remains the same. This will create all the frames with the same size.

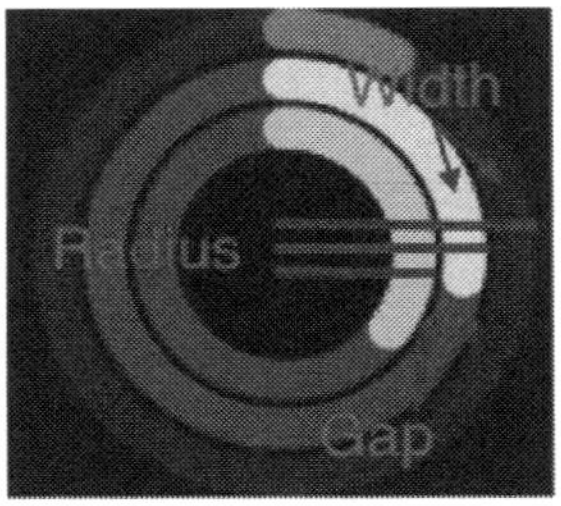

Build and run. When it's done generating, go grab all your frames from Finder, like before:

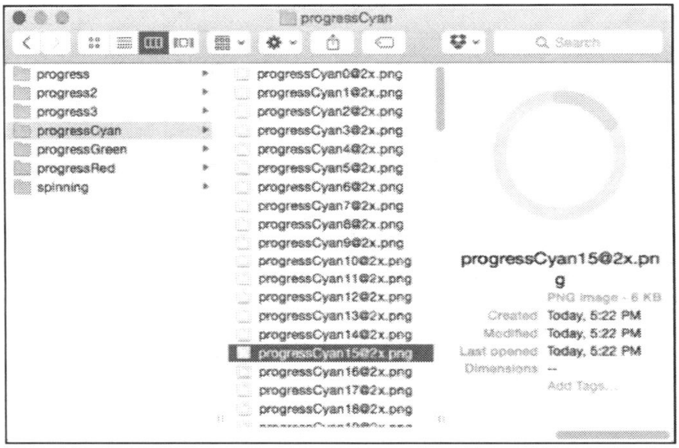

Adding your arcs to the interface—with animations!

Locate the **FitnessArcs** starter project and open it up in Xcode. This is a small project that you'll use to demonstrate animating your arcs.

Open **Interface.storyboard** and have a poke around. The initial interface is set up for you, with three nested groups, and three labels in the innermost group:

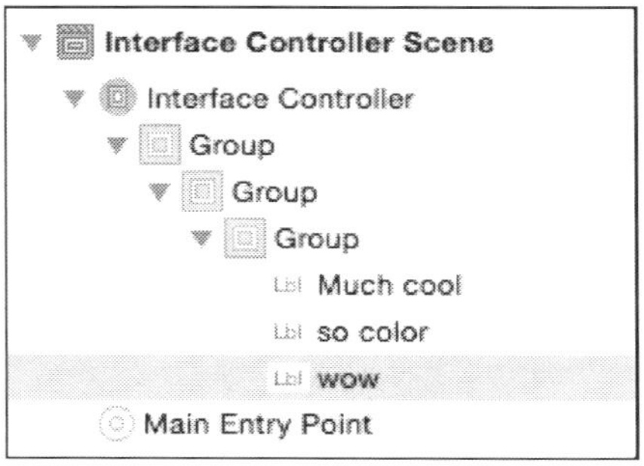

Now drag the folders containing all the arcs you generated and add them to both the **WatchKit App** group and target.

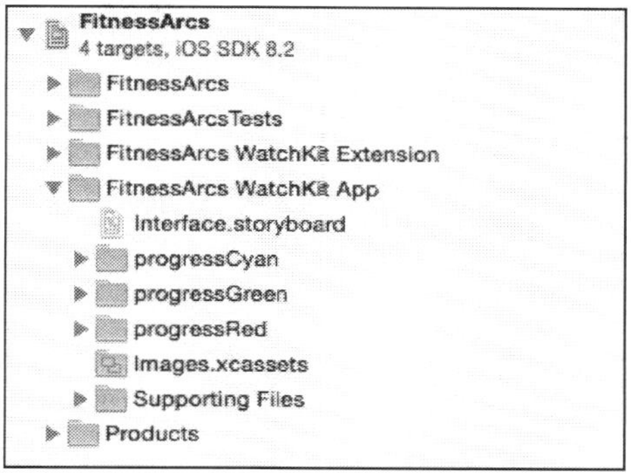

Open **InterfaceController.swift** found in the **WatchKit Extension** group and add the following snippet to the end of `awakeWithContext(_:)`:

```
redGroup.setBackgroundImageNamed("progressRed")
cyanGroup.setBackgroundImageNamed("progressCyan")
greenGroup.setBackgroundImageNamed("progressGreen")

redGroup.startAnimating()
cyanGroup.startAnimating()
greenGroup.startAnimating()
```

There's not much to say here, but recall that you set animations using `setBackgroundImageNamed(_:)` if the frames exist in the bundle.

Make sure the **FitnessArcs WatchKit App** scheme is selected and **build and run**. You'll see the bars animate around in circles—not what you want, but it's not bad for the first try!

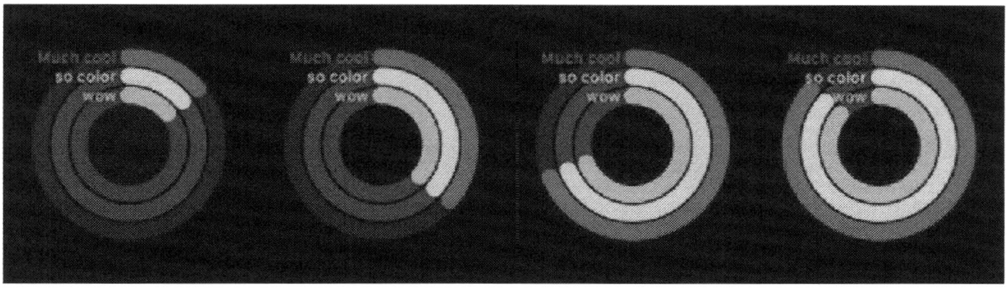

You don't want a continuous animation like this. You want the bars to start at 0, animate to a certain value and then stop.

Fortunately, `startAnimatingWithImagesInRange(_:duration:repeatCount:)` provides exactly what you need!

Delete the `startAnimating()` lines and replace them with the following:

```
redGroup.startAnimatingWithImagesInRange(
  NSMakeRange(0, 30), duration: 1, repeatCount: 1)
cyanGroup.startAnimatingWithImagesInRange(
  NSMakeRange(0, 45), duration: 1, repeatCount: 1)
greenGroup.startAnimatingWithImagesInRange(
  NSMakeRange(0, 85), duration: 1, repeatCount: 1)
```

Here, 30, 45 and 85 are arbitrary numbers for the "progress" these arcs indicate. A `repeatCount` of 1 tells the arc to animate once and stop, which is precisely what you want.

Build and run. Watch the arcs simultaneously animate to their endpoints and stop there. Gorgeous!

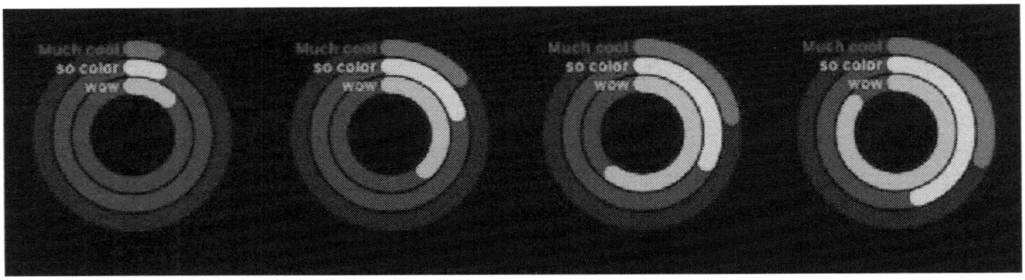

Where to go from here?

At this point, you not only have a thorough understanding of images and animations in WatchKit, you even have the tools and tricks to create some stunning and delightful interfaces!

Don't stop there, though—go the extra mile and add the little icons at the top of each arc to the Health & Fitness-style arcs. Here's a hint: draw the icon on *every frame* of the arcs. Your final app will be nearly identical to the image on the following page:

WatchKit may be much more restrictive than UIKit, but you don't have to let that stop you from creating beautiful and stunning interfaces.

Chapter 13: iCloud

By Audrey Tam

In Chapter 8, "Sharing Data" you used a shared container to synchronize recipes between the containing iOS app and the Watch app. But imagine this: You edit your grocery list on your iPad, but aren't wearing your Apple Watch at the time, and then you go grocery shopping with your iPhone and Apple Watch. If SousChef used only app groups to share the grocery list between your iOS devices and your Apple Watch, you wouldn't have the most up-to-date grocery list while you're out shopping. And if you want to make some of the tastiest Yorkshire puddings you'll ever have, then you're going to need an up-to-date grocery list!

iCloud to the rescue! Sharing the grocery list via Apple's iCloud service means that the iPhone, iPad and Watch can all share the same grocery list. Turns out you won't be forgetting the eggs and flour after all.

In this chapter, you'll move the data used by the `GroceryList` class to iCloud, allowing you to sync it between multiple devices. Whenever the user of the containing iOS app is signed into iCloud, it will use the iCloud document to be sure the grocery list is up to date; when there's no iCloud account, it will use the document stored in the shared container.

In this chapter, you'll learn how to:

- Implement a `UIDocument` subclass, and find or create a new document in both the shared and iCloud containers;
- View and manage your iCloud document on your iOS device;
- Turn iCloud access on and off in the simulator;
- Keep a `UIDocument` in sync between both the shared and iCloud containers.

Getting started

An app that uses iCloud storage keeps documents in a local iCloud-specific *container*, which periodically syncs with the user's iCloud Drive.

This container is often referred to as **ubiquitous**, which simply means that it exists everywhere simultaneously. You'll see a few property and method names that contain "ubiquitous" as you move through the rest of the chapter.

> **Note**: A big advantage of using iCloud is that most users sign into their iCloud accounts on all of their iOS devices the first time they switch them on, so your app doesn't have to present login forms or handle authentication.

Open the project you've been working on throughout the rest of this book, or alternatively open the starter project for this chapter and complete the setup instructions in Chapter 8, "Sharing Data":

1. Personalize `SOUSCHEF_BUNDLE_PREFIX`;
2. Set the **Team** to your iOS developer account in the three main targets and let Xcode create your provisioning profiles;
3. Enable the **App Groups** capability for both the **SousChef** and **SousChef WatchKit Extension** targets, and select the appropriate groups;
4. Update `kAppGroupIdentifier` in **RecipeStore.swift**.

Then, with the SousChef project selected in the Project Navigator, select the **SousChef** target and enable **iCloud** in the **Capabilities** pane:

1. Set the switch to **ON**;
2. Select **Services\iCloud Documents** and *uncheck* **Key-value storage**;
3. Make sure both **Containers\Use default container** and your default container name are selected.

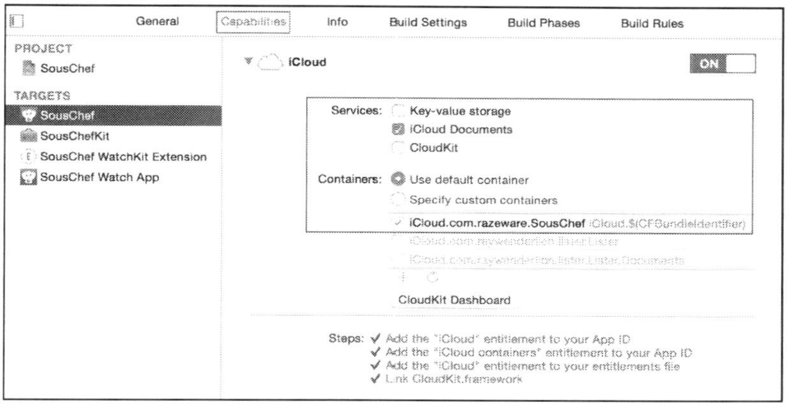

Now, do the same thing for the **SousChef Watchkit Extension** but select **Specify custom containers** along with your **SousChef** target's default container. To emphasize that you won't be using the WatchKit extension's default container, uncheck its checkbox:

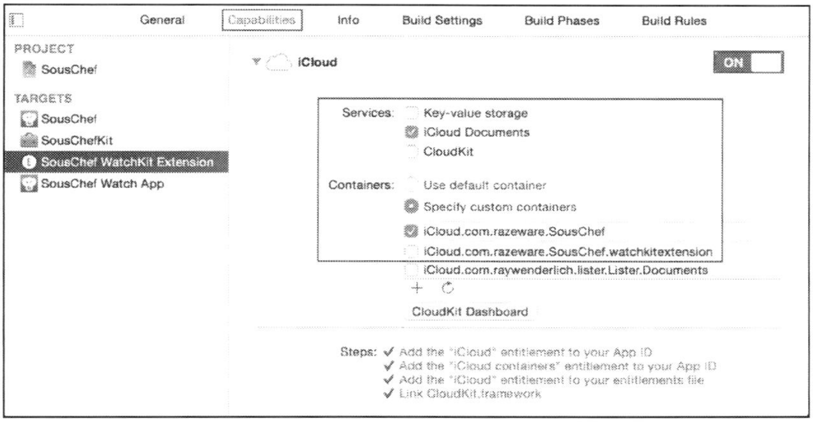

Each target gets its own iCloud container by default, so this step ensures the WatchKit extension will use the same container as the main app.

Open **SousChefKit\Storage\GroceryList.swift** and, in the `GroceryListConfig` struct, edit `groupID` and `iCloudID` to match the containers you set up in the target's App Group and iCloud capabilities; for example:

```
public static let groupID = "group.com.razeware.SousChef"
public static let iCloudID = "iCloud.com.razeware.SousChef"
```

> **Note**: These keys are case sensitive; make sure you enter them exactly as they're shown in *your* **Capabilities** pane.

Select the **SousChef** scheme and **build and run**. Add a recipe's ingredients to the grocery list. Your Groceries view will look similar to the following screenshot:

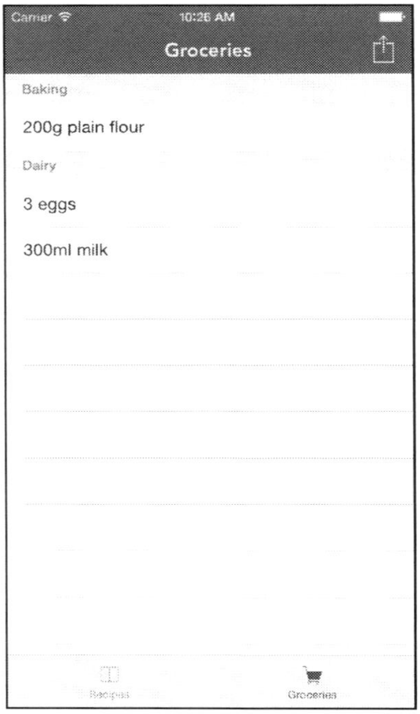

Mic's Yorkshire Puds—yum!!

Now select the **SousChef Watch App** scheme and **build and run**. The groceries you added in the iOS app aren't in the Watch app—don't worry, at this point this is very much expected behavior.

Add a different recipe's ingredients in the Watch app. Re-launch the iOS app just in the simulator—the Watch's groceries aren't shown there, either:

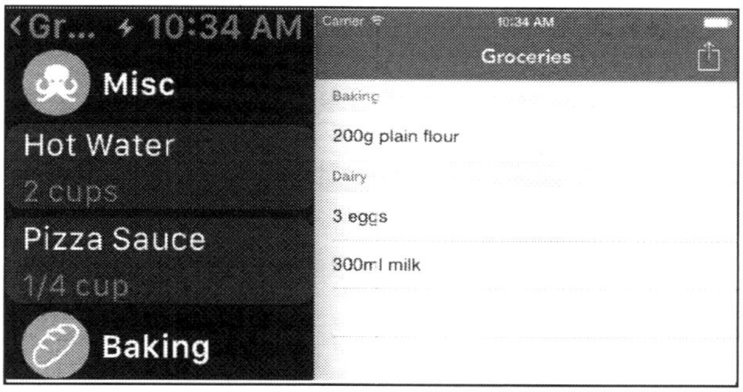

Pizza, not puds, on the Watch!

It should be pretty obvious by now that the two apps aren't sharing the grocery list, so you'll fix that first.

Sharing data as a UIDocument

You'll start by making `GroceryList` a subclass of `UIDocument`. You might be wondering why you haven't done this earlier, but up until now there hasn't been a requirement to share the grocery list. This requires several changes to GroceryList.swift and minor changes to the controllers that interact with the grocery list.

Storing this document in iCloud requires you add lot of code in `AppDelegate`, so it's quicker to test the `UIDocument` code with a shared app group document, which is what you'll do in this section. All of the `UIDocument` code works the same with both iCloud and app groups, and the final app will use the app group's document as a fallback whenever it doesn't have access to iCloud.

Open **SousChef\SousChefKit\Storage\GroceryList.swift**, find the `GroceryList` class and make it a subclass of `UIDocument`:

```
public class GroceryList: UIDocument
```

Doing this now enables you to use `UIDocument` methods to set up the grocery list document in `AppDelegate`. However, now that `GroceryList` inherits from `UIDocument`, Xcode will complain that `init()` should override its superclass's `init()`.

You don't need to override `UIDocument`'s initializer in this case; just find both `init()` and `init(useSample:)` and delete them.

Don't pay too much attention to the `reload()` statement in `init()`—that simply reloads the grocery list for each of the controllers that use `GroceryList`. Instead, you'll call the `UIDocument`-equivalent method in each of these controllers.

Setting up a UIDocument in an app group

The next step is to check for an existing grocery list document when the app starts. If it doesn't exist, create a new one.

Open **AppDelegate.swift** and add the following method:

```
func createNewGroceryListDoc() {
  let newGroceryListDoc = GroceryList(fileURL:
    GroceryListConfig.url)
  newGroceryListDoc.saveToURL(newGroceryListDoc.fileURL,
    forSaveOperation: UIDocumentSaveOperation.ForCreating,
      completionHandler: { success in
    if success {
      println("createNewGroceryListDoc: success")
    } else {
      println("createNewGroceryListDoc: failed")
    }
  })
}
```

This method uses the grocery list URL, which can be either the app group's URL or the iCloud URL. You call `UIDocument`'s designated initializer to allocate a new document with this URL and save it using the option `UIDocumentSaveOperation.ForCreating`. It is this save operation that creates the new, empty document.

Next, add the following convenience property to the class, just below `recipeStore`:

```
let fileManager = NSFileManager.defaultManager()
```

You'll use this property to check if you already have a grocery list document saved.

Now, add the following method:

```
func setupGroceryListGroupDoc() {
  GroceryListConfig.url = GroceryListConfig.groupURL
  // check for existing doc; create one if none exists
  if !fileManager.fileExistsAtPath(
    GroceryListConfig.url.path!) {
    println("setupGroceryListGroupDoc: create empty group doc")
    createNewGroceryListDoc()
  }
}
```

The first line sets the URL that the app uses to initialize the grocery list document—in this method, the app uses the app group's container URL, not the iCloud container URL. If the document already exists, that's all the setup you need to do in `AppDelegate`. If not, you call `createNewGroceryListDoc()` to create the document.

Now, in `application(_:didFinishLaunchingWithOptions:)`, call `setupGroceryListGroupDoc()`, just before returning `true`:

```
setupGroceryListGroupDoc()
```

You also need to add all of this code to the WatchKit extension to make sure it uses the same file.

Open **SousChef WatchKit Extension\Interface Controllers\InitialInterfaceController.swift** and add the same two methods and `fileManager` property to the class.

Since there's no `application(_:didFinishLaunchingWithOptions:)` in WatchKit interface controllers, add the following method to the class instead:

```
override func willActivate() {
  super.willActivate()
  setupGroceryListGroupDoc()
}
```

Now you have the same setup function for the UIDocument in both the iPhone app and the Watch app.

Implementing your data as a UIDocument

To implement `GroceryList` as a `UIDocument`, you must override two `UIDocument` methods:

- `loadFromContents(_:ofType:error:)` is invoked when reading the document; it receives the grocery list as an instance of `NSData` and initializes `GroceryList`'s data structures with it. This method is called by `openWithCompletionHandler(_:)`, which you'll call in the grocery and recipe controllers.
- `contentsForType(_:error:)` is invoked when writing the document; it provides a snapshot of the document as an instance of `NSData`, and is called by `saveToURL(_:forSaveOperation:completionHandler:)`, which is invoked whenever you call `sync()` in the grocery and recipe controllers.

Open **GroceryList.swift** and look at the methods in its **Persistence** section; they call the following methods:

- `syncedGroceryItems()`: returns the groceries from the data contained in the saved document.
- `saveCurrentState()`: saves the current groceries as data to the saved document.

Those two methods appear to match up perfectly with the two methods you need to override for `UIDocument` subclasses! The `data` constant of `syncedGroceryItems()` is the `contents` argument of `loadFromContents(_:ofType:error:)`, and the `data` constant of `saveCurrentState()`: is the return value of `contentsForType(_:error:)`:

```
// MARK: Persistence
public func sync() { saveCurrentState() }
public func reload() {
  list = syncedGroceryItems()
  table = updatedTable(list)
}

// MARK: Private
private func syncedGroceryItems() -> GroceryItems {
  if let data = NSData(contentsOfFile:
    savedGroceriesPath) {
    if let rawGroceries =
      NSKeyedUnarchiver.unarchiveObjectWithData(data)
      as? GroceryItems {
      return rawGroceries
    }
  }
  return GroceryItems()
}
private func saveCurrentState() {
  let data =
    NSKeyedArchiver.archivedDataWithRootObject(list)
  if !NSFileManager.defaultManager().createFileAtPath(
    savedGroceriesPath, contents: data, attributes: nil) {
    println("saveCurrentState: error saving grocery list")
  }
}
```

With a little rearranging, the two `UIDocument` methods fit nicely into the grocery list's read/write workflow.

First, replace the implementation of the following two methods:

```
// 1
private func reload(contents: NSData) {
  list = syncedGroceryItems(contents)
  table = updatedTable(list)
}
// 2
private func syncedGroceryItems(contents: NSData)
  -> GroceryItems {
  if contents.length > 0 {
    if let rawGroceries =
      NSKeyedUnarchiver.unarchiveObjectWithData(contents)
      as? GroceryItems {
      return rawGroceries
    }
  }
  return GroceryItems()
}
```

And edit `saveCurrentState()` to call `saveToURL(_:forSaveOperation:completionHandler:)`:

```
// 3
private func saveCurrentState() {
  saveToURL(fileURL, forSaveOperation:
    UIDocumentSaveOperation.ForOverwriting, completionHandler: {
      success in
    if success {
      println("saveCurrentState: document updated to container
        \(self.fileURL)")
    }
  })
}
```

These three methods lay the groundwork for implementing the two `UIDocument` methods, which you'll do very soon:

1. `reload(contents:)` is a revised version of the existing `reload()` method, which will receive its `contents` argument from `loadFromContents(_:ofType:error:)`. It passes `contents` to a revised `syncedGroceryItems(contents:)` method to create a `list`, then updates `table`, as before.

2. In `syncedGroceryItems(contents:)`, the `contents` argument replaces the need to call `NSData(contentsOfFile:)` as used by the existing `syncedGroceryItems()` method. The remaining contents of these two methods are identical.

3. `saveToURL(_:forSaveOperation:completionHandler:)` is a `UIDocument` method that will save its underlying `data` to the specified URL. It receives the grocery list as an instance of `NSData` from `contentsForType(_:error:)`, which you'll implement next.

Now add the following two `UIDocument` methods to the **Persistence** section:

```
// 1
override public func loadFromContents(contents: AnyObject,
  ofType typeName: String, error outError: NSErrorPointer)
    -> Bool {
  reload(contents as NSData)
  return true
}
// 2
override public func contentsForType(typeName: String, error
  outError: NSErrorPointer) -> AnyObject? {
  return NSKeyedArchiver.archivedDataWithRootObject(list)
}
```

From the viewpoint of these two methods:

1. `loadFromContents(_:ofType:error:)` simply passes its `contents` argument to `reload(contents:)`, which sets the `list` and `table` properties.
2. `contentsForType(_:error:)` returns the grocery list as an instance of `NSData`, which the `saveToURL(_:forSaveOperation:completionHandler:)` uses to save the document.

Before you clear out the now-unused code from **GroceryList.swift**, you need to check the other project files for any calls to `reload()`, as this is the only public method you've replaced.

Open **GroceriesController.swift** and find `viewWillAppear(_:)`. Remove the call to `reload()` here and your project should now build without any errors.

Your `UIDocument` subclass is now ready for the relevant controllers to use it to manage their data. But are the controllers ready to use *it?*

Updating controllers to manage a UIDocument

There are four controllers that interact with the grocery list.

There are two in the containing iOS app:

1. `GroceriesController` is responsible for displaying the grocery list, and allows the user to mark items as purchased and remove them from the list.

2. `RecipeDetailController` displays a recipe's ingredients, and allows the user to add them to the grocery list.

The remaining two controllers are in the Watch app:

1. `GroceryInterfaceController` does the same as `GroceriesController`.
2. `RecipeIngredientsInterfaceController` lets the user add all of a recipe's ingredients to the grocery list.

You need to make only three changes to each of these four controllers to update them to be compatible with the new `UIDocument` based `GroceryList`:

First, you need to initialize `groceryList` from its URL rather than creating a new instance each time. In all four controllers, replace:

```
groceryList = GroceryList()
```

With the following:

```
groceryList = GroceryList(fileURL: GroceryListConfig.url)
```

> **Note**: Xcode might complain that this isn't a valid initializer—just select **Product\Clean** to remove any old builds and remind Xcode that `GroceryList` is now a subclass of `UIDocument`.

The second step is the "meat in the sandwich", and it's a long one: call `openWithCompletionHandler(_:)`, either when the groceries view will appear or when the user adds recipe ingredients to the grocery list. Because the user can edit the grocery list on different devices, it's important to re-open the document each time the user needs it—you want to be sure the user always has the most up-to-date version of the grocery list.

Open **GroceriesController.swift** and replace the implementation of `viewWillAppear(_:)` with the following:

```
override func viewWillAppear(animated: Bool) {
  super.viewWillAppear(animated)

  groceryList.openWithCompletionHandler { success in
    if success {
      println("GroceriesController: opened groceryList")
      let purchasedItems = self.groceryList.purchasedItems()
      let uniqueIndexPaths = NSMutableSet()
```

```
      purchasedItems.map({ (var anItem) -> Void in
        if let indexPath =
self.groceryList.indexPathForItem(anItem) {
          uniqueIndexPaths.addObject(indexPath)
        }
      })
      self.selectedIndexPaths = uniqueIndexPaths.allObjects as
[NSIndexPath]
      self.tableView.reloadData()
    } else {
      println("GroceriesController: open groceryList failed")
    }
  }

  tableView.reloadData()
}
```

Rather than a simple load of the grocery list, `openWithCompletionHandler(_:)` tells the `UIDocument` to open its document asynchronously. The rest of the code in the completion handler is the same as before, to set up the list of purchased items.

Open **GroceryInterfaceController.swift** and delete the call to `updateTable()` in `awakeWithContext(_:)`—you're going to move this into `willActivate()` instead.

Override `willActivate()` and call `openWithCompletionHandler(_:)`, which again opens the document and updates the table when finished:

```
override func willActivate() {
  super.willActivate()
  groceryList.openWithCompletionHandler { success in
    if success {
      println("GroceryIC: opened groceryList")
      self.updateTable()
    } else {
      println("GroceryIC: open groceryList failed")
    }
  }
}
```

Now, open **RecipeDetailController.swift** and move the contents of `onPromptAddGroceries(sender:)` into a new method named `addGroceries()`:

```
func addGroceries() {
  let name = recipe?.name ?? "this recipe"
  let alert = UIAlertController(title: "Grocery List", message:
    "Do you want to add all of the ingredients for \(name)
    to your grocery list?", preferredStyle: .Alert)
```

```
    alert.addAction(UIAlertAction(title: "Add Items", style:
    .Default, handler: { _ in
    if let items = self.recipe?.ingredients {
      for item in items {
        self.groceryList.addItemToList(item)
      }
      self.groceryList.sync()
    }
  }))
  alert.addAction(UIAlertAction(title: "Cancel", style: .Cancel,
    handler: nil))
  presentViewController(alert, animated: true, completion: nil)
}
```

Next, call `openWithCompletionHandler(_:)` in `onPromptAddGroceries(sender:)`, as shown below:

```
func onPromptAddGroceries(sender: AnyObject) {
  groceryList.openWithCompletionHandler { success in
    if success {
      println("RecipeDetailController: opened groceryList")
      self.addGroceries()
    } else {
      println("RecipeDetailController: open groceryList failed")
    }
  }
}
```

This opens the grocery list only if the user selects the "add ingredients" option, and adds the ingredients only after opening the grocery list.

Next, open **RecipeIngredientsInterfaceController.swift** and move the contents of `onAddToGrocery()` into a new method named `addToGrocery()`:

```
func addToGrocery() {
  if let items = self.recipe?.ingredients {
    for item in items {
      groceryList.addItemToList(item)
    }
    groceryList.sync()
  }
}
```

Once again, call `openWithCompletionHandler(_:)` in `onAddToGrocery()`, as shown below:

```
@IBAction func onAddToGrocery() {
```

```
    groceryList.openWithCompletionHandler { success in
      if success {
        println("RecipeIngredientsIC: opened groceryList")
        self.addToGrocery()
      } else {
        println("RecipeIngredientsIC: open groceryList failed")
      }
    }
  }
```

You are now opening the shared document correctly between all the controllers, but you aren't closing them when done. This is the third and final step before you can test syncing between your Watch and its containing app.

To close the `UIDocument`, call `closeWithCompletionHandler(_:)` in `viewWillDisappear(_:)` in both **GroceriesController.swift** and **RecipeDetailController.swift**:

```
  override func viewWillDisappear(animated: Bool) {
    super.viewWillDisappear(animated)
    groceryList.closeWithCompletionHandler(nil)
  }
```

That leaves just two more places! Go to **GroceryInterfaceController.swift** and **RecipeIngredientsInterfaceController.swift** and override `didDeactivate()` in both:

```
  override func didDeactivate() {
    super.didDeactivate()
    groceryList.closeWithCompletionHandler(nil)
  }
```

Now that you've got your grocery list data managed by `UIDocument`, which both apps can access and all four controllers can use, there's only one thing left to do… test it out!

Testing your new sharing capability

Select the **SousChef** scheme and then **build and run**. Add some ingredients to the grocery list. Then, switch the scheme to the **SousChef Watch App** scheme and **build and run**. Go to each app's groceries page to confirm that they do in fact have exactly the same grocery list.

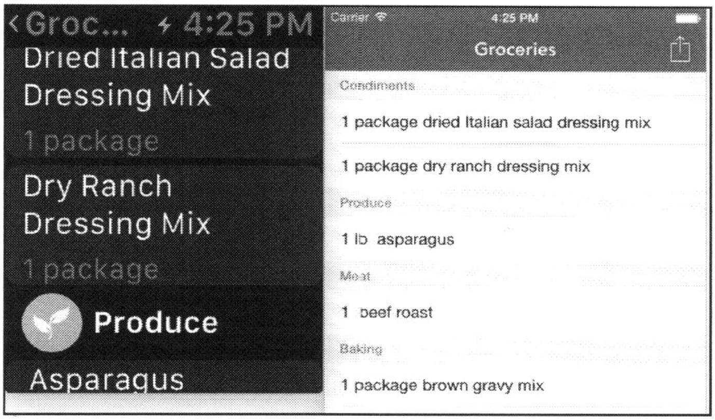

Back in the Watch app, add some more ingredients, then mark some as purchased.

Note: You might need to tap twice, to mark the first ingredient as purchased, but then a single tap should be enough to mark subsequent ingredients as purchased. Remember that the simulator reflects the performance of the real device as closely as possible, so response may not be immediate, and sometime might be dropped all together due to the Bluetooth song-and-dance that has to take place.

In the containing iOS app, tap the Recipes tab and then tap the Groceries tab to reopen the grocery list. Confirm that it contains the changes you made in the Watch app.

Make changes to the containing iOS app's grocery list, then back out and reopen the grocery list in the Watch app to see the changes. Your grocery list now syncs between both apps! Congratulations.

I'm feeling a little hungry… I'll just grab some roasted asparagus and meet you back here in a jiffy.

Up next—moving the grocery list into the cloud!

Sharing in iCloud

First things first; make sure you've set up your iOS simulator to use iCloud.

Boot it up and then go to **Settings\iCloud** and sign in to your iCloud account.

> **Note:** The iCloud account you use in the simulator doesn't have to be associated with your iOS developer account, but it must not use two-step verification—Apple's term for *two-factor authentication*. The simulator doesn't support this security system, which requires a verification code sent to one of your trusted devices, in addition to your password.

Setting up the iCloud document requires a few extra steps to construct its URL, and these involve asynchronous operations:

1. First, you need to construct and start an asynchronous metadata query to search for the document in the iCloud container.

2. If the query finds the iCloud document, you need to construct its URL based on the metadata.
3. If the query doesn't find the iCloud document, you need to make an asynchronous call to `URLForUbiquityContainerIdentifier(_:)` to configure the iCloud container, and then call `createNewGroceryListDoc()` to create a new document.

Earlier, you created a shared app group document by calling `createNewGroceryListDoc()`, which sets up a new document based on the `GroceryListConfig` URL. Now you'll use the same method, but with the iCloud URL instead.

Open **SousChef\AppDelegate.swift** and add the following method:

```
func setupGroceryListCloudDoc(query: NSMetadataQuery) {
  if query.resultCount > 0 {
    // construct cloudURL from metadata
    let item: NSMetadataItem = query.resultAtIndex(0)
      as NSMetadataItem
    let groceryListCloudURL =
      (item.valueForAttribute(NSMetadataItemURLKey) as NSURL)
    GroceryListConfig.cloudURL = groceryListCloudURL
    GroceryListConfig.url = GroceryListConfig.cloudURL
  } else {
    // construct cloudURL from URLForUbiquityContainerID
    dispatch_async(dispatch_get_global_queue
      (DISPATCH_QUEUE_PRIORITY_DEFAULT, 0)) {
      if let iCloudContainerURL =
        self.fileManager.URLForUbiquityContainerIdentifier(
          GroceryListConfig.iCloudID)
      {
        println("setupGroceryListCloudDoc: new cloud doc")
        let groceryListCloudURL = iCloudContainerURL.
          URLByAppendingPathComponent("Documents").
            URLByAppendingPathComponent(
              GroceryListConfig.filename)
        GroceryListConfig.cloudURL = groceryListCloudURL
        GroceryListConfig.url = GroceryListConfig.cloudURL

        self.createNewGroceryListDoc()
      }
    }
  }
}
```

This code checks the query results and updates the `GroceryListConfig.cloudURL` from the metadata. If there are no results, you create an iCloud document just as you did before using `createNewGroceryListDoc()`, but this time using the iCloud URL.

You need to call this method after a query to the iCloud container. Add the following property below `fileManager`:

```
var groceryListQuery = NSMetadataQuery()
```

You declare the query as a property so that the handler can access it when the query is complete.

Next, add the method that both constructs and starts the query:

```
func queryGroceryListCloudContainer() {
  groceryListQuery.searchScopes =
    [NSMetadataQueryUbiquitousDocumentsScope]
  groceryListQuery.predicate = NSPredicate(format: "(%K = %@)",
    argumentArray: [NSMetadataItemFSNameKey,
      GroceryListConfig.filename])
  NSNotificationCenter.defaultCenter().addObserver(self,
    selector: "metadataQueryDidFinishGathering:",
      name: NSMetadataQueryDidFinishGatheringNotification,
        object: groceryListQuery)
  groceryListQuery.startQuery()
}
```

The query's search scope is `UbiquitousDocuments`—that is, the iCloud container. The predicate sets it to search for an item in the container whose name matches the grocery list's filename. When the query finishes, `metadataQueryDidFinishGathering(notification:)` receives the notification.

Add the notification handler that you just assigned to the query:

```
@objc private func metadataQueryDidFinishGathering(notification:
  NSNotification) {
  groceryListQuery.disableUpdates()
  groceryListQuery.stopQuery()
  NSNotificationCenter.defaultCenter().removeObserver(self,
    name: NSMetadataQueryDidFinishGatheringNotification,
      object: groceryListQuery)
  setupGroceryListCloudDoc(groceryListQuery)
}
```

First, you do some standard query housekeeping; disable updates, stop the query, and stop observing the notification. Then you call `setupGroceryListCloudDoc(query:)`, the iCloud equivalent of `setupGroceryListGroupDoc()`.

Note: In an app that manages a collection of documents, you would register for `NSMetadataQueryDidUpdateNotification` and set the query predicate to a more general search, such as for certain file extensions. You would disable updates to "lock" the query result while you handle the found documents, then enable updates again once you've finished. You also wouldn't stop the query.

Now in `application(_:didFinishLaunchingWithOptions:)`, you'll call `queryGroceryListCloudContainer()` if iCloud is available, and `setupGroceryListGroupDoc()` if it isn't. Add the following **in place of** the call to `setupGroceryListGroupDoc()`:

```
if let currentToken = fileManager.ubiquityIdentityToken {
  println("iCloud access with ID \(currentToken)")
  queryGroceryListCloudContainer()
} else {
  println("No iCloud access")
  setupGroceryListGroupDoc()
}
```

Note: Checking for `ubiquityIdentityToken` is the quickest and easiest way to determine whether iCloud is available. If the user switches to another iCloud account, the token changes.

Just as you did when you set up the shared app group, you need to add all of this new code from **AppDelegate.swift** to **InitialInterfaceController.swift**.

Here's a checklist of what you need to add or replace:

1. `setupGroceryListCloudDoc(query:)`
2. The `groceryListQuery` property
3. `queryGroceryListCloudContainer()`
4. `metadataQueryDidFinishGathering(notification:)`
5. In `willActivate()`, replace the call to `setupGroceryListGroupDoc()` with the `if-else` code that checks for iCloud access

> **Note**: It's essential that both the Watch app and the containing iOS app use the same iCloud container, so double-check that now before continuing!

OK, are you ready to see some results? Perform exactly the same steps as you did in the section "Testing your new sharing capability" where you tested the syncing via a local shared container. Feel free to jump back a few pages and refresh your memory; I'll happily wait for you...

Once again, your grocery list syncs between the two apps! The console messages show that now you're using the iCloud document:

```
iCloud access with ID <264931d6 4dc648a3 6d3fa0eb 6284b87e
  e75ffa8d>
GroceriesController: opened groceryList
saveCurrentState: document updated to container
file:///Users/amt1/Library/Developer/CoreSimulator/Devices/3E4A3
E7E-D065-44BA-BE81-
637D690F5079/data/Library/Mobile%20Documents/iCloud~com~razeware
~SousChef/Documents/com.rw.souschef.groceries.json
```

Testing your work in iCloud

The `println()` messages in the console confirm that you're using iCloud storage, but you can also check this on your physical iPhone.

You can see the iCloud document on an iOS device that's signed into the same iCloud account as the simulator.

On that device, go to **Settings\iCloud\Storage\Manage Storage**, and scroll down in the **Documents & Data** section until you find SousChef. Here it is with an empty grocery list:

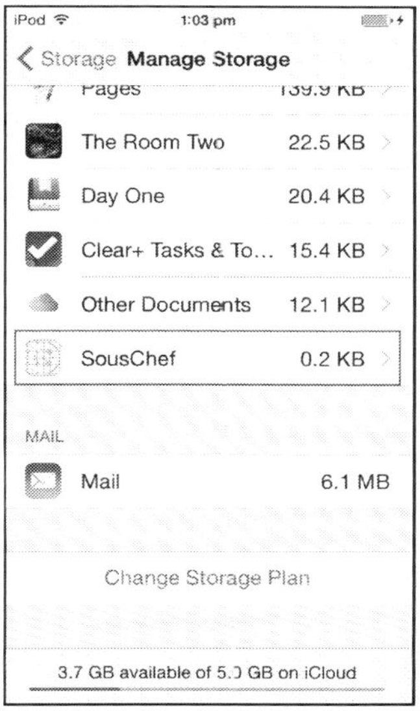

Add some groceries in either app; then, on your iOS device, go back to **Storage** and then reopen **Manage Storage** to see that the file is now bigger:

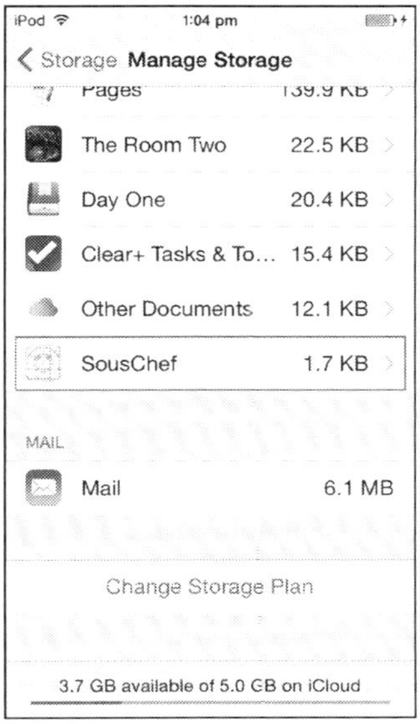

In **Manage Storage**, tapping on **SousChef** opens its detail view, where you can delete the document on your iOS device—tap **Edit**, then tap **Delete All**. Confirm your action in the alert view, and you should see the **Manage Storage** view after the deletion is complete.

You can also delete the iCloud document via **Xcode\Debug\iCloud\Delete Container Contents**, but neither of these actions is guaranteed to delete the iCloud document in the simulator. The only reliable way to do that is to sign out of iCloud on the simulator, delete the document from iCloud and then sign back in to iCloud on the simulator.

> **Note**: If you see more than one document in the SousChef container, you should definitely delete these files, and reset the simulator, to start with a clean slate.

Syncing with intermittent iCloud access

If there's no iCloud access, the iPhone app and the Watch app can fallback to using the document in the local shared container to keep the grocery list in sync between the two devices. But for this to work, you need the document in the shared container to contain the same grocery list information as the iCloud document that's no longer available. Likewise, when iCloud access is restored, you want the iCloud document to contain any changes the user made to the document stored in the shared container.

> **Note**: It is highly unlikely that your average user will make a habit of turning iCloud access off and on—at most, they might forget to log in to iCloud after resetting their device. But this scenario is easy to test on the simulator, and also provides a chance to demonstrate some of the other methods available to manage iCloud documents.

Here's part one of the plan: To keep the document in the shared container up to date, you'll use the iCloud document when there's iCloud access, and copy it to the shared container whenever it syncs.

Open **GroceryList.swift** add the following convenience property and private method:

```
let fileManager = NSFileManager.defaultManager()

private func copyCloudToGroup() {
  let groupURL = GroceryListConfig.groupURL
  if fileManager.fileExistsAtPath(groupURL.path!) {
    fileManager.removeItemAtPath(groupURL.path!, error: nil)
  }
  dispatch_async(dispatch_get_global_queue(
    DISPATCH_QUEUE_PRIORITY_DEFAULT, 0)) {
    let fileCoordinator = NSFileCoordinator(filePresenter: nil)
    fileCoordinator.coordinateReadingItemAtURL(self.fileURL,
      options: NSFileCoordinatorReadingOptions.WithoutChanges,
      error: nil) { newURL in
      let success = self.fileManager.copyItemAtURL(self.fileURL,
        toURL: groupURL, error: nil)
      if success {
        println("copyCloudToGroup: success")
      } else {
        println("copyCloudToGroup: failed")
      }
    }
  }
}
```

This method deletes the document file in the shared container if it exists and replaces it with the version currently available in iCloud.

Now in `saveCurrentState()`, add the following code inside the `if success` block:

```
// if doc is in cloud, save it to App Groups container as backup
if self.fileManager.isUbiquitousItemAtURL(self.fileURL) {
  self.copyCloudToGroup()
} else {
  println("saveCurrentState: doc is in group container")
}
```

Now for part two of the plan: When iCloud access is restored, you'll move the document in the shared container to the iCloud container, then open and sync it to save a new copy back to the shared container. You'll do this whenever iCloud is available, not just when the availability changes. Thanks to part one of the plan, the document in the shared container always has the most current grocery list.

Open **AppDelegate.swift** and add the following method:

```
func moveGroupDocToCloud() {
  let defaultQueue =
    dispatch_get_global_queue(
      DISPATCH_QUEUE_PRIORITY_DEFAULT, 0)
  dispatch_async(defaultQueue) {
    let success = self.fileManager.setUbiquitous(true,
      itemAtURL: GroceryListConfig.groupURL, destinationURL:
        GroceryListConfig.cloudURL, error: nil)
    if success {
      println("moveGroupDocToCloud: moved doc to cloud")
      // open and sync cloud doc to save group doc, in case user
      // doesn't update cloud doc before losing cloud access
      let groceryList = GroceryList(fileURL:
        GroceryListConfig.cloudURL)
      groceryList.openWithCompletionHandler { success in
        if success {
          println("moveGroupDocToCloud: opened groceryList")
          groceryList.sync()
        } else {
          println("moveGroupDocToCloud: open groceryList
            failed")
        }
      }
    }
    return
  }
}
```

This accomplishes the goal of copying the local document to iCloud, and upon completion, it opens and syncs the `groceryList` between devices.

Now add code to call `moveGroupDocToCloud()` if the local document exists. In `setupGroceryListCloudDoc(query:)`, add this `if` clause to the end of the `if query.resultCount > 0` block, just after setting `GroceryListConfig.url`:

```
if fileManager.fileExistsAtPath(
  GroceryListConfig.groupURL.path!) {
  // remove cloud doc and move group doc to cloud container
  fileManager.removeItemAtURL(groceryListCloudURL, error: nil)
  moveGroupDocToCloud()
}
```

And add similar code to the end of the `else` branch, replacing the call to `self.createNewGroceryListDoc()` with the following lines:

```
if self.fileManager.fileExistsAtPath
  (GroceryListConfig.groupURL.path!) {
  println("setupGroceryListCloudDoc: moving group doc to cloud")
  self.moveGroupDocToCloud()
} else {
  println("setupGroceryListCloudDoc: creating empty cloud doc")
  self.createNewGroceryListDoc()
}
```

Like before, add all of this new code from **AppDelegate.swift** to **InitialInterfaceController.swift**. Here's a checklist of what you need to add:

- `moveGroupDocToCloud()`
- `if`-(`else`-)clause to check for the local document, in the main `if` and `else` closures of `setupGroceryListCloudDoc(query:)`

How to toggle iCloud in the simulator

To test iCloud availability, you'll need to toggle the iCloud Drive setting. To do this in iOS Simulator, go to **Settings\iCloud\iCloud Drive** and toggle the switch for SousChef (image on following page):

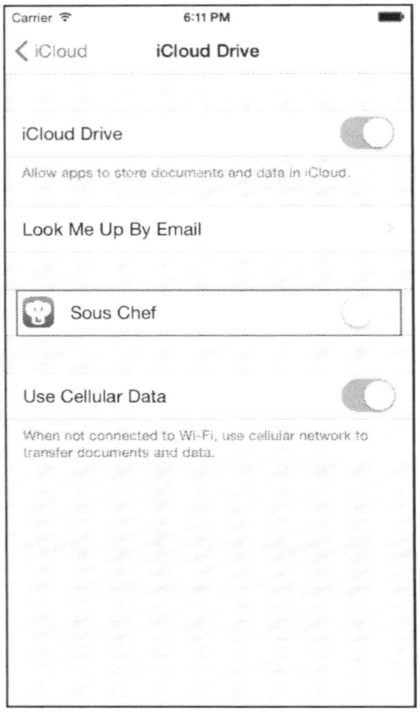

Testing intermittent syncing

With iCloud on, run the containing iOS app and add some ingredients to the grocery list.

Then stop the app and turn off iCloud as per the instructions above. Then run the containing iOS app again, and change the grocery list: console messages will show the app is now using the document in the shared container:

```
No iCloud access
GroceriesController: opened groceryList
saveCurrentState: document updated to container
file:///Users/amt1/Library/Developer/CoreSimulator/Devices/3E4A3
E7E-D065-44BA-BE81-
637D690F5079/data/Containers/Shared/AppGroup/B962FC31-8286-4326-
A014-E89304A7734A/com.rw.souschef.groceries.json
saveCurrentState: doc is in group container
```

Then stop the app and turn *on* iCloud. Run the containing iOS app one last time, and console messages will show that the app is once more using the iCloud document.

```
iCloud access with ID <264931d6 4dc648a3 6d3fa0eb 6284b87e
e75ffa8d>
```

```
moveGroupDocToCloud: moved doc to cloud
moveGroupDocToCloud: opened groceryList
saveCurrentState: document updated to container
file:///Users/amt1/Library/Developer/CoreSimulator/Devices/3E4A3
E7E-D065-44BA-BE81-
637D690F5079/data/Library/Mobile%20Documents/iCloud~com~razeware
~SousChef/Documents/com.rw.souschef.groceries.json
copyCloudToGroup: success
```

Confirm this by checking that the grocery list contains the changes you made on both the iOS simulator and the Watch simulator.

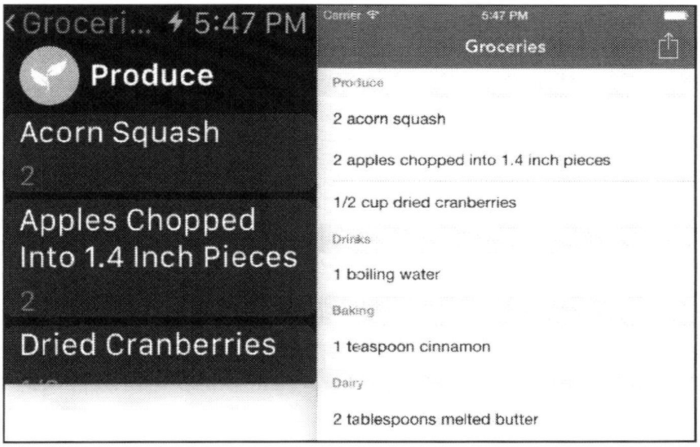

And you've done it! Reward yourself by whipping up some of Mic's Yorkshire Puds—I've had my eye on those the whole time I've been writing this chapter!

Where to go from here?

In this chapter, you've learned how to sync a `UIDocument` subclass between a Watch app and its containing iOS app, in either the shared container or the iCloud container. Using iCloud storage requires a little more work than sharing data locally, but provides a convenient service to users with multiple devices. You also learned how to move and copy a `UIDocument`, to keep it in sync between both the shared and iCloud containers—this means that on those rare occasions when the app has no iCloud access, the user doesn't lose their data, which can only be a good thing!

There are a couple of things you didn't do in this chapter, but which Apple recommends for apps that use iCloud storage:

- Always let the user choose between iCloud and local storage;
- Periodically check for the user switching iCloud accounts.

To see how to do this, download Apple's sample app Lister. Note that Lister doesn't attempt to keep iCloud and local documents in sync—it doesn't move a document if it already exists in the other container. Nor does it migrate documents from one iCloud account to another—it only informs the user to sign in to the previous account if she wants to access the documents stored there.

Keep reading to learn about potential performance bottlenecks when writing WatchKit apps, and how to tackle them, as well as tips on taking advantage of the super-efficient communication options between the Watch app and its containing iPhone app. There's even a new project to help you cook up that wonderful Crock Pot Roast, to go with Mic's yummy Yorkshire Puds!

Chapter 14: Performance, Tips & Tricks

By Jack Wu

When Apple released WatchKit, you probably heard many people talk about how much it reminded them of the early days of iOS. Perhaps you've heard tales of how difficult it was back then to make an app do just about anything, and how developers had to optimize everything for memory simply to keep an app from getting killed.

WatchKit is as new and fresh right now as iOS was in those stories. There are data transfer limitations, memory limitations and storage limitations—*all* the good stuff!

This is an opportunity to learn a new technology from the ground up. These limitations will force you to gain a better understanding of the framework, and the platform as a whole. You will scour through the documentation, looking for the best way to accomplish your tasks. You will have a chance to innovate and forge new ways achieving things through these limitations.

Then, in the future when WatchKit is easier and the limitations are no more, you will still know the best practices and principles that you've gathered over time.

And that is exciting!

This chapter looks into the performance bottlenecks of the current iteration of WatchKit, and provides some tips and tricks for tackling them and improving your Watch app's overall user experience. At the very least, this chapter aims to providing a starting point for when you need to push your Watch app to the next level.

In this chapter, you will first look at some code snippets and scenarios that show you what *not* to do. Then, you will look for a solution to the performance issues covered and implement it in a sample app.

So jump right in! Maybe this chapter will become the opening to all your future WatchKit stories. :]

Performance in WatchKit

These days, you can write an iOS app without worrying too much about performance, and you will most likely be fine. Both users and developers are used to activity indicators in apps and generally don't complain about them.

WatchKit is very different in this regard. Apple puts it best:

> "If you measure interactions with your iOS app in minutes, you can expect interactions with your WatchKit app to be measured in seconds."

That's right—*seconds*. If the user had a minute, she would probably reach for her phone instead. On the Watch, even a slight delay in responsiveness may be enough for users to put down their wrists, and it's your job to prevent that from happening.

Performance on Watch apps is especially critical because the Watch will suspend an app immediately if the user stops interacting with it. That means your expensive operations might never complete.

Performance limitations usually arise from bottlenecks, which occur when an app is over-utilizing some resource, thereby holding up the entire app. The main bottlenecks to look out for are:

- **Communication** bottlenecks. When you send too much data from the iPhone to the Watch, you can run into this particular bottleneck.
- **Permission** bottlenecks. These aren't really performance bottlenecks, but they can occur if you try to access a service that requires the OS to request permission, such as location services.
- **Networking** bottlenecks. If your Watch app is waiting on any network activity, that's almost certainly a bottleneck.

These bottlenecks aren't necessarily unique to WatchKit, but are more noticeable due to the limitations of the hardware and the way the Watch interacts with your phone. You want to eliminate these bottlenecks as much as possible. The following sections cover the most common causes of these bottlenecks and how to deal with them. Afterward, you'll look to solve performance issues from a higher level.

Communication bottlenecks

WatchKit tries to minimize the amount of communication between the iPhone and the Watch. One of the ways it does this is by resizing images to match interface objects whenever it can.

In some cases, this isn't possible. When you send an image to the Watch, WatchKit doesn't know how you intend to use it. This results in the full-sized image being transferred wirelessly over to the Watch, which can obviously take a long time.

You, the developer, must step up here and always provide images that are sized properly for your interface. The easiest way to make sure you aren't sending any unnecessarily large images to the Watch is to resize them all to fit within the Watch's screen size.

The AVFoundation framework includes a very handy method that will calculate the size you need. Here's how you can use it:

```
let size = AVMakeRectWithAspectRatioInsideRect(image.size,
  contentFrame).size
```

If you would rather not import AVFoundation into your project simply to use this simple function, here's a helper method that performs the calculation:

```
func sizeWithAspectRatioInsideRect(aspectRatio: CGSize,
  boundingRect: CGRect) -> CGSize  {
  let widthRatio = boundingRect.size.width / aspectRatio.width
  let heightRatio =
    boundingRect.size.height / aspectRatio.height
  let ratio = min(widthRatio, heightRatio)
  let transform = CGAffineTransformMakeScale(ratio, ratio)
  return CGSizeApplyAffineTransform(aspectRatio, transform)
}
```

And, once you've added it to your project, you can use it like so:

```
let size = sizeWithAspectRatioInsideRect(image.size,
  boundingRect: contentFrame)
```

Either of these methods will provide you with an image size that will fit into the content frame of the interface controller.

After you calculate the size you want, you can then resize the image using this handy extension on `UIImage`:

```
extension UIImage {
  func resizedImageWithSize(newSize: CGSize) -> UIImage {
    UIGraphicsBeginImageContextWithOptions(newSize, false,
      0)
    drawInRect(CGRect(origin: CGPointZero, size: newSize))
    let scaledImage =
      UIGraphicsGetImageFromCurrentImageContext()
    UIGraphicsEndImageContext()
    return scaledImage
```

```
  }
}
```

Resizing every image before you send it over to the Watch may seem likely to cause a performance hit itself. Just remember that the Watch app's code runs as an extension on the phone's powerhouse processor, and the overhead will be small compared with transferring a larger image wirelessly.

Permission bottlenecks

Permission bottlenecks will most commonly occur when requesting location data, although there are many other services that require a user to grant permission before they can be used such as the Address Book. You simply need to avoid triggering permission prompts from WatchKit and direct users to the containing iOS app.

Here's a small example of a bottleneck in a `WKInterfaceController`:

```
override func awakeWithContext(context: AnyObject?) {
  super.awakeWithContext(context)

  let locationManager = CLLocationManager()
  locationManager.delegate = self
  locationManager.requestWhenInUseAuthorization()
  locationManager.startUpdatingLocation()
}

func locationManager(manager: CLLocationManager!,
   didUpdateLocations locations: [AnyObject]!) {
  if let location = locations.first as? CLLocation {
    coordinateLabel.setText("\(location.coordinate.latitude),
      \(location.coordinate.longitude)")
  }
}
```

Here the code creates a new `CLLocationManager`, assigns its delegate and finally requests location updates—textbook code for retrieving a location in iOS.

As innocent as this looks, if the user hasn't granted permission to use location services in the app, the app won't show the user any prompts and it will never call the delegate method. The user will stare at the Watch for a few seconds, tap its screen, shrug and put it away unamused.

Unfortunately, because the Watch app runs separately from the containing iPhone app, it will never be granted the location permission. The two apps do not share a permission set, and there's no way for the user to accept a permission dialog for a Watch extension.

If your Watch app needs access to things like location services that require a users permission, consider getting the data you need in your iPhone app and sending that data to the Watch app yourself. Refer back to Chapter 8, "Sharing Data" to look for ways to add location information to a shared data store. There are also tips later in this chapter for communicating directly between the iPhone app and the Watch app.

Networking bottlenecks

Networking is a core component of many apps now. If your phone app fetches and displays frequently updated data from a server, it makes sense that your Watch app should do the same, right?

Yes and no. Remember that interactions with the Watch happen in seconds. Unfortunately, so do network requests.

Requesting new data upon the start of the app is sometimes unavoidable, so simply "not doing it" won't be an option here.

Your iOS app should already have some sort of caching, so upon startup the Watch display shouldn't be completely empty because it can use that cached data. It should at the very least have some outdated data, often the same data that was loaded in the previous session.

The question then becomes—*How can you do better?* You want to update the cache even when the user isn't using your app. There are two good ways of tackling this:

1. **Notifications**: If your iOS app's data updates only a few times a day, you can trigger updates using silent push notifications. This way, your app can *always* be up to date!
2. **Background Fetch**: If your data updates frequently, as a Twitter feed does for example, it is pretty much impossible to be completely up to date, as updates can come in several times a minute. Background fetch, introduced by Apple in iOS 7, provides a reasonable solution for this case.

There are other chapters in this book that cover notifications, so this section will focus on background fetching.

With background fetch, iOS will try to learn a user's usage patterns in the hope of fetching new data before the user asks to see it. The system will provide your app 30 seconds whenever it predicts that conditions are safe to fetch data. You can then inform the system whether or not new data is available.

To implement background fetch in your app, you must first go to the **Capabilities** pane in your project's settings, turn on **Background Modes**, and check **Background fetch**, as shown here:

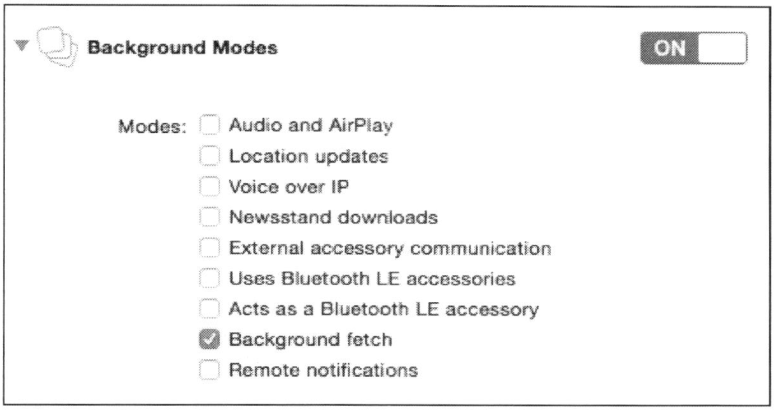

Before you get to the actual fetching, you need one more line of code in your app delegate's `application(_: didFinishLaunchingWithOptions:)` method:

```
application.setMinimumBackgroundFetchInterval(
  UIApplicationBackgroundFetchIntervalMinimum)
```

This tells the system that you want to fetch using the minimum interval—that is, as frequently as possible.

Now you're ready to perform some fetching! Whenever it's your turn to fetch, `application(_:performFetchWithCompletionHandler:)` will be called on your app delegate.

Here's an example implementation:

```
func application(application: UIApplication,
  performFetchWithCompletionHandler completionHandler:
  (UIBackgroundFetchResult) -> Void) {
  fetchNewDataWithCompletion() { data, error in
    if let data = data {
      // Received new data
      self.updateCacheWithNewData(data: data)
      completionHandler(.NewData)
    } else if let error = error {
      completionHandler(.Failed)
    } else {
      completionHandler(.NoData)
    }
  }
}
```

As you can see, by calling the completion handler your provided with the correct outcome, you can help the system effectively schedule your fetches.

With background fetching in place, users should be able to see the most up-to-date data whenever they open the app. While not a true performance boost, to the user it appears that your app just loaded infinitely faster. :]

Other bottlenecks

A final bottleneck worth considering is the decompression time of images. Apple insists that you use **PNGs** in your resource bundles.

It may be tempting to use JPEGs instead of PNGs for opaque images, as JPEGs are quite a bit smaller in space.

Don't do it. Xcode runs PNGCRUSH on your PNGs, which reduces their size, and much, much more importantly, reduces their **decompression time.** Apps can load PNGs noticeably faster than JPEGs due to this optimization, so that file size trade-off might not be as good as it first appears!

A bigger solution

You can see that although WatchKit extensions *can* do quite a bit, they really *shouldn't* be doing all that much. They are companions to the main app.

That doesn't mean you should throw out your super-awesome Watch app idea, though. Just save it for the future, when hopefully Apple will allow us to build native Watch apps. :]

As iOS app companions, WatchKit extensions are amazing for displaying succinct parts of the app, and are an simple way to manipulate data in the app. Your Watch app doesn't need to talk to a server—it simply needs to talk to the containing iOS app.

With this in mind, you can take advantage of the fact that the WatchKit extension can communicate with the main app really efficiently—after all, they both run on the phone!

The rest of this chapter will focus on communication between the WatchKit extension and the iOS app, and provide a compelling example of how much value a companion can provide.

Communicating between the WatchKit extension and iOS app

There are a few different ways to communicate between the WatchKit extension and the iOS app. You should already be familiar with communicating through shared files or user defaults using an **app group**. This will be the main way you share data between the extension and the main app.

Here are two more ways they can communicate:

1. Using `WKInterfaceController`'s `openParentApplication(_:reply:)`.

2. Using the **Darwin Notifications**.

`openParentApplication(_:reply:)` is the only method that's exclusive to WatchKit. It allows the Watch to launch the companion iOS app in the background, even if it was in a suspended or terminated state!

`openParentApplication(_:reply:)` allows you to pass some data between the two apps. The data is limited in such a way that it has to be compatible with the property list format, but you don't need to worry too much about sending large amounts data, since the method doesn't transfer anything wirelessly since both the iOS app and extension are running on the same device. `openParentApplication(_:reply:)` is a class method of `WKInterfaceController`, so can only be called from the extension.

The Darwin Notification Center has been around for a while, but developers rarely use it due to the more powerful `NSNotificationCenter`. If you are familiar with `NSNotificationCenter`, you'll find the Darwin Notification Center to be a simplified version where you can't observe a specific object, or even pass a user object. You simply register for a notification name and receive a callback whenever it's posted.

With these tools in your tool belt, you have everything you need to have your WatchKit extension and iOS app run in unison.

It might still be unclear what exactly you're trying to accomplish with all this communication, so this is a great time to introduce this chapter's sample project—**MeatCooker V2.**

Cooking with two apps

Let's face it—you can't cook meat with only one device to assist you. Even if you could, you couldn't submit MeatCooker without a functioning iOS app, anyway. :]

Find **MeatCookerV2-Starter** and open the project in Xcode. This project is the same as the one in Chapter 3, "UI Controls" but has been re-architected to enable saving the timer configuration to the disk.

Also, shiny new controls have been created in the main iOS app to mimic the look of the Watch app.

Build and run the iOS app and have a poke around. Then **build and run** the WatchKit app, which should look identical to the project from the earlier chapter:

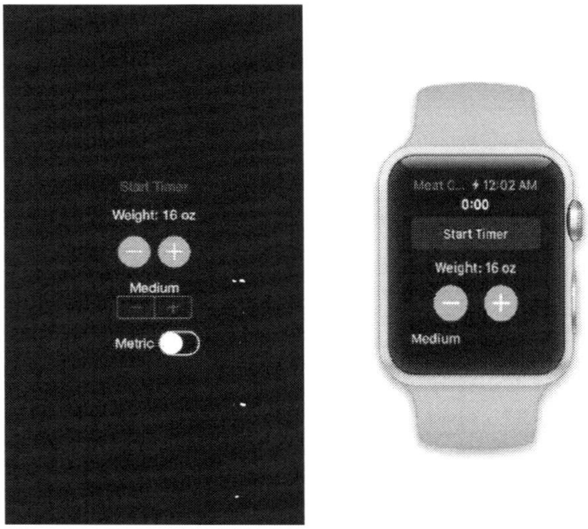

Immediately, the issue at hand rears its ugly head: timer changes on either the Watch or the iPhone are not reflected on the other device. The Watch app is effectively standing alone, and it shouldn't be.

Syncing up

The goal is to have both apps always be up to date and in sync with each other. Therefore, there are four cases to consider:

1. The Watch app updates while the iPhone app is active.
2. The Watch app updates while iPhone app is inactive.
3. The iPhone app updates while Watch app is active.
4. The iPhone app updates while Watch app is inactive.

Since you need to pass data both ways, you'll need to write it to an app group. If both apps load this data upon launch, you've effectively covered the cases where either app is inactive when a change occurs.

For the cases where both apps are active, you need to let the other app know that a change has occurred. When the change happens on the phone app, you can make use of the Darwin Notification Center to notify the Watch. If the change happens on the Watch, you have a choice of doing the same, or using `openParentApplication(_:reply:)`.

MeatCooker will make use of the Darwin Notification Center in this case as well, since it's consistent with how the iOS app behaves and easier to implement.

So the plan is:

1. When either app launches, you'll load the configuration in the app group and register for notifications.
2. Whenever a change happens, you'll write a new configuration to the app group and post a notification.
3. When either app receives a notification, you'll reload the configuration from the app group.

Sounds pretty good—that means it's time to start coding!

The app group

You are probably quite familiar with app groups now. The first thing to do will be to change the app group to one of your own. You can use the same one you used for SousChef—I won't tell. ;]

If you've forgotten how enable app groups in your project, refer back to Chapter 8, "Sharing Data".

After you've changed the app group on both the MeatCooker and MeatCooker WatchKit Extension targets, find and open **Configuration.Swift.**

This is the model class that's shared between both the iOS app and the WatchKit extension. It holds a configuration of the timer and also defines some constants that will be useful for persisting it. Find the `Constants` struct and change `AppGroup` to your app group:

```
public static let AppGroup =
  "group.com.raywenderlich.souschef.documents"
```

That's my SousChef app group—*shhhhh*.

Persisting the configuration

Take a quick look at **InterfaceController.swift** and **ViewController.swift**. You'll notice they're structured almost identically, with some method stubs all set up for you to fill in.

The first steps will be to write the configuration to the app group and load it upon startup. You've already done this once before, so no need to go slow here.

Open **MeatCooker WatchKit Extension\InterfaceController.swift** and locate `configurationUpdated()`. Currently, all it does is update the interface with the new configuration. Replace it with this:

```
private func configurationUpdated() {
  NSKeyedArchiver.archiveRootObject(
    configuration.dictionaryRep(),
    toFile: Configuration.savePath())
  displayConfiguration()
}
```

There's just one extra line. Here you use `NSKeyedArchiver` to write the dictionary representation of the configuration to disk.

Next, to load the configuration upon launch, replace `loadConfiguration()` in **InterfaceController.swift** with the following:

```
private func loadConfiguration() {
  if let dictionary = NSKeyedUnarchiver.unarchiveObjectWithFile(
    Configuration.savePath()) as? [NSObject: AnyObject] {
    configuration = Configuration(dictionaryRep: dictionary)
  } else {
    configuration = Configuration()
  }
  displayConfiguration()
}
```

This is yet another small change. Here you un-archive the dictionary from the app group and use it to initialize the configuration, if one exists. If not, you create a new, default configuration.

So far, so good. You need to implement both of these changes in the containing iOS app, as well.

Open **MeatCooker\ViewController.swift** and once again find `configurationUpdated()` and `loadConfiguration()`. Replace them with exactly the same code you used above.

Build and run the WatchKit app. Change some values, stop it, and **re-run** it again. The app should have preserved the changes you made.

Now **run** the containing iOS app without first stopping the Watch app. The initial configuration will be the same as on the Watch:

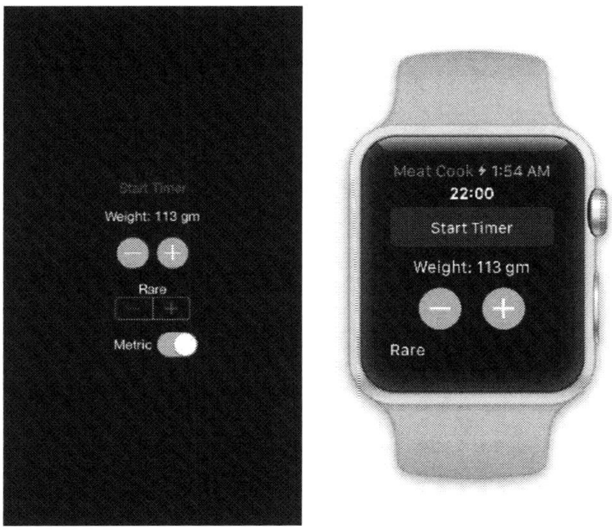

Not bad for a small change! However, once you start changing the values on either app, they will quickly go out of sync. It's time to fix that.

The Darwin notification center

You can only access the Darwin Notification Center using C APIs. Unlike most C APIs, the fact that you need to be able to get a C function pointer means that you *cannot* use Darwin Notifications natively in Swift.

Since the API is a bit messy, I've implemented `DarwinNotificationHelper` in Objective-C, for your convenience!

Open **DarwinNotificationHelper.h** and take a glance at the two instance methods. They're pretty simple! Now open **DarwinNotificationHelper.m** and peek at their implementation.

`registerForNotificationName:callback:` nicely wraps `CFNotificationCenterAddObserver()` and executes a callback every time the notification is triggered.

`postNotificationWithName:` wraps `CFNotificationCenterPostNotification()` so you don't have to worry about all that bridging. :] You call this to post a notification, which will call the registered callback. This works a lot like `postNotificationName(_:object:)` on `NSNotificationCenter`.

Using the Darwin Notification Center is almost exactly the same as using the `NSNotificationCenter`, so you're going to jump right in!

Watches first! Open **MeatCooker WatchKit Extension\InterfaceController.swift** again and find `registerForNotifications()`. Add the following line to its body:

```
DarwinNotificationHelper.sharedHelper().
  registerForNotificationName(
  Configuration.Constants.Identifier, callback: { () -> Void in
  self.loadConfiguration()
})
```

Here you register for the notification identifier defined in `Configuration.Constants` and provide a closure that's called whenever the notification is received, which itself calls `loadConfiguration()` to load the new configuration whenever the app receives a notification.

Next, find `configurationUpdated()` again. After you save the new configuration to the app group, you should notify the containing iOS app. To do so, replace the existing implementation with the following:

```
NSKeyedArchiver.archiveRootObject(configuration.dictionaryRep(),
  toFile: Configuration.savePath())
DarwinNotificationHelper.sharedHelper()
  .postNotificationWithName(Configuration.Constants.Identifier)
displayConfiguration()
```

This is another single line change. Here you post the relevant notification so the containing iOS app can update its configuration.

Again, find the same two methods, `registerForNotifications()` and `configurationUpdated()`, in **MeatCooker\ViewController.swift** and update them in exactly the same as you did above.

And that's it! Now both apps are listening for the same notification and posting it whenever their configurations are updated.

Build and run the Watch app, and then **run** the containing iOS app. Make some changes in either the Watch or the iOS app and "watch" in amazement as the other device is immediately updated.

Now you're ready to cook!

Companions

MeatCooker's WatchKit extension feels great to use now, like a true companion. By having shared data in an app group and frequently updating it, performance will be much less of a concern because all you have to do is read that cache.

Not all apps can make use of these principles, but being familiar with how the WatchKit extension and the iOS app can communicate effectively and efficiently will definitely help your WatchKit extension provide a rich user experience. At the end of day, isn't that what we're all here for?

Where to go from here?

This chapter was authored before anyone outside of Apple had even touched the Apple Watch. As Apple shows us more and more, you can count on this chapter to grow and grow.

The next step is to go add WatchKit extensions to all your apps. At the very least, you'll have some great stories to tell in the future about your good times with the initial release of WatchKit. :]

Chapter 15: Localization

By Ben Morrow

With the painless global distribution provided by the App Store, you can release your app in over 150 countries with only a single click. You never know where it might take off and how that might change the fortunes of your company.

Here's a story I love:

When the Evernote app launched in 2008, it unexpectedly became very popular in Japan. Since the app was built in English, the company's leaders decided they could expand sales even faster if they optimized the interface for Japanese. The team scrambled, and with a bit of local help, they were able to offer Evernote in the new language.

Interestingly, as time went on, this move began to affect the company in larger ways. The team started traveling in Japan and noticed that some partner companies were over 100 years old. That's when CEO Phil Libin rallied the team, saying:

> "Let's build a company that has the long-term planning and thinking of some of these great Japanese companies, combined with the best of the Silicon Valley startup mentality. We don't just want to build a 100-year company, we want to build a 100-year startup."[3]

---

[3] "Interview with Phil Levin," doeswhat.com, Feb 25, 2012: http://doeswhat.com/2012/02/25/interview-with-phil-libin-evernote/

Before you can run like Evernote, you've first got to learn to walk. To grow your reach internationally, you'll have to make sure you've optimized the language, number formatting and layout of your app for many different regions and cultures.

In this chapter you're going to learn how to localize your app so you can reach that larger audience, and understand what techniques and tools are available to aid that process.

Getting started

For the vast majority of this chapter, you'll be making localization changes to the SousChef project, allowing the text in the app to change like magic to match the user's current language. But first, to make it easy to demonstrate localization, you're going to set up a new interface controller in your storyboard to work on, and then it's up to you to apply what you learn to the rest of SousChef – are you up for the challenge?

> **Note**: As with the rest of this book, this chapter builds on the chapters that precede it. If you're beginning with the starter project for this chapter because you've skipped previous chapters or simply want a fresh start, you'll need to set up the necessary provisioning profiles and enable App Groups and iCloud in order to share recipes between the containing iPhone app and the Watch app.
>
> For more information on what's required, see Chapter 8, "Sharing Data" and Chapter 13, "iCloud".

Open the SousChef project and drag a new **interface controller** from the **Object Library** onto the **Interface.storyboard** canvas.

Next, drag the **Main** app entry arrow to the **new interface controller**:

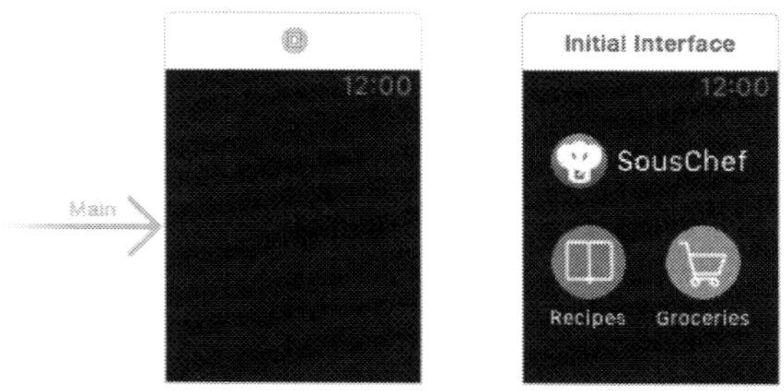

This change will make it so that when you run the WatchKit app in the simulator, the initial interface controller will be the one you've just created. Don't worry, though; when you're done with this chapter, you'll move the starting point back to the original initial interface controller.

Great! The Watch app now uses your new interface controller on launch. Before moving on to localization, you'll take a few minutes to set up this new interface controller.

Setting up the interface

Drag a **Date** and two **Labels** from the **Object Library** onto the new interface controller. Change the text of the two labels to **<greeting>** and **<report>** so that your interface looks like this:

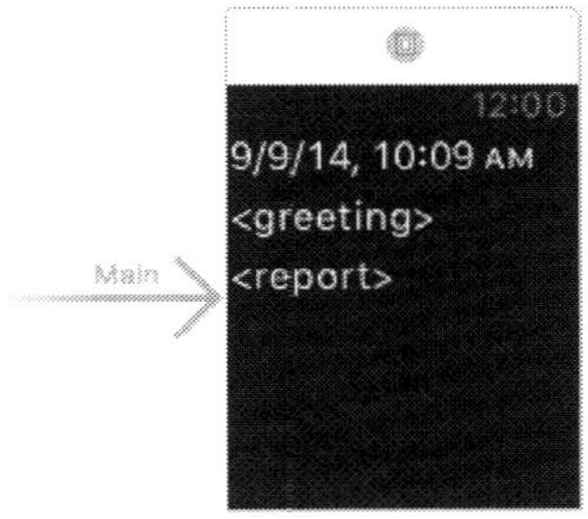

Change the **Lines** to **0** on the **<report>** label to let the label take as many lines as it needs to display the full text.

Line space is always an important consideration when you're localizing your app. Because languages have different average word lengths—for example, German is a lengthy language compared with English—you always want to make sure you allow enough space in your interface to accommodate longer text.

This means labels and buttons might take up more than one line. It also means that sometimes, instead of placing buttons side by side, you'll have to stack them on top of each other.

Since you already have the time provided by the operating system in the upper-right corner of the screen, you don't need it displayed by **Date** label. In the Attributes Inspector change the label's Time property to **None**:

> **Note**: In WatchKit, a `WKInterfaceDate` object displays the current date and/or time. This allows you to show what's current without having to do any configuration at runtime. You can't, however, display a past or future date. To do that, you'd need to use a regular label and `NSDateFormatter`. For your purposes here, the current date works nicely.

Now that you've got your interface ready to roll, you need to create a new interface controller subclass so you can programmatically change the contents of the labels from code.

Right-click on the **Interface Controllers** group in the Project Navigator and choose **New File...**, then select **iOS\Source\Cocoa Touch Class** and click **Next**. Make sure you're subclassing `WKInterfaceController`, and name the new class **ReportInterfaceController**. Click **Next** and then click **Create**.

Open **Interface.storyboard**, select your new interface controller and, using the **Identity Inspector**, change its **Class** to `ReportInterfaceController`:

While you're at it, set its **Identifier** in the **Attributes Inspector** to **ReportInterfaceController**:

As you learned in Chapter 11, "Notifications", you need to do this so that later you can refer to this interface controller in code.

Next, you'll create outlets in the now familiar way. Open the Assistant editor and make sure it's displaying the `ReportInterfaceController` class. Then, **ctrl-drag** from both the **<greeting>** and **<report>** labels to `ReportInterfaceController`, just below the class definition. Name your outlets `greetingLabel` and `reportLabel`, respectively.

Great! Now you'll get down to business with some code. Add a new constant just inside the class definition:

```
let greeting = "Hello there!"
```

Then at the bottom of `awakeWithContext(_:)`, add:

```
greetingLabel.setText(greeting)
```

Build and run.

Very nice! You've successfully populated a label with code—so now you'll learn how to localize it!

Internationalizing your app

Is it localization or internationalization?

Internationalization means modifying code to use APIs such as `NSLocalizedString(_:value:comment)` so that your app can display different languages. It's up to you, the app developer, to perform internationalization.

By contrast, **localization** means translating the words in your app's user interface, text strings and images into different languages.

Internationalization and localization together ensure your app looks as good in Chinese or Arabic as it does in English.

Separating text from code

Most of the time when you start this process, the text in your app will be hard-coded in your storyboard. To localize the language, you need to separate this text into a separate file. So, rather than hard-coding the text, you'll simply reference it from the new file in your bundle.

For each supported language, Xcode uses a file with the **.strings** extension to store and retrieve all of the text strings used within the app. A simple method call will look up and return the requested string based on the current language of the iOS device.

Apple provides a handy command line tool called **genstrings** that will create the .strings file by inspecting your code. So the first thing you need to do is prepare your app for genstrings.

To get started, open **ReportInterfaceController.swift** and change the definition of `greeting`:

```
let greeting = NSLocalizedString("greetingLabelText",
  value: "Hello!", comment: "Top of report")
```

By using this code, instead of setting the text directly, you'll read in the value from a .strings file you will create soon. This macro takes three parameters:

1. **Key:** A variable-like name to look up in the strings file. You might be tempted to use the English word as the key, but before long, you'll run into a situation where the app might need a button and a label with the same word in English. In another language, the conjugation might need to be different, depending on the activity. By using a variable-like name, you can ensure that each button and label has its own string.
2. **Value:** This is the default text in your base language. In this case, that's English. If the app has a problem accessing the .strings file, this is the text it will use in the interface object.
3. **Comment:** The optional comment is an aid for the translator, especially in large projects. The best practice is to describe the context in which the string is used so that the translator can look at screenshots and see where the text corresponds. Later, you'll learn just how this is important.

Adding an evaluated string

Now it's time to get cooking with the grocery stats.

Inside `awakeWithContext(_:)`, below `greetingLabel.setText(_:)`, add:

```
// 1
let totalGroceries = 10_000
// 2
let quantityReport = NSString(
  format: NSLocalizedString("reportLabelText",
    value: "In the last week, you bought %@ groceries",
      comment: "Full groceries report summary"),
  // 3
  String(totalGroceries))
// 4
reportLabel.setText(quantityReport)
```

Here's what's happening:

1. For now, you hardcode the number of groceries to 10,000. If you've got eagle eyes, you'll notice a cool Swift feature: to make numbers readable, you can optionally use an underscore without affecting the value.
2. You use the `NSString` initializer that lets you specify a format, and inside you use `NSLocalizedString(_:value:comment)`, just like you did for the greeting. The difference here is the use of `%@`, which is a placeholder for an evaluated string.
3. You transform `totalGroceries` from an `Int` to a `String` so that it's ready to be injected into the overall string.
4. Finally, you send the data to your label.

Build and run.

And with that, you get the full report—and apparently, a whole lot of groceries. ;] Next, you need to make sure your app is ready for localization.

Preparing for localization

Once you start localizing your files, Xcode is very particular about where they are stored and what they are named. If your interface isn't using the correct translation, be on the lookout for the "gotchas" that I'll describe along the way.

The first "gotcha" you might run into is that Xcode wants your storyboard to be in the right place in the folder structure. Browse to the **SousChef Watch App** folder in Finder.

If **Interface.storyboard** is not inside a folder called **Base.lproj**, you'll need to rearrange things manually. Create that folder and put the storyboard file inside. Then in the Project Navigator, delete Interface.storyboard and in its place, drag in the one from the new folder you just created.

Ensure that "Copy items if needed" is **unchecked**:

Click **Finish**. Now that your storyboard is in its correct location, you're ready to begin localizing your project.

Generating the .strings file

You can always add a .strings file manually, but thankfully the folks at Apple have provided a tool that you can run anytime you need to sync your code with your translated text.

First, find your way to the physical location of **ReportInterfaceController.swift**. The quickest way is to **right-click** on the file in the Project Navigator and then select **Show in Finder**.

Next, open Terminal. Type `cd` followed by a space. This is the Unix command for **c**hange **d**irectory.

Before you press Enter, drag **ReportInterfaceController.swift** from Finder into the Terminal window. This will copy the location of that file. Now **delete** the **filename** so that you're left with only the directory on the end. It should be either the Watch App or the WatchKit Extension folder, depending on where you saved the file.

Press **Enter**. If you did it correctly, the prompt prefix will change to the name of the folder:

```
Computer:SousChef WatchKit Extension username$
```

Finally, type:

```
genstrings *swift
```

Press **Enter**. This command runs through all of your filenames ending with "swift" and checks the contents for instances of `NSLocalizedString(_:value:comment:)`, from which it generates a Localizable.strings file for you.

The genstrings bug in Xcode 6.2

At this point, you may see an error message. At the time of writing, the most current release of Xcode, version 6.2, includes a bug involving genstrings and Swift. You can read about the problem on the Apple Developer Forums here:

- https://devforums.apple.com/message/1092119

When you enter the `genstrings` command in Terminal, you may see an error message like this:

```
Bad entry in file ReportInterfaceController.swift (line = 15):
Argument is not a literal string.
```

The fix is to delete the `value` parameter from the `NSLocalizedString(_:value:comment:)` calls. Back in Xcode, open **ReportInterfaceController.swift** and remove the `value` parameters so that your two calls look like this:

```
NSLocalizedString("greetingLabelText",
```

```
    comment: "Top of report")

  NSLocalizedString("reportLabelText",
    comment: "Full groceries report summary")
```

Build and run your project.

Now you no longer see the English text, but only the key names. Run the genstrings command once again. You can do that easily by pressing the **up** arrow key on your keyboard while in the Terminal app window.

```
genstrings *swift
```

This time, you shouldn't see any errors. To verify that it worked, look back in your project folder in Finder. You should now see a new **Localizable.strings** file.

Right now, though, Xcode doesn't know about the new file. To get it into Xcode, simply drag it from Finder into the **Supporting Files** group of the **SousChef WatchKit Extension** group in the Project Navigator:

Again, ensure that "Copy items if needed" is **unchecked** and that the file will be added to the **SousChef WatchKit Extension** target:

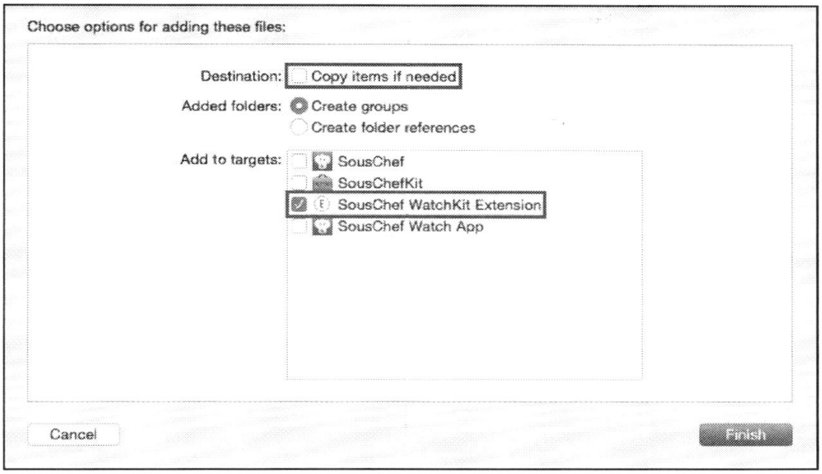

Awesome! You'll now see **Localizable.strings** available in the Project Navigator. Open it and prepare to go through what you see there.

About the .strings file

In your shiny new **Localizable.strings** is a strict but fairly simple format. First, notice that genstrings automatically populates a comment above each line:

```
/* Comment */
```

You can see how helpful it is to provide a little context about where the translated text will go in the app.

Then you'll see a key/content pair:

```
"KEY" = "CONTENT";
```

These work like a dictionary. If you had been able to keep the `value` parameter, the content would have been filled in already with English, but since you had to skirt around the bug, you'll have to edit the text manually. To officially start your strings file, edit the `greetingLabelText` line so that its value is "Hello!":

```
"greetingLabelText" = "Hello!";
```

Next, edit the `reportLabelText` line to have the following value:

```
"reportLabelText" = "In the last week, you bought %@ groceries";
```

> **Note**: Even though you've been writing Swift code for the entire book, don't be deceived—the strings file is not in Swift! You *will* need to have the semicolon at the end of every line.

Build and run.

You're back in action with the full report in English! In the next section, you'll learn how to put all your localization preparation into action so you can see the report in Spanish.

Adding a localization

To add support for another language, select the **SousChef** project and in the **Info** tab, you'll see a section for **Localizations**. Click the + button and choose **Spanish (es)**:

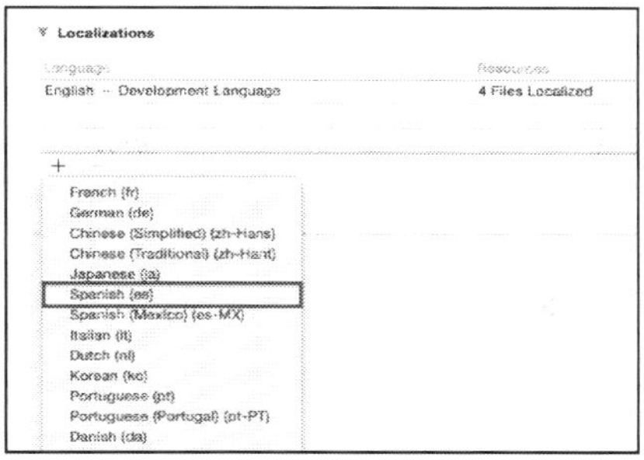

The next screen asks you which files you want to localize, showing only your storyboards and .xib files. Keep them all selected and click **Finish**:

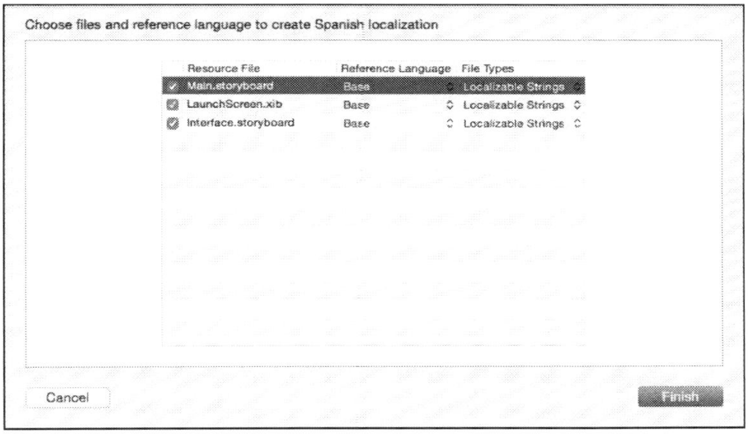

At this point, Xcode has set up directories behind the scenes that contain separate storyboards for each language you selected. To see this for yourself, expand **Interface.storyboard** in the Project Navigator by clicking the disclosure triangle:

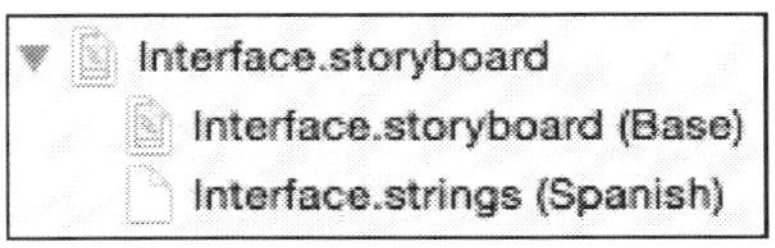

But wait, what about the .strings file? Select **Localizable.strings** using the Project Navigator and open the **File Inspector**. There you will see a button labeled **Localize...**. To let Xcode know you want it to localize a file, click this button:

Leave the value as **Base** and click **Localize**:

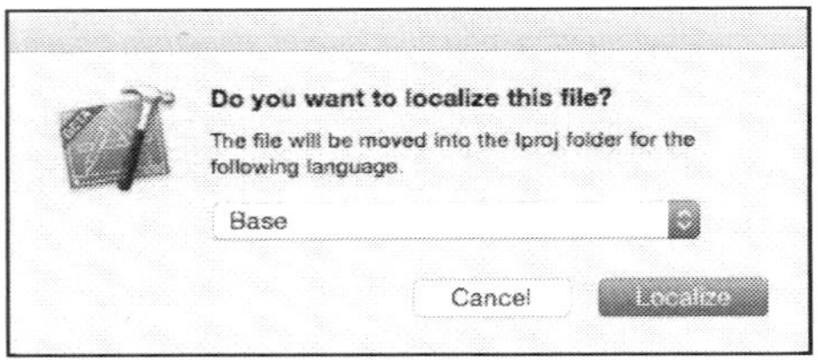

Now the **File Inspector** panel will show which languages this file supports. Add the **Spanish** localization by checking that box:

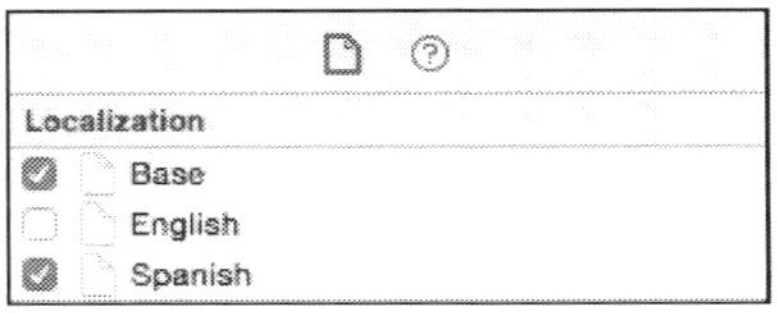

English isn't checked because English is also the Base language, which is checked.

In the Project Navigator, a disclosure triangle will appear next to **Localizable.strings** indicating there are now different versions available. You now have two versions of this file, one for Base and one for Spanish:

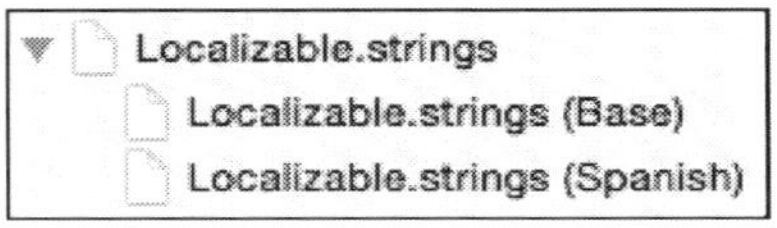

To add your first bit of Spanish to your app, select **Localizable.strings (Spanish)** and replace its contents with the following:

```
/* Top of report */
"greetingLabelText" = "¡Hola!";

/* Full groceries report summary */
"reportLabelText" =
  "En el última semana, compraste %@ comestibles";
```

¡Felicidades! Your app is now bilingual.

To test it out, launch the iOS Simulator and open Settings.app:

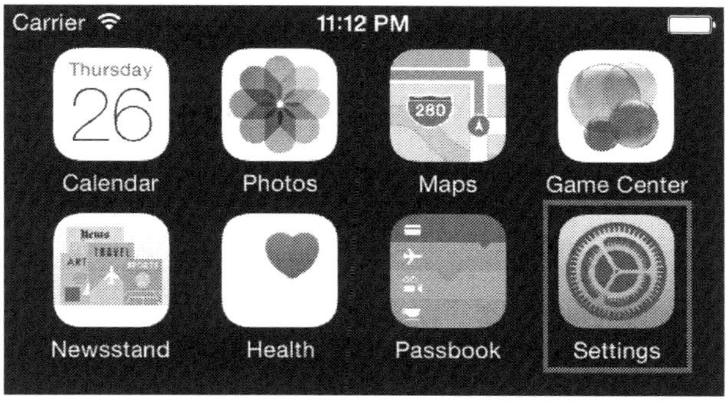

Navigate into the language settings and select Spanish:

General\Language & Region\iPhone Language\Español

Tap **Done** and then **Change to Spanish**:

In Xcode, stop the Watch app if it's still running. Build and run. You'll see the following:

Presto change-o! Your report is now in Spanish.

Jolly good show – or rather, alegre buen espectáculo!

> **Note**: You might have to unlock the phone in order to activate the Watch app. To do that, simply press the virtual home button - **shift+cmd+h** - and swipe to unlock.
>
> You might also run into another "gotcha": You simply don't see any Spanish. If that's the case, perform an ultraclean in Xcode - **cmd+shift+fn+k**. Then, uninstall the app from the simulator by doing a long press on the icon on the home screen and tapping the jiggling "x". Then build and run again.

Locales and number formatting

You might be thinking that it would be silly to buy 10,000 groceries in one week, but it's important to test your app in extreme cases. Is it possible that someone could buy a ton of groceries if they use the app in a commercial setting? Sure, and it's even more possible if the report was generated for the past year instead of the past week.

So, it's a good practice to test large numbers in your app because you never know precisely how it will be used.

Speaking of big numbers, you need to fix the way the app displays them. Most people in the US would prefer to see 10,000 - with a comma - while in many Spanish-speaking countries, most people would prefer to see 10.000 - with a period.

This will be a one-two punch, requiring both a number formatter and a region setting. Fortunately, Apple has a class for just this purpose called `NSNumberFormatter`.

In **ReportInterfaceController.swift**, find `awakeWithContext(_:)` and replace the code for setting the `reportLabel` with the following:

```
let totalGroceries = 10_000
let numberFormatter = NSNumberFormatter()
numberFormatter.numberStyle = .DecimalStyle
if let numberString =
  numberFormatter.stringFromNumber(totalGroceries) {
  let quantityReport = NSString(
    format: NSLocalizedString("reportLabelText",
      comment: "Full groceries report summary"),
    numberString)
  reportLabel.setText(quantityReport)
}
```

The only difference between this code and what you had before is that here, you let `NSNumberFormatter` format the number with `.DecimalStyle`, which will add the friendly thousands separator. Build and run.

You've got the comma! But remember, you're currently using the Spanish language, so you should be seeing a period.

Is a period too much to ask?

Back in the iOS Simulator, open **Ajustes** - which is Spanish for Settings - and change the locale by navigating to:

General\Idioma y region\Region\Spain

Stop the app if it's still running, and then build and run.

Perfect! The number now uses a period as the thousands separator.

Without any extra code, `NSNumberFormatter` has automatically formatted your numbers for the appropriate region. When working with numbers and dates, resist the urge to re-invent the wheel; it usually pays to do things the Apple way.

As a bonus, notice the date has changed to use the correct regional formatting, with the day before the month. Too cool!

Before you bask in the glory of being multilingual, you have a little bit of cleaning up to do. In **Interface.storyboard**, move the **Main** entry point arrow back to the **Initial Interface**:

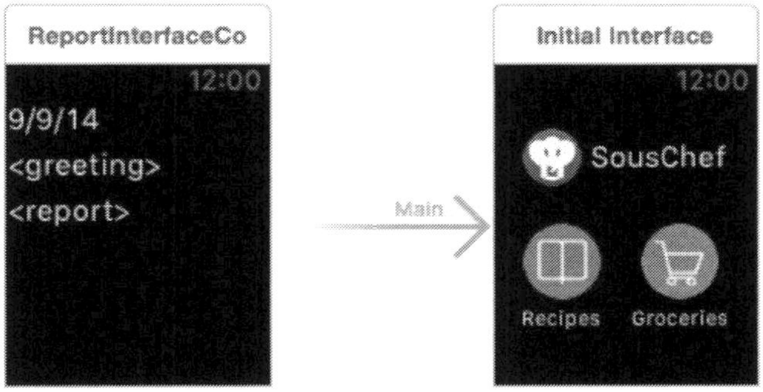

Next, set your language and region back to English and US, respectively. In **iOS Simulator** on the **phone**, open the **Ajustes** (Settings) app and do the following:

1. Navigate to **General\Idioma y region\ Region\United States**;
2. Tap **Back** (‹ Idioma y region);
3. Navigate to **Idioma del iPhone\English**;
4. Tap **OK**;
5. Tap **Cambiar a English**.

Back in Xcode, Stop the app if it's running and then build and run again.

SousChef is back in the house—er, the kitchen.

Where to go from here?

You've now got a firm understanding of how to work with languages and locale formatting.

This is a vast topic, though, so if you want to dive deeper, Apple's WatchKit programming guide covers some of the steps you need to take for localization:

- https://developer.apple.com/library/prerelease/ios/documentation/General/Conceptual/WatchKitProgrammingGuide/TextandLabels.html#//apple_ref/doc/uid/TP40014969-CH19-SW1

For localizing the words themselves, you may be able to get away with using Google's free translation service at http://google.com/translate, but the results are very hit or miss. If you can spare a few bucks, there are several third-party vendors listed at the bottom of Apple's Internationalization and Localization page. Pricing varies from vendor to vendor, but is typically less than 10 cents per word:

- https://developer.apple.com/internationalization/

If you're looking to be at the top of your game, here are a few ideas to extend the SousChef app:

1. Make a button on the initial interface to launch your report interface as a modal.
2. Internationalize the button labels for **Recipes** (Spanish: *recetas*) and **Groceries** (Spanish: *comestibles*) on the initial interface. **Note**: While it's possible to localize text in a storyboard, the best practice is to set up outlets and set text programmatically like you did in this chapter. While you're localizing these two labels, challenge yourself to see if you can remember all the steps. If you get stuck, follow along with the "Separating text from code" section in this chapter.
3. Modify the app so that the number of purchases in the report pulls from the real history of your grocery list.
4. Did I mention you can use the Localizable.strings file for image names, too? See if you can display a different image for Spanish speakers by using `setImageNamed(:_)` with `NSLocalizedString(_:value:comment)` in your app.

Now that your app is ready to for use across the world, may your WatchKit skills take you far and wide! :]

Conclusion

We hope you had a ton of fun working through this book. If you did decide to cherry-pick chapters according to your own interests and projects, then fair enough—you surely learned a lot and got your WatchKit projects started off on the right foot. And if, as intended, you read this entire book from cover to cover, then take a bow—you're officially a WatchKit ninja!

You now have a wealth of experience with WatchKit and know what it takes to build rich, engaging and performant apps for the Apple Watch, using a host of exciting concepts and techniques that are unique to Apple's new platform. If you're like us, learning about all these cutting-edge technologies and concepts has you overflowing with ideas. We can't wait to see what you build!

If you have any questions or comments, please do stop by our forums at http://www.raywenderlich.com/forums.

Thank you again for purchasing this book. Your continued support is what makes the tutorials, books and other things we do at raywenderlich.com possible—we all truly appreciate it!

Best of luck with your Apple Watch adventures,

- Ryan, Audrey, Soheil, Ben, Matt, Jack, Scott, Mike, Eric, B.C., Mic, Ray and Vicki

(The raywenderlich.com Tutorial Team and friends!)

Appendix I: Setting Up Notifications in the iPhone App

By Matthew Morey

Chapter 11 covers in great detail how to enhance notifications to take full advantage of the Watch interface, but it's also important to understand how the same notifications behave on the SousChef iPhone app.

The SousChef iPhone app supports two kinds of notification; a local one that allows the user to create a kitchen timer for recipe directions, and a remote one that informs the user when a new recipe is available.

This part of the appendix will focus on the kitchen timer local notification, as well as some of the notification basics. The second part of the appendix will focus on remote notifications; both the client-side APIs and the server technologies you need to push notifications to the client.

Notifications

Open the SousChef project, select the **SousChef** scheme and then **build and run**.

On first launch, iOS presents a dialog asking the user for permission to present user-facing notifications. Tap **OK**.

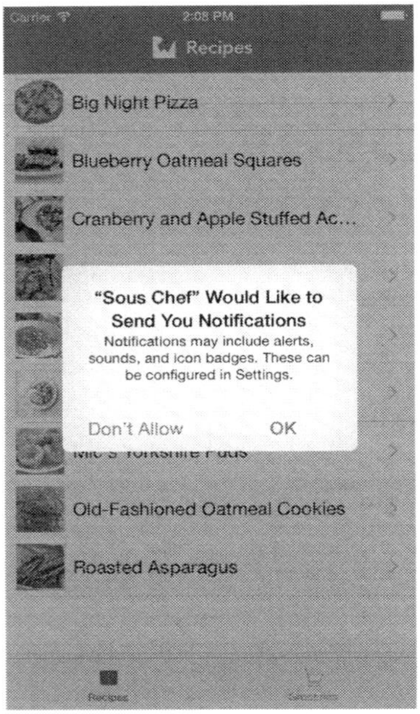

If you don't see this dialog, it means you've already run the app, probably in an earlier chapter, and already responded to the permission dialog. To see the dialog again, delete the SousChef iPhone app from the simulator and then **build and run** again.

If you tap **Don't Allow**, notifications will not work and you will not be able to follow the rest of this chapter.

In that case, open the Settings app and find the settings for SousChef, where you can enable notifications.

Viewing the local notification

After granting permission, select the **Blueberry Oatmeal Squares** recipe from the list. Then tap on **Directions** in the navigation bar, and you'll see a list of steps to follow in order to prepare the recipe.

Tap on the **first step** in the recipe, which conveniently includes a timer; any step that includes time as part of its description allows you to invoke a timer. The app will display the following prompt:

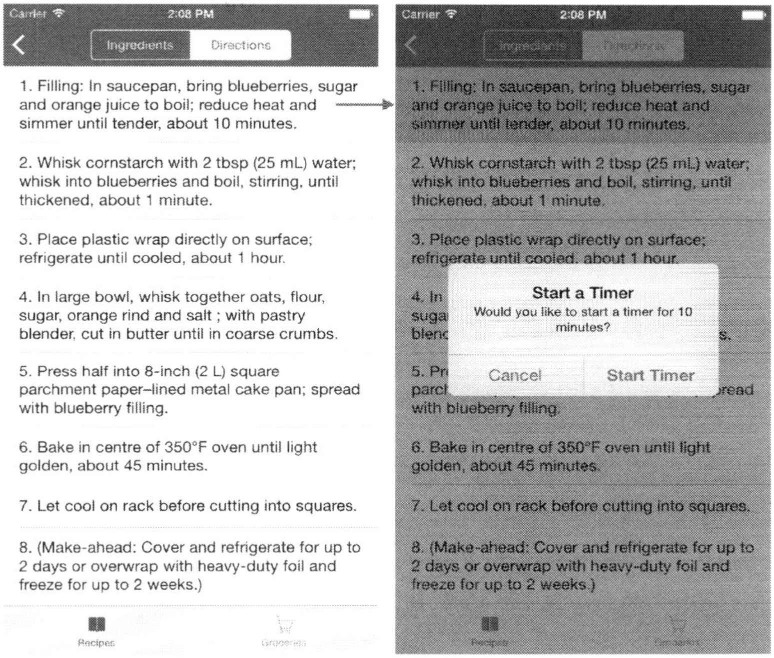

Tap on **Start Timer** to activate the kitchen timer. Select **Hardware\Home** to put the app in the background.

Now take a break. Maybe this app is making you hungry, or maybe you have someone you want to call only when you have an excuse to get off the phone—this is your opportunity!

As long as you don't return to the SousChef app before the timer runs out, the app will stay in the background and the notification will appear as a banner at the top of the device. If the device is locked when the notification happens it will appear on the lock screen. It is also possible to configure notifications to appear as alerts or to disable them completely in the Settings app.

The default configuration is for the notification to appear as a banner. Pull down on the banner to show the actions for the notification.

For the kitchen timer notification, there's a single action, **View Directions**.

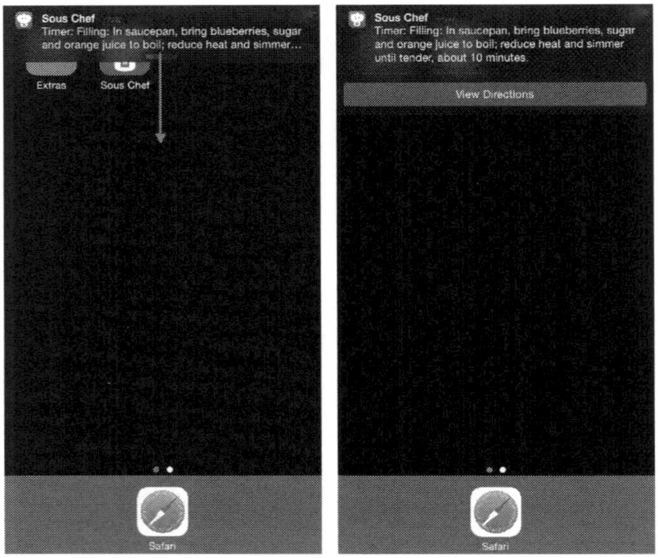

If the app is in the foreground when the timer expires, the app will display an alert that includes the recipe name and the directions associated with the expired timer. Just like the banner version of the notification, there is a single action, **View Directions**.

Tapping on **View Directions** will take you directly to the recipe associated with the expired timer.

Viewing the remote notification

The iPhone app also supports a second type of notification that is sent when new recipes are available for download. When a new recipe is available, the app gives the user the opportunity to view that recipe right away.

Unlike the kitchen timer notification, which is local, the new recipe notification is a remote notification.

The iPhone app schedules local notifications using `scheduleLocalNotification(_:)`, a method on `UIApplication`, and delivers them to the same device.

A server is responsible for sending remote notifications, commonly called push notifications, to Apple's Push Notifications Service, which then delivers the notification to the users' device.

For now, you won't be able to see a new recipe notification for yourself, as it requires setting up a server, which is covered in detail in the second section of the appendix.

For now, just know that the SousChef iPhone app does support the "new recipe" remote notification, which looks like this:

Now it's time to put on your chef hat and see what code ingredients you require to make these notifications work on the iPhone app.

Under the hood

Now that you know what the notification UI looks like it is time to see the actual code. A lot of this code is very similar to what you wrote back in Chapter 11 when creating the custom notifications for the Watch app. Due to the overwhelming similarities you won't be writing any code yourself, but instead you just need to follow along.

Open **SousChef\AppDelegate.swift** and find `registerUserNotificationSettings()`:

```
func registerUserNotificationSettings() {
  // 1
  let viewDirectionsAction = UIMutableUserNotificationAction()
  viewDirectionsAction.identifier = "viewDirectionsButtonAction"
  viewDirectionsAction.title = "View Directions"
  viewDirectionsAction.activationMode = .Foreground
  viewDirectionsAction.authenticationRequired = false

  let viewRecipeAction = UIMutableUserNotificationAction()
  viewRecipeAction.identifier = "viewRecipeButtonAction"
  viewRecipeAction.title = "View Recipe"
  viewRecipeAction.activationMode = .Foreground
  viewRecipeAction.authenticationRequired = false

  // 2
  let timerCategory = UIMutableUserNotificationCategory()
  timerCategory.identifier = "timer"
  timerCategory.setActions([viewDirectionsAction],
    forContext: .Default)

  let newRecipeCategory = UIMutableUserNotificationCategory()
  newRecipeCategory.identifier = "new_recipe"
  newRecipeCategory.setActions([viewRecipeAction],
    forContext: .Default)

  let categories = NSSet(array: [timerCategory,
```

```
    newRecipeCategory])

  // 3
  let settings = UIUserNotificationSettings(
    forTypes: .Alert | .Sound, categories: categories as
    Set<NSObject>)
  UIApplication.sharedApplication()
    .registerUserNotificationSettings(settings)
}
```

This method is called from `application(_:didFinishLaunchingWithOptions:)` upon app launch. Let's go through this code step by step to find out what it does:

1. First, the method creates two separate notification actions. A notification action is exactly what it sounds like; it represents an action the user can take when presented with a notification. The method creates `viewDirectionsAction` for use with the "kitchen timer" local notification and allows the user to immediately go to a recipe's directions when a kitchen timer expires. The "new recipe" remote notification uses `viewRecipeAction`, which allows the user to immediately view the new recipe. Both are set to the foreground activation mode, meaning the device on which the user tapped the button will determine whether that tap will launch the iPhone app or the Watch app.

2. Next, the method creates two notification categories, `timerCategory` for the "kitchen timer" local notification and `newRecipeCategory` for the "new recipe" remote notification. Because apps can have multiple notification types, categories are used to differentiate one notification from another. To each category, the method adds the appropriate actions created in the previous step.

3. Finally, the method calls `registerUserNotificationSettings(_:)` to register the notification categories and settings. For the SousChef app, the method requests alert and sound types. If this is the app's first launch, then the app shows the familiar user permissions dialog:

Now locate `application(_:didRegisterUserNotificationSettings:)`, also in **AppDelegate.swift**:

```
func application(application: UIApplication,
  didRegisterUserNotificationSettings
    notificationSettings: UIUserNotificationSettings) {
  if (notificationSettings.types & UIUserNotificationType.Alert)
    != nil {
    application.registerForRemoteNotifications()
  }
}
```

The app automatically calls this method after calling `registerUserNotificationSettings(_:)`. If your user has approved alert style notifications, then the method also registers them for the "new recipe" remote notifications by calling `registerForRemoteNotifications()`.

iOS treats notifications differently according to whether your app is in the foreground or background when the user receives the notification.

If your app is in the background, as it typically is, the OS will take care of displaying the notification text and potential actions to the user. If the user decides to open your app or invoke one of the actions in the notification, iOS will call `application(_:handleActionWithIdentifier:forLocalNotification:completionHandler:)`, which is shown here:

```
func application(application: UIApplication,
  handleActionWithIdentifier identifier: String?,
    forLocalNotification notification: UILocalNotification,
      completionHandler: () -> Void) {
  if identifier == "viewDirectionsButtonAction" {
    if let userInfo = notification.userInfo {
      showRecipeWithUserInfo(userInfo, andInitialController:
.Steps)
    }
  }
  completionHandler()
}
```

In the case of SousChef, if the user invokes the "View Directions" action, the app will take them directly to the recipe via `showRecipeWithUserInfo(_:andInitialController:)`. If the user invokes any other action or simply opens the notification, the app will open and this method will simply call the completion handler it's handed.

If your app is in the foreground when the user receives a notification, the OS won't show any of the standard notification UI from above. Instead, the OS will call `application(_:didReceiveLocalNotification:)` and rely on you to display what you need to the user.

Handling local notifications when the app is open

Locate `application(_:didReceiveLocalNotification:)` to see what happens when a local notification is received when the app is in the foreground:

```
func application(application: UIApplication,
  didReceiveLocalNotification notification: UILocalNotification)
{
  if let userInfo = notification.userInfo {
    if let category = userInfo["category"] as? String {

      // 1
      if category == "timer" {

        // 2
        let title = userInfo["title"]! as! String
        let message = userInfo["message"]! as! String
        let alert = UIAlertController(title: title,
          message: message, preferredStyle: .Alert)
        alert.addAction(UIAlertAction(title: "Cancel",
          style: .Cancel, handler: nil))
        alert.addAction(UIAlertAction(title: "View Directions",
          style: .Default, handler: { _ in
          self.showRecipeWithUserInfo(userInfo,
            andInitialController: .Steps)
        }))

        // 3
        let tabBarController =
          window?.rootViewController! as! UITabBarController
        let recipesNavigationController =
          tabBarController.viewControllers![0]
            as! UINavigationController
        recipesNavigationController.presentViewController(alert,
          animated: true, completion: nil)
      }
    }
  }
}
```

That's quite the chunk of code; let me break it down:

1. Check if the received notification is of the "kitchen timer" category.
2. If it is, create an alert view to display the directions for the expired timer. The alert has two buttons, Cancel and View Directions. If the user taps View Directions, then `showRecipeWithUserInfo(_:andInitialController:)` is called passing the relevant info about the associated recipe.
3. Finally, the alert is presented to the user by calling `presentViewController(_:animated:completion:)`:

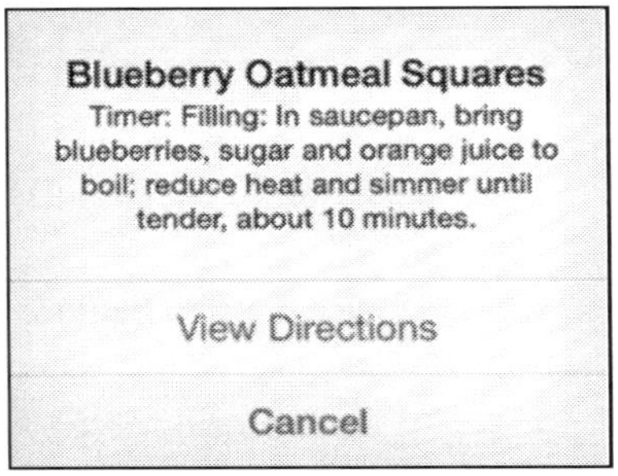

Whether the user receives the notification in the foreground or the background, you probably noticed both methods eventually show the recipe directions to the user by calling `showRecipeWithUserInfo(_:andInitialController:)`, which does the following:

```
func showRecipeWithUserInfo(userInfo: [NSObject : AnyObject]!,
  andInitialController initialController:
    RecipeDetailSelection){

  // 1
  if let title = userInfo["title"] as? String {

    // 2
    let matchingRecipes =
      recipeStore.recipes.filter({$0.name == title})

    // 3
    let tabBarController =
      window?.rootViewController! as! UITabBarController
    let recipesNavigationController =
      tabBarController.viewControllers![0]
        as! UINavigationController
    let mainStoryboard = UIStoryboard(name: "Main", bundle: nil)
    let recipeDetailController =
      mainStoryboard.instantiateViewControllerWithIdentifier(
```

```
        "RecipeDetail") as! RecipeDetailController
    recipeDetailController.recipe = matchingRecipes[0]
    recipeDetailController.initialController = initialController

    // 4
    recipesNavigationController.pushViewController(
      recipeDetailController, animated: true)
  }
}
```

This method, called by both `application(_:handleActionWithIdentifier:forLocalNotification:completionHandler:)` and `application(_:didReceiveLocalNotification:)`, receives a dictionary and an initial controller type to display, in this case either ingredients or directions. This is how it works:

1. Check the `userInfo` dictionary for the title key, which stores the name of the recipe associated with the expired "kitchen timer" local notification.
2. Find the correct recipe based on the value of title key. You use the new `filter(_:)` method in Swift to find the recipe with the matching name.
3. Instantiate a new controller of type `RecipeDetailController`. The method sets `recipe` to the correct recipe.
4. Finally, the new controller is pushed onto the navigation stack.

Now you know how the iPhone app processes the "kitchen timer" notifications. But how are they scheduled in the first place?

Scheduling local notifications

Open **SousChef\RecipeDirectionsController.swift** and find `tableView(_:didSelectRowAtIndexPath:)`:

```
override func tableView(tableView: UITableView,
  didSelectRowAtIndexPath indexPath: NSIndexPath) {
  let timer = recipe.timers[indexPath.row]
  if timer > 0 {
    promptToStartTimerForStepIndex(indexPath.row)
  }
}
```

As you can see, you check if there's a timer associated with the selected recipe direction by testing if its value is greater than 0.

If there is, then call `promptToStartTimerForStepIndex(_:)`, which is shown here:

```
func promptToStartTimerForStepIndex(stepIndex: Int) {
  let alert = UIAlertController(title: "Start a Timer",
    message: "Would you like to start a timer for
      \(recipe.timers[stepIndex]) minutes?",
        preferredStyle: .Alert)
  alert.addAction(UIAlertAction(title: "Cancel",
    style: .Cancel, handler: nil))
  alert.addAction(UIAlertAction(title: "Start Timer",
    style: .Default, handler: { _ in
    self.startTimerForStepIndex(stepIndex)
  }))

  presentViewController(alert, animated: true, completion: nil)
}
```

Here you present an alert with **Cancel** and **Start Timer** buttons:

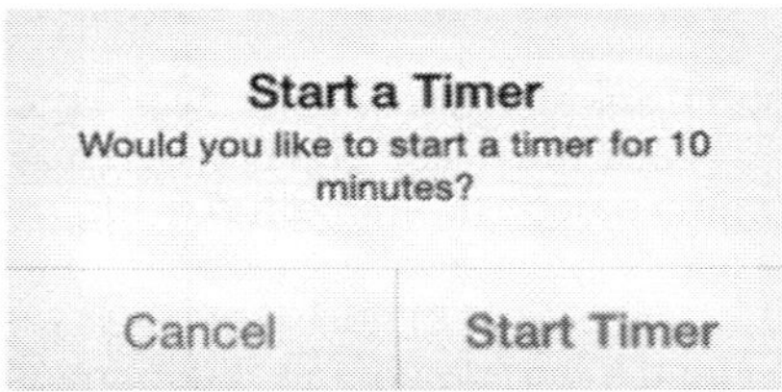

If the user taps the Start Timer button, then the method calls `startTimerForStepIndex(_:)`:

```
func startTimerForStepIndex(stepIndex: Int) {
  let userInfo: [NSObject : AnyObject] = [
    "category" : "timer",
    "timer" : recipe.timers[stepIndex],
    "message" : "Timer: \(recipe.steps[stepIndex])",
    "title" : recipe.name
  ]

  let appDelegate =
    UIApplication.sharedApplication().delegate as! AppDelegate
  appDelegate.scheduleTimerNotificationWithUserInfo(userInfo)
}
```

This helper method creates a `userInfo` dictionary that contains the title, message, and timer length for the tapped recipe step. The dictionary is passed to `scheduleTimerNotificationWithUserInfo(_:)` in AppDelegate.swift:

```
func scheduleTimerNotificationWithUserInfo(
  userInfo: [NSObject : AnyObject]!) {
  let application = UIApplication.sharedApplication()
  if (application.currentUserNotificationSettings().types &
    UIUserNotificationType.Alert) != nil {
    let message = userInfo["message"] as! String
    let title = userInfo["title"] as! String
    let timer = userInfo["timer"] as! Int
    let fireDate =
      NSDate(timeIntervalSinceNow: NSTimeInterval(timer * 60))

    let notification = UILocalNotification()
    notification.fireDate = fireDate
    notification.alertTitle = title
    notification.alertBody = message
    notification.soundName = UILocalNotificationDefaultSoundName
    notification.category = "timer"
    notification.userInfo = userInfo

    application.scheduleLocalNotification(notification)
  }
}
```

Finally, `scheduleTimerNotificationWithUserInfo(_:)` is responsible for building the local "kitchen timer" notification and scheduling it by calling `scheduleLocalNotification(_:)`.

Nice work! Now you know how the SousChef notifications look, behave and work on the iPhone app.

Where to go from here?

In this part of the appendix, you reviewed how notifications work in the SousChef iPhone app. You got to see how notifications look to the user, and you learned how to handle incoming notifications and schedule local notifications.

If you'd like to understand how to set up remote notifications from both the client and server sides, then the next section of the appendix, "Setting Up a Push Notification Server", is for you.

To learn more about the new iOS 8 features specific to notifications, such as actions, check out Apple's Local and Remote Notification Programming Guide:

https://developer.apple.com/library/ios/documentation/NetworkingInternet/Conceptual/RemoteNotificationsPG/Introduction.html - //apple_ref/doc/uid/TP40008194-CH1-SW1.

Appendix II: Setting Up a Push Notification Server

By Scott Atkinson

Chapter 11, "Notifications", showed you how to customize the display of, and take actions on local and remote notifications in the SousChef Watch app. It also described how to create a local "kitchen timer" notification.

Then, the "Setting Up Notifications in the iPhone App" section of the appendix reviewed all the code in the SousChef iPhone app that handles the registration, categorization, and receipt of those notifications.

You may have been asking yourself: "Great, but how do I send a push notification in the first place?" In this section of the appendix, we'll walk you through everything you need to know about setting up your very own push notification service.

Here's what you'll learn:

- How to create the necessary Apple credentials for your push service;
- How to set up a push server using Parse.com.

You've waited long enough—so let's get started!

Prerequisites

The process of setting up your own push notification service using Parse and configuring your app for receiving push notifications is not terribly difficult. But there are a number of things you'll need to have in place before you get started. In particular, you'll need:

1. An active iOS developer account with administrative privileges;
2. An actual iOS device, not a simulator, to receive push notifications;
3. A GitHub account where you've forked the **recipes** repo introduced in Chapter 8, "Sharing Data".

You'll also need a Parse.com account, which you'll create later in the chapter. Parse will act as the server that communicates with the Apple APNS servers. In this chapter, you'll build a JavaScript-based service that initiates the push notifications, and let Parse and Apple handle the rest.

Apple's Push Notification service

Getting a notification from a service out to the Internet and then to a specific mobile device is actually pretty tricky. You need to know how to connect to that device, establish a trusted connection with it and then send a payload that it can understand and react to. And, since any given app or service has the potential to send multiple notifications to possibly millions of devices, it has to scale well and be always available.

Luckily, since iOS 3, Apple has provided many of these features via the Apple Push Notification service (APNs). In its simplest form, APNs is a point-to-point transport layer between your app's service and the millions of devices that may use your app to receive notifications. Several things are required for it to work properly:

- Your service can send messages to APNs;
- Each device that could receive a push notification has a unique identifier or token;
- There's a "topic" that identifies the app that is intended to receive a given push message, which is generally your app's Bundle ID;
- There is a set of certificates to establish trust between your server and APNs, and between APNs and each mobile device.

Provisioning your app for push notifications

In Chapter 8, "Sharing Data", you configured SousChef for various capabilities and entitlements. Xcode then created an App ID in the Apple Provisioning Portal and configured it with the capabilities you'd selected. In this section, you'll add push services to this App ID and then create an APNs certificate that establishes the trust between the client and server.

First you need to locate the App ID generated by Xcode. Open **Safari** and navigate to the Apple Provisioning Portal, and then select **App IDs** from the **Identifiers** section. Scroll through the list to locate the App ID you created in Chapter 8, "Sharing Data".

You should see something like this:

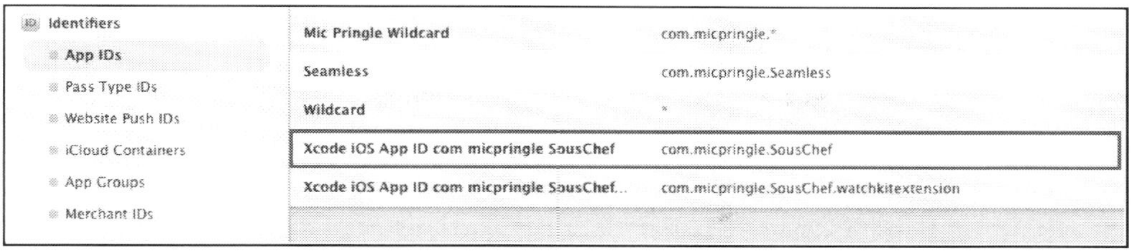

Once you locate the correct App ID, **click** on it and then click the **Edit** button. Scroll down to the **Push Notifications** section, tick the checkbox and then click **Done**.

Nice job—you've enabled push notifications for Sous Chef! That was easy, right?

Creating an APNs certificate

Now you'll continue the work of generating the correct credentials to enable you to send a push notification.

You need to create an APNs development certificate, which your service on Parse will use to create a secure connection to Apple's APNs servers.

Back in the Apple Provisioning Portal, click **All** in the **Certificates** section, followed by the + button to create a new certificate. You'll be presented with a number of options. You want an **Apple Push Notification service SSL (Sandbox)** certificate, found under the **Development** section. Select that option and then click **Continue**.

On the next screen, choose the same App ID that you edited earlier:

By choosing the SousChef App ID, you are associating the app with the certificate. When the Parse server makes a connection to the APNs server using this certificate, the

APNs server will know that the server is sending out notifications specifically for the SousChef app.

Next, you'll be asked to generate a **Certificate Signing Request** (CSR). The provisioning portal has a helpful set of instructions for creating the CSR, but I've outlined the steps below as well.

First launch the **Keychain Access** application located in **Applications\Utilities**. Then, from the **Keychain Access** menu, select **Certificate Assistant\Request a Certificate from a Certificate Authority**:

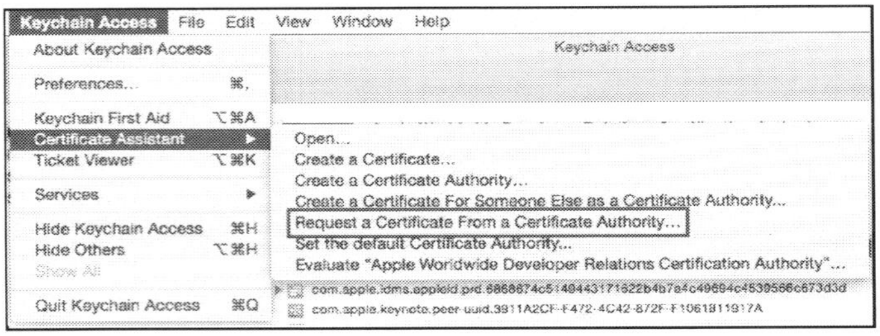

The Certificate Assistant will now appear. In the dialog, enter the following:

- **User Email Address**: Use any valid email address you have.
- **Common Name**: Enter a descriptive name that will make it easy to locate the certificate in the Keychain Access app. Again, reverse domain name notation is probably best.
- **CA Email**: Leave this field blank.
- **Request is**: Select "Saved to Disk".

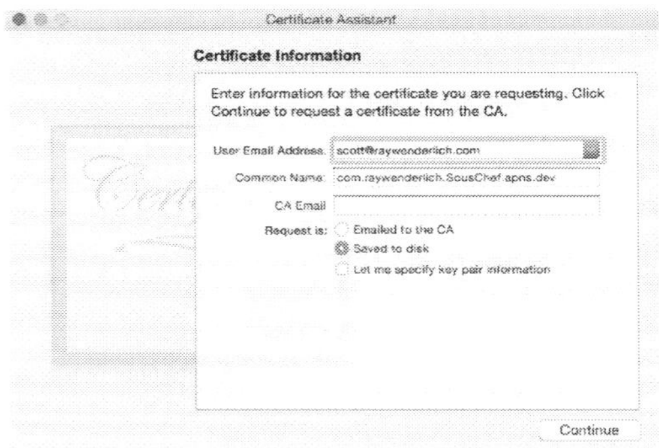

Now click **Continue**. You'll be asked to save the CSR; save it using the recommended filename and return to the provisioning portal. On the **About Creating a Certificate**

Signing Request page, click **Continue**. Then **Choose File…** and find the CSR file you just saved. Finally, click the **Generate** button.

It may take a couple of minutes for your certificate to be generated. Once it's done, click the **Download** button. Finally, find the downloaded file and **double-click** it. This will save the certificate to your keychain.

To verify that the certificate has been saved, open **Keychain Access**, select the **Certificates** category in the left navigation pane and scroll through the list to find the certificate.

It should look like this:

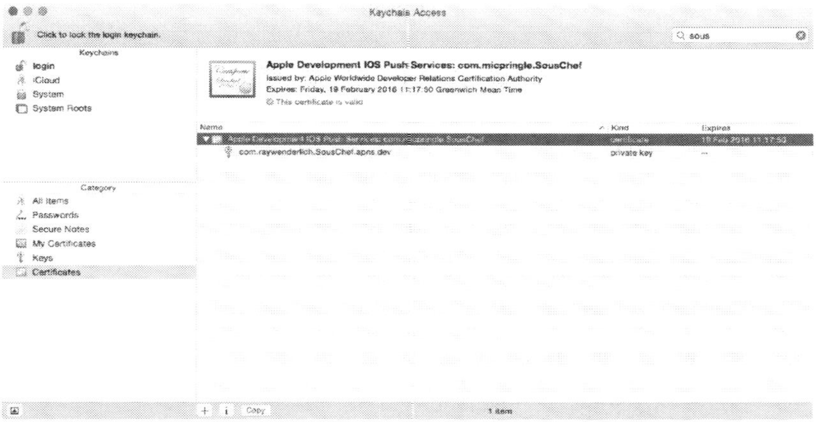

> **Note**: In the screenshot above, the certificate has a "private key" entry. Since the downloaded certificate was saved to the same keychain that generated the CSR, the certificate's private key was associated with the certificate. If you were to download the certificate to another machine and save it to that machine's keychain, it would not include the private key; thus, you wouldn't be able to install it on your push server.
>
> Be sure to make a backup of the full certificate by following the instructions in the next section, "Exporting your certificate", from the machine that originally created the certificate in case you need to reinstall the certificate on another machine—for instance, if you purchase a new Mac.

Excellent! At this point, you've got all the pieces necessary to set up and send push notifications from APNS.

Exporting your certificate

You'll need to export a copy of your APNs certificate so it can be installed on Parse. Parse uses **.p12** certificate files, which contain both the certificate and the private key.

Open **Keychain Access** from the **Applications\Utilities** folder. In the left pane, click **Certificates**. Then enter **souschef** in the search bar and press **Enter**. The certificate you imported from the provisioning portal should appear in the search results. Now, select the certificate and choose **File\Exports Items…**. In the save dialog enter **SousChefDevCert** for the file name. In the **File Format** field, select **Personal Information Exchange (.p12)**. Finally, click **Save**. You'll be asked to enter a password. Leave this field blank and click **OK**. It should look like this:

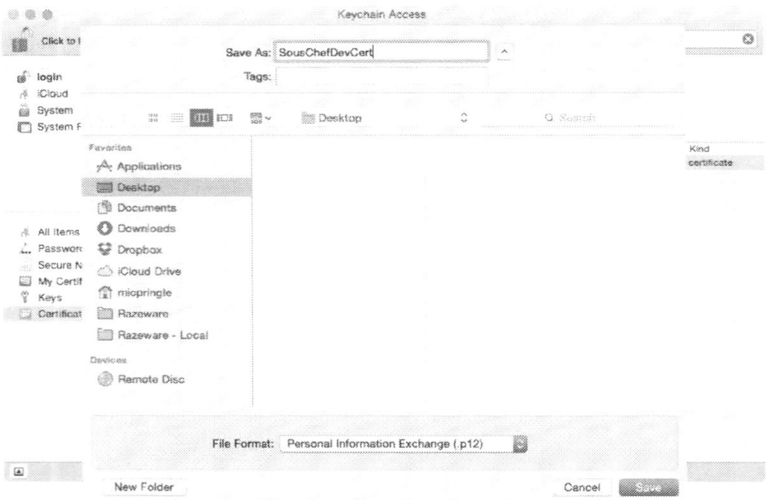

That's it! You just saved a .p12 certificate file ready to be uploaded to Parse.

Creating a push service

In order to send push notifications you need some sort of server that will be able to send the notifications to your user's devices at any time. In this section, you'll set up a service that can send "New Recipe Available" notifications from the **Platform as a Service** (PAAS) provider parse.com.

Parse.com

Parse.com provides a number of tools that make building a server-backed app super simple. In this section, you'll take advantage of three Parse technologies:

- Push notifications (of course).
- Object data store: This allows for saving pieces of data. You'll use it to store recipes.
- Cloud Code: Parse was originally developed to work directly between mobile clients and Parse services. Later, Parse added support for the ability to execute custom code directly on its servers. You'll use Cloud Code to pull the Recipes.json file from your GitHub repo, parse it, and store the recipes in the object data store.

First, you'll need to sign up for a Parse account. Parse is free as long as your apps use a relatively small amount of resources. For the purposes of this tutorial, this shouldn't be an issue.

If you don't have an account already, head over to Parse.com and click **Sign up**. Enter your **name**, **email address** and **password**.

If you already have an account, log in and then click **Create a new app**.

On the next screen, enter **SousChef** as the app name and select **Individual Developer** from the second drop-down. Click **Start using Parse**:

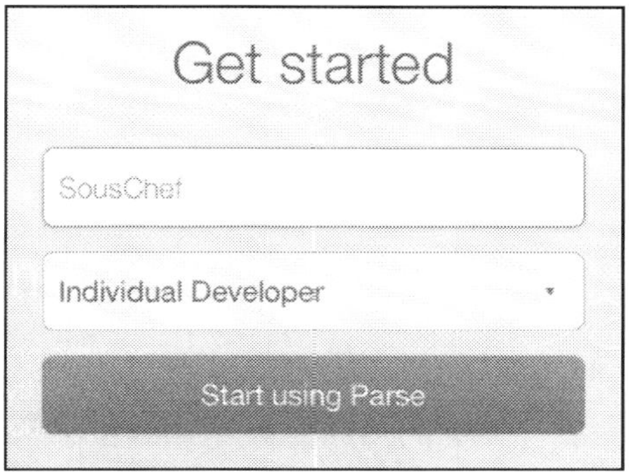

Your server architecture

In Chapter 8, "Sharing Data", you configured SousChef to pull the Recipes.json file down from GitHub. Your Parse service will watch this repo for changes, grab the latest Recipes.json when it changes, and send push notifications to registered devices.

This process is detailed in the following diagram:

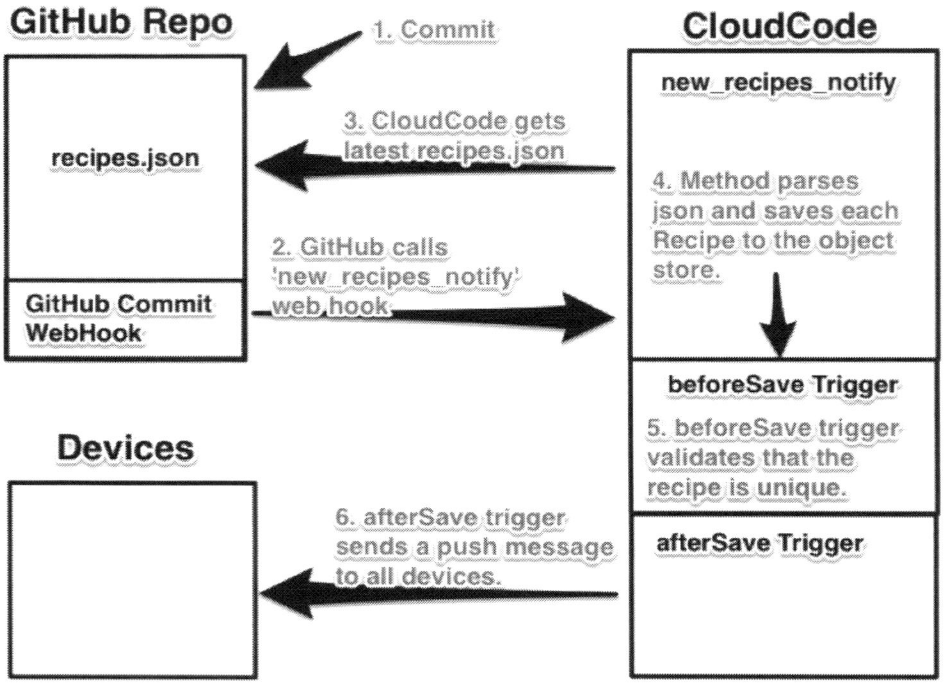

Set up your recipes object store

You need a place to track your recipes so you can determine if a recipe is new and whether you've sent out a push notification for that recipe yet. By default, Parse's security is somewhat open. In particular, clients with the appropriate access tokens will be able to create new classes. Let's turn that off.

In the Parse console for your app, click on **Settings** and then make sure **General** is selected in the left hand pane. Scroll down the page to the **App Permissions** section, and set **Allow client class creation** to **No**:

Now, click the **Core** tab at the top of the screen (the first button), then **Add Class**. In the dialog that appears, enter **Recipe** and click **Create Class**.

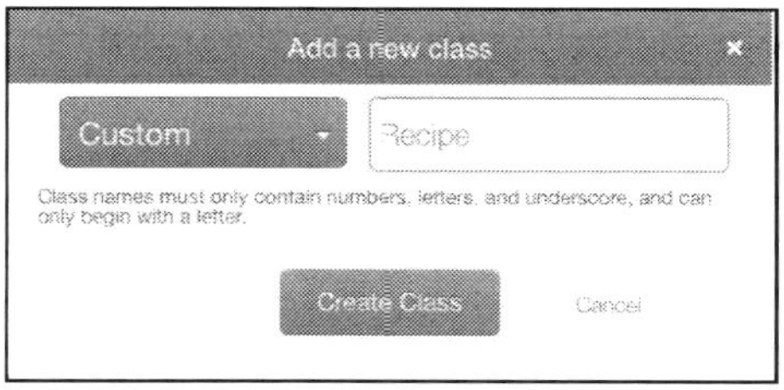

That's it; you've created a placeholder for your class. You don't need to define properties for it—the first time Cloud Code saves an instance of the class, it will add the necessary properties automatically.

Create and test a Cloud Code application

Now that you have a `Recipe` class ready to store recipes from the JSON file on GitHub, you'll want to create the Cloud Code files. Cloud Code is simply a server-based JavaScript client for the Parse SDK, so you'll be working with JavaScript in this section.

First you need to download the Parse command line tools. In **Terminal**, enter the following command.

```
curl -s https://www.parse.com/downloads/cloud_code/installer.sh
| sudo /bin/bash
```

You'll need to enter your administrator password to install the tools, so do that when prompted.

Once installation is complete, you'll create a Cloud Code directory structure using the command line tools.

Still in **Terminal**, navigate to the directory directly above the location of the **SousChef.xcodeproj** and enter the following command:

```
parse new SousChefCloudCode
```

Enter the **email address** and **password** you when signing up for Parse. Then select **SousChef** from the menu. It should look like this:

```
Email: your@emailaddress.com
Password:
1:SousChef
Select an App: 1
```

The Parse command line tool will create a Cloud Code directory structure. You'll be working with the main.js file located in the **cloud** folder. Switch to that folder now:

```
cd SousChefCloudCode/cloud
```

Open **main.js** using your favorite text editor. You'll see the classic "Hello, World" function.

Back in **Terminal**, enter the following:

```
parse deploy
```

This command deploys all Cloud Code in the current directory to Parse. Before you test your code, you'll need to get your Parse API keys. You'll use them to set headers in `curl` requests you make to test your code.

Switch back to your browser. In the Parse control panel, click the **Settings** tab, then the **Keys** option in the sidebar. Find the **Application ID** and **Rest API Key** values. Copy those to somewhere where you can easily access them.

Back in **Terminal**, enter the following `curl` command, replacing **APPLICATION_ID** and **REST_API_KEY** with the values you just copied from the Parse control panel:

```
curl -X POST \
  -H "X-Parse-Application-Id: APPLICATION_ID" \
  -H "X-Parse-REST-API-Key: REST_API_KEY" \
  -H "Content-Type: application/json" \
  -d '{}' \
  https://api.parse.com/1/functions/hello
```

This command adds three HTTP headers to a HTTP `POST` call to the https://api.parse.com/1/functions/hello endpoint. Notice that the endpoint is named "hello". This is the same name that was defined in the Javascript file you opened a few moments ago.

You should receive a response that looks something like this:

```
{
  "result": "Hello world!"
}
```

Implement your push server

OK, now that you've tested your Cloud Code, and Parse is returning responses, let's create something that actually serves a purpose.

Open **main.js** and replace its contents with the following:

```
// ****** Send Push on New Recipe Creation ******
Parse.Cloud.afterSave("Recipe", function(request) {
  // 1
  var recipeName = request.object.get("name");
  var imageURL = request.object.get("imageURL");

  // 2
  Parse.Push.send({
  // 3
    where: new Parse.Query(Parse.Installation),
    // 4
    data: {
      alert: "New "+recipeName+" recipe is now available.",
      category: "new_recipe",
      title: recipeName,
      recipe: {
        name: recipeName,
        imageURL: imageURL
      }
    }
  }, {
    // 5
    success: function() {
      console.log("Push Sent\n");
    },
    error: function(error) { console.error("Push Error
      "+error.code+" : "+error.message);
    }
  });
});
```

Whoa, that's a lot of code! It's actually pretty easy. First, you declare `Parse.Cloud.afterSave` on the `Recipe` class. You can think of this as callback that's executed after a `Recipe` object is saved to Parse. Let's walk through the method step by step:

1. You grab the pertinent information from the recipe (the `name` and `imageURL`) that you'll send as the payload of the push notification.
2. Next, you begin the process of sending the push notification.
3. The `where` parameter of the closure defines which device tokens will receive the message. In your case, you want all devices to receive it. Creating a new `Query` on the `Installation` object will return *all* device tokens—more on the `Installation` object later.
4. You build a JavaScript dictionary that will represent the payload of your push notification.
5. Finally, you handle the results of the push by logging either the success or failure to the Parse console.

That wasn't too bad, right? Save **main.js** and deploy to Parse again by entering the following in **Terminal**:

```
parse deploy
```

Installing your APNS certificates in Parse

Before Parse can communicate with APNS, you need to upload the certificate you created earlier. In the Parse control panel, click **Settings**, and then select **Push** from the list on the left. Scroll down to the **Push Notification Settings** section and ensure that the **Client Push enabled** slider is set to **Yes**:

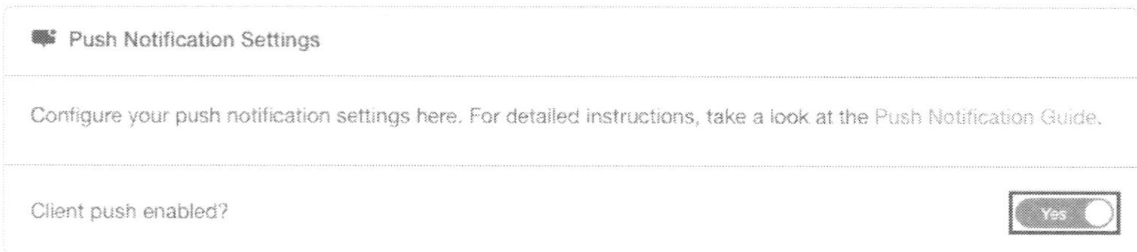

Now, scroll to the **Apple Push Certificate** section and click **Select your certificate**. Navigate to the **SousChefDevCert.p12** file you exported earlier and click **Open**. The file will be uploaded to Parse. It will look like this when you're done:

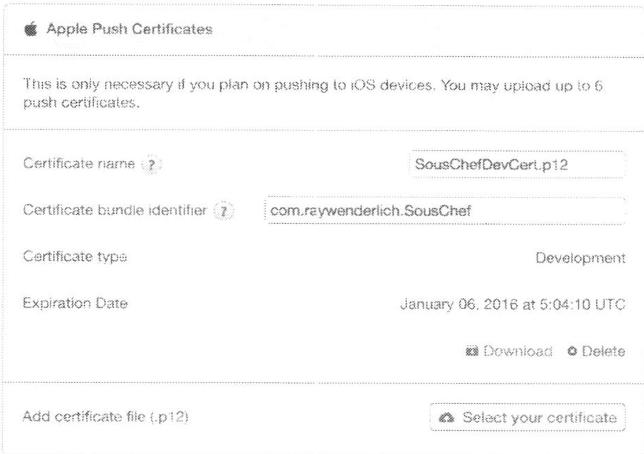

At this point, it's technically possible to create a `Recipe` object from the Parse console and have it send a push notification. But, to keep things moving, let's add a mechanism to pull a JSON file into Parse's object store.

Back in Chapter 8, "Sharing Data", you added the necessary methods to `RecipeStore` to pull a JSON file down from GitHub. You're going to use the same file and pull it into Parse for further processing. You'll build this as a web hook so that GitHub can call it when `Recipes.json` changes. Let's get to it!

Open **main.js**, add the following to the top of the file:

```
var express = require('express');
var _ = require('underscore');
```

Parse supports a number of modules in Cloud Code. In this case, you've imported the ExpressJS middleware and the Underscore.js utility library. You'll use both of these to download and process `Recipes.json` from GitHub repo.

Next, add the following in **main.js**:

```
var recipesJSONURL =
'https://raw.githubusercontent.com/YOUR_GITHUB_USERNAME/recipes/
master/Recipes.json';

// Subclass a parse object to be a Recipe object
var Recipe = Parse.Object.extend("Recipe");
```

Here, you define the `recipesJSONURL` string to point to the JSON file stored in your GitHub repo. You need to adjust this string to point to your own repo because you'll need to make changes to it later. This is the same URL that you used in Chapter 8,

"Sharing Data". After that, you define the Recipe subclass to make your code more readable.

Now, at the bottom of **main.js**, add the following:

```
// ****************** Web Hook ******************
var app = express();

// Global app configuration section
app.use(express.bodyParser()); // Populate req.body
```

Here you define app as an Express application. Then, you tell the app to parse the body of the HTTP request and deliver it to your web hook—you'll actually ignore that body in this web hook.

You'll now define a HTTP POST-based web hook called new_recipes_notify.

At the bottom of **main.js**, add the following:

```
app.post('/new_recipes_notify', function(req, res) {
  // Get Recipes from GitHub Repo
  Parse.Cloud.httpRequest({
    url: recipesJSONURL,
    headers: {
      'Content-Type': 'application/json;charset=utf-8'
    },
    success: function(httpResponse) {
      handleJSON(res, httpResponse);
    },
    error: function(httpResponse) {
      // Something bad happened with the request
      res.status(500);
      res.send("Error\n");
    }
  });
});
```

The web hook is pretty straightforward. First you build your own HTTP request to grab Recipes.json from GitHub. The HTTP request is executed immediately. In the success block of httpRequest, you parse the JSON using handleJSON(). If the HTTP request fails, the web hook simply returns a 500 error to its caller.

OK, now let's parse that JSON recipe data! Below the web hook method you just added, enter the following:

```
function handleJSON(res, httpResponse) {
  // 1
  var fileJSON = JSON.parse(httpResponse.text);
```

```
    if (fileJSON.length <= 0) {
      // No records were available for parsing
      res.status(500);
      res.send("Error\n");
      return;
    }
    // 2
    _.each(fileJSON, function(itemJSON) {
      // 3
      var recipe = new Recipe();

      // 4
      recipe.save(itemJSON, {
        success: function(savedRecipe) {
        },
        error: function(savedRecipe, error) {
        }
      });
    });
    // 5. Everything worked out
    res.send("Success\n");
  }
```

Here's what's going on:

1. First, you assume the HTTP response body contains JSON, so you parse it using `JSON.parse()`.
2. If there is valid JSON data, which should be an array of `Recipe` objects, then you iterate over the array using `Underscore.js`.
3. For each entry, you create a Parse `Recipe` object.
4. Since Parse is JavaScript-based itself, populating the new object's properties is as simple as passing the parsed JavaScript object in `save`.
5. If everything works, you pass a "Success" message back as the response to the web hook's caller.

You may have noticed something: There wasn't any code in this call to send a push notification. Remember that when you implemented `Parse.Cloud.afterSave()`, you did the pushing there. Since you're saving `Recipe` objects in the web hook, the `afterSave()` callback will get executed for each one that's saved, thereby generating a push notification.

There's just one more thing to do before deploying, and that's telling the web hook to start listening for requests. At the bottom of **main.js**, add the following:

```
// Begin listening for calls to the web hook
app.listen();
```

Once you deploy, your web hook will start listening for requests.

You're going to add one more method to the server to prevent it from saving and pushing out duplicate recipes. Since you'll be processing the same **Recipes.json** file many times over, this is important. The method you'll implement is another Parse object creation trigger similar to `afterSave()`; you'll call this one `beforeSave()`.

In **main.js**, add the following code **above** `afterSave()`.

```
// ***************** Prevent Duplicates *****************
Parse.Cloud.beforeSave("Recipe", function(request, response) {
  if (!request.object.get("name")) {
    // 1
    response.error('A Recipe must have a name.');
    return;
  }
  if (!request.object.isNew()) {
    // 2
    response.success();
    return;
  }
  // 3
  var query = new Parse.Query(Recipe);
  query.equalTo("name", request.object.get("name"));

  // 4
  query.first({
    success: function(object) {
      if (object) {
        // 5
        response.error("A Recipe with this name
          already exists.");
      } else {
        // 6
        response.success();
      }
    },
    error: function(error) {
      response.error("Could not validate uniqueness of
        this Recipe object.");
    }
  });
});
```

This method is fired right *before* `Recipe` objects are saved to the object data store.

Here's what's happening:

1. The `request` object that's passed to the function contains an `object` property that represents the object this Parse is attempting to save. The method gets the `name` property from the `Recipe` object. If one doesn't exist, the method fails and doesn't save the `Recipe`.
2. All Parse objects expose an `isNew()` property. If the object is *not* new, it is saved.
3. Parse also provides `Query` objects. Here, you create a `Query` on the `Recipe` class. It will look for other objects that have the same `name`.
4. `first()` simply executes the `Query` and returns the first matching object it encounters. If there are no matches, the `object` parameter will be empty.
5. You simply check for the presence of the `object`. If it exists, you should *not* save the new recipe.
6. Otherwise, you should save the new recipe, as it isn't a duplicate.

That's it! You can now deploy your code with the knowledge that your users won't get spammed with extra push messages. So, once more in **Terminal**, enter the following:

```
parse deploy
```

And that's it, your custom Cloud Code to handle sending the push notifications is all set up and ready to go.

Making the call

Right now, you have many of the pieces in place to create `Recipes` and send push notifications. But what's missing is a URL on which to call the web hook and a way to make the call from GitHub. You'll fix that now.

You'll first need to enable web hosting in Parse. To do this, open the Parse control panel and then select **Settings**. Choose **Hosting** from the sidebar. At the top of the main panel, you'll see a place to enter a unique **ParseApp Name**. You can use whatever unique name you'd like.

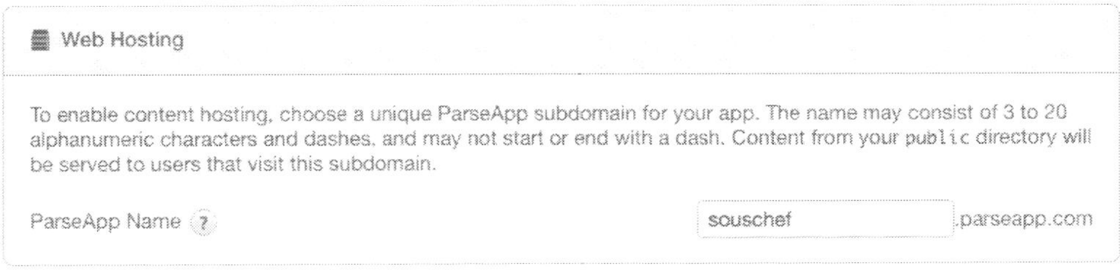

It will now be possible to trigger your web hook from outside of Parse. To test this, in **Terminal**, enter the following `curl` command:

```
curl -X POST http://souschef.parseapp.com/new_recipes_notify
```

You'll need to replace the ParseApp name with the one you chose.

Here, you simply `POST` to the `new_recipes_notify` web hook that you created. At this point, you should see a "Success" response in **Terminal**. Also, a number of `Recipe` objects will have been created in Parse.

To verify that they were created, return to the Parse control panel. Click **Core**; then select **Recipes** from the sidebar. You should see a table of `Recipe` objects.

> **Note**: You didn't actually `POST` any data to the web hook. Since the web hook really just pulls from GitHub, there is nothing it needs to do its job. In a live application, this would most likely be insufficient, but it will work for now.

You now need to fire the web hook each time you commit changes to your `Recipes.json` file in GitHub. Luckily, GitHub makes it easy to do this.

Open your web browser and browse to your recipes repo on GitHub. Click on the settings button, and then choose **Webhooks & Services** from the **Options** menu. Finally, click **Add webhook**.

Here, you'll set up a web hook that's fired each time you commit to your repo.

Enter your Parse web hook URL for the **Payload URL**.

I'm using `http://souschef.parseapp.com/new_recipes_notify` but you will need to substitute this with the actual URL you set up earlier.

Select `application/json` for the **Content Type**. Leave everything else with the defaults and click **Add Webhook**. It should look like the following:

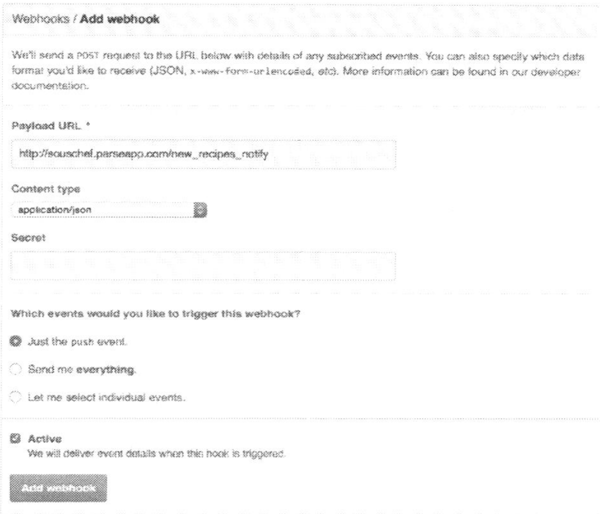

To see if it works, simply commit a change to the repo on GitHub containing a new recipe. Feel free to consult Chapter 8, "Sharing Data" if you can't remember how to do this.

Committing a change will now trigger the web hook, which in turn calls the `new_recipes_notify` method on Parse.

You can verify that this has worked by refreshing the Parse object data store browser. You should see that a new `Recipe` has been added!

Parse says: Token? What Token?

You've written all the code you need for Parse to send push notifications, and you've exercised that code. But, you may have noticed you haven't received a push notification on your device yet.

In this section, you'll make a few modifications to the SousChef app to register your device with Parse so you can receive push notifications.

Open your SousChef project in Xcode. In the resources for this chapter, you'll find a new file **ParsePushRegistrationService.swift**. Add this file to your project under the iPhone app group.

The file contains a class that does all of the work of registering your device for push messages. Parse calls this registration an `Installation` object.

Take a look through the class. You won't be making any code changes to it, but you'll need to update it with your Parse API keys.

At the top of the file, locate the `parseApplicationID` and `parseRestAPIKey` variables. Remember the two Parse keys you copied and stored earlier? Copy the **Application ID** into the `parseApplicationID` property, and the **REST API Key** into the `parseRestAPIKey`.

Still in Xcode, open **AppDelegate.swift**. Find `application(_: didRegisterForRemoteNotificationsWithDeviceToken:)`. Replace the existing implementation with the following code:

```
let parseRegistrationService = ParsePushRegistrationService()
parseRegistrationService.subscribe(deviceToken, completion: {
  (success, error) -> Void in
  if success {
    println("Successfully registered device with Parse")
  } else {
    println("There was an error registerring device with Parse")
  }
})
```

Here, you simply create a `ParsePushRegistrationService` object. Then, you call the `subscribe(_:completion:)` method on it, passing the `deviceToken` your handed by the system. Finally, in the `completion` closure, you check to see if all went well. In either case, you simply print the results to the console.

And that's it! Select the **SousChef** scheme and **build and run** on an actual iPhone. Once the app has finished launching, check the console to see if the device was correctly registered.

Additionally, in the Parse control panel, you can view the Installations data to see your registration. Click **Core**, then **Installation** in the sidebar, and you'll see the Installation object belonging to your iPhone. It should look something like this:

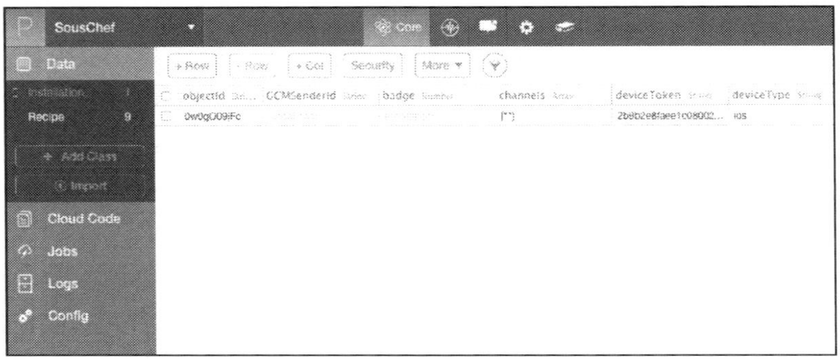

Finally, you'll probably want to see a push notification arrive on your iPhone, right? Head back over to GitHub and add another recipe to your recipes.json file, then watch your iPhone:

Where to go from here?

Congratulations! If all went well, you are now receiving push notifications in SousChef!

You may find that Parse doesn't meet your needs. If that's the case, don't panic! There are plenty of other tools you can use. Here are a number of other projects and services that offer push notifications:

- Houston: https://github.com/nomad/houston
- Urban Airship: http://urbanairship.com/
- Amazon Simple Notification Service: http://aws.amazon.com/sns/
- Helios: http://helios.io/
- PushSharp: https://github.com/Redth/PushSharp

41801439R00228

Made in the USA
Charleston, SC
07 May 2015